Weeds
IN THE URBAN LANDSCAPE

Weeds
IN THE URBAN LANDSCAPE

WHERE THEY COME FROM, WHY THEY'RE HERE, AND HOW TO LIVE WITH THEM

RICHARD ORLANDO

North Atlantic Books
Berkeley, California

Published by
North Atlantic Books
Berkeley, California

Cover photo © edography/Shutterstock.com
Cover design by Jasmine Hromjak
Interior design by Happenstance Type-O-Rama

Printed in the United States of America

Pen and ink drawings copyright 2018 Estate of Tom Yutani

Weeds in the Urban Landscape: Where They Come from, Why They're Here, and How to Live with Them is sponsored and published by the Society for the Study of Native Arts and Sciences (dba North Atlantic Books), an educational nonprofit based in Berkeley, California, that collaborates with partners to develop cross-cultural perspectives, nurture holistic views of art, science, the humanities, and healing, and seed personal and global transformation by publishing work on the relationship of body, spirit, and nature.

North Atlantic Books' publications are available through most bookstores. For further information, visit our website at www.northatlanticbooks.com or call 800-733-3000.

Library of Congress Cataloging-in-Publication Data

Names: Orlando, Richard, 1942- author.
Title: Weeds in the urban landscape : where they come from, why they're here, and how to live with them / Richard Orlando.
Description: Berkeley, California : North Atlantic Books, [2018] | Includes bibliographical references and index.
Identifiers: LCCN 2017043940 (print) | LCCN 2017049376 (ebook) | ISBN 9781623172121 (e-book) | ISBN 9781623172114 (pbk.)
Subjects: LCSH: Weeds—West (U.S.)—Identification. | Weeds—Control—West (U.S.) | Urban gardening—West (U.S.)
Classification: LCC SB612.A2 (ebook) | LCC SB612.A2 O75 2018 (print) | DDC 632/.50978—dc23
LC record available at https://lccn.loc.gov/2017043940

1 2 3 4 5 6 7 8 9 SHERIDAN 23 22 21 20 19 18

Printed on recycled paper

North Atlantic Books is committed to the protection of our environment. We partner with FSC-certified printers using soy-based inks and print on recycled paper whenever possible.

To Kitty Hughes,
the love of my life

CONTENTS

PREFACE

Why I Wrote This Book

$\mathcal{I}$ first thought about writing this book when I began teaching a course on urban weeds at Merritt College, a community college in Oakland, and soon discovered that there was no single work available that would serve as an adequate text. I quickly cobbled together a reader, consisting of excerpts from various sources, as well as some articles I wrote myself and a list of all the weeds I knew that grew in the cities of the San Francisco Bay Area. I resolved to follow this with a book that would serve as a complete text for my class, and for similar classes that are taught in landscape horticulture programs in many other community colleges. These classes teach identification of weeds that grow in urban landscapes, and strategies and techniques for controlling them.

My class was originally called Weed Identification and Control and was almost entirely limited to these two tasks—identifying and naming the weeds, then learning all the options for controlling them. But what are weeds, and how do they differ from plants that are not weeds? The answer I was taught was that they were simply unwanted plants, but I soon discovered that the real answer was a lot more complex. Weeds belong to a specific group of plants that follow us around, that are supremely well adapted to colonizing the bare, disturbed ground that humans have created since the beginnings of civilization. They have a history, inextricably intertwined with our history, and referred to in our folklore and literature. This realization added a new and fascinating dimension to how I viewed my course. I incorporated information on the historical, folkloric, and literary aspects of weeds into my lectures and reader. I renamed the course Weeds in the Urban Landscape, a name that I have also chosen as the title of my book.

There are many textbooks available for weed identification and control classes, but these are mostly oriented toward weeds growing in agricultural situations; none of them work well for students who are trying to focus on the assemblage of weeds present in urban areas and the particular problems associated with them. I hope my book will fill this gap and also be of interest to general readers who are curious about this wonderfully varied and interesting group of plants that pop up everywhere and are usually labeled merely as "weeds," a term often uttered with a dismissive sneer.

The book assigned at Merritt when I took the late Emile Labadie's weeds course in the 1970s was W. W. Robbins's *Weeds of California,* which still serves well as a field guide to weeds in my home state and includes most of those found in cities. It has been out of print since 1970, more than forty-five years, a period that has seen many changes in both urban and rural weed populations, as well as botanical nomenclature; yet, it is still very useful, if you can find a used copy. Robbins's book contains some information on weed control techniques, but mostly focuses on identification.

Shortly after *Weeds of California* ceased being printed, the University of California began publishing the *Grower's Weed Identification Handbook,* a collection of sheets with descriptions and color photographs set in a ring binder, so that more could be added as they were produced. By 1978, this publication covered over 200 weeds; the last revision I know of contained 312 species, including most of those present in urban areas. Used copies of this publication are still available but are very expensive.

In 1991, a group of cooperative extension scientists who belonged to the Western Society of Weed Science collaborated to produce an identification guide to weeds of the western states that they titled *Weeds of the West.* This is a hefty volume, containing clear, vibrant photographs of all the weeds it describes. I considered assigning it as a text but found that it contains many weeds that are present only in rural areas and is missing many that are common in West Coast cities.

In 2007, Joseph DiTomaso, a renowned UC Davis weed scientist, and coauthor E. A. Healy published their massive two-volume *Weeds of California and Other Western States.* Illustrated with many color photos, this book is the most comprehensive and accurate guide to the weeds present in rural, wild land, and urban areas of California and adjoining states. It is a definitive reference work, but it is too massive to serve as a handy field guide, or even as a textbook.

My book has a threefold purpose. It will serve as an identification guide to weeds I have observed growing in urban environments of the San Francisco Bay Area and other West Coast cities. It will also help gardeners and pest control specialists working in these environments implement integrated control strategies, that is, set priorities, determine what tools are available, and devise comprehensive plans for achieving the needed level of control. But my motivation for writing this book goes beyond these utilitarian concerns. I truly believe that developing an understanding of the natural and historical contexts in which weeds developed and continue to thrive is essential for defining our relationship to a natural environment that we have irrevocably altered, and that we now dominate. The current era, called by some the Anthropocene, is a time in which we must learn to live lightly, and in harmony with our fellow creatures. I think all of our activities need to be informed by this perspective.

I plan to use this book in my course, which is aimed at students preparing for careers in landscape horticulture. I am hoping that other instructors teaching similar courses will find it useful, and that it will help home gardeners to identify and manage the plants that appear unbidden in their yards. I also hope it will give them something more: a perception of their gardens as complex and diverse ecosystems, where a whole array of life forms intermingle and life processes occur, and an appreciation of all of these life forms—even the weeds.

I have been accused of having never seen a weed I didn't like, and I am willing to acknowledge that this is almost true. Weeds developed as an integral part of our ongoing attempts to domesticate plants we consider useful and beautiful, and they continue to move about with us as we continue to move about and modify our environment. They are our familiars, and, if not exactly brothers and sisters of the plants that we favor and cultivate, are definitely first cousins. They belong in our gardens, and there is no telling them otherwise. My attitude toward weeds is not a "let it be," or a "let nature take its course" philosophy—in our built and planted environment, nature is definitely taking courses we have set for it, and will continue to do so.

I have killed many thousands of weeds in my lifetime and shall continue to do so with gusto, secure in the knowledge that I shall never succeed in eradicating them. I enjoy the process, and I enjoy the weeds that remain after I have done all I can to manage them. I admire their tenacity, their adaptability, their in-your-face wildness—and find some every bit as beautiful as the plants we choose to grow. Some are more threatening than others and need to be dealt with at lower population thresholds, but I think all are best managed by prudently limiting their populations rather than by waging war on them. I'm hoping this book will help other gardeners do this, and enjoy doing it.

ACKNOWLEDGMENTS

I want to acknowledge and thank the many people whose assistance, encouragement, generosity, ideas, critical feedback, and enthusiasm for this project made it possible for me to initiate and complete it. If I had needed to rely on my efforts alone, this book would not be in print.

My gratitude goes first and foremost to Kitty Hughes, my wife, partner, intimate friend, sympathetic critic, and soul mate for nearly a quarter century. I could not have written the book without her love, encouragement, criticism, editorial help, and commitment.

Next, my appreciation goes to my two grandchildren, Jane Loewinsohn, age five, and her little brother, Sonny, age two, who have helped me immeasurably by continually modeling the qualities of enthusiasm, inquisitiveness, analysis, experimentation, and delight in new experiences. They, along with the rest of my immediate family—their parents, Steve and Briana Loewinsohn, my son, Dante Orlando, my sister, Flora Orlando, and my niece, Lena Orlando—are the nucleus of my extended family, my "village."

I first encountered the pen and ink drawings by Toshimasa (Tom) Yutani in a copy of his self-published book, *Garden and Roadside Weeds of Southern California,* given to me by an old friend, Rob Shulman, when I told him I was writing this book. I immediately fell in love with these images; I found them clear, accurate, and elegantly simple, not consciously artistic, but definitely works of art. I wanted them to appear in my book. I was able to contact his daughter, Amy, who liked the idea and, along with her brothers Fredrick, Ray, and Dennis, gave me permission to use them. I want to thank them all.

My views about weeds changed profoundly when I read the works of five writers who taught me the broader context in which weeds should be understood: Herbert Baker, who taught me that weeds have specific biological characteristics that set them apart from other plants and are not just "plants out of place"; Edgar Anderson, Marston Bates, and Carl Sauer, who revealed to me that these plants have a history that directly correlates with our history over the last ten thousand years; and Maud Grieve, who made me aware of the rich cultural context in which weeds are embedded.

I taught weed classes for nearly four decades in the Landscape Horticulture Department at Merritt College, a community college in Oakland, California; that is where I conceived the notion of writing this book. Most of what I convey in it is based on research I did to prepare for those classes. I am grateful for the ongoing support and mentoring I received from my fellow instructors. Foremost is the late Jane Andrews, who was a former junior high school English teacher when I met her. She had developed a keen interest in gardening, taken courses at Merritt, and was offered a part-time teaching job at the same time that I was hired. We cotaught the weeds class for a number of years, until she was ready to retire and I was ready to solo. Others who stand out are the late Emile Labadie, who founded the department and taught nearly all the classes that were offered there for many years (he was my weed instructor when I was a student at Merritt); Barry Friesen, the department head who succeeded Emile and whose methodical approach and meticulous attention to detail informed his teaching and practice of horticulture, setting an example for instructors and students alike; and Tom Lemieux, who taught the weeds class after Emile Labadie retired and developed the set of weed identification sheets that, with additions by Jane Andrews and me, are still in use, and that gave me a good deal of the information I needed to write this book. Tom Branca and Chris Grampp were department heads who vastly expanded the scope and diversity of class offerings, turning Merritt Horticulture into a nationally recognized department. Judy Donaghey taught many classes for many years and was widely acknowledged by students and fellow teachers for her generous support and mentoring; and Stu Winchester, who never saw a plant he couldn't identify, helped me get out of many identification dead ends.

Thanks are also due to several nonteaching staff members. Molly Sealund, our longtime garden manager, was dedicated to keeping the myriad weeds that inhabit the department grounds under control, yet was always willing to leave them alone until I taught about them. Successive department secretaries who have been mother hens and father roosters to the entire department were Denise Lea, Milfie Howell, Janet Zepel, and Maril Bull. Maril is the current secretary, finally receiving a salary after many years of unpaid volunteer work.

Most of all, I would like to acknowledge my students, whose enthusiasm for the subject energized me, whose inquisitiveness kept me working on my research, whose skepticism kept me honest, and whose feedback helped me become a better teacher. They came from many backgrounds; few were "typical" beginning college students (if there is such a thing); most were older—middle-aged or beyond. Many were professionals seeking new professions; some were gardeners and landscapers seeking to expand their knowledge and skills; a few had PhDs. A good number were retired, seeking new horizons. Many taught me far more than I taught them. There are too many to name, so I won't.

Last, but not least, I wish to thank all my associates in the Grounds Department at the University of California at Berkeley, where I worked for twenty-seven years as a gardener and lead gardener. When I started there, the prevailing attitude was "do as you're told, don't make waves, put in your eight hours, and go home." As time went on, we managed to develop a more engaged, collegial, and friendly work environment, due both to pushback from workers who had had enough of being passive and to managers who were receptive to feedback from workers and wanted to create a more congenial environment. The first of these managers was Ken Schmitz; those who followed him continued to emulate the example he set.

Our managers encouraged us to obtain certification in pest management and arboriculture, paid our certification fees, and paid for the continuing education classes we needed to maintain them. They also allowed me to adjust my work schedule to accommodate my teaching. The support I received from the Grounds Department for my teaching ultimately led to the inception of this book.

I would also like to mention Gary Imazumi, the last manager under whom I worked. I started out as his boss, his crew leader; he became my boss; we were always colleagues.

TOM YUTANI

$\mathcal{T}$oshimasa (Tom) Yutani passed away on January 9, 2010. He was a respected horticulturist and lecturer and most notably an expert in Southern California weed and pest control. He was born in Ookala near Hilo, Hawaii, on March 6, 1907. By the age of six he demonstrated an artistic talent that many decades later would be valuable for the pen and ink weed drawings in his books. Six years later, when he was twelve, Toshimasa rejoined his family, who had already returned to Japan. He eventually graduated from Shobara Agriculture High School and became a respected elementary and high school teacher. Following his desire to return to the United States, he moved to Northern California at the age of twenty. He worked as a flower grower, where, through astute observation and experimentation, he learned what chemicals were needed and how to apply them to grow beautiful pest-free flowers. Many of those flowers were sought after for the early Pasadena Rose Parades.

Following a brief visit to Japan in 1936 to visit his parents, Toshimasa returned to rose growing in San Leandro. He was married to his wife, Harue, in 1938, starting a wonderful marriage of seventy-one years. His successful and rewarding career was cut short by the internment during World War II. Following the war he moved his young family to Detroit, Michigan, and then settled in Whittier, California, in 1952. After working for several years as a gardener, he opened a retail nursery out of his garage. His Highway Garden Service nursery was successful mostly due to his expertise and knowledge of horticulture and weed and pest control.

He retired as a nurseryman in 1974 and embarked on a second career as a weed and gardening expert. He was continually studying and received a certificate in landscape design. He again was the teacher that he was meant to be—lecturing to members of the Southern California Gardeners' Federation on pruning, grafting, and weed and pest control. Through the decades, he spent countless hours growing, identifying, and drawing weeds. He never left the house without his plastic bag and trusty trowel to dig up new weeds he spotted.

Each weed would be grown and nurtured until he was able to identify it; then he would draw it with pen and ink and in watercolor. He eventually identified and drew over three hundred weeds for nine editions of his self-published and authoritative book, *Garden and Roadside Weeds of Southern California.*

Over the years, while holding the title of lecturer, Toshimasa was very active in the Southern California Gardeners' Federation. With them, he shared his technical and practical knowledge of the identification and control of weeds through his numerous monthly columns, workshops, and lectures. In 1979 he wrote the book *The Gardener's Manual* for the Federation—covering basic botany, soil science, diagnosis of plant problems, pruning techniques, and related subjects. He served from January to December 1984 as the representative for professional gardeners on the California Department of Food and Agriculture pest control panel in Sacramento. In 1986, Toshimasa received a certificate of excellence from the California Weed Conference in recognition of the many contributions he had made to weed science through his very popular weed books, lectures, discoveries of new weed species, and weed collection exhibits at numerous training meetings and conferences. In 1991, the Pesticide Applicators Professional Association honored his contributions and dedication to the study and control of weed species by presenting him with their Southern California Educator of the Year award. He continued his lectures and contributions through the mid-1990s. He took personal pride in his self-taught knowledge; even though he did not have a college degree, his expertise was sought after and respected by his colleagues at the University of California at Davis and horticultural agencies with the state of California.

In his one hundredth year he and his wife, Harue, were recognized as Parents of the Year during Nisei Week. In that same year, 2007, he was further honored when his weed paintings were displayed in the exhibit *Landscaping America: Beyond the Japanese Garden* at the Japanese American National Museum in Los Angeles.

He passed away at age 102 following the death of his beloved wife. He left four children (Fredrick, Amy, Ray, and Dennis); seven grandchildren (Kevin, Marti, Tommi, Jennifer, Kimberly, Lynelle, and Jeanine); and eight great-grandchildren (Corey, Charlie, Sara Elizabeth, Ethan, Connor, Lily, James, and his namesake, Milo Toshimasa).

—AMY YUTANI

Part 1
THE BACKGROUND

1

WHAT IS A WEED?

*T*he most widely taught definition of a weed, "any plant out of place," is the one I learned first. I still consider it a valid definition, but incomplete, for it does not tell us the most important things we need to know about this group of plants. It is highly subjective, as it addresses the issue of where we would like to see plants growing, rather than why they grow where they do. Who is to say that any plant thriving in a well-cultivated, sunny corner of our gardens, or even one stubbornly persisting in the dry, compacted, gravelly ground of our driveways, is "out of place"? While any plant *can* be considered a weed when it grows where we do not want it, there seem to be some plants that we *almost always* regard as weeds. This is due to their rapid growth and proliferation—they tend to pop up everywhere there is room for them to grow. In other words, weeds are plants with characteristics that we regard as *weedy*.

The best definition I have found of weediness is that given by the late Herbert Baker, who was a professor of botany at the University of California at Berkeley. Baker was one of a small group of Berkeley botanists with a special interest in cultivated plants—and he considered weeds to be cultivated plants, observing that, in general, they grow only in proximity to humans and their activities. He began to consider the characteristics that made these plants good at what they do, and, in "Characteristics and Modes of Origins of Weeds," a chapter he wrote in *The Genetics of Colonizing Species,* a book he coedited with

G. Ledyard Stebbins in 1965, he added as an appendix the following list, which he titled "The Ideal (?) Weed."

1. Has no special environmental requirements for germination.

2. Has discontinuous germination (self-controlled) and great longevity of seed.

3. Shows rapid seedling growth.

4. Spends only a short period of time in the vegetative condition before beginning to flower.

5. Maintains a continuous seed production for as long as growing conditions permit.

6. Is self-compatible, but not obligatorily self-pollinated or apomictic [asexual].

7. When cross-pollinated, this can be achieved by a nonspecialized flower visitor or by wind.

8. Has very high seed output in favorable environmental circumstances.

9. Can produce some seed in a very wide range of environmental circumstances. Has high tolerance of (and often plasticity in face of) climatic and edaphic [soil-related] variation.

10. Has special adaptations for both long-distance and short-distance dispersal.

11. If a perennial, has vigorous vegetative reproduction.

12. If a perennial, has brittleness at the lower nodes, or of the rhizomes or rootstocks.

13. If a perennial, shows an ability to regenerate from severed portions of the rootstock.

14. Has ability to compete by special means: rosette formation, choking growth, exocrine production [secretion of germination-blocking compounds] (but no fouling of soil for itself), etc.

Reflecting on this list, we can see that weeds are plants with adaptations that make them tough, fast growing, and persistent; but that the primary characteristic that distinguishes them from other plants is their ability to produce large quantities of readily germinating seed, thus giving them an edge over equally tough, fast growing, and persistent plants that are more restrained in their seed production and germination. To exploit this advantage, however, they need a condition that is not always available in nature but is plentiful in the vicinity of human activity: bare, disturbed soil.

Disturbing the ground has always been a characteristic activity of our species, and it became a major activity beginning about ten thousand years ago. Edgar Anderson, whose fascinating study of the relationship between plants and humans, *Plants, Man, and Life,* hypothesizes that the crop plants that fed the growth of civilization in the Near East and Europe—and the weeds that inevitably accompanied them—originated in Neolithic times on dump heaps near habitations of semisettled hunters and gatherers in the foothills of the Near East right after the end of the last ice age. I'll explain this process further in the next chapter, "A Brief History of Weeds and Crop Plants."

2

A BRIEF HISTORY OF WEEDS
AND CROP PLANTS

*W*hen I first read that the Tollund man's stomach contents consisted of seeds of chickweed, knotweed, and fat hen, I was delighted and gratified. This ancient Dane had been killed by strangling, his neck broken. His body was then tossed into a peat bog, an environment that allowed it to be perfectly preserved until it was extracted more than two thousand years later. Before meeting his fate, he had eaten a meal of weed seeds—the seeds of some of the very weeds that I have contended with frequently during my career as a gardener and horticulture instructor. Here was a personal connection with the ancient past, with somebody who, like me, realized that weeds are not just pest plants, but have many virtues, including nutritious seeds.

I have always tried to teach my students that, however much of a nuisance and a hindrance weeds might be in the garden, they are nonetheless an essential part of the urban landscape and ecology; and that, like our crops, our domestic animals, and the rats, mice, lice, and cockroaches that share our dwellings, barnyards, and fields, they have a history that is contemporaneous with the history of our species. The Tollund man seemed to be living (so to speak) proof of this notion, someone so knowledgeable about and comfortable with the weeds of the field that he actually preferred them to the conventional fare of his time and place, the barley and other grains that formed the staple diet of his contemporaries.

Further inquiry showed the story was more complicated. Whoever wrote the piece about the chickweed, knotweed, and fat hen undoubtedly shared some of the same connection fantasies I enjoyed nurturing and had either misunderstood the account of the stomach content analysis or selectively chosen details that supported the story he wanted to believe. In fact, according to more scholarly sources, the Tollund man's stomach contained seeds of over forty species of plants, sixteen of them wild. The bulk of these seeds, however, were barley, false flax (*Canelina sativa,* a mustard family oil seed undoubtedly included for its high fat content; it probably originated as a weed in cultivated linseed, but was no doubt cultivated as an oil seed crop by the Tollund man's time), and knotweed, a buckwheat relative that grows abundantly almost everywhere. Another meal that was found in the stomach of a Dane interred in a bog in Borremose, however, consisted entirely of wild seeds, primarily spurry and knotweed.

The Tollund man had not, as the spurious account relates, been strangled, then unceremoniously tossed into the bog, a fate suitable for a common criminal. He had been hanged, then placed carefully into the bog, his limbs arranged, his facial muscles carefully manipulated to give him a serene expression. This was not the execution of a criminal, nor the murder of an outsider; it seems to have been the ritual sacrifice of a highly regarded member of the community, an act no doubt intended to insure the germination and fruition of the seeds of the very barley and its attendant weeds that filled his stomach.

Before the advent of agriculture, no barley grew in Denmark. This should not surprise anyone who is aware that grain agriculture began in the ancient Middle East during the Neolithic era and disseminated slowly, reaching the fringes of western Europe in the Bronze Age. What many might find more surprising is that weeds as we now know them were not present, either; they arrived along with the cultivated grains of the Middle East. In some cases, plants of the same species as these weeds grew wild in the forests and mountains of Europe; but, as pollen studies by a Swedish botanist named Göte Turesson indicate, the common plants that grow in the meadows of Europe are genetically distinct from those that occur in nearby wild lands—the genes of the meadow weeds indicate a Central Asian origin. The late Edgar Anderson, formerly a professor of botany at UC Berkeley, writes in his wonderful and unfortunately out-of-print book *Plants, Man, and Life:*

> Grown in Turesson's garden, the meadow plants of Europe more closely
> resembled the varieties of these same plants which are native far to the

east in such places as the Altai Mountains than they did the transplants from European mountains. The meadow strains of yarrow, buttercups and daisies may be older than European culture. In part at least they must have spread into Europe when the earliest cattle raisers began to press out of Central Asia. They will be as exact evidence for European prehistory as long barrows and bell beakers, when our information about them is as precise. (p. 78)

Elsewhere in the same book, Anderson describes the whole complex of plants that comprise our crop lands and gardens, along with their associated weeds, as "transported landscapes." As early humans moved about, they were accompanied by a whole entourage of creatures they had come to depend on, or learned to coexist with—not only their crop plants and domesticated animals, which they carried with them deliberately, but also the creatures that had adopted *them* during their lengthy process of developing agriculture and animal husbandry and building habitations and cities, roads and canals, seaports and fortifications. To again quote Anderson:

> It is not until one sits down to work out precise answers to such questions that he realizes that unconsciously as well as deliberately man carries whole floras about the globe with him, that he now lives surrounded by transported landscapes, that our commonest everyday plants have been transformed by their long associations with us so that many roadside and dooryard plants are *artifacts* [italics mine]. An artifact, by definition, is something produced by man, something which we would not have had if man had not come into being. That is what many of our weeds and crops really are. Though man did not wittingly produce all of them, some are as much dependent upon him, as much a result of his cultures, as a temple or a vase or an automobile. (p. 9)

The history of the movement of crops and their accompanying weeds throughout the world can be deduced by analyzing pollen deposited in peat bogs and the sediment of lake beds. Pollen grains have a glossy, plastic-like coating that makes them highly resistant to decay; they are small and light, which enables them to be blown by the wind and deposited like a fine rain over land and water. Scientists who painstakingly analyze these pollen layers and correlate them with geological and archaeological data can give us a precise record of the sequence and duration of vegetative changes in the ancient world and provide us with insight into the role of humans in bringing about some of these changes.

An example Anderson gives is ribgrass, *Plantago lanceolata,* more familiar to contemporary Americans as buckhorn plantain. Citing another Scandinavian botanist, a Dane named Johannes Iversen, who studied pollen extracted from peat bogs, Anderson tells us that there was no ribgrass present in Danish peat until the first farmers arrived at the beginning of the Bronze Age. Where ribgrass pollen first begins to appear, there is also a layer of charcoal, indicating extensive burning, undoubtedly to clear land for farming. Just above the charcoal layer, pollen of such previously abundant woodland plants as ivy disappears completely for a time, while pollen of plants such as ribgrass, previously sparse, appears in great abundance and steadily increases in quantity layer after layer. Cereal pollens increase, and birch pollen rapidly becomes more abundant (birch is a pioneering plant that follows fire). All of this is consistent with the so-called slash and burn agriculture that is still practiced (or has been until recently) in the mountains of Central and South America and in eastern Asia.

These Bronze Age farmers limited their activities to clearing oak woodlands, where the soil was richer, then planting grain; but by the Iron Age more extensive land clearing was occurring, indicating a surge in population. Farmers moved from the richer soils of the rapidly diminishing oak woodlands into the sandier pinelands. When these fields were abandoned, the ground was colonized by heather and other scrubby vegetation, forming the extensive heaths that still cover much of the sandy regions of northern Europe today.

The path established by the movement of cereal grains—wheat, barley, rye, and oats—from the Near East into Europe was completed about two thousand years before the beginning of the Common Era, and by this time all the grains from the Fertile Crescent, along with most of their accompanying weeds, as well as the domestic animals and the rats, mice, lice, and cockroaches that compose the human entourage, were present throughout Eurasia and North Africa, from India to Ireland, from Ethiopia to Scandinavia. Grain agriculture provided the material basis for the culture that produced the Tollund man, the Roman Empire, the magnificent cathedrals of the Middle Ages, the spread of Islamic religion, culture and learning throughout the Near East and North Africa, and the exploration and colonization of the New World.

Many books have been written on the origins and development of crop plants, our primary source of food since the beginnings of civilization. Probably the most seminal is Carl Sauer's *Agricultural Origins and Dispersals*. Sauer was a geographer, but much has also been written by botanists, such as W. W. Robbins, Herbert Baker, and Edgar Anderson, of UC Berkeley, and N. W. Simmonds of the University of Edinburgh. More recent contributions include two best-selling books: *Guns, Germs, and Steel*, by Jared Diamond, an ornithologist whose work in New Guinea prompted him to consider the question of how western Europeans came to dominate the rest of the world; and *1491*, by Charles C. Mann, a journalist who summarized a good deal of research on how Native Americans intensively managed their environments to maximize production of food from both agricultural and wild plants.

Reading these works, one might conclude that all of human history can be summed up in one contemporary cliché—you are what you eat. As for all organisms, eating is central to our being. The quest for food has shaped cultures and civilizations, engendered religious beliefs, triggered wars, built empires, and stimulated scientific inquiry, geographic exploration, and technological innovation. Food, and the partaking of food, have been depicted and celebrated in our art, our literature, even our music. Now of course there is much more to history, as well as to art, literature, and music—but, at bottom, we are living organisms, and organisms at all levels spend most of their time, essentially, seeking, gathering, and ingesting food.

Edgar Anderson points out that, during most of our quarter million years on earth, *Homo sapiens* survived as hunters of big game animals. We developed technologies that enabled us to survive and thrive in a variety of environments and climates, crafting ever finer and sharper stone spear points and other tools and learning how to sew clothing and build shelters suited to the rigors of the ice ages. This process reached its peak during the last glacial advance, when the big game we hunted consisted of creatures such as horses, bears, bison, giant ground sloths, even mammoths. We became such efficient hunters of these animals that we may have contributed significantly to their extinction at the end of the last ice age—although this theory is vigorously debated. In any case, the retreat of the glaciers led to substantial changes in ways we fed ourselves. Sea levels rose, rainfall increased, large lakes and estuaries formed. People settled by these bodies of water and switched to hunting smaller game such as waterfowl and fishing, gathering shellfish, and foraging wild plants.

The most important of these wild plant foods for the ancestors of West Asians and Europeans were the seeds of grasses growing in the foothills of the mountains of the Near East, which form an arc known as the Fertile Crescent to the north and east of the Tigris and Euphrates Valleys. These grasses were the progenitors of the staple crops of Western civilization: wheat, rye, barley, and oats. It was a fairly short step from gathering plants in the wild to growing some of them near their dwellings and selecting seed from those with the best characteristics to save for replanting. The first evidence of deliberate cultivation comes from about nine thousand years ago, in foothill communities such as Jericho in Israel and Catal Huyuk in Turkey, areas that get enough rainfall to allow dry farming. Grain agriculture did not spread to the great river valleys until around 3000 BCE, when the development of irrigation technology and a social structure that could support large-scale irrigation projects allowed farming in these essentially desert regions.

Anderson describes the process by which crop plants were selected in a chapter titled "Dump Heaps and the Origins of Agriculture." New Stone Age people, living in semipermanent settlements and eating a more diverse diet, did what we all do when we live close together: they dug up the ground and accumulated garbage. The disturbed ground surrounding our dwellings, and our dump heaps, made very fertile by decaying plant residues, animal parts, and other substances, provided a rich environment for the seeds and pits from the fruits of our gathering to germinate and thrive. They were what Anderson describes as open habitats—zones where high fertility, loose and constantly shifting soil, and continual introduction of the seed of various plants gathered from the wild allowed new hybrids to develop; from these, people could select more desirable varieties for propagation. Weeds hybridized with weeds; descendants of plants that had been gathered for food hybridized with each other and with weeds.

Now weeds, by definition, are plants that are adapted to colonizing bare ground. Their ancestors, the theory goes, evolved to take advantage of bare ground left by retreating glaciers. They would have become fairly insignificant or even extinct as stable plant communities evolved on this ground, and would have thrived only in naturally disturbed areas such as riverbanks, gravel bars, landslides, and lava flows—except that we continued to do what the glaciers had stopped doing—that is, disturb the ground with all our moving about, hunting and gathering, building and mining. We saved these plants, and allowed them to evolve further, by continuing to provide them with the disturbed habitat they needed.

Evolution of agriculture from dump heaps didn't first occur in the Near East, but in the tropics, in Southeast Asia, where bananas and root crops such as yams and taro were grown, producing foods rich in starch but deficient in protein. It was still necessary to depend on hunting and fishing to provide complete nutrition, although later the domestication of dogs, pigs, chickens, geese, and water buffalo, as well as the introduction of rice, enabled farmers to produce a complete diet through agriculture alone. Fishing continued, of course, but fish farming also developed.

In general, as the practice of growing crops moved from south to north, agriculture switched from vegetative propagation of root crops to seed propagation of grasses. Grass seeds like wheat, rye, barley, and rice have a high protein content and are very storable and easily transportable. The geographic nature of temperate Eurasia—a broad, contiguous expanse of land, largely plains running from east to west in the latitudes most suitable for grain growing—facilitated the rapid spread of these crops.

In *Agricultural Origins and Dispersals,* Carl Sauer refers to several centers he calls *hearths,* where the world's major crop plants were developed. These hearths and their associated food sources are as follows:

India and the Malay Peninsula: yams, taro, bananas, pigs, ducks, geese, and chickens were domesticated here.

Southwest Asia (Kashmir, Turkestan, Turkey, and Iran): the grain crops grown in the Fertile Crescent moved quickly into this area. A number of fruits and vegetables were domesticated here: apples, pears, and peaches, as well as several mustard family vegetables. Horses were possibly domesticated here as well.

The Mediterranean Basin: grain crops, olives, figs, lentils, and peas were domesticated, as well as cattle, sheep, and goats.

The mountains of central China: the oldest grain crop was Asian rice, *Oryza sativa,* cultivated since the fourth millennium BCE. Barley was introduced from India via Tibet somewhat later, and wheat was brought from western Asia. Yaks were the only native domestic animal. Rice spread throughout Asia during millennia of selection and reached Europe and Africa before the European discovery of the New World. Europeans introduced it into South and Central America, and cultivation began in North America during the seventeenth century.

Ethiopia: teff (a grass, *Eragrostis tef,* whose seeds are milled into a flour that resembles wheat flour) and millets were domesticated, and barley was introduced.

Sub-Saharan Africa: cowpeas, black-eyed peas, millets, and sorghums were domesticated, as well as African rice, *Oryza glaberrima;* yams and bananas came from Asia.

The highlands of North and South America: corn, potatoes, squash, beans, and tomatoes were domesticated here. Also developed were broad-leaved grain crops such as amaranth and quinoa, whose seeds are becoming more and more popular today in other parts of the world due to their abundant high-quality protein. In the lowlands, manioc, or yuca (cassava), sweet potato, arrowroot, peanuts, and yams were grown. Dogs, turkeys, and llamas were the animals domesticated in this region. After the arrival of Columbus, corn spread rapidly throughout the world, becoming a staple crop in large parts of Asia and Africa, where its high yield and significant protein content filled serious dietary gaps.

All of these centers are characterized by the tremendous *variability* of their crop plants. This phenomenon reaches its extreme in Central and South America, where there are more varieties grown than are found in the rest of the world put together.

The clustering of many varieties of crops in small areas of the world is a phenomenon that was first noticed by a Russian geneticist named N. I. Vavilov, whose story is told by Edgar Anderson. Vavilov began his career in Russia, then went to Cambridge before World War I to study wheat breeding. While there, he noticed that a few areas of the world contained the greatest numbers of crop plant varieties, and that this diversity always included the most primitive forms. Vavilov hypothesized that this diversity indicated that these regions were the centers of origin of these crop plants, centers from which they diffused to other areas where only the most adapted varieties came to predominate. This hypothesis applies to a lesser extent to the weeds that evolved along with the crop plants.

After the Russian Revolution, Vavilov continued to serve the country he loved as a Soviet bureaucrat and director of research. He sent expeditions to all the centers he had identified (what Carl Sauer calls *hearths*) to find and bring back varieties best suited to Russia's various environments. However, he soon ran afoul of Stalinist authorities, who were inimical to theories based on genetics, and who, during the 1930s, were determined to root out every trace of dissent from the party line. He was tried and sent to a labor camp in Siberia, where he died.

As I stated previously, most of the crops—and weeds—grown in Europe, and later in America, originated in the Fertile Crescent region of the Near East and in adjacent parts of the Mediterranean Basin and Central Asia. This was where the crops that provided the material basis for ancient and subsequent European civilizations were developed: wheat, rye, oats, barley—especially wheat. A closer look at wheat reveals a lineage involving the crossbreeding of the genus *Triticum,* containing primitive forms of wheat, with the weedy genera *Aegilops* and *Agropyron.* This allowed the supplanting of varieties with few-seeded heads that shattered easily (einkorn), with larger-headed, tighter, nonshattering tetraploids (Persian wheat and emmer, a.k.a. farro). Further crosses with *Agropyron* created the hexaploid bread wheats, such as spelt and kamut. More recently, additional crosses with *Aegilops* produced the "modern" varieties that we grow today.

Farmers started growing these grain crops about 7000 BCE in the Near East; their spread was amazingly rapid, facilitated by the vast swath of plains that runs almost the entire length of the Eurasian continent in the latitudes suited to grain growing. According to Jared Diamond in *Guns, Germs, and Steel,* grain crops (and, I should point out, their weeds) were in Hungary by 5400 BCE and were moving rapidly into western Europe (this is about two thousand years before the rise of the river valley civilizations in the Near East). By time of Jesus, crops of Fertile Crescent origin were grown from the Pacific coast of Japan to Ireland.

Wheat, rye, and barley were the staple crops that provided the material basis for the development of the ancient civilizations of the Near East and the Greek and Roman civilizations of ancient Europe. They also provided sustenance for the civilizations of the Middle Ages, when, as Lynn White indicates in a chapter of *Medieval Technology and Social Change* called "The Agricultural Revolution of the Early Middle Ages," two technological innovations, the moldboard plow and the improved horse harness, allowed cultivation of the heavier but richer soils of northern Europe, which in turn fed a growing population. After Columbus's voyage, these crops moved into the New World to feed the Europeans who conquered and colonized that region. Wherever these crops were introduced, they were accompanied by the weeds with which they had coevolved.

European colonization of the Americas brought grain agriculture and animal husbandry, along with all their attendant weeds, to that part of the world, but the original Americans already had their own grain agriculture and their own array of weeds, so a great movement of crops and weeds took place. This widespread transfer, which has come to be known as the Columbian Exchange, profoundly changed agriculture in both Europe and America. Maize, or Indian corn, could be grown in parts of Europe where wheat cultivation was difficult, and nutrition for European mountain dwellers such as central Italian peasants was greatly improved by the substitution of corn meal for chestnuts, a staple food for many people too poor to afford wheat. The peasant diet was further enriched by the introduction of New World crops such as squash, beans, tomatoes, peppers, gourds, and prickly pears.

The establishment of grain agriculture in the New World was essential for the domination of this area by Europeans but did little to benefit the Native Americans, who had already worked out their own methods of self-sufficient food production. The ability of the colonists to feed their rapidly growing population, based on growing their own grains as well as Indian corn in areas better suited to this crop, helped them to drive the native populations into smaller and remoter areas, a process that was abetted by the decimation of these people from European diseases to which they had no resistance. The growing demand in Europe for Native American crops such as tobacco, sugar cane, and cotton (actually hybrids of New and Old World cottons) led to large-scale plantation agriculture in the Americas, which involved the use of slave labor, at first by enslaved Native Americans and later by slaves imported from Africa.

Along with the mosaic of native and European crops, there developed a mosaic of native and European weeds, at least in the parts of the Americas where the original Americans practiced intensive agriculture: Mexico and Peru, and the Northeast, Southeast, and Southwest regions of the United States. Even today, these areas possess a greater number of native weeds than are found in places such as the Great Plains, the Pacific Northwest, and California, where there was no significant farming activity.

Native Californians did not practice agriculture extensively, but it was not unknown to them. Southern California Indians traded with the inhabitants of the Southwest Pueblo area, so they knew about corn, beans, and squash, and some, like the Cahuilla, even occasionally planted these crops in the vicinity of desert springs, returning later in the year to see if these gardens had produced anything; but this was a fairly sporadic and haphazard practice, for in fact the original Californians could easily produce more food than they needed by gathering acorns and wild grass seed, and by hunting the abundant game animals that surrounded them and fishing in the rivers and ocean. In the far north, the Karoks grew tobacco, which they used only for ceremonial purposes; they didn't grow food crops.

But the lack of agriculture does not mean that the Native Californians did not manage or modify the land in any way; they did, and they substantially altered the vegetation patterns, although not nearly to the extent that the European invaders did. The Indians cleared areas of brush or forest to facilitate viewing and flushing game; they cut back plants to produce long, pliable stems for basketry (a practice known to English speakers as *coppicing*); and they weeded and propagated certain favored wild food plants, such as camas, a native bulb that grows in moist mountain meadows. The California that Spanish-speaking colonists from Mexico began settling in 1769 was by no means pristine—the landscape had been extensively modified by the native inhabitants, who comprised the densest population north of central Mexico at the time; their numbers are estimated at perhaps as many as 350,000. This population began declining precipitously when the Hispanic settlers appeared. Most Native Californians died of European diseases to which they had no resistance, but starvation, massacres, loss of cultural identity, and a decreasing birth rate all contributed to the population's decline. By 1880, the identifiable native population of the state had sunk to a low of 20,000. At present, it stands at about 200,000, representing both a substantial rebound in the number of Native Californians and Native American migration from other parts of the country.

The introduction of European weeds into California began with the arrival of the Mexican colonists in 1769. They altered the landscape in ways far more substantial than the modest changes the native inhabitants had wrought. Only sixteen weeds were introduced in the fifty-five years of Spanish rule of California that preceded Mexican independence, but among these were a number of annual grasses and forbs, such as wild oats, hare barley, Italian ryegrass, and redstem filaree, that would soon predominate in areas formerly occupied by native forbs and grasses. Spread by grazing cattle, these European annuals established themselves on the hillsides and plains that had been previously dominated by native grasses, forbs, and shrubs, some of which the Indians used for food and basketry.

Thus were born the storied green and golden hills of California, hills covered with glistening, tall grasses rippling in the wind, grasses that sentimental Californians like to imagine form a timeless, unchanging landscape, but that in fact appeared in the state no earlier than 1769 (there is some evidence that a few weeds may have arrived earlier, a fairly plausible possibility, since the Spanish had settled Mexico more than two hundred years before they got around to inhabiting California; so some weeds might well have traveled along Indian trade routes).

We know about the presence of weeds during the so-called Spanish period largely because of some studies done by two botanists named Hendry and Bellue, who analyzed pollen residues taken from adobe bricks used to build missions and pueblos during this period (adobe is clay and straw; some of the oldest bricks possibly contained bedding straw unloaded from the first ships from Mexico). Besides the three grasses I have already mentioned (wild oats, hare barley, and Italian ryegrass), the pollen studies revealed the presence of redstem filaree, small mallow, annual bluegrass, curly dock, black mustard, lamb's quarters, bur clover, and prickly sowthistle. All these weeds grew from seed carried in the ballast of ships, in the bedding and feed straw of domestic animals, or in contaminated crop seed. This seed was dispersed by clearing activity around settlements and by cattle grazing in the grasslands and shrublands of coastal California.

During the Mexican era, which lasted only twenty-three years—from 1825 to 1848—sixty-three more weeds were introduced. This was due to a growing population and vastly expanded cattle grazing, which fed a lively commerce in hides. Ripgut brome and other brome grasses came in, intensifying the transformation of California's grasslands from native grasses and forbs to European annual grasses; giant reed established itself in riparian zones, where it offered serious competition to the native vegetation; and a good many broad-leaved weeds that are all too familiar to us today, such as field bindweed, wild radish, scarlet pimpernel, chickweed, yellow mustard, milk thistle, and dandelion, made their appearance.

Most of what we know about the introduction of weeds during the Mexican era comes from botanical surveys carried out during these years, mostly by botanists on visiting ships (Collie and Lay, on the *H. M. S. Blossom,* in 1827–28; Hinds, on the *H. M. S. Sulphur,* in 1837–38), as well as exploratory expeditions originating in the United States, such as the Pacific Railroad exploration (Bigelow) in 1837. Another source is material collected by two Russian botanists working near Fort Ross in Sonoma County in 1841. All this activity indicates that there was a growing interest in California by foreign powers, an interest that was to culminate in its annexation to the United States after the conclusion of the Mexican War in 1848.

Anglo settlement had grown at a modest pace during the Mexican era, with emigrants from the eastern United States buying land, or even receiving it as grants from the Mexican government. This trickle turned into a flood beginning in 1849 with the discovery of gold on the American River. Gold seekers flooded in not only from the United States, but from all over the world. The wealth extracted from the gold mines created a full-blown mercantile and agricultural economy in very short order, and in 1850 California was granted statehood without having ever passed through the territorial phase, a period that in other parts of the country lasted for years, even decades.

During the years between the discovery of gold in 1849 and what is generally considered the end of the gold rush in about 1860, fifty-five more species of weeds were introduced. During the following decades, the introduction of weedy plants continued unabated; by the later part of the twentieth century, there were 846 alien species naturalized in California. Comparing this with the 134 species that were present in 1860, we can see that during the second hundred years of the settlement of the state by nonnatives, about seven times as many weeds were introduced as during the first hundred. This correlates directly with the geometric growth of disturbed land connected with human economic activity: grazing, farming, building roads and railroads, constructing cities, dredging harbors, and building dams, canals, and levees.

In recent years, increasing numbers of plant species have been escaping from gardens and nurseries and invading wild lands, mostly landscape plants that are so well adapted to the California environment that they spread aggressively inside and outside of garden walls. Plants such as French broom, pampas grass, mayten trees, Bermuda buttercup, eucalypts, Cape ivy, and even English ivy have become major weed pests that threaten entire native ecosystems. These horticultural invaders, along with a number of the more classic Mediterranean weeds that have the same invasive tendencies—poison hemlock, milk thistle, and yellow starthistle, for instance—have been lumped into the category of invasive exotics to differentiate them from the bulk of the traditional weeds that persistently and aggressively invade bare ground but do not offer much competition to native plants in a stable environment. Dealing with these invaders has become a major focus of groups seeking to preserve and restore native ecosystems. This work presents challenges much more difficult and complex than dealing with traditional weeds growing in crop and garden settings.

3

IMPORTANT WEED FAMILIES

INTRODUCTION

When teaching my classes on weeds, I've always stressed the importance of being able to recognize quickly to which family the weed in question belongs as the first step in identifying the species. There are keys to plant families, but since the vast majority of our common weeds belong to one of about a dozen, the ability to recognize immediately their key characteristics speeds up the process considerably. Once we know the family, we can move more quickly through keys, or select from pictorial guides that have been organized into family groups. In the following pages, I describe the characteristics of ten important weed families and conclude with a list of all families represented by the weeds in this book.

THE CARNATION FAMILY—CARYOPHYLLACEAE

This family of mostly herbaceous plants is found in all temperate areas of the world and in tropical mountains, but it is represented most heavily in the Mediterranean Basin. It includes a number of our familiar garden flowers, such as carnations, pinks, and catchflies, as well as some of our most common and widespread weeds, such as common and mouse-eared chickweed, spurry, and four-leaved allseed.

The family is characterized mainly by low-growing, sprawling, or mat-forming herbaceous plants with opposite leaves, simple and entire, usually lacking petioles, growing from somewhat swollen nodes. Flowers are regular and perfect, with five petals, often fringed or deeply cleft—so deeply on some species that they appear to have ten petals. They usually grow in clusters called *cymes*. The fruits are capsules containing several to many seeds.

A substantial number of weeds are included in the pink family, the most common and universal of which are the chickweeds, members of the genera *Stellaria* and *Cerastium*. Some silenes, or catchflies, are also represented, as well as sand spurry, *Spergularia rubra,* and corn spurry, *Spergula arvensis.* Four-leaved allseed, *Polycarpon tetraphyllum,* is a very common weed in urban areas, and rose campion, *Lychnis coronaria,* and corn cockle, *Agrostemma githago,* which are grown as garden flowers, often volunteer freely to the point of becoming pests.

With the exception of a variety of the weedy corn spurry, *Spergula arvensis,* which is sometimes grown as a fodder plant in dry, sandy soils, there are no food crops or culinary herbs in this family. It does, however, give us a number of familiar garden flowers, the most common of which are in the genus *Dianthus.* Carnations, *Dianthus caryophyllus,* are long-stemmed, mostly double flowers; the more compact varieties are grown as garden perennials; long-stemmed cultivars are raised in greenhouses for the cut flower trade. Close cousins are the clove pinks or gilliflowers, representing several other species of *Dianthus.* These are often single, generally shorter stemmed than carnations, and with foliage that tends to form mats. Other garden flowers in this family are baby's breath, *Gypsophila;* snow-in-summer, *Cerastium tomentosum;* catchflies or campions, in the genus *Silene;* corn cockles, genus *Agrostemma;* soapwort, or bouncing bet, genus *Saponaria;* and rose campion, *Lychnis coronaria.* The last three sow themselves freely, and can easily become weedy pests.

THE COMPOSITE FAMILY—ASTERACEAE, COMPOSITAE

Compositae is the ancient name for the world's largest plant family; however, some botantists think Orchidaceae, the other of the two, may be larger. Under the system of botanical nomenclature adopted during the first two decades of the twentieth century by the International Botanical Congress, families must be named after the genus considered most typical, so this group is now called the Asteraceae. Compositae, however, is still considered a valid name, a concession to history made by the Congress for all plant groups that were recognized as families prior to the publication of Linnaeus's *Species Plantarum.* The aster family consists of about 1,100 genera and 25,000 species, which are most abundant in semi-arid regions of the tropics and subtropics; composites are scarce only in tropical rain forests. In *The Jepson Manual,* it is divided into fifteen groups, each containing a number of common flowering characteristics. Some of the genera in the family are found in more than one group. This makes field identification from keys even more difficult than it was when the aster family was divided into tribes; but it fits in well with the newly emerging cladistics system, based on common ancestors determined by DNA analyses. For practical purposes, I'll group the composites into two groups: those with milky sap, such as lettuce, dandelions, and sowthistles, sometimes called the lettuce tribe (Cichoreae), and those with resinous sap. Members of this family are, for the most part, herbaceous annuals and perennials, or semiwoody shrubs—very few are trees. Leaves for the most part are simple, usually lobed or toothed and without stipules. Stems of composites all have resin canals or latex ducts—these substances help keep the plants from drying out, making them particularly suited to semi-arid environments. The latex or resin in the stems also helps deter grazing and browsing, allowing composites to thrive in grasslands.

The characteristic inflorescence of the composites is what gives the family its name. It is called a *capitulum,* and it consists of a cluster of small, individual flowers called *florets,* which are surrounded by a ring of protective bracts, known collectively as the *involucre.* The whole structure resembles a single flower, and it functions as one biologically, attracting pollinators such as insects and birds.

The florets are of two types, ray and disk. Using a daisy "flower" as an example, the ray florets are the "petals" at the edge, each one a complete floret with a pronounced projection; the disk florets are clustered in the center, and lack the petallike appendages. Some composite inflorescences consist entirely of disk florets, a few completely of ray florets; most typical, however, is a combination of the two, with the disk florets at the center, surrounded by ray florets. All are perfect florets, with both male and female parts, but their sex organs do not develop at the same time—there is a staminate and a pistillate stage. The anthers, fused to form a tube, ripen their pollen before the ovules develop inside the pistil and deposit pollen into the tube. The style then elongates without opening, growing through the anthers and pushing the pollen grains upward, where they become available to passing pollinators or to the wind. Once the pollen is dispersed, segments of the style separate to expose stigmatic surfaces, which can then receive pollen dispersed from other plants. If this does not happen, the style arms may continue to grow and recurve sufficiently to contact their own anthers and receive whatever pollen is left on these. This system is weighted in favor of cross-pollination, but enables self-pollination should cross-pollination fail.

There are many food, medicinal, and ornamental plants in the composite family. Examples of food plants are lettuces, chicories, endives, sunflowers, and artichokes. Safflower seeds provide cooking oil, and the yellow flower parts are used in the Near East as a saffron-like spice and coloring agent often referred to as Turkish saffron. Medicinal composites are too numerous to enumerate here, but they include many of our common weeds. Ornamentals include various daisies and daisylike plants such as coneflowers, sneezeweed, and black-eyed Susan; cornflowers, marigolds, dahlias, cinerarias, and ageratum; and plants grown mostly for their foliage, especially silvery-leaved ones such as santolina, dusty miller, and artemisias. Two of the latex-bearing composites, *Parthenium argentatum* and *Taraxacum bicorne,* have been used as minor sources of rubber. Some of the ornamentally attractive composites have escaped from cultivation and become aggressive weeds.

One of the major divisions of the large composite family (Compositae, or Asteraceae) is a group of plants that exude a white, sticky latex when the leaves or stems are broken. Known in Latin as the Chichoreae in some systems, this group is commonly called the lettuce tribe after its best-known member, *Lactuca sativa,* or garden lettuce. Garden lettuce does not usually behave as a weed, but several of its close cousins, members of the genus *Lactuca*, definitely qualify, as do a host of somewhat more distant relations, including dandelions, chicory, salsify, bristly oxtongue, and sowthistles (often mistaken for dandelions). The primary function of the latex seems to be its deterrent effect on grazing by herbivores, a property that enables these plants to form a close association with grasses. Development of wild lettuce for food involved selection for plants that produced less latex.

The weeds in the lettuce tribe are among the most ancient of the "classic" field and garden weeds, and many have closely related counterparts among the crop plants, as we have seen in the case of lettuce. Various forms of chicory—endive, escarole, radicchio, and some narrow-leaved chicories known in commerce as garden dandelions—are grown for use as salad and cooked greens. Many of the wild members of this tribe are also edible: wild dandelions are still commonly gathered for use as salad and cooked greens, and until fairly recently sowthistles and wild chicory were eaten as spring greens, raw in salads or as potherbs in porridges and stews. Sowthistle was considered good rabbit and pig food in Europe long after people ceased to eat it.

Lettuce tribe herbs have medicinal properties, mostly based on substances in the latex. The principal use of dandelion latex has been as a diuretic, although it has also been taken as a tonic to aid digestion by causing stomach muscles to contract, as a cough medicine, as a mild laxative, and as a sedative and narcotic, as has latex derived from the wild lettuces. The early seventeenth-century herbalist Nicholas Culpeper claimed that the juice of the sowthistle was efficacious for inducing lactation in new mothers, a notion undoubtedly related more to ideas of sympathetic magic than to any empirical evidence.

THE GOOSEFOOT FAMILY AND THE AMARANTH FAMILY– CHENOPODIACEAE, AMARANTHACEAE

The chenopods, or goosefoots, are a family of herbaceous plants well adapted to growing in saline habitats. They typically have broadly triangular leaves (resembling goose feet), often with a mealy white underside. Goosefoots tend to be deep-rooted and are very drought tolerant, even when growing outside of salt marshes. The flowers are typically tiny and greenish with a mealy appearance and are arranged in spikes or cymes.

Chenopods grow in salt marshes and other saline and alkaline habitats throughout the temperate and subtropical zones of the world. They are particularly abundant around the Mediterranean, Caspian, and Red Seas, on the Central and East Asian steppes, along the edge of the Sahara, on the alkaline prairies of the United States, in the Karoo of South Africa, in Australia, and on the Argentine Pampas. Several have become weeds around human habitations, environments that often have somewhat salty soil.

In horticulture and agriculture, goosefoots are mostly represented by various forms of *Beta vulgaris*, the species that gives us beet roots, as well as sugar beets, fodder beets (mangels), Swiss chard, and the spinach beet, or perpetual spinach. Spinach itself, *Spinacia oleracea,* is also a goosefoot, as is *Chenopodium quinoa,* grown in Peru since ancient times for its spinachlike leaves and grain-like fruits. Known as quinoa, these fruits (usually referred to as seeds) are becoming an increasingly popular food outside their place of origin, deservedly so, as they contain a high percentage of high-quality protein and have a pleasant, nutty flavor as well. *Chenopodium ambrosioides,* a salt marsh weed known in Mexico and Central America as *epazote,* is used there as a culinary herb, particularly with black beans. *Chenopodium amaranthicolor,* with green and violet foliage, is grown as an ornamental.

The genus *Atriplex* contains a number of salt-tolerant shrubs with broadly triangular leaves. *Atriplex hortensis,* garden orache, was developed from a wild source as a warm-season spinach substitute and is still sometimes grown by tradition-minded gardeners. There are a number of saltbush weeds that sometimes appear in crop fields or gardens.

Another closely allied family, the Amaranthaceae, or amaranth family, gives us a number of mostly summer annual weeds, commonly known as pigweeds, as well as some attractive ornamentals, such as the celosias and the dark red-foliaged (and flowered) *Amaranthus caudatus,* love-lies-bleeding. Various amaranths have traditionally been grown throughout Central and South America as greens and grains, producing leaves and fruits somewhat similar to those of quinoa. They were brought by the Spanish to Europe and Asia during the Columbian Exchange. The grain amaranths, often plants growing six or eight feet or higher, are currently experiencing a revival as a productive source of high-quality protein that can be grown under less than ideal conditions, much like quinoa; unlike quinoa, however, they are a warm- rather than a cool-season plant. Thus, the two are complementary, providing year-round access to both high-protein grains and edible greens. Whether they become widely accepted enough to be a viable crop in parts of the world that cannot produce enough wheat, rice, or corn remains to be seen.

THE GRASS FAMILY–POACEAE, GRAMINEAE

The Poaceae, or Gramineae, is one of the largest and most widespread plant families, and one of the most recently evolved. Fossil evidence for grasses is rare before about fifteen million years ago, when they grew increasingly abundant and began occupying an increasingly large number of habitats. There are now about nine thousand species of grasses distributed among six hundred genera and growing almost everywhere in the world: they sprout in rock crevices on mountaintops; grow at the bottom of lakes, rivers, and the ocean itself; and occupy polar tundra and tropical forest, moist meadows and dry prairies, rain forests and deserts.

The great grasslands of the world occur in the latitudes between the temperate forest zone and the desert regions immediately north and south of the tropics of Cancer and Capricorn. In these zones, grass species coevolved with the animals that fed on them. Grazing by these large herbivores allowed the grasslands to persist and expand, since grasses recover more efficiently from grazing than broad-leaved plants do from browsing; so the grassy plains were able to support vast herds of ungulates—and a healthy population of the carnivores that fed upon them. Our hominid ancestors, originally forest dwellers subsisting largely on fruits, nuts, and tubers, became primarily grassland dwellers as they learned to hunt the large beasts that lived there and to supplement their meat diets with seeds of wild grasses. Following herds across these wide-open spaces enabled growing human populations to expand their territories, and by the beginning of the Paleolithic they had spread from their original home in Africa to Asia and Europe; they were in Australia by 40,000 BCE and in the Americas by perhaps 18,000 years ago.

After the last ice age, and following the decline of the great grazing herds, the grassy uplands of the Near East provided humans with another subsistence opportunity—the highly nutritious seeds of a number of wild grasses, gathered at first, later cultivated and improved, and ultimately providing the basic food source for the great civilizations that grew up in this region. Along with the development of grain crops came the domestication of some of the large grazing animals—cattle, sheep, goats, and horses—which provided further sources of food, as well as traction power.

Grasses are *monocotyledons,* containing a single cotyledon, or seed leaf, inside their seeds, as opposed to the two seed leaves of the broad-leaved plants, colloquially known as *dicots*. Compared to the dicots, the monocots are a fairly recent development in the evolution of flowering plants.

In addition to grasses, monocots contain the families of sedges and rushes, as well as palms, agaves and aloes, orchids, and many families of bulbous and rhizomatous plants formerly lumped into the lily and amaryllis families. They are mostly herbaceous, with long, narrow, parallel-veined leaves; when woody, the stems lack the distinct zonation of dicot stems. Whereas dicot stems are divided into heartwood, sapwood, xylem, phloem, cambium, and bark, woody monocot stems consist of "vascular bundles" that are distributed around a pithy or hollow core and contain a more or less uniform distribution of xylem and phloem tubes.

Since weeds coevolved with cultivated food plants, it is not surprising that a significant number of them are in the grass family. These are often difficult to distinguish from one another, and from desirable cultivated grasses. An understanding of the basic structure of these plants and their inflorescences provides the basis for using the many keys that have been devised to aid in their identification.

Like most other monocots, grasses have simple, narrow, parallel-veined leaves; they are mostly herbaceous (bamboo is a notable woody exception), annual and perennial, with fibrous roots, cylindrical hollow or pithy stems, and leaves growing from the basal crown, or opposite each other at nodes along the stems. Growth meristems are at the bases of the leaves and at nodes on the stems, a feature that allows grasses to recover quickly from grazing and mowing. Growth at the stem nodes is differential—that is, one side can grow faster than the other, allowing bent stems to easily grow upright again. Thus, grasses are adapted both to grazing and trampling.

Grass roots are generally fibrous and extensive, making them good plants for stabilizing soil. Inflorescences are compound, consisting of spikes or racemes, flower structures in which the smallest flower-bearing portions (known as *spikelets*) are held closely along a central stem, or of panicles or corymbs, more complex branched inflorescences.

The spikelets consist of a number of layers of leafy structures, which enclose one or more sets of both male and female flower parts, and which, after pollination, form a fruit called a *grain,* or *caryopsis.* The layers of leafy structures all have names—learning these is essential in order to use identification keys effectively. The outermost layer consists of two thin, papery bracts known as *glumes,* structures that may or may not remain attached to the plant when the grain drops off. Beneath these is a bract known as a *lemma*, which often has a thin, needlelike appendage called an *awn.* Awns come in a variety of lengths, depending on the species of grass—they can be straight, bent, or twisted. Between the lemma and its opposite bract, called the *palea,* the flowering parts are located—the stamens and anthers, pistils and styles. All these parts comprise the *floret,* the subdivision of the spikelet that produces the grain. The whole spikelet, which may consist of one or more florets, is enclosed by the glumes.

Grasses have characteristic vegetative features—leaf and stem structures—that aid in their identification. Tips of the leaf blades may be gradually tapered or bluntly pointed; the blade may be flat or may curve out from the midrib near the tip (*boat-shaped* is the term often used in keys). Outside the leaf, where it wraps its base around the stem, forming a *sheath*, is a thickened area known as a *collar*—this can be lighter than the rest of the leaf, smooth and glossy, or hairy. There are often projections from the sheath, earlike appendages known as *auricles*—these can vary considerably in shape and appearance.

If the leaf blade is peeled back where it emerges from the stem (at the junction of the leaf and sheath), a thin appendage known as a *ligule* is often visible.

This may be membranous, or it may consist of a fringe of hairs that can vary in appearance from species to species.

When grass stems first begin to emerge from the crown, the leaves are tightly clustered, forming a structure known as a *bud-shoot*. Slicing through this shoot can enable one to see whether these leaves are wrapped in a circular fashion (rolled in the bud) or in a more angular manner (folded in the bud).

Most keys depend more on analyzing floral structures than on the vegetative parts—keys involving the latter were mostly developed to aid in identifying turf grasses, which, because they are mowed, rarely produce flowers. Horticulturists, however, can make good use of both floral and vegetative keys when trying to identify the many species of grass that form a significant part of our weedy flora.

THE MUSTARD FAMILY–BRASSICACEAE, CRUCIFERAE

The mustard family, which contains some of our most important crop plants as well as many of our most common weeds, has been known since medieval times as Cruciferae, or cross-bearers, a reference to the flowers, which consist of four symmetrical petals, forming a corolla that resembles a Celtic or Maltese cross. In the early twentieth century, this family was named Brassicaceae, after what is considered its most typical genus, *Brassica*—but, in accordance with International Botanical Congress rules, the old name is still valid. Frequently used common names are mustard family, cabbage family, or simply crucifers.

The four-petaled flowers develop in racemes or panicles at the ends of stems. As the stems elongate, new flowers form at the tips, while the older blossoms develop into fruiting bodies, either long and narrow fruits known as *siliques* (rhymes with *sleek*), or shorter and wider fruits known as *siliculas* (has a chunky sound). These are usually dehiscent, meaning they split open and allow the seed to fall to the ground or actually propel it some distance.

This progressive development of flowers and fruiting bodies along a stem is one of the characteristics that allow us to recognize this family fairly easily. Another characteristic is prominently lobed leaves, often hairy, often with a pungent, characteristically "cabbagey" smell and taste, sometimes accompanied by some heat, as in the mustards.

Most crucifers are herbaceous annuals or perennials; a few are shrubs, even fewer climbers. They are found worldwide, but most are in the north temperate regions, with the heaviest concentrations of genera in the Mediterranean area and in Southwest and Central Asia, the regions where wheat-based grain agriculture developed. Crop plants in this family fall mostly into two species: *Brassica oleracea*, which includes kales, cabbages, broccoli, cauliflower, kohlrabi, and Brussels sprouts; and *Brassica rapa,* which gives us turnips, broccoli raab, and various Chinese "cabbages" and greens, including bok choy, nappa cabbage, Chinese broccoli, and numerous other greens, often referred to as "mustard greens." Other varieties are grown for oil seed. The condiment known as mustard is, these days, mostly derived from cultivated forms of *Sinapis alba,* although, in the recent past, other species such as black mustard *(Brassica nigra)* were frequently used. The hot seeds of these plants were traditionally mixed with must from the bottoms of wine barrels, forming hot must, or, in Latin, *musta ardens.*

Other crop plants in the mustard family include swedes, turnip-like plants grown for cattle feed and derived from *Brassica napus.* Other forms of the same species give us the rapes, plants used both for fodder and for oil seed. The many forms of radishes are varieties of *Raphanus sativus;* watercress is a cultivated form of *Rorippa nasturtium-aquaticum.*

The crucifers include a number of garden flowers, many of them very easy to grow, freely volunteering plants that border on weediness. Examples are wallflowers; sweet alyssum; golden alyssum; candytuft; stocks, honesty, or money plant; and rock garden plants such as aubretia and rock cress.

THE NIGHTSHADE, OR POTATO, FAMILY–SOLANACEAE

The nightshades form a large family consisting mostly of herbaceous or subwoody plants. They are represented in temperate and tropical zones on all continents except Antarctica and are most heavily concentrated in Australia and Central and South America, where about forty genera are endemic. Worldwide, there are about two to three thousand species, distributed through ninety genera. The family contains many of mankind's most useful plants, employed for food, ornament, and medicine. Important food plants include potatoes, tomatoes, eggplant, and hot and sweet peppers.

Eggplant is the only solanaceous crop with roots in the Old World—it originated in India in ancient times and moved quickly into China (by about 500 BCE). It was brought to Persia and Africa by Arab traders before the Middle Ages but was not introduced into Europe until the fifteenth century and did not become widespread until the seventeenth. All the other crops in the nightshade family originated in the New World and were introduced into Europe shortly after the discovery of America, part of the so-called Columbian Exchange. One of these was tobacco, which became immensely popular very quickly and developed into a lucrative crop for American planters.

A number of other nightshade genera, in both the New and Old Worlds, have been used since ancient times as both poisons and medicines. Among the most famous (or notorious) are jimson weed, *Datura stramonium,* a plant of undetermined origin that has long been used as a sedative and narcotic and that has become a worldwide weed; it came into widespread use among Europeans in the sixteenth century. People living in Europe claimed jimson weed came from the New World, while European settlers in America thought it came from Europe. Its most likely origin is Central Asia, where it is particularly abundant. Other species of *Datura* were used by Native Americans, including California Indians, to induce dreams and visions. Some European nightshades used as sedatives or pain killers are belladonna, or deadly nightshade, *Atropa belladonna;* black henbane, *Hyoscyamus niger;* and mandrake, *Mandragora officinarum.* Belladonna got its name from its use by fashionable ladies at the time of the Renaissance to enhance their beauty by dilating their pupils; it is still the source of atropine, an antidote to a number of nerve poisons and a component of every combat medic's kit.

Mandrake, or Satan's apple (*Mandragora officinarum),* is a Mediterranean herb used since ancient times as a sedative and soporific, as an emetic and purgative, and as an antidote to madness and possession by demons. The roots of this herb tend to fork and produce side shoots and many root hairs, suggesting a resemblance to a hairy human. Illustrations in old herbals often depict it as a male with a long beard or a female with a very bushy head of hair. The demonic appearance of these roots tended to evoke a number of lurid superstitions about the plant: it was believed to grow under the gallows of murderers, and digging up the roots growing in these locations was considered deadly—the mandrake was thought to utter a shriek and terrible groan upon extraction, a noise that killed anyone hearing it. Some recommended removing these roots from the ground by tying a dog to the plant and allowing it to pull out the plant, thus causing the dog to perish instead of its master. Most herbalists probably chose to dig out roots growing in other locations.

The medicinal actions of solanaceous plants are produced by alkaloids of the tropane group, which are therapeutic in small doses, poisonous in large, as is the case with many medicinal plants. It has been claimed that all nightshade plants, even edible ones, have some toxic portions. This seems to be largely true for the edible ones: some wild solanums have edible leaves, but poisonous berries; tomatoes are edible, but their leaves and roots poisonous; the top growth of potatoes is poisonous, but the tubers have become a worldwide staple.

Nightshades can be recognized most easily by their flowers, which are complete, regular, and five-petaled, partly or almost completely fused, with five stamens attached to the corolla tube and alternating with the petals. Anthers tend to be large and conspicuous, often yellow, often protruding beyond the petals (if you can recognize a tomato flower readily, you should be able to place most solanaceous weeds in the correct family). Sepals are partly fused, often persistent, sometimes engulfing the fruit, as in the ground cherry, or tomatillo. Other diagnostic features are simple, usually alternate leaves, often pointed, sometimes lobed; annual or perennial upright or vining herbs, sometimes with woody bases; flowers growing in the axils, usually in cymes.

Ornamentals in this family include petunias, salpiglossis, nicotiana, schizanthus, nierembergia, solandra; various viny and shrubby solanums grown for their ornamental flowers; and shrubs such as the marmalade bush, *Streptosolen jamesonii;* angel's trumpets, *Brugmansia* spp.; and night-blooming jessamine, *Cestrum nocturnum.* A number of peppers are grown for their ornamental fruits; the Chinese lantern, *Physalis alkekengi,* is grown as an ornamental because of its papery red fruits, which are dried for use in flower arrangements.

THE PARSLEY FAMILY—APIACEAE, UMBELLIFERAE

The Apiaceae, or Umbelliferae, most commonly known as the parsley or carrot family, is a large and widespread group of mostly herbaceous plants that occur most often in upland temperate zone habitats. Their most common identifying characteristics are hollow stems, pronounced taproots, finely dissected compound leaves, and small flowers in flat-topped clusters known as *umbels.* The plants are often aromatic. Some of these characteristics make members of this family suitable for culinary, medicinal, and horticultural purposes. The aromatic seeds of umbellifers such as fennel, anise, caraway, dill, cumin, and coriander are used as spices, and the oils that produce these aromas have some medicinal uses. Careful selection for large, tender roots has given us carrots and parsnips, the most common temperate zone root vegetables from this family. In the tropics, the tubers of the great earthnut, *Bunium bulbocastanum,* are eaten, as well as those of the pignut, *Conopodium majus.* Native Americans in the northwestern United States and Canada have traditionally used the starchy, edible roots of various species of *Lomatium* as staple foods. The stems, leaves, and petioles of plants in this family are also eaten—celery and parsley are the most common examples, but angelica and lovage also have a long history of culinary use.

Umbellifers are often thought of as good companion plants in kitchen and ornamental gardens because their large inflorescences tend to attract beneficial insects. It has also been proposed that the fragrance of some umbelliferous plants might dilute the odors of nearby plants, or of the pheromones of pest insects attracted to those plants. A number of apiaceous plants are grown as ornamentals: various species of *Eryngium,* or sea holly, drought-tolerant Mediterranean natives; *Astrantia,* or masterwort; *Bupleurum fruticosum,* or shrubby hare's ear; *Ferula* spp.; *Aegopodium podagraria* Variegata, or bishop's weed; and various species of *Heracleum,* or cow parsnip, the most spectacular of which is *Heracleum mantegazzianum,* or giant hogweed. *Heracleum lanatum,* California's native cow parsnip, has also found favor in some native gardens, although it does seem to have some weedy characteristics.

There are a number of important weeds in the parsley family, the most problematic of which are probably *Foeniculum vulgare*, fennel; *Conium maculatum,* poison hemlock; and *Daucus carota,* Queen Anne's lace.

THE PEA FAMILY—FABACEAE, LEGUMINOSAE

Legumes, an old common name for a large family of plants that is well represented in horticulture and agriculture, are so called in reference to a common name for their fruits, one-chambered pods with seams top and bottom, containing a number of seeds—peas and beans come to mind most readily. Some of these pods are dehiscent, some not.

Fabaceae is a large, cosmopolitan family consisting of trees, shrubs, vines, and herbs. It is divided into several subfamilies, only one of which, the Papilionoideae, is extensively represented in the temperate zones. Members of this group are easily recognized by their flowers, typical "pea" blossoms with five irregular petals: an upstanding dorsal petal (the standard); two lateral petals (the wings); and two fused lower petals (the keel), which enclose the stamens and pistil. Virtually all the legumes that are grown as ornamentals, or for food, fodder, and other economic uses, as well as most leguminous weeds, are in this group. Most of these have alternate, compound pinnate, or trifoliate leaves.

Two other legume subfamilies are the Mimosoideae, which includes *Mimosa* and *Acacia,* and whose flower petals are small and equal; and the Caesalpinioideae, which includes the tropical and subtropical genera *Caesalpinia, Poinciana, Bauhinia,* and *Cassia,* as well as *Cercis,* well represented in the temperate zones by the redbuds. Species in this subfamily have a number of regular and irregular flower types.

Herbaceous legumes are a major source of food for people and animals, and their ability to inject nitrogen into the soil through bacterial action in nodules on their roots further enhances their food-producing ability. All our peas, beans, lentils, and favas—collectively called *pulses*—are members of this family. Their high-protein seeds have long provided nourishment for people and animals in the Old and New Worlds. *Genista tinctoria* produces a yellow dye; species of *Indigofera* yield a dark blue known as indigo. Tamarind, native to India, produces pods that are eaten as a fresh fruit; the dried fruits are infused to make a refreshing drink.

Some legumes not grown for food have other uses. At least two acacias are considered valuable timber trees: *Acacia melanoxylon,* the blackwood acacia of Australia, and *Acacia koa,* the Hawaiian koa tree. *Acacia decurrens,* the black, blue, or green wattle, provides a bark used in tanning. Various species of *Cassia* yield senna, used as a laxative or purgative. Clover and alfalfa are important fodder and green manure crops.

Ornamentals in this family include lupines, various brooms, sweet peas, wisteria, the golden chain tree, locusts, and many other trees, shrubs, and vines.

Leguminous weeds include a number of herbaceous plants that are sown deliberately as forage plants or cover crops, including clovers and bur clovers, vetches, and birdsfoot trefoil. Two widely grown Australian acacias, *Acacia decurrens* and *A. melanoxylon,* have escaped cultivation and become serious wild land pests in California and the Pacific Northwest. The same is true for French and Scotch broom, *Genista monspessulana* and *Cytisus scoparius,* as well as gorse, *Ulex europaeus.*

THE ROSE FAMILY–ROSACEAE

Rosaceae is a large and widespread family of herbaceous and woody plants divided into a number of subfamilies, or tribes. It consists of more than 3,000 species spread among approximately 120 genera. This family is distributed throughout the world's temperate and tropical zones but is most heavily represented in the north temperate regions. It includes many important food and ornamental plants, such as the stone fruits: peaches, plums, apricots, cherries, and almonds; the pome fruits: apples, pears, and quinces; strawberries and bramble berries (blackberries, raspberries, boysenberries, etc.); and ornamentals such as roses, hawthorn, cotoneaster, pyracantha, toyon, Japanese quince, alchemilla, potentilla, geum, and ornamental plums, cherries, and crabapples.

The rose family is most readily recognized by its flowers—regular and five-petaled, with numerous protruding stamens. Receptacles are urn shaped or cylindrical. Flowers are typically insect pollinated and frequently large and showy. Leaves may be simple or compound, usually alternate, with a pair of stipules at the base. Thorns or prickles are fairly common.

Many members of this family are vigorous, fast-growing plants, sometimes with rhizomatous root systems. They produce abundant seed. Most weedy rosaceous plants are, in fact, escapes from ornamental gardens and fruit orchards. Seedling apple and pear trees are often found near abandoned houses and fruit orchards, as are a number of ornamental roses, especially those used as rootstock, such as the species *Rosa multiflora* and *R. canina*. Rootstocks are often more vigorous than the scions grafted to them and so tend to persist under conditions inimical to the scions. The most likely surviving rootstocks to be found in neglected urban gardens are relatively modern hybrids such as Ragged Robin (a.k.a. Gloire des Rosomanes), a double crimson rose with a white center; Dr. Huey, double and almost purple; and a double, light pink Chinese tea rose known as Fung Jwan Lo. *R. rubiginosa*, eglantine, an old European climbing rose with single pink flowers and apple-scented foliage, is sometimes found forming thickets around abandoned houses, as is Harison's Yellow, a hybrid of a Scottish wild rose. Cuttings of both of these were often carried westward by nineteenth-century pioneers; Harison's Yellow may very well be the legendary "yellow rose of Texas."

R. multiflora has become a rampant invasive in the eastern United States, where it can form dense thickets along roadsides as well as take over pastures and invade woodlands. It is much less troublesome in the arid West, where it tends not to stray too far from the site where it was planted. The West Coast counterpart to *R. multiflora* is *Rubus armeniacus,* the Himalayan blackberry, which was introduced as a fruit crop in the Pacific Northwest and quickly got out of hand. It can often be seen growing in woodlands and chaparral, frequently alongside native blackberries and often forming thickets on roadsides and in meadows.

The widely grown ornamentals cotoneaster (mostly *Cotoneaster pannosa* and *C. franchetii*); the closely related pyracantha, *Pyracantha coccinea;* and the red-leaved plum, *Prunus cerasifera,* are often spread by birds and water and can invade woodlands some distance from their places of origin. Escaped red-leaved plums quickly revert to a green-leaved form with yellow fruit; in mountain canyons, they bloom a month or more later than in the Bay Area, where they often begin blossoming as early as late January and complete their bloom by early March.

COMPLETE LIST OF FAMILIES REPRESENTED BY WEEDS IN THIS BOOK

Acanthaceae, the acanthus family

Alliaceae, the onion family

Amaranthaceae, the amaranth family

Anacardiaceae, the sumac family

Apiaceae, Umbelliferae, the parsley family

Apocynaceae, the dogbane family

Araceae, the arum family

Araliaceae, the aralia family

Asparagaceae, the asparagus family

Asteraceae, Compositae, the aster family

Boraginaceae, the borage family

Brassicaceae, Cruciferae, the mustard family

Cannabinaceae, the hemp family

Caryophyllaceae, the carnation or pink family

Chenopodiaceae, the goosefoot family

Convolvulaceae, the morning glory family

Cyperaceae, the sedge family

Dennstaedtiaceae, the bracken fern family

Dipsacaceae, the teasel family

Equisetaceae, the horsetail family

Euphorbiaceae, the spurge family

Fabaceae, Leguminosae, the pea family

Geraniaceae, the geranium family

Iridaceae, the iris family

Juncaceae, the rush family

Lamiaceae, Labiatae, the mint family

Lythraceae, the loosestrife family

Malvaceae, the mallow family

Myrtaceae, the myrtle family

Onagraceae, the evening primrose family

Orchidaceae, the orchid family

Oxalidaceae, the sorrel family

Papaveraceae, the fumitory or poppy family

Plantaginaceae, the plantain family

Poaceae, Gramineae, the grass family

Polygonaceae, the buckwheat family

Portulacaceae, the purslane family

Primulaceae, the primrose family

Ranunculaceae, the buttercup family

Rosaceae, the rose family

Rubiaceae, the coffee family

Scrophulariaceae, the figwort family

Simaroubaceae, the quassia family

Solanaceae, the nightshade family

Tropaeolaceae, the nasturtium family

Urticaceae, the nettle family

Valerianaceae, the valerian family

Verbenaceae, the verbena family

Violaceae, the violet or pansy family

4

ABOUT BOTANICAL AND COMMON NAMES

*W*hen I first began to study horticulture, I had never taken a botany course. I had become a self-employed gardener to earn a living while deciding "what I really wanted to do with my life," but I quickly became fascinated by the complex and intriguing world of cultivated plants. The Bay Area, with its mild and moist climate where plants from virtually every part of the world will thrive, was an ideal place for me to learn about them. Although gardeners here tend to emphasize the plants of the Mediterranean Basin and other areas of the world with similar climates, the cool, foggy summers and nearly frost-free winters enable plants from such diverse environments as tropical cloud forests, the humid woodlands of the Northern Hemisphere, and rugged mountain and desert areas to thrive as easily as those from warm temperate, dry-summer regions such as South Africa, Greece, and Australia, whose climates most closely resemble that of California. We virtually have the world in our gardens, and as someone who had become obsessed with creating a detailed mental image of the world's vegetative cover, working as a gardener in the Bay Area seemed an ideal way to do this.

When I realized this, I started supplementing my freelance gardening and self-study with horticulture classes at Merritt College in Oakland, California, and soon found it necessary to memorize the Latin-based, two-part botanical names that I was told would enable me to distinguish every plant species from all others and to determine how it is related to other plants. Some people in my classes struggled with this requirement; I did not. I attribute this not only to my innate love of naming and categorizing but also to the years I spent grappling with Latin in high school and college. We were told that memorizing these names was the only way we would be able to identify the plants we encountered in our work with precision; common names, we were told, often described plants inaccurately, were misleading about relationships, varied widely from one place to another, and were often applied to more than one species. Cork oaks and she-oaks, for instance, grow in different hemispheres, and the she-oak is not even closely related to the true oaks; the apple is a member of the rose family, as is the cherry, but the Argyle apple is a eucalyptus, and the Surinam cherry is a member of the myrtle family (as is the eucalyptus). The stinking rose (garlic) is in the onion family.

The trouble with botanical names, as I was soon to find out, is that many of them change frequently. Botanists are always making discoveries that lead them to reassess the relationships between plants and have gravitated between two moieties, the *lumpers* and the *splitters*. Lumpers tend to see common characteristics that are possessed by different species and so tend to aggregate them into fewer groups; splitters tend to perceive fine distinctions and so create more groups. This is a battle that can never be won so long as the outcome depends on differing subjective perceptions. However, in recent years studies of cellular chemistry have led to increased agreement on evolutionary relationships, and this has resulted in even more shifting of plants between genera, creation of new genera, and shifting of plants from one family to another. This new approach has been a boon to those studying the evolution of the plant kingdom but has left horticulturists in somewhat of a dilemma: we took the trouble to learn botanical names so we could communicate with precision, and now we find that many of the names we know no longer apply. To make things even harder, we sometimes find that the names we learned draw a blank from older horticulturists and nursery growers, who continue to use names even older than the ones that were discarded in favor of the now obsolete names that we use.

The horticulturists' answer to this dilemma, ironically enough, has been a return to the common names that we once discarded in exchange for the supposed precision of botanical nomenclature. With Latin names changing so rapidly and unpredictably, a widely agreed-upon common name, we theorized, could provide the sort of precision horticulturists need in order to communicate about their plants. But then the question becomes, how can we come to universal agreement about what these proper common names should be and which frequently changing botanical names they relate to? There are no international congresses to settle disputes over common names, and if there were, horticulturists would become as hopelessly enmeshed in controversy as botanists seem to be. The common currency of common names that we so sorely need is going to have to be developed simply through usage over time; there will be no absolute precision, but hopefully we will come to speak the same language most of the time, and gardeners, landscape architects, and nursery growers will be able to use a name and be reasonably sure about what plant it represents. We will be inventing a new language of commerce, a horticultural Swahili, as it were.

There is, however, much more to common names than their use in plant commerce. All the history, folklore, and cultural values associated with garden plants and weeds lie in the clusters of common names that have adhered to them over the centuries. Wild morning glory or field bindweed are the two common names most likely to engender recognition of *Convolvulus arvensis,* a very persistent and threatening weed, but we learn so much more about it when we hear it called Jack-run-in-the-country, or withywind, creeping Jenny, devil's garters, or hedge bells. Bedstraw, the common name most usually associated with *Galium odoratum,* tells us something about one of the many uses for this plant; but cleavers, devil's garters, catchweed, loveman, and Robin-run-in-the-grass tell us so much more. Homesick English colonists who settled Australia seized upon the most tenuous resemblances to the plants they had left behind to attach the most unlikely names to the strange flora of that continent: they called *Eucalyptus cinerea* the Argyle apple, named *Acacia decurrens* the green wattle, christened *Grevillea robusta* the silk oak. Some common names indicate medicinal uses, for instance, self-heal, feverfew, plaster clover, eyebright, bruisewort, and fleabane. Some plants have become so well loved and familiar over the centuries that they have acquired proper names: herb Robert, herb John, herb Good Henry, for instance.

There are many plants that are new to horticulture or less well known, which have not acquired common names. If we are to accept the premise that all plants must have at least one common name so we can talk about them easily, we must create some. This naming is often accomplished by an adaptation or literal translation of the Latin name: thus, *Ehrharta erecta* is often called simply ehrharta grass, *Escallonia rubra* is red escallonia, *Homeria collina* simply homeria. As time goes by, some of the plants so named will hopefully acquire more colorful and allusive common names.

I am not suggesting that horticulturists ignore botanical names; these still provide the most accurate way to communicate about plants with some precision, to understand how they relate to other plants, and to communicate about them across linguistic boundaries. Still, well agreed-upon common names can be very useful tools for identifying plants in commerce, and all common names should be valued for what they tell us about the historical and cultural associations of the plants we gardeners encounter in our daily work.

Part 2
THE WEEDS

5

THE "CLASSIC" WEEDS

INTRODUCTION

Throughout this book, I have used the term *classic weeds* to designate a grouping of plants that includes our oldest and most common and abundant weeds, those that go back to the beginnings of agriculture in the Near East and Europe. These are the weeds that grow in our most frequently disturbed ground: farm fields, pastures, roadsides, construction sites, urban gardens, sidewalk cracks, tree wells. With some notable exceptions, these tend not to invade areas of native vegetation—when they occur there at all, they stay close to trail sides and campsites.

Many of these weeds have culinary and medicinal uses, and since they have been the familiars of the peoples of Europe and the Near East for many centuries, there is an extensive and rich body of folklore associated with them. I give some examples of this in my discussions of individual weeds—these are largely drawn from Mrs. M. Grieve's wonderful book, *A Modern Herbal,* which was written in England during the 1930s, when a good deal of this folklore was still very much alive. How much persists today is a good question, which I cannot answer. Many of the common names still in use refer to this folklore, and Mrs. Grieve's book is an excellent source for those who want to know the stories behind these names.

ARROWLEAF SALTBUSH

Atriplex prostrata—arrowleaf saltbush, spearscale— saltbush family

Arrowleaf saltbush is an annual native to Eurasia that has naturalized in North America, including California, and grows in marshy, saline areas along

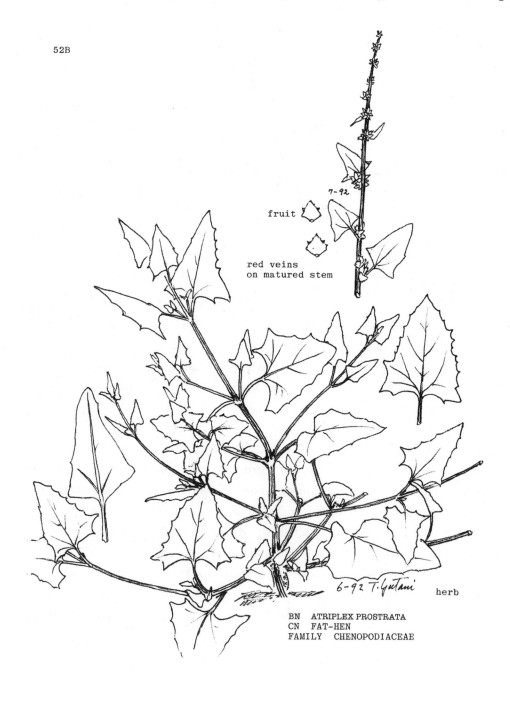

52B

7-92

fruit

red veins
on matured stem

6-92 T. Gyatani herb

BN   ATRIPLEX PROSTRATA
CN   FAT-HEN
FAMILY   CHENOPODIACEAE

the coast and on alkaline soils in the Central Valley. A member of the goosefoot family, it closely resembles lamb's quarters and sometimes shares the name *fat hen* with that plant. Like lamb's quarters, it has a high tolerance for salts in the soil.

Also known as spearscale or halberd-leaved orache, *Atriplex prostrata* is a branching plant that grows from 1 to 2 feet tall or more. Its leaves are its most distinctive characteristic: they are triangular, but the base of the leaf has two outward-curving, pointed appendages that make it resemble an arrowhead or spear point. The leaves are 1 or 2 inches long, often as wide, entire or wavy-margined, opposite on the lower stem, alternate above, mealy on the surface (as are the stems). The flowers are tiny, greenish, and mealy, occurring in spikes, with male and female blooms growing either on the same spike or separately, but always on the same plant. The pistillate flowers are surrounded at their bases by two bracts, which subsequently cover the fruits, hard capsules with rough, pointed appendages. Seeds are brownish, often somewhat wrinkled.

Arrowleaf saltbush is listed as a weed, and it may invade crops to some extent, but it does not often travel much beyond its preferred salt marsh locations in the Bay Area. It is a host for the beet leafhopper, which makes it a threat to crops growing near alkaline soils in the Central Valley.

A number of atriplexes, native and exotic, are listed in *The Sunset Western Garden Book* as useful shrubs and ground covers for alkaline and saline soils; at least one of these, *A. semibaccata,* the Australian saltbush, has escaped and become a weed in some places. Garden orache, a cultivated European atriplex that has been grown as a warm-weather green since Roman times, is still sometimes available in seed exchanges. It grows from 4 to 6 feet tall and has triangular leaves with a flavor somewhat resembling that of spinach. It is susceptible to the beet leaf miner.

BEDSTRAW

Galium aparine—bedstraw, goosegrass—Rubiaceae, madder or coffee family

This common and abundant weed has acquired many colorful common names during its long association with European peasants, names that indicate a long history of practical uses and folkloric associations. Besides bedstraw, it has been referred to in English-speaking countries as cleavers, catchweed, barweed, hedgeheriff, hayriffe, eriffe, hayruff, grip grass, scratweed, mutton chops, robin-run-in-the-grass, loveman, goosebill, everlasting friendship, and sticky Willy. I'll explain some of these names later.

Bedstraw is considered native to most of the cold and temperate parts of the Northern Hemisphere, including, possibly, California. If it was in California before European settlement, I doubt that it was very widespread—its current abundance was no doubt (in my opinion, anyway) due to its presence in the suite of weeds brought here by Europeans.

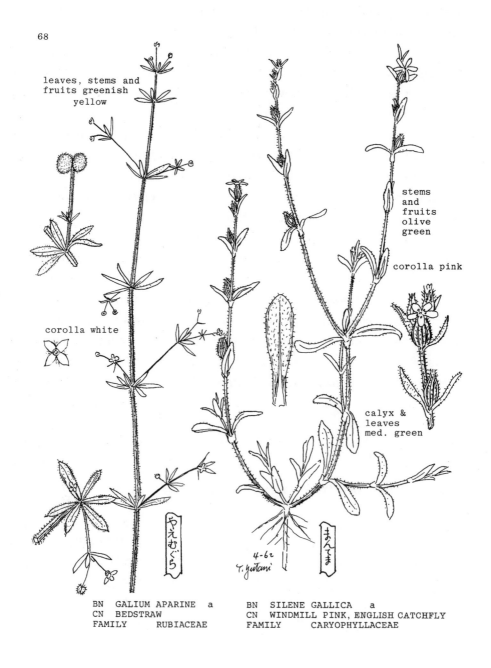

68

leaves, stems and
fruits greenish
yellow

stems
and
fruits
olive
green

corolla pink

corolla white

calyx &
leaves
med. green

4-62
T. yutani

BN   GALIUM APARINE   a
CN   BEDSTRAW
FAMILY   RUBIACEAE

BN   SILENE GALLICA   a
CN   WINDMILL PINK, ENGLISH CATCHFLY
FAMILY   CARYOPHYLLACEAE

Bedstraw is a winter annual or short-lived perennial with a climbing or sprawling habit. The stems are square in cross section, 2 to 6 feet long, and covered with tiny recurved prickles that allow the plant to cling to almost anything it touches. These same prickles appear on the edges of the leaves, as well as on the flowers and fruits. These structures explain the plant's ability to scramble through shrubs and hedges, on whose surface growth it often forms extensive mats, and are referred to by a number of the common names the plant has acquired. Whorls of narrow, oblanceolate (wider at tip than base) leaves grow in evenly spaced whorls along the stems.

Bedstraw flowers are small (less than ¼ inch across), four-petaled, and white or greenish white; they grow in small clusters arising from the leaf axils. The globular calyces of the flowers are covered with prickles, as is the globular fruit, a characteristic that greatly facilitates seed dispersal.

Bedstraw usually grows in moist soil in shady areas, although it likes to get its tops up into the sun. It can be a nuisance in plantings of woody ground covers and low shrubs, which provide the roots with the shade and moisture they need and furnish a platform for the plant to reach sunlight, allowing it to flower, set seed, and move around in the landscape by attaching itself to passersby.

Historically, goosegrass has had many culinary, medicinal, and practical uses. It was often fed to livestock and poultry and eaten by people as a boiled spring green or potherb. The seeds, roasted and ground, are said to make an excellent coffee substitute, and they have been used as such in Sweden. Decoctions of the entire plant have been drunk as teas, both culinary and medicinal. Bedstraw is a powerful diuretic. It has been used to treat skin diseases, heal scalds and burns (including sunburn), remove freckles, shrink tumors, reduce swelling, treat colds, prevent scurvy, and cure insomnia. Dioscorides, the ancient Greek herbalist, reports that the Greek shepherds of his day used the matted stems of the plant to make a rough sieve to strain sheep's milk. Linnaeus reported a similar use in country districts in Sweden, a tradition that continued well into the twentieth century. The dried stems were also used as a mattress stuffing.

Legend has it that this plant was one of the original "cradle herbs" that were present in the manger where the baby Jesus lay—a good possibility, since it was often fed to livestock. Hence, another of its traditional names is our lady's bedstraw. The names *hedgeheriff, hayriffe, eriffe,* and *hayruff* are derived from the Anglo-Saxon term for a tax collector, although they were often applied to other sorts of livestock thieves. This official would hide in a hedge along a roadway near the dwelling of the delinquent farmer, waiting for him to drive his sheep down the road. When the flock passed, he would reach out from the hedge and appropriate as many sheep as were needed to settle the debt.

BINDWEED

Convolvulus arvensis—field bindweed, wild morning glory—Convolvulaceae, morning glory family

Field bindweed is an aggressively vigorous, perennial Eurasian weed that has probably been known to farmers in that part of the world since the beginning of agriculture. It has accumulated a wealth of folklore, much of which is reflected in its many colorful common names, such as creeping Jenny, cornbind, rope-bind, withywind, bearwind, Jack-run-in-the-country, devil's garters, hedge bells, and, of course, creeping Charlie. It is a trailing and twining vine, with stems that grow to about 3 feet. They can twine around the stems of other plants and even around each other, elevating themselves to a height where they can continue to wind around the lower branches of shrubs. These stems can make a complete turn in less than two hours.

Bindweed likes sun and warmth but can tolerate part shade. It is primarily a weed of crop lands and pastures, but it often invades urban gardens. Once established, it is extremely difficult to eradicate, for reasons I'll explain shortly.

The leaves of field bindweed grow alternately on the stems, attached by short petioles. They are entire, light green, shaped somewhat like a spearhead *(hastate),* rounded to slightly pointed at the tip, indented and pointed at the base. The flowers, which grow in the leaf axils, are white with some pink, funnel shaped, with five mostly fused petals, resembling garden morning glories but somewhat smaller—about 1 to 1½ inches across. They produce globular, two-celled capsules, each cell holding two seeds.

What enables field bindweed to spread so aggressively and persist so tenaciously is its remarkable root system. Newly emerged seedlings produce taproots that can grow to a depth of 10 feet or more. Laterals branch from this taproot, originating from adventitious buds. More buds develop on these laterals; these generate rhizomes, which produce new crowns. These laterals are annual—but if they succeed in producing crowns, the crowns are perennial. It is therefore important to eliminate bindweed plants before new crowns emerge, preferably in the seedling stage. Bindweed plants with fewer than five true leaves will die if cut to the ground. Herbicides are widely used in agriculture, sometimes in urban gardens; they are effective in suppressing the growth of this weed but will never eradicate it. Cutting back or breaking off the tops of established plants actually stimulates underground bud formation, so a combination of cutting back and persistent digging will be needed. Digging, of course, helps spread the rhizomes.

Medicinally, field bindweed has been used as a purgative. All members of its family have this property.

There are several species of wild morning glory that are native to California—none of them are weedy. They can often be seen twining through shrubs in the wild, but they will generally stay out of gardens (they can be introduced, if desired). The species that grows in the Bay Area is *Convolvulus occidentalis;* it can be readily distinguished from field bindweed by its leaves, which are broader and much more triangular (sagittate, shaped like an arrowhead) than the spearhead-shaped (hastate) leaves of bindweed.

Garden morning glories—mostly in the genus *Ipomaea* (which includes sweet potatoes) are tropical perennials that are usually grown as annuals in colder climates. In warm areas such as coastal California, they can retain their perennial nature and regenerate from their roots, as well as germinate readily from seed. They can easily become persistent, unwanted weeds in these areas.

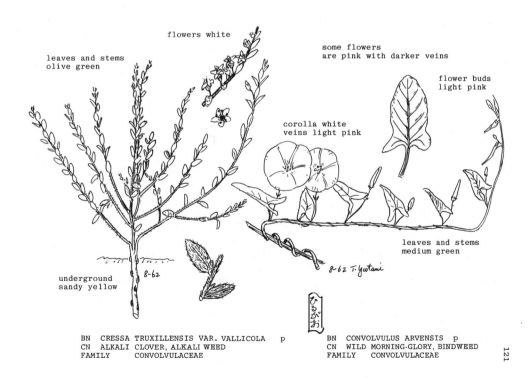

flowers white

leaves and stems olive green

some flowers are pink with darker veins

flower buds light pink

corolla white veins light pink

leaves and stems medium green

underground sandy yellow

8-62

8-62 T. Yutani

BN   CRESSA TRUXILLENSIS VAR. VALLICOLA   p
CN   ALKALI CLOVER, ALKALI WEED
FAMILY   CONVOLVULACEAE

BN   CONVOLVULUS ARVENSIS   p
CN   WILD MORNING-GLORY, BINDWEED
FAMILY   CONVOLVULACEAE

121

THE CHICKWEEDS

Stellaria media—common chickweed—Caryophyllaceae, the carnation family

Cerastium fontanum ssp. *vulgare*—perennial mouse-eared chickweed—Caryophyllaceae

Cerastium glomeratum—annual mouse-eared chickweed

One of the most common winter annuals, appearing in abundance after the first substantial autumn rain, is *Stellaria media,* common chickweed, also known as star chickweed, alsine media, or passerina. This is a sprawling plant with bright green, almost chartreuse, stems and leaves. These leaves are generally ¼ to ½ inch long, oval and entire, and set opposite one another on the stems. They are smooth and shiny *(glabrous),* bright green on top, paler beneath, pointed at the tips. Flowers are small (¼ inch or less), white, five-petaled, but with each petal deeply cleft, which gives the flowers their starlike appearance. These flowers are solitary in the leaf nodes, or in few-flowered leafy clusters at the ends of the stems. The fruit is a many-seeded oval capsule with dull,

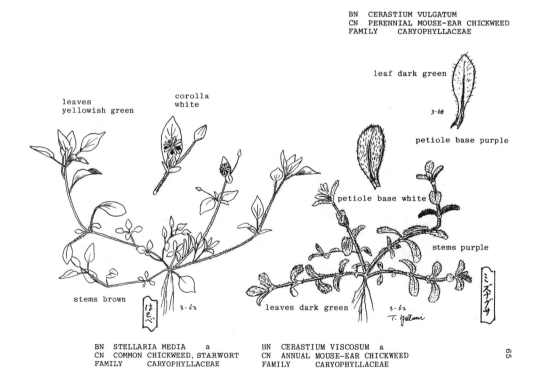

BN CERASTIUM VULGATUM
CN PERENNIAL MOUSE-EAR CHICKWEED
FAMILY CARYOPHYLLACEAE

leaf dark green

3-68

petiole base purple

corolla white

leaves yellowish green

petiole base white

stems purple

stems brown 3-62

leaves dark green 3-62

T. Yutami

BN STELLARIA MEDIA a
CN COMMON CHICKWEED, STARWORT
FAMILY CARYOPHYLLACEAE

BN CERASTIUM VISCOSUM a
CN ANNUAL MOUSE-EAR CHICKWEED
FAMILY CARYOPHYLLACEAE

65

reddish-brown seeds. The roots are fibrous. Under very ideal conditions, the plant can root at the nodes and become a short-lived perennial.

Chickweed grows best in moist areas with rich soil, and it is particularly abundant in the shade, where its chartreuse-green leaves are especially attractive. It can be controlled easily by pulling or hoeing, but allowing it to become the dominant seasonal ground cover in areas that grow little else but weeds can be an attractive option. It withers almost completely at the end of the rainy season, needing very little cutting back.

Chickweed is quite edible, with a mild, pleasant flavor, and has been eaten both as a potherb and a salad green, often mixed with more bitter greens such as dandelion leaves. A caution—chickweed is said to be capable of accumulating nitrates in toxic quantities. Birds like both the seed and the foliage. Medicinally, chickweed has been used to make poultices and has been taken internally for constipation, coughs and hoarseness, and liver ailments. In the past, it was mixed with elecampine *(Inula)* as a cure for rabies and was sometimes prescribed by herbwives to combat obesity.

Although in a different genus, the mouse-eared chickweeds somewhat resemble common chickweed, but they are darker green and have oblong, rounded, or obovate leaves, which are sessile and covered with short hairs and somewhat sticky. The flowers resemble those of the common chickweed but are a little smaller; the sepals are hairy and sticky and almost as long as the flower petals.

Perennial mouse-eared chickweed, *Cerastium fontanum* ssp. *vulgare,* is a low-growing plant that tends to form mats and can become a persistent weed in lawns. It flowers in cymes, with individual blossoms on pedicels that are two to four times as long as the calyces of the flowers. Annual mouse-eared chickweed, *Cerastium glomeratum,* does not form mats; it is a more upright plant growing from a single crown. Its flowers grow in very close clusters, with pedicels no longer than the flowers. Annual mouse-eared chickweed can grow in lawns, but it is more often found elsewhere.

MATS AND TUFTS

Polycarpon tetraphyllum—four-leaved allseed—Caryophyllaceae, pink family

Spergularia rubra—sand spurry—Caryophyllaceae

Spergula arvensis—corn spurry

Sherardia arvensis—field madder—Rubiaceae, coffee family

In this section, I'm departing from my usual practice of grouping weeds by families to discuss four mat or tuft-forming plants that somewhat resemble the three chickweeds described in the last section. These four weeds are all annual, with sprawling stems and deep taproots. All produce an abundance of small seed and thrive in hot, dry situations and compacted soil. Cracks in pavement, where the seed tends to lodge, provide an ideal environment.

Polycarpon tetraphyllum, four-leaved allseed, has spreading but somewhat erect stems that extend about 6 inches or less from the crown and form a dense tuft. It has oval leaves with smooth margins, about an ⅛ inch long or less, opposite on the stems. Each leaf has a small lobe at its base, approximately the same shape as the leaf itself, but smaller, creating the illusion of two smaller leaves growing on the stem perpendicular to the larger leaves—thus, "four-leaved."

Dense clusters of tiny greenish flowers form at the tips of the stems, followed by clusters of tiny fruits—the flowers and fruit seem to cover the entire plant—thus, "allseed." These fruits are dehiscent—they split open when mature—so the seed scatters. New plants germinate in abundance, forming colonies where there is little competition from other weeds.

Four-leaved allseed is native to Europe. In the United States, it is found mostly on the West Coast and in the southeastern states. It grows well in

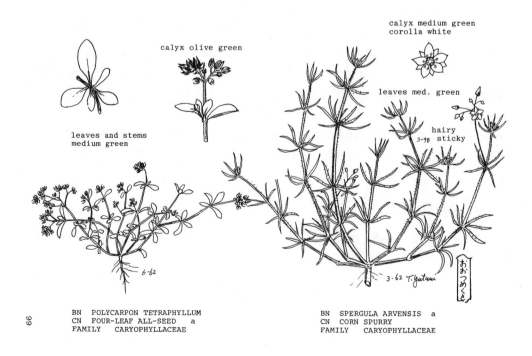

calyx olive green

leaves and stems
medium green

calyx medium green
corolla white

leaves med. green

hairy
sticky

BN POLYCARPON TETRAPHYLLUM
CN FOUR-LEAF ALL-SEED   a
FAMILY   CARYOPHYLLACEAE

BN SPERGULA ARVENSIS a
CN CORN SPURRY
FAMILY   CARYOPHYLLACEAE

sidewalks and on compacted ground but can easily spread to cultivated areas. It is not difficult to control if one learns to recognize it and removes it before it sets seed.

Spergularia rubra, sand spurry, is a low, sprawling European native with wiry stems about 4 to 10 inches long. The stems produce dark green, needlelike, somewhat succulent leaves on opposite sides of the nodes. Alternating sets of leaves are often set at more or less right angles to each other, giving a whorled appearance. New branches sprout from the leaf nodes, causing the plant to form a dense mat.

This weed is a very drought tolerant winter annual that survives and flowers throughout the summer and sometimes lives for another year or so, especially in mild winter climates. Like many of the other mat- or tuft-forming plants, sand spurry likes hot, dry situations and compacted soils, conditions not hospitable to most of the taller weeds that might otherwise suppress it. It does especially well in sandy places but will grow in almost any soil. It has fibrous roots or a slender taproot, which enables it to thrive in sidewalk cracks.

The flowers of sand spurry are borne in few-flowered cymes at the tips of the stems and in the leaf nodes. Individual blossoms are pink, with five ovate petals with pointed tips, less than ¼ inch across, and prominent yellow stamens. These are followed by three-valved capsules containing many dull brown, wedge-shaped seeds.

Sand spurry is native to Europe and Asia.

There are several other *Spergularia* species found in California, a number of them native. These somewhat resemble sand spurry, but they confine themselves to coastal environments, such as sand dunes, salt marshes, seaside bluffs, and alkaline flats. Sand spurry also grows in such locations, as well as in farm fields and gardens and along roadsides. Anyone concerned with preserving or restoring coastal environments will need to learn to distinguish sand spurry from the other *Spergularia* species that grow there.

Corn spurry, *Spergula arvensis,* is another European native also known as sand weed, poverty weed, cow quake, pick purse, and devil's gut. Like its cousin, sand spurry, it qualifies as a sprawler, but it is different in other respects. It produces long, slender, branched stems, about 6 to 18 inches long. The plant is anchored by a shallow, slender taproot, which produces fibrous branches. It can be either upright or sprawling. It often clambers over surrounding vegetation—think of it as a kind of miniature bedstraw.

Corn spurry's leaves are slender, threadlike, and bright green, with blunt tips; they grow in whorls around the stems. They are about an inch long, and form two whorls at each node. Flowers are about ¼ inch across, white-petaled, in terminal clusters. The fruit is a single-celled capsule.

This weed prefers sandy or gravelly soil but does not occur in the same hot, dry situations as sand spurry. It is largely a weed of grain fields and competes well with grasses. It grows in meadows and cultivated ground. Like sand spurry, it is basically a winter annual but can survive mild winters and become a short-lived perennial.

Sherardia arvensis, field madder, is an elegantly formed little winter annual that produces dense mats or tufts about 1 to 4 inches high, consisting of branched stems up to 12 inches long. It is in the coffee family, and, with its whorls of six leaves spaced evenly along the stems, it looks something like a miniature version of its close cousin, bedstraw. These leaves are from ⅛ to ½ inch long, narrowly lanceolate with sharply pointed tips, bright green in color. The flowers are tiny, tubular, and starlike; pink, lavender, or purple; occurring in clusters surrounded by fused bracts at the tips of the stems. Each flower produces two one-seeded nutlets. The plant is anchored by a slender taproot.

Sherardia grows in moist ground, often with grasses. It can be found in lawns, meadows, grasslands, and orchards. As a lawn weed, it is often tolerated for its fine, attractive foliage, which helps vary the texture of the grass monoculture, and for its lovely little flowers. Field madder is a beautiful and very unthreatening weed.

I close with a comment quoted verbatim from a weed identification sheet that my former student Nora Elliott wrote as part of a class project: "Linnaeus named this pretty little weed after William Sherard (1659–1728), a noted English botanist. With the help of Dillenius (1684–1747), he produced *Hortus Elthamensis* (1732), which illustrated and described the plants of James (perhaps his father?) Sherard's garden at Eltham."

MORE MATS AND TUFTS

Matricaria discoidea—Pineapple weed—Asteraceae, sunflower family

Chamaesyce prostrata—Prostrate spurge—Euphorbiaceae, spurge family

Chamaesyce maculata—Prostrate spotted spurge

Matricaria discoidea—pineapple weed—is a European native closely related to German chamomile, *Matricaria recutita,* from which chamomile tea is made (I have made a tea with a very similar flavor from *M. matricarioides*). It is similar

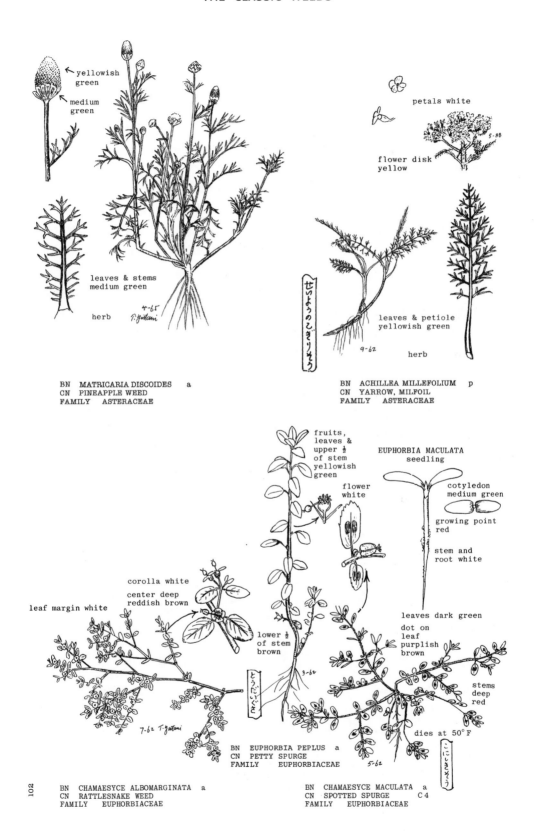

yellowish green

medium green

leaves & stems medium green

herb

4-65
T. Yutani

petals white

5-88

flower disk yellow

せいようのこぎりそう

leaves & petiole yellowish green

9-62

herb

BN   MATRICARIA DISCOIDES   a
CN   PINEAPPLE WEED
FAMILY   ASTERACEAE

BN   ACHILLEA MILLEFOLIUM   p
CN   YARROW, MILFOIL
FAMILY   ASTERACEAE

fruits, leaves & upper ½ of stem yellowish green

flower white

EUPHORBIA MACULATA seedling

cotyledon medium green

growing point red

stem and root white

corolla white

center deep reddish brown

leaf margin white

lower ½ of stem brown

leaves dark green

dot on leaf purplish brown

stems deep red

dies at 50° F

とうだいぐさ

3-62

7-62 T. Yutani

BN   EUPHORBIA PEPLUS   a
CN   PETTY SPURGE
FAMILY   EUPHORBIACEAE

5-62

こにしきそう

BN   CHAMAESYCE ALBOMARGINATA   a
CN   RATTLESNAKE WEED
FAMILY   EUPHORBIACEAE

BN   CHAMAESYCE MACULATA   a
CN   SPOTTED SPURGE   C 4
FAMILY   EUPHORBIACEAE

102

in form to four-leaved allseed, but with somewhat taller and more compact tufts. The stems are thicker and densely covered with bright green leaves, usually about ⅓ inch long (sometimes up to 2 inches), with very narrow, nearly linear lobes. The whole plant feels very soft to the touch. Dense, conical flower clusters about ½ inch tall consisting of masses of tiny bright yellow flowers form at the tips of the stems. They resemble tiny pineapples.

Pineapple weed truly loves full sun and very dry, compacted soil. It thrives on gravel roads and road shoulders and makes limited inroads into cultivated areas, where it probably cannot withstand competition from weeds more adapted to these situations. If it does appear in the garden, it can mix well with other flowering plants and ground covers, and you might well consider retaining a limited amount.

Chamaesyce prostrata and *Chamaesyce maculata*—prostrate spurge and prostrate spotted spurge—are separate species, but are virtually identical in appearance except for one difference: prostrate spotted spurge has a reddish spot in the middle of its leaf; prostrate spurge does not. The leaves of spotted spurge are also somewhat larger—½ inch long by ⅛ inch wide, as opposed to ⅜ inch long by ¼ inch wide for prostrate spurge. Both have ovate leaves, opposite on long (to 12 inches), sprawling stems that form a dense mat. Both plants are summer annuals, well adapted to full sun and dry, compacted soil, but

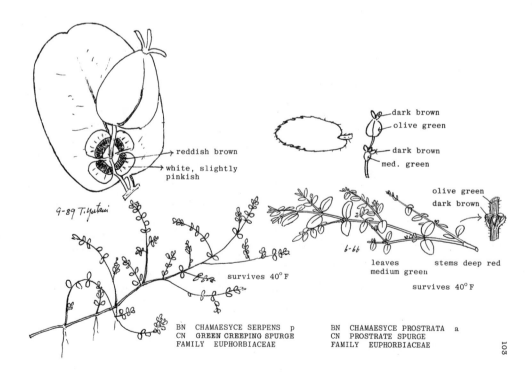

reddish brown

white, slightly pinkish

9-89 T.Yutani

survives 40° F

BN CHAMAESYCE SERPENS p
CN GREEN CREEPING SPURGE
FAMILY EUPHORBIACEAE

dark brown
olive green

dark brown
med. green

olive green
dark brown

6-66

leaves   stems deep red
medium green

survives 40° F

BN CHAMAESYCE PROSTRATA a
CN PROSTRATE SPURGE
FAMILY EUPHORBIACEAE

103

thrive in all light conditions and soil types. They have a long central taproot that can grow to 2 inches. Flowers are tiny and pink, without petals or sepals, and grow in clusters in the leaf axils. The fruits are tiny three-lobed capsules, pinkish in color, and produced in great abundance—if one pulls a plant that has matured, the ground will be covered densely with the tiny, seedlike fruits. Like four-leaved allseed, these spurges love cracks in sidewalks, but they will spread readily to other areas of the garden. Like other spurges, they contain a milky sap that can be poisonous to livestock and cause skin rashes as well. They are native to the Americas: *C. maculata* to the eastern United States; *C. prostrata* to the West Indies and South America.

FENNEL

Foeniculum vulgare—fennel, sweet fennel, fenkel—Apiaceae, Umbelliferae, parsley family

Fennel is a tall (6 to 8 feet), upright, free-flowering perennial, a beautiful weed that is often kept in gardens because of its elegant form, soft, ferny, fragrant foliage, and abundance of bright yellow flowers. If this is not enough, it also attracts a large yellow butterfly with black markings, the anise swallowtail. Allowing this plant anything like free rein, however, is a bad mistake. It seeds prolifically, and one fennel plant that appears in a neglected yard or vacant lot often creates a solid mass that can engulf the entire space in a few years. If you like this plant, you need to restrain it, early and often.

Fennel is native to the Mediterranean Basin and grows best in Mediterranean climates. It is herbaceous, but with very sturdy taproot and stems; since it often grows more than head high, it can be thought of as a virtual shrub. Fennel leaves are about a foot long, compound, and finely dissected into many threadlike segments; these do not lie flat along the midrib, but form a sort of plume. The petioles are somewhat swollen and clasp the stems. The flower heads are large compound umbels, 3 to 6 inches across, and consist of small (perhaps ¼ inch across), bright yellow, five-petaled flowers. The fruits are oblong, slightly flattened laterally, with pointed ends and prominent ribs. These smell and taste like licorice, as do the leaves and stems.

Removing a well-established fennel plant is a formidable task. Cut it at the base and it will resprout; even removing crowns to a depth of a foot does not always prevent new plants forming from the remnants of the roots. It is far easier to deal with newly germinated plants, by mechanical or chemical means.

If you want to keep just one, see to it that it remains just one, and remove flower heads before they set seed.

Fennel is also sometimes called anise, or sweet anise, a name more properly ascribed to a white-flowered annual relative, *Pimpinella anisum,* often grown in gardens and in commerce for its fragrant, sickle-shaped fruits. The flavors are similar, as are the medicinal virtues; but anise has a purer licorice

129

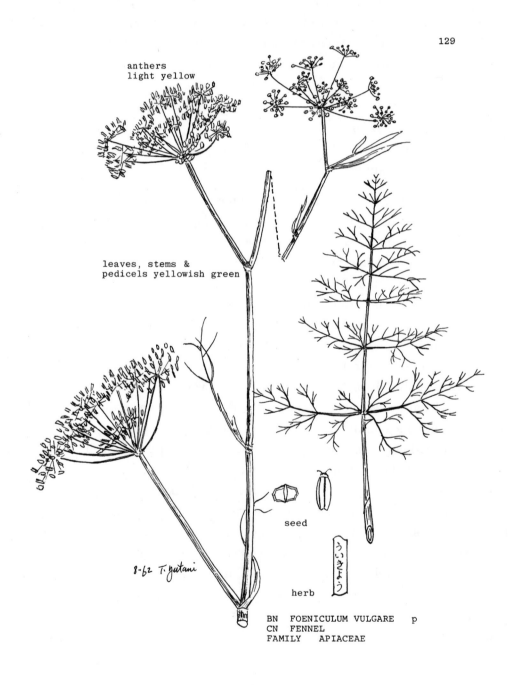

anthers
light yellow

leaves, stems &
pedicels yellowish green

8-62 T. Gutani

seed

herb

BN   FOENICULUM VULGARE   p
CN   FENNEL
FAMILY   APIACEAE

taste (fennel has overtones of camphor) and is not weedy, so is often preferred for culinary purposes and for ease of management. If anise "seeds" are not available, however, fennel fruits are an appropriate substitute. The leaves of fennel (or anise) are often used as a culinary herb, especially with fish. Shoots that form in the leaf nodes can be picked when young and tender and eaten in salads—these are known to Italians as *cartucci*.

A cultivar of fennel sometimes listed as *Foeniculum vulgare* ssp. *Azoricum*, whose enlarged petioles form a sort of bulb at the base of the plant, is grown by gardeners and farmers as a vegetable. The bulbs are cut up into pieces that can be eaten cooked or raw; uncooked, they are crunchy and aromatic, something like a licorice-flavored celery. Referred to as *anice* in Italy (not *finocchio*), this vegetable, served raw, is an antipasto staple at every Italian and Italian American holiday dinner.

Medicinally, fennel has been used since ancient times. Pliny, the Roman natural historian and admiral, ascribed no less than twenty-two cures to it and claimed that serpents eat it "when they cast their old skins, and they sharpen their sight with the juice by rubbing against the plant." This according to Mrs. Grieve, who also quotes a Middle English rhyming herbal that refers to the same process:

Whaunce the heddere [adder] is hurt in eye
Ye red fenel is hys prey,
And yif he mowe it fynde
Wonderly he doth hys kynde.
He schall it chow wonderly,
And leyn it to hys eye kindely,
Ye jowls shall sand and hely ye eye
Yat beforn was sicke et feye

Medieval and early modern herbals ascribe to fennel the power to strengthen sight; other uses are as a carminative (to expel gas), as an aromatic, and for alleviating bronchial ailments. Oil of fennel has been listed in the United States Pharmacopeia for these uses; when European fennel became unavailable during World War II, it was grown as a crop in the United States to supply the pharmaceutical market here, a practice that no doubt introduced it as a weed to areas where it had not grown formerly.

Other claims for medicinal efficacy, perhaps less valid, were also made by the early modern herbalists. Culpeper recommends fennel as a diuretic; as an aid to lactation; for dissolving kidney stones; for curing hiccups and nausea, liver and spleen ailments, gout and cramps, and snake bites; and for losing weight.

POISON HEMLOCK

Conium maculatum—poison hemlock—Apiaceae, Umbelliferae, parsley or carrot family

> If asses chance to feed upon hemlock, they will fall so fast asleep they will seem to be dead, insomuch that some, thinking them to be dead, indeed have flayed off their skins, yet after the hemlock had done operating they have stirred out of their sleep, to the grief and amazement of the owners.
>
> —WILLIAM COLE, *The Art of Simpling*

Although it seems, according to Cole, that hemlock ingestion may not always be fatal to donkeys, it has long been known as a deadly poison for humans (might the above perhaps be an apocryphal story?). The most famous instance of hemlock poisoning in history, the enforced suicide of Socrates mandated by the Athenian government as a punishment for "corrupting youth," is described by his friend and disciple Plato as follows:

> He walked about until his legs began to fail, . . . and then he lay on his back, . . . and the man who gave him the poison . . . pressed his foot hard and asked him if he could feel; . . . and he said "no"; and then his leg, and so upwards and upwards, and showed us that he was cold and stiff. And he felt them instead and said, "when the poison reaches the heart, that will be the end." He was beginning to grow cold about the groin . . . when he said—these were his last words—"Crito, I owe a cock to Asclepius—will you remember to pay the debt?" "The debt shall be paid," said Crito; "is there anything else?" There was no answer . . . but in a minute or two a movement was heard, and the attendants uncovered him; his eyes were set, and Crito closed his eyes and mouth. Such was the end, Echecrates, of our friend; concerning whom I may truly say, of all the men of his time whom I have known, he was the wisest and justest and best.
>
> —PLATO, *Phaedo,* translated by Benjamin Jowett

Hemlock is a nerve poison, causing paralysis and respiratory failure. Poisoning has often occurred when various parts of the plant have been mistaken for edible members of the parsley family. The leaves have sometimes been taken for parsley, the roots for parsnips, the seed for anise or fennel. The plant is very common and can be quite abundant, so it is important to be able to recognize the characteristics that distinguish it from other members of the Apiaceae. The upright, branching plant often grows 6 to 10 feet tall, allowing it to be confused with fennel, another large and quite edible member of this family. Leaves of hemlock are large (as long as 1 to 2 feet) and pinnately compound with leaflets further subdivided, giving the leaves a fernlike appearance. They are light green, and flat in profile, unlike fennel leaves, which are also compound, but with filament-like leaflets that branch from the central midrib at various angles, forming a "bushy" rather than flat leaf structure. Flowers of hemlock are white, in umbels about 3 inches across; those of fennel are yellow, forming larger umbels up to 5 inches across. Hemlock has a stout, white taproot, but it is generally only biennial; fennel is strongly perennial.

As described by its specific epithet *maculatum,* hemlock stems and petioles have purple spots, a characteristic that distinguishes it from all other members of this family. These spots are apparent in fairly young seedlings, making it possible to distinguish them from the seedlings of edible umbellifers with which they might be confused, most notably coriander and chervil. Traditionally, these spots were thought to represent the mark on Cain's brow. The scent of this plant also distinguishes it—this is often described as a "mousy" odor, meaning, based on my experience, the smell of a dead mouse that has departed not too recently.

Some of the common names for hemlock refer to its distinguishing characteristics. It has been known as spotted corobane, spotted parsley, and poison parsley; it has also been referred to as beaver poison, musquash root, herb Bennet, kex, and kecksies.

The old Latin name for this plant is *cicuta,* which was used until the eighteenth century, when Linnaeus restored the ancient Greek name *conium,* from a Greek verb meaning "to whirl," a reference to its capacity to produce vertigo. All parts of the plant are poisonous, but the concentration of alkaloids varies from plant to plant, so it is difficult to know how much is fatal—best to learn to recognize it and avoid confusing it with fennel.

Like many poisonous plants, hemlock is medicinal in minute quantities. The extract of the alkaloid, called coniine, is official in Britain and the United States, and its sedative and antispasmodic properties have made it useful as an antidote for convulsive poisons such as strychnine. During the Middle Ages, it was often prescribed for rabies, as were many other herbal medicines.

Goats are said to be immune to hemlock poisoning—donkeys also, apparently, at least to a limited extent. In Europe, larks and quails were said to eat the seeds with no ill effects, but these birds would then sometimes poison hunters who ate their flesh. Hemlock also tends to invade pastures, especially well-irrigated pastures, and has caused livestock poisoning. Although it generally likes fairly moist conditions, it has been known to escape from pastures and crop lands and invade native habitats, so it is classified as an invasive alien, or ecological weed, in much of the country.

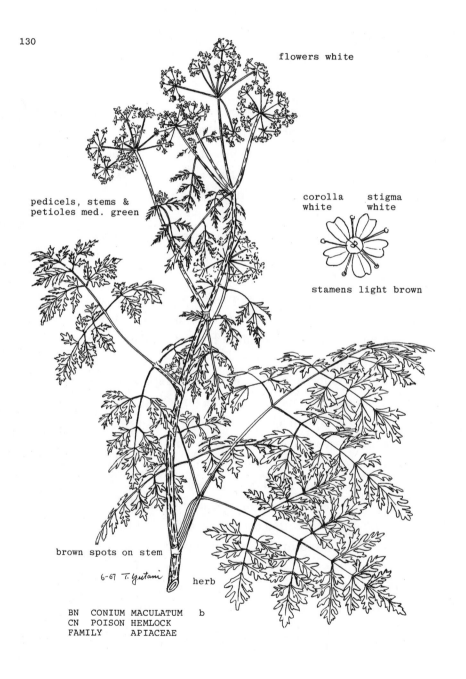

130

flowers white

pedicels, stems & petioles med. green

corolla white

stigma white

stamens light brown

brown spots on stem

6-67 T. Yutani

herb

BN   CONIUM MACULATUM   b
CN   POISON HEMLOCK
FAMILY   APIACEAE

FOUR SMALL UMBELLIFERS

Torilis nodosa—hedge parsley—Apiaceae, Umbelliferae, parsley family

Anthriscus caucalis—bur chervil—Apiaceae

Scandix pecten-veneris—shepherd's needle—Apiaceae

Cyclospermum leptophyllum—marsh parsley—Apiaceae

These four weeds have very similar foliage and are difficult to tell apart in their seedling stages but easier to distinguish when mature. They tend to grow in different environments, but their ranges overlap, and any number of them are sometimes found growing together.

Hedge parsley, *Torilis nodosa,* is an erect, slender winter annual that persists throughout the summer and sometimes overwinters. This European native seems to have appeared fairly recently in California—the 1970 edition of *Weeds of California* (the last one published, alas) reports it as "becoming widespread within California, although no place very abundant." In 2012, I would characterize it as fairly common, sometimes abundant, at least in the Bay Area. It grows in sun or shade, moist or dry soil, but because of its sturdy stems and leaves it is very well adapted to dry situations. Seedlings have fibrous roots, but these soon give way to a deep taproot, which makes the plant ideally suited to growing in sidewalk cracks. It also adapts very well to lawns—it recovers from mowing by forming rosette-like growth and flowering at crown level. Unchecked, it can form dense colonies that outcompete grass. Unmowed, the plant usually grows about a foot tall, but sometimes as high as 2 feet.

Hedge parsley leaves are triangular, pinnately compound twice-over (bipinnately compound), alternate, 3 to 5 inches at the base, becoming smaller as the stem elongates. Petioles and ribs are rough and hairy, slightly bristly (scabrous), as are the stems. Flowers are tiny, white, in small compound umbels that grow from the stems opposite the leaves. The fruit is ovoid and bristly, hooked and ribbed when growing on the outside of the plant, merely ribbed when on the inside. The hooks allow the fruits to travel on clothing and animal fur.

Often confused with hedge parsley is another common umbellifer, bur chervil, *Anthriscus caucalis.* A European native, it was reported in *Weeds of California* as "thus far rare in California." True to its weedy nature, it is now, more than forty-five years later, fairly common in the Bay Area, especially in the moist, shady locations that are favorable to its growth. It can invade stream-side woodlands, where it mingles easily with native vegetation, providing a lush, attractive, and not too threatening addition to the riparian flora.

Seedlings of bur chervil are hard to distinguish from many other umbellifers—but as a mature plant, it is a branching, lacy, or ferny-appearing herb that grows from about 18 inches to 2 feet tall. It is not bristly like torilis, and it is brighter green, less pyramidal in shape.

Leaves of bur chervil are alternate and pinnately compound, with very finely divided leaflets (bipinnate) that are soft and tender to the touch. The whole plant begins to wither at the first onset of warm, dry weather in late spring, when torilis is just beginning to thrive and flower. Flowers are in small umbels on short stems, somewhat larger than those of hedge parsley, ranging from ⅓ to about ¾ inch across. They bloom fairly early in the spring, followed by the fruits, which are unribbed but with bristles and consist of two one-seeded units.

Bur chervil is very closely related to culinary chervil, *Anthriscus cerefolium*, and has a very similar fragrance and flavor. Some have speculated that it was perhaps brought here by recent immigrants from Europe as a culinary herb, and escaped from gardens.

Another umbellifer that is very hard to distinguish from bur chervil and hedge parsley when young is the shepherd's needle (a.k.a. Venus's comb or needle weed). This is *Scandix pecten-veneris,* a Mediterranean native that has long been common in the eastern United States and has recently entered California. This plant, a winter annual, grows to about the same size as hedge parsley, 5 to 16 inches, but is not as pyramidal—most of its branches originate near the base of the plant and form a more rounded structure. The leaves more closely resemble those of bur chervil: they are pinnately dissected two or three times, but with very narrow and pointed segments. Leaf blades are 1 to 5 inches long. The flowers of bur chervil are very small, in compound umbels on stalks no longer than an inch. Flower petals are white, mostly unequal in size. The fruits that follow are very distinctive and are what most readily allow this plant to be distinguished from bur chervil and hedge parsley. They are linear or linear-oblong, laterally flattened, and extended by a long beak that is prominently ribbed and bristled. The tip of the "needle" is blunt and somewhat recessed, appearing hollow. These bristles can cause sores in the mouths of animals that eat the plant.

Shepherd's needle has a taproot. It grows in sun or part shade and generally likes moist, fairly rich soil. It is often found in pasture lands. It grows along the coast from the Bay Area south to Santa Barbara County.

Marsh parsley, *Cyclospermum leptophyllum* (formerly *Apium leptophyllum*), is another small annual in the Apiaceae family that is easy to distinguish from the last three. It is a water-loving plant that is native to South America but has spread worldwide; it grows mostly in very moist to wet ground and is commonly found in cracks in street gutters, in lawns, and at the edges of marshy areas. This plant has a stout taproot capable of forming a new crown when the top is cut back; it is prostrate when young, but can ascend to 18 inches when blooming on compound umbels. The basal leaves are 3 to 4 times pinnately compound, on long petioles, with the ultimate divisions narrowly linear, about an inch long or less; the entire leaf can be about 2½ inches, but is usually smaller. As the branching umbel forms, smaller leaves with short petioles develop at the nodes. The flowers are very small, white to greenish yellow; they are followed by tiny oval fruits.

When marsh parsley appears in lawns, it should be regarded as a sign of overwatering, but correcting this situation will not magically eliminate the weed—its stout taproot renders it remarkably drought tolerant, as is the case with many marsh plants. Once it is eliminated from the lawn, however, the drier conditions created by cutting back on irrigation can help the grasses outcompete any new marsh parsley seedlings that might appear.

QUEEN ANNE'S LACE

Daucus carota—wild carrot, Queen Anne's lace—Apiaceae, parsley family

The wild carrot has a history similar to that of the wild radish: it is native to the Mediterranean and western Asia, is descended from a wild form that was brought here as a weed, but has most likely crossbred with cultivated carrots. As a food crop, carrots were first developed in Afghanistan, probably in ancient times. In California, wild carrots grow in all the usual waste places: roadsides, crop lands, unused fields, meadows. They are quite happy in dry soil and full sun, since they possess a substantial taproot. They are far more common in rural than in urban areas, but recently their numbers in Bay Area cities have increased noticeably.

Queen Anne's lace is a large, open, spreading plant, a biennial that can reach a height of 7 feet in good soil but usually grows between 2 and 3 feet. The main stem is hollow, ridged, and bristly-hairy.

The leaves of Queen Anne's lace are lacy and soft, three times pinnate, with narrowly lanceolate to linear leaflets. Overall, the leaves are triangular in shape, opposite on the lower portions of the stems, alternate above. Flowers are in cup-shaped umbels, with dense clusters of tiny individual flowers on long peduncles; the base of the umbel is surrounded by pinnate bracts that resemble the finely divided leaves. Indeed, the whole plant has a lacy look.

Individual flowers are tiny, usually white, at times pinkish; they are followed by bristly, ribbed achenes. The plant blooms throughout the summer and well into the fall.

In N. W. Simmonds's *Evolution of Crop Plants*, the Dutch horticulturist O. Banga gives us a fairly detailed history of the development of carrots as a crop (see bibliography). Cultivated carrots spread from Afghanistan west and east; they were in Asia Minor by the eleventh century, in Arab Spain in the twelfth, and had reached northwestern Europe and England by the fifteenth century. Originally, they were not orange, but purple or yellow. The purple color was due to a compound known as anthocyanin; the yellow form was a mutant that lacked this color. Purple carrots were generally regarded as having a superior flavor, but tended to give their color to soups and sauces, a fact that distressed the chefs who were developing haute cuisine during the early modern era. Clearly, a form was needed that lacked the anthocyanin but was as tasty as the purple carrots.

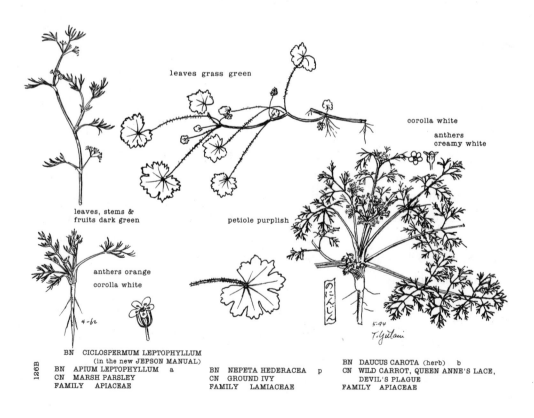

leaves grass green

corolla white
anthers creamy white

leaves, stems & fruits dark green

petiole purplish

anthers orange
corolla white

4-62

5-94
T. Yutani

BN CICLOSPERMUM LEPTOPHYLLUM
(in the new JEPSON MANUAL)
BN APIUM LEPTOPHYLLUM a
CN MARSH PARSLEY
FAMILY APIACEAE

BN NEPETA HEDERACEA p
CN GROUND IVY
FAMILY LAMIACEAE

BN DAUCUS CAROTA (herb) b
CN WILD CARROT, QUEEN ANNE'S LACE,
DEVIL'S PLAGUE
FAMILY APIACEAE

126B

This feat was accomplished by Dutch breeders in the early seventeenth century. Working with the yellow carrot, they managed, through selection and crossbreeding, to increase the carotene content sufficiently to produce orange carrots, much more eye-catching than the pale yellow ones, and tastier as well. The Dutch dominated carrot breeding during the seventeenth and eighteenth centuries and were succeeded by the French in the nineteenth. Several other Western countries, as well as Japan, made significant contributions during the twentieth century.

Medicinally, carrots have been used as a laxative, diuretic, and stimulant; they also have been known to help remove obstructions such as gall and kidney stones (the term is *deobstruent*). An infusion of the leaves is a traditional remedy for dropsy, kidney disease, and bladder disorders. The seeds have been used to treat flatulence, dysentery, coughs, colic, and jaundice, and as a stimulant. Poultices made from the roots have been applied to ease the pain of cancerous ulcers. The leaves have antiseptic qualities and were traditionally applied with honey to cleanse running sores and ulcers. Red varieties of carrots have been found to contain lycopene, a possible cancer inhibitor, and all orange carrots contain carotene, a desirable component of diets because of its antioxidant qualities.

Carrots contain substantial amounts of sugars and so can be used to make alcoholic beverages. Carrot wine and jelly are traditional in Britain, and carrot spirits were distilled in France and Germany—the residue was often fed to hogs. In Germany, an adulterant or substitute for coffee was once made by roasting cut-up carrot roots until they carbonized, then grinding them; a similar use is made of roasted chicory roots in the American South.

TRUE GERANIUMS

Geranium dissectum—birdsfoot geranium, cutleaf geranium—Geraniaceae, geranium family

Geranium carolinianum—Carolina geranium

Geranium molle—dove's foot geranium

Geranium robertianum—herb Robert

Plants in the genus *Geranium* are generally low growing and herbaceous, and mostly native to the Northern Hemisphere, unlike the succulent-stemmed South African plants in the genus *Pelargonium* (also in the geranium family), which are often referred to as "geraniums." There are four common weedy species in the Bay Area, and a few others that have some potential for weediness. All are low growing, usually less than a foot high, with 5-foot palmate leaves on long petioles, small five-petaled pink or magenta flowers, and beaked fruits similar to those of the erodiums, but with much shorter beaks. Geraniums are commonly referred to as cranesbills; the erodiums are known as storksbills.

Perhaps the most abundant geranium weed in Bay Area cities is *Geranium dissectum,* commonly called the cutleaf or birdsfoot geranium. This is a winter

101

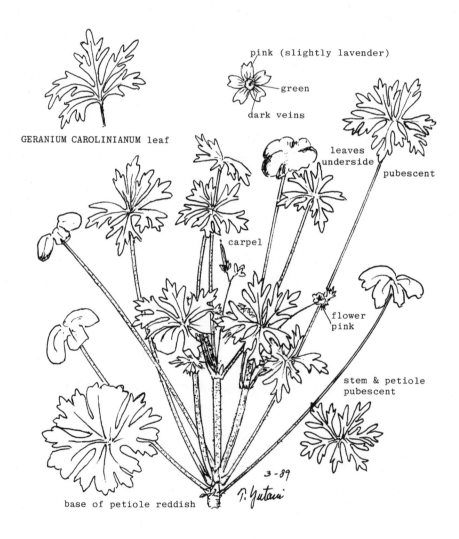

GERANIUM CAROLINIANUM leaf

pink (slightly lavender)

green

dark veins

leaves underside

pubescent

carpel

flower pink

stem & petiole pubescent

base of petiole reddish

3-89

BN GERANIUM DISSECTUM a
CN CUT-LEAVED GERANIUM
FAMILY GERANIACEAE

annual that begins its life as a small ascending rosette consisting of a number of deeply lobed leaves on long petioles. The tips of the lobes are divided again into three parts, giving the whole leaf a very dissected, almost lacy appearance. Petioles and lobes are sparsely hairy. In this early stage, the plant forms a mounding rosette, usually 6 to 8 inches high, but capable of growing to a foot or more in rich soil.

When this geranium reaches the flowering stage, a central stem appears and begins to elongate—this is known as the *cauline* stage, from the Latin word for stem. The leaves that grow on the stem, known as *cauline leaves,* are even more deeply and finely dissected than the rosette leaves (this is true of other annual geraniums as well). Quarter-inch magenta flowers appear in small cymes, followed by beaked, dehiscent fruits—they split open to release their seeds.

The cutleaf geranium grows in moist soil in full sun or light shade and can be an attractive plant during its rosette growth and the first part of its flowering stage. If it mixes well with the plants close to it, there is no need to remove it until just before it is ready to set seed.

Similar in appearance to the cutleaf geranium, but with somewhat less deeply lobed leaves and white to light pink, rather than magenta, flowers is the Carolina geranium, *Geranium carolinianum,* a winter annual native to much of North America, including California. It is a good deal less common than its cutleaf cousin.

The foliage of both of these geraniums resembles the leaves of many of the ornamental garden species and varieties; most of these, however, have larger flowers and are perennial.

The dove's foot geranium, *Geranium molle,* is similar in growth habit to the other two, but with leaf lobes that are distinctly more rounded and less incised. Leaves and stems are thickly covered with fine, dense hairs. These characteristics make it easy to distinguish from the other two. The petioles are often reddish (but not always), and there are sometimes red dots at the tip of each lobe. Flowers are about ¼ inch across, five-petaled, dark pink, with purple anthers and stigmas. This plant prefers shade and moist soil, often grows to a foot or more, and can form a very attractive seasonal ground cover under trees or in other shaded areas. The leaves will always feel soft and plush, a characteristic that is very helpful for identifying this plant. *Geranium molle* is native to Europe, and its attractiveness may well have aided its spread.

Another European geranium, herb Robert, *Geranium robertianum,* is often planted as an ornamental, but its aggressive colonizing habits render it a serious

weed, especially in wild lands. This plant spreads by underground stems, forming dense colonies on shaded ground in wooded areas. It is easily recognized by
its deeply dissected leaves, somewhat larger and more robust than those of *G.
dissectum*, its wine-red stems, and its mottled magenta flowers. When the leaves
are crushed, they emit a disagreeable odor. Herb Robert can be an easy and
attractive ground cover in large-scale landscaped areas shaded by big trees, and
it has been used that way in places such as Golden Gate Park; but care must be
taken to keep it from spreading to wild areas or to more cultivated portions of
the landscape where it is sure to become a pest.

This plant's common name reflects an old English tradition, going back at
least to the Middle Ages, of giving certain plants personal names. Thus, the
cowslip *(Primula veris)* is known as herb Peter, poison hemlock *(Conium maculatum)* as herb Bennet, and one of the goosefoot weeds *(Chenopodium bonus-
henricus)* as herb Good Henry.

Some of the European geraniums have medicinal uses that are discussed
in a number of the old herbals. *Geranium dissectum* and *G. Molle* have been
used as sources of alum, derived mostly from the roots and leaves. This compound has the property of closing pores and so can be applied externally to stop

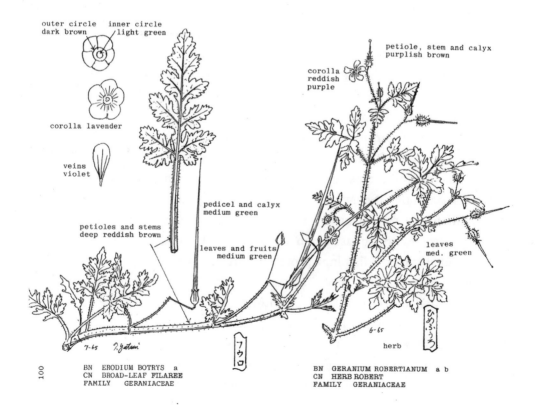

outer circle   inner circle
dark brown   light green

corolla lavender

veins
violet

petioles and stems
deep reddish brown

pedicel and calyx
medium green

leaves and fruits
medium green

petiole, stem and calyx
purplish brown

corolla
reddish
purple

leaves
med. green

herb

100

BN   ERODIUM BOTRYS   a
CN   BROAD-LEAF FILAREE
FAMILY   GERANIACEAE

BN   GERANIUM ROBERTIANUM   a b
CN   HERB ROBERT
FAMILY   GERANIACEAE

bleeding and help heal wounds, as well as internally to stop bleeding and to control diarrhea.

LAMB'S QUARTERS

Chenopodium album—lamb's quarters—Chenopodiaceae, goosefoot family

The goosefoot family contains a number of herbaceous plants that have long been used for food and medicine. Perhaps the best known of these are spinach, beets, and Swiss chard (a type of beet grown for its leaves), familiar vegetables of European origin. Recently, the highly nutritious grains of quinoa, a South American chenopod, have come into widespread use in Europe and America. The leaves of various chenopods can also be eaten—including those of the weedy species.

The best known of the goosefoot weeds is lamb's quarters, *Chenopodium album*, a herbaceous winter annual of European origin. This is an upright, branching plant that usually grows between 1 and 4 feet tall, although some specimens have been known to reach 6 feet. The leaves are somewhat variable in shape, but generally rhombic (i.e., irregularly four-sided), like a goose's foot. They range from ½ inch to about 3 inches long and are prominently three-veined, alternate, and glaucous bluish-green above, white mealy *(farinose)* beneath and on the stems. The margins of the lower leaves are toothed or serrate, those of the upper entire.

The flowers of lamb's quarters are small and greenish, in slender, densely flowered spikes growing in the leaf axils, and clustered into a panicle at the tips of the stems. The fruit is an achene enclosed by five keeled sepals. This plant likes full sun and grows in a wide range of environments. It is especially fond of loose soil, such as is found in tilled gardens and fields and on dump heaps and piles of manure or open compost heaps.

Lamb's quarters have edible tops that are sometimes gathered by foragers in Europe and America. These greens are usually eaten cooked and taste something like spinach, but with a not unpleasant gamey overtone. The weed is often eaten by domestic animals, or gathered by their owners and fed to them; the names *lamb's quarters* and *fat hen* probably refer to the use of this plant as animal feed. In Iron Age Europe, the seeds of fat hen and some other weeds such as knotweed were sometimes mixed with cultivated grains such as barley (if you read the introduction to this book, you may recall that the Tollund man's last meal contained these seeds).

Lamb's quarters are still grown for food in Africa and Asia, notably in northern India, where it is the basis of several curry dishes. Other common names for *Chenopodium album* are white pigweed, white goosefoot, fat hen, meal weed, frost blite, bacon weed, and wild spinach.

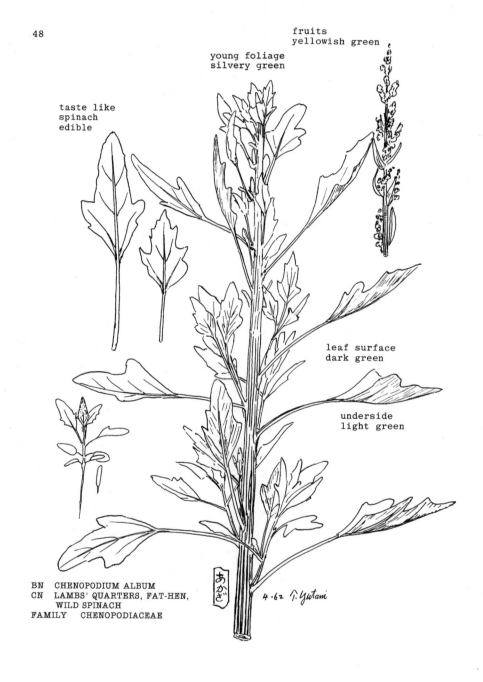

48

fruits
yellowish green

young foliage
silvery green

taste like
spinach
edible

leaf surface
dark green

underside
light green

BN   CHENOPODIUM ALBUM
CN   LAMBS' QUARTERS, FAT-HEN,
       WILD SPINACH
FAMILY   CHENOPODIACEAE

あかざ

4-62 T. Yutani

ENGLISH DAISY

Bellis perennis—English daisy—Asteraceae, Compositae, daisy family

The English daisy has long been regarded as both a weed and a wild plant valued for its medicinal uses. This European native grows in meadows and other grassy areas and along roadsides and stream banks. It is especially well adapted to lawns, due to its low, rosette-forming habit and its ability to proliferate by forming new crowns from short rhizomes, a process known as *tillering,* also common to bunch grasses.

Kept in check by providing lawn grasses with optimal growing conditions, English daisies, along with dandelions, can be an asset to a lawn: their white flowers, sometimes tinged with pink, always with yellow centers, can provide visual interest and varied texture to a lawn that might otherwise be a monotonous mass of identical blades of grass. These flowers are about ¾ inch across and grow on stems no longer than 4 inches. They emerge from rosettes of somewhat succulent, oval or obovate toothed leaves that narrow at the base to a petiole with a leafy margin. The rosette form of this species enables it to recover quickly from grazing and mowing.

The roots of English daisy are fibrous, growing from a stout, perennial crown. The plant also produces short rhizomes, which generate new crowns. These crowns clump together and can form large, solid masses in lawns where the grasses do not have a strong competitive advantage; in a well-maintained and properly irrigated lawn, they will remain more scattered. By tolerating a scattering of dandelions and English daisies in a lawn, incorporating clover, and perhaps adding some carefully selected small bulbs and low-growing perennials, one can approach the medieval ideal of the lawn as a "flowery mede."

One of the best perennials to add to a lawn is the English daisy. Cultivars have been developed from the wild plant; these have larger flowers, usually double flowers, often in shades of red and pink, and are usually used as edgings in borders, but will also do well in lawns. These cultivars do not tiller as aggressively as the wild form and will not last indefinitely in lawns; but they can be used to add variety to the lawn population.

English daisy has also been referred to as bruisewort or bone flower in England, and as bairnwort in Scotland (perhaps a reference to its efficacy in treating childhood cuts and scrapes), names referring to its long-standing use as a wound treatment. It has also been used to treat fevers, inflammation of the liver, and, as the seventeenth-century herbalist John Gerard puts it, of "alle the inwarde parts." A decoction of the roots has been given as a treatment for scurvy (antiscorbutic). The juice of the plant is acrid, limiting its culinary value; it has nevertheless been used as a potherb in some places.

The word *daisy* means "eye of the day." An old English saying goes, "When you can put your foot on seven daisies, summer is come."

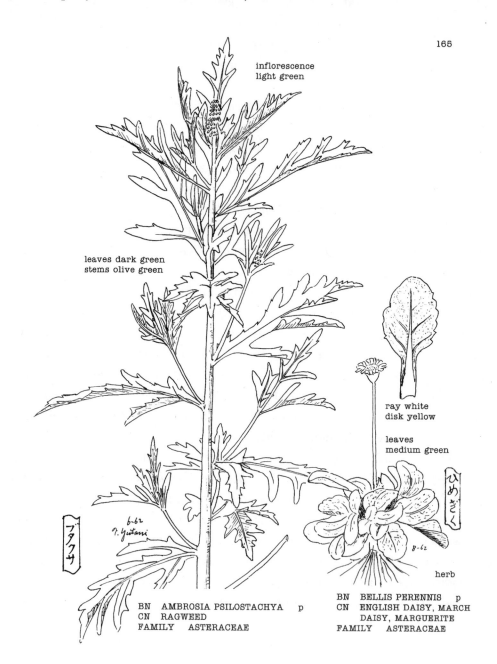

165

inflorescence
light green

leaves dark green
stems olive green

ray white
disk yellow

leaves
medium green

herb

BN   AMBROSIA PSILOSTACHYA   p
CN   RAGWEED
FAMILY   ASTERACEAE

BN   BELLIS PERENNIS   p
CN   ENGLISH DAISY, MARCH
      DAISY, MARGUERITE
FAMILY   ASTERACEAE

MUGWORT

Artemisia vulgaris—mugwort—Asteraceae, Compositae, aster family

Mugwort is an upright herbaceous perennial that grows from 3 to 6 feet tall. It has a distinctive fragrance and flavor, somewhat on the bitter side, and has been used for many centuries as a flavoring, as food for animals, and as a medicine.

The leaves are 2 to 8 inches long, dark green above, covered with dense white hairs beneath. Their overall shape is ovate, but with deeply cut, narrow, pointed lobes—the term for this is *bipinnately lobed.* They grow on stems that are often reddish-purple. The green inflorescences consist of tiny receptacles that are globular or cylindrical in shape, with the yellowish flowers barely protruding from them. They grow on narrow, raceme-like panicles and produce abundant seed. The whole plant is anchored by a sturdy taproot.

Artemisia can grow in sun or shade and is found in many habitats: gardens, roadsides, fields, woods, and vacant lots. It is native to Eurasia, northern Africa, and Alaska and is widely naturalized in North America. Until this mystery is resolved, I'll continue to refer to the plant I have described as *Artemisia vulgaris.*

One of the traditional uses for mugwort, which may have given the plant its name, was as a flavoring for beer. In England, mugwort and ground ivy (*Glechoma hederacea,* in the mint family) were the principal flavorings for beer until hops were introduced from Belgium in the fourteenth century, during the Hundred Years' War. Or, says Mrs. Grieve, the name may have come from the French word *moughte,* "moth" or "maggot," because the plant has been used as a moth repellent at least as far back as the time of Dioscorides.

Dioscorides also reported the use of the dried leaves, flowers, and roots for various medicinal purposes. It was used as a bronchial dilator to treat asthma, often by inhaling the smoke; as a diuretic to facilitate urination; as an emmenagogue to stimulate the onset of menses; and as a nervine to mitigate palsy and epileptic fits. It was also prescribed for indigestion, to calm upset stomachs, and to lower fevers. Bathwater was often infused with mugwort leaves to give it an invigorating effect. In Japan, the down from the undersides of the leaves was made into a cure for rheumatism.

In Cornwall during the nineteenth century mugwort was used as a tea substitute by the working classes during a period when the price of tea leaves had risen substantially. In other parts of Europe, it has been used as a culinary herb, often to stuff goose.

Some other common names for *Artemisia vulgaris:* felon herb (I can't explain this), St. John's plant, cingulum sancti Johannis, and St. John's girdle, a reference to the medieval belief that John the Baptist wore a girdle of it in the wilderness to protect himself from fatigue, sunstroke, attacks by wild beasts, and evil spirits. Medieval peasants may have emulated him whenever they traveled far from home; on St. John's Eve, wearing a crown of mugwort was a tradition designed to confer protection from evil spirits, diseases, and other misfortunes for the coming year.

GROUNDSEL

Senecio vulgaris—groundsel—Asteraceae, Compositae, sunflower family

Groundsel is one of the most abundant winter annual weeds wherever it grows, which is in most temperate areas settled by Europeans. It has a long oral and written history and is known by an impressive assortment of names: ragwort, grimsel, grundy swallow, ground glutton, simpson, sention, old-man-of-the-spring. The name *groundsel* and its linguistic cousins derive from the Anglo-Saxon word *groundeswelge,* meaning "ground-swallower." *Simpson* and *sention* probably come from the Latin *senecio,* from *senex,* old man, a reference to the tuft of fuzzy white achenes, which remind some of the soft, white hair covering the scalps of elderly people. When these blow away, what remains is a receptacle resembling the bald heads of other elders. According to Mrs. Grieve, one of the "old herbalists" describes it thusly: "the flower of this herb hath white hair and when the wind bloweth it away, then it appeareth like a bald-headed man."

It is the abundant seed produced by the flowers of this plant that causes it to literally swallow the ground in areas where it grows unchecked. The seed produces plants that can grow 18 to 24 inches tall in good soil, but are generally found at 6 to 8 inches or less. These are upright, often single-stemmed, bearing oblong leaves, deeply and irregularly lobed, the lobes toothed. Leaves are generally 1 to 3 inches long, those at the base of the plant with petioles, the upper ones clasping the stems, which are often reddish.

158

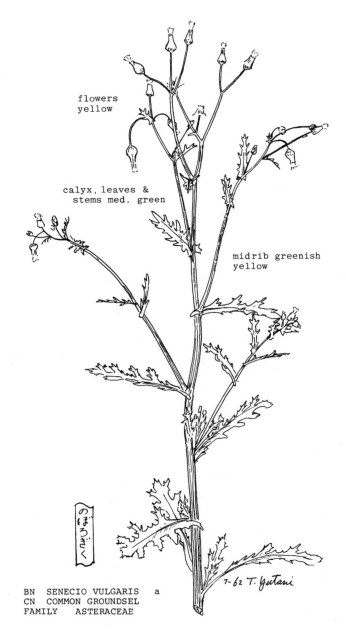

flowers
yellow

calyx, leaves &
stems med. green

midrib greenish
yellow

BN   SENECIO VULGARIS   a
CN   COMMON GROUNDSEL
FAMILY   ASTERACEAE

7-62 T. Gutani

Groundsel begins flowering when young and small, often when barely more than an inch tall. Inflorescences are yellow, shaped like a pig snout, consisting entirely of disk flowers. They are about ½ inch long and subtended by green bracts with black tips. They produce achenes tipped with silky white pappi, the old person's hair, which are carried by the wind to produce new infestations. The overall appearance of these flowers is very similar to those often found in the lettuce tribe, but groundsel is in a different tribe of the aster family, the Senecioniae, which does not produce latex.

Groundsel attracts birds, which like to eat the seeds. It is well known as one of the principal components of canary seed. The whole plant has traditionally been used as rabbit food. It also has a number of medicinal uses. The ancient Greek writer Dioscorides recommends it for stomach pains, jaundice, and epilepsy. Gerard and other early modern herbalists advocate combining it with a number of other herbs for healing wounds. Culpeper cites it as a purgative, saying it is gentler acting than most. It has also been used as a poultice for gout, chapped hands, headaches, and worms.

DANDELIONS AND CAT'S EARS

Taraxacum officinale—dandelion—Asteraceae, Compositae, aster family

Hypochaeris radicata—hairy cat's ear, coast dandelion—Asteraceae

Hypochaeris glabra—smooth cat's ear

Probably the best known of all the weeds, in America and Europe at any rate, is the dandelion, *Taraxacum officinale.* This perennial composite is ubiquitous in lawns but also grows very well in other locations: by roadsides, along ditch banks, as a miniature rosette in dry, compacted soil, as a lush, vigorous plant with a height of a foot or more in loose, rich, moist soil.

The dandelion is easily recognized by its rosette of narrow, sharply lobed leaves; its flat-topped, bright yellow inflorescence consisting entirely of ray flowers in a receptacle, with only one inflorescence (commonly regarded as a flower) per stem; and its deep, brittle taproot, the smallest piece of which is capable of generating a new plant.

The leaves of dandelions are not always deeply incised; some forms have shallow lobes, others are almost entire. These occasional variations should not be a source of confusion to anyone who knows the other characteristics of the plant.

The rosette form, a spiral of leaves placed very closely on the stem and lying flat on the ground, is an adaptation possessed by many young herbaceous plants that allows them to compete with nearby plants by essentially excluding them from the ground occupied by their own circle of leaves, thus giving their leaves full exposure to the sunlight they need for photosynthesis. Most rosette-forming plants grow this way only in their juvenile stage, when they are producing and storing the carbohydrates they will need to flower and fruit; at flowering time, they develop elongated stems, abandoning the rosette for a more upright, branching form.

The dandelion does not do this—it retains its rosette form for its entire life. Thus, it is a supremely adaptable lawn weed—the flat rosette is barely touched by lawn mowers, which may cut off the flowers, but the plant puts out new ones very quickly. If the lawn is sparse, with many small patches of bare ground, the dandelion will seed itself quickly and prolifically in these bare areas. The secret to keeping it from dominating a lawn is to maintain healthy, vigorous turf by choosing appropriate grasses, mowing high, aerating the soil when it becomes compacted, irrigating sufficiently and evenly, and maintaining an adequate level of fertility. The latter can be accomplished by leaving grass clippings on the lawn and allowing them to decay and release their nutrients and by introducing clover into the turf. If all this is done, there should be no need for synthetic fertilizer.

The fruit of the dandelion is an achene, essentially a seed with a hard coating, to which is attached a delicate, branched, umbrellalike structure known as a *pappus*. The pappus acts as a sort of parachute, allowing the achene to drift for great distances on the wind. Closely crowded on the receptacle, these

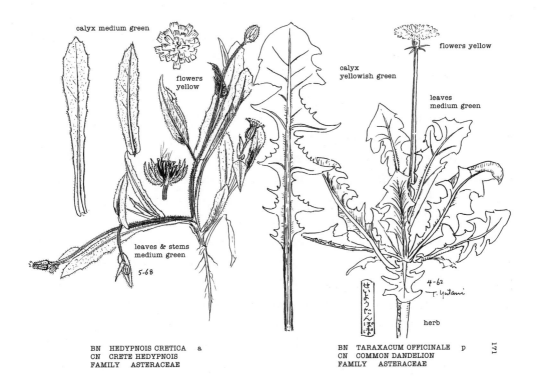

calyx medium green

flowers
yellow

leaves & stems
medium green

5-68

BN   HEDYPNOIS CRETICA   a
CN   CRETE HEDYPNOIS
FAMILY   ASTERACEAE

flowers yellow

calyx
yellowish green

leaves
medium green

4-62
T. Yutani

herb

BN   TARAXACUM OFFICINALE   p
CN   COMMON DANDELION
FAMILY   ASTERACEAE

171

achenes with pappi form a delicate white globular structure, a "blowball," as the herbalist Gerard describes it, which will disperse into the air at the slightest puff of wind. This blowball is a common feature of many other composites and of virtually all plants in the lettuce tribe.

The common name *dandelion* comes from a French phrase meaning "lion's tooth," *dent de lion*—this refers to the very jagged margins of the leaves. Other common names applied to this plant are swine snout, in reference to the shape of the flower bud before it opens, and priest's crown, from the appearance of the flower receptacle after all the achenes have blown away. In France this plant is known as *pissenlit,* a reference to its diuretic qualities. In England, it has been called *pissabeds,* and in Italy *piscialetto.*

Dandelions possess both culinary and medicinal qualities. The leaves can be cooked, or eaten in salads when young and tender. They are somewhat more bitter than endive, but have a similar flavor. Dandelion leaves are very high in vitamins A and C and in iron. Dandelion root, like that of its close cousin chicory, can be roasted and ground as a coffee substitute. Its main medicinal uses are as a diuretic and tonic. The latex has been used for removing warts and as a mosquito repellent. During World War II, it was considered as a source of latex for making synthetic rubber, but this turned out to be too expensive to be practical.

Closely related to and resembling the dandelion, the hairy cat's ear, false dandelion, or coast dandelion, *Hypochaeris radicata,* is a familiar sight along roadsides, where its buttery yellow flowers on tall stems are a visual delight all summer long in areas with dry climates, and make this a weed with considerable ornamental value. It can, however, be a persistent pest in lawns and in other plantings where its presence is not desired. Like the dandelion, it is perennial and spends its entire life as a rosette; it differs from the dandelion by having lobed instead of serrated leaves, which are covered with fine, short hairs. Like the dandelion, it has one inflorescence per stem, but these are rather more flattened, with petal tips more squared, and resting atop somewhat longer stems. The rosettes also tend to tiller, forming clusters; the dandelion does this only when it regenerates from a root that has been broken off. To permanently eliminate a specimen of either of these weeds, it is necessary to dig out the entire root, a difficult task.

Hypochaeris glabra, the smooth cat's ear, is much smaller than its hairy cousin; it has shorter stems and smaller flowers and rosettes and, as its name implies, lacks hairs on the leaves. It, too, can improve the appearance of dry, compacted ground, and there is no need to control it in such situations.

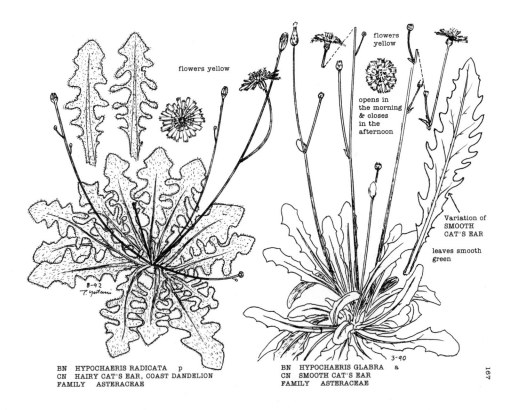

flowers yellow

flowers yellow

opens in
the morning
& closes
in the
afternoon

Variation of
SMOOTH
CAT'S EAR

leaves smooth
green

BN   HYPOCHAERIS RADICATA   p
CN   HAIRY CAT'S EAR, COAST DANDELION
FAMILY   ASTERACEAE

BN   HYPOCHAERIS GLABRA   a
CN   SMOOTH CAT'S EAR
FAMILY   ASTERACEAE

WILD LETTUCES

Lactuca serriola—prickly lettuce—Asteraceae, Compositae, daisy family

Lactuca virosa—wild lettuce, opium lettuce

Lactuca saligna—willow-leaved lettuce

Of the three members of the genus *Lactuca* that are commonly found in the urban environment, *Lactuca serriola,* known as prickly lettuce, is by far the most common. Like the other two, it is a winter annual that persists throughout the summer. It starts out as a rather attractive rosette of hairy, somewhat wrinkled leaves, usually about 5 or 6 inches long, but sometimes up to a foot long in rich, moist soil. There are some soft prickles on the leaf margins and along the midrib on the underside of the leaf. The leaf shape is usually obovate to oblanceolate, but the leaves on some plants may be lobed. The plant, firmly secured by a taproot, remains in the rosette form during the cool winter months, when it is often very attractive; clusters of prickly lettuce rosettes growing under native oaks can be quite lovely, despite their status as alien invaders.

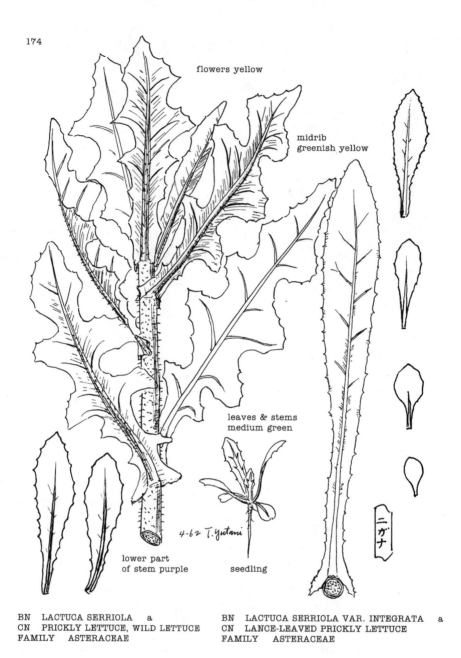

174

flowers yellow

midrib
greenish yellow

leaves & stems
medium green

4-62 T. Yutani

lower part
of stem purple

seedling

ニガナ

BN   LACTUCA SERRIOLA   a
CN   PRICKLY LETTUCE, WILD LETTUCE
FAMILY   ASTERACEAE

BN   LACTUCA SERRIOLA VAR. INTEGRATA   a
CN   LANCE-LEAVED PRICKLY LETTUCE
FAMILY   ASTERACEAE

Late in the spring, this plant undergoes a transformation. The rosette sprouts a central stem, which begins to elongate, ultimately becoming 3 or 4 feet tall. The leaves that sprout on these stems are smaller and narrower than the rosette leaves, and any lobes present become more pronounced. They orient themselves with their margins perpendicular to the ground, rather than parallel as in the rosette. As the plant matures, it develops a large inflorescence of small (about ¼ inch diameter), creamy yellow flowers, which ultimately turn into dandelion-like fuzzball heads consisting of achenes with pappi.

Lactuca serriola is theoretically edible and was once used as a potherb, but it is somewhat tough and bitter for modern tastes. Its close relative, *Lactuca sativa,* is a much better food choice; it has been grown for salad and cooked greens since 4500 BCE. It may have been derived from *L. serriola,* but there are other possibilities, such as *L. serriola* being a hybrid of *L. sativa* and some other wild lettuce (there are other instances of weeds deriving from crop plants, such as wild oats). The seventeenth-century herbalist John Gerard, notes Mrs. Grieve, has this to say about the virtues of cultivated lettuce: "Lettuce cooleth the heat of the stomacke, called the heart-burning; and helpeth it when it is troubled with choler; it quencheth thirst, and causeth sleep. Lettuce maketh a pleasant sallad, being eaten raw with vineger, oile, and a little salt: but if it be boiled it is sooner digested, and nourisheth more."

Lactuca virosa, generally named in the literature as wild lettuce, bitter lettuce, or opium lettuce, is quite similar to *L. serriola,* so like it, in fact, that they are difficult to tell apart—the most apparent difference is color of the achenes: those of *L. serriola* are white, of *L. virosa* black. This species is the most powerfully medicinal of the three and is the one referred to in herbals going back as far as Pliny and Dioscorides. The medicinal compounds are found in the latex, the sticky white substance that oozes from the leaves and stems when they are broken. Taken internally, this substance is somewhat narcotic, said to resemble a feeble opium, and has been used as an opium adulterant in the United States. Medicinally, the latex from wild lettuce has been employed as a sedative and narcotic and as a mild diuretic and diaphoretic; it has been dissolved in wine as an anodyne and combined with more active drugs for dropsy. It has been used to ease colic, induce sleep, and allay coughs.

Lactuca virosa was cultivated for its medicinal latex in Scotland, France, Austria, and Germany until well into the twentieth century. Collectors would cut off the heads of mature plants, then scrape the latex that oozed out into porcelain vessels; this was done several times daily until the plant was exhausted. The content of the vessels, known as *lactucarium,* was allowed to harden; the cups were then warmed to enable the product to be separated from the molds. It was dried, cut into quarters, and sold for adulterant or medicinal purposes.

Augustus, the first emperor of Rome, is said to have attributed his recovery from a dangerous illness to the effects of lettuce. He declared it a god, built an altar to it, and erected a statue in its honor.

A smaller, less common lettuce found in the urban environment is *Lactuca saligna,* the willow-leaved lettuce, a plant that forms a rosette consisting of linear to lanceolate leaves that are strongly lobed, with a long, pointed terminal lobe. These leaves are seldom more than 6 inches long. The plant elongates and flowers in the same manner as *Lactuca serriola,* but remains overall a much smaller plant, usually attaining a height of only a foot or so. Its flowers are a brighter yellow than those of *L. serriola,* and grow in smaller clusters.

OTHER WEEDS WITH MILKY SAP

Helminthotheca echioides—bristly oxtongue, oxtongue bugloss—Asteraceae, Compositae, daisy family

Tragopogon porrifolius—salsify, oyster plant—Asteraceae

Cichorium intybus—chicory—Asteraceae

Bristly oxtongue, *Helminthotheca echioides,* is a close relative of dandelion, prickly lettuce, and sowthistle, and resembles all three in a number of ways. It has a biennial growth cycle—biennials, in theory, grow for their entire first year in rosette form, then elongate in the second year, producing flower stems with leaves smaller than those of the rosette. After blooming and setting fruit, the plants die. The bristly oxtongue performs a variation on this pattern, as do many biennials that grow in Mediterranean climates. It starts out as a rosette of narrow, somewhat lobed leaves, dark green and covered with warty bumps and straight, stiff, hairlike prickles, anchored by a stout taproot. Typically, this rosette is 6 to 8 inches across—it may lie flat on the ground; or, in a crowded growth situation, the leaves may extend upward at an angle. Late in the spring, the plant bolts, producing a solid, branching, bristly stem, with smaller leaves attached, that ends in a cluster of dandelion-like flowers, but of a somewhat lighter yellow. Achenes with pappi form, clustered into little puffball structures similar to those of sowthistles. In late autumn, this top growth dies back, and the taproot sprouts a new rosette, thus renewing the whole process for at least another year.

I have found no record of medicinal uses for bristly oxtongue; however, Mrs. Grieve points out the name *helminthotheca* derives from a Greek name for a small worm, and speculates that it might have once been used as a vermifuge. It is edible, if not palatable; some sources from the Middle Ages indicate that the very young leaves of this plant were used as potherbs, as were the leaves of dandelions and various other winter annuals.

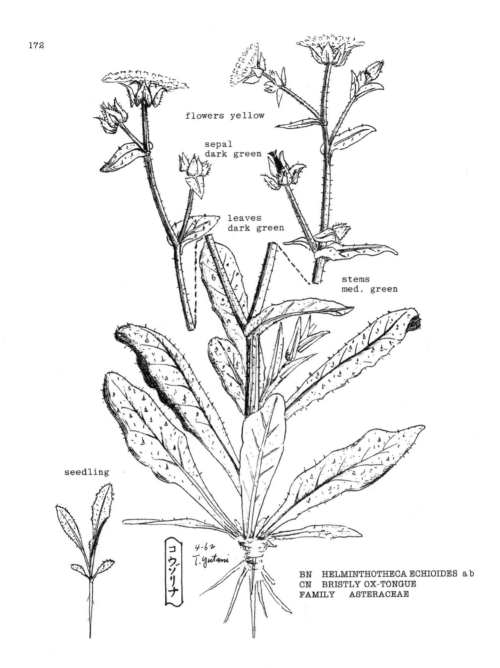

172

flowers yellow

sepal
dark green

leaves
dark green

stems
med. green

seedling

コウゾリナ

4-62
T. Yutani

BN   HELMINTHOTHECA ECHIOIDES a b
CN   BRISTLY OX-TONGUE
FAMILY   ASTERACEAE

Salsify, or oyster plant, *Tragopogon porrifolius,* a perennial also known as goat's beard, resembles nothing so much as a giant dandelion when in bloom. Before sending up flower stems, its leaves grow in an upright, narrow rosette, which makes it easy to mistake for a monocot. The leaves are about a foot long, alternate, entire, smooth, very narrow, and tapering to a fine point from a clasping base. The flower stem can grow as tall as 3 feet and bears smaller clasping leaves. Flower clusters are solitary, 2 to 4 inches in diameter, consisting entirely of purple ray flowers. This inflorescence is subtended by narrow, erect bracts that extend beyond the rays. The "flowers" open in the morning, closing later in the day, forming a long pig snout–like bud. Fruits are achenes with long pappi, forming a dandelion-like puffball 2 inches or more in diameter.

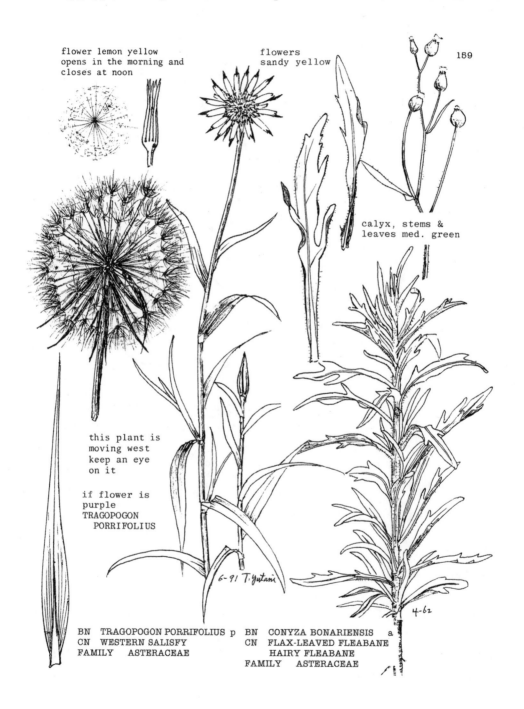

flower lemon yellow
opens in the morning and
closes at noon

flowers
sandy yellow

159

calyx, stems &
leaves med. green

this plant is
moving west
keep an eye
on it

if flower is
purple
TRAGOPOGON
PORRIFOLIUS

6-91 T. Yutani

4-62

BN   TRAGOPOGON PORRIFOLIUS p   BN   CONYZA BONARIENSIS   a
CN   WESTERN SALISFY   CN   FLAX-LEAVED FLEABANE
FAMILY   ASTERACEAE   HAIRY FLEABANE
                                   FAMILY   ASTERACEAE

Salsify is cultivated in gardens for its dense taproots, which, when cooked, have an oyster-like flavor. It has escaped from farms and gardens and become a not terribly abundant or threatening weed. It can be seen along roadsides and in meadows and grasslands, growing in sun or part shade. Old herbals report some medicinal uses: Culpeper recommends it for gall bladder problems and jaundice and considers it "cooling, bitter, astringent, antibilious, deobstruent, and slightly aperient."

A close relative of salsify, John-go-to-bed-at-noon, *Tragopogon pratensis,* also known as noon flower or goat's beard, grows as a wildflower in Europe. It closely resembles the oyster plant but is smaller, with yellow flowers. Culpeper cites the same medicinal uses as for salsify, but considers it more effective. The roots were once boiled and eaten; they have a flavor that resembles asparagus rather than oysters.

Chicory, *Cichorium intybus,* also known as blueweed, succory, wild succory, hendibeh, or barbe de capucin, is uncommon in urban areas, but is often seen as a roadside weed in the country. It is perennial, with a sturdy, dandelion-like taproot. Stems are 2 to 3 feet long, with numerous, wide-spreading branches that are sparsely covered with hairy, lobed, clasping leaves somewhat resembling those of prickly lettuce. The lower leaves, at first forming a rosette, are large and spreading, but they diminish in size as they sprout up the stem. Blue flower heads grow from leaf axils, in clusters of two or three.

Wild chicory is the parent of various cultivars of garden chicories, or radicchio, grown as cooking or salad greens, as well as for the roots, which, roasted, have been used as a coffee substitute or extender. In some parts of the American South, such as New Orleans, coffee with chicory is preferred by many people to the unadulterated version. Chicory root is also used to produce Belgian endive (the endives proper derive from a wild plant native to East Asia). The ancient Romans used chicory as a salad green, as well as for fodder. It is still grown as a pasture plant in parts of Europe. Medicinally, chicory has been used for stomach and pulmonary ailments, jaundice and other liver problems, gout, gravel, rheumatism, and inflammations of the skin and eyes. The leaves have been used to produce a blue dye.

SOWTHISTLES

Sonchus oleraceus—common sowthistle—Compositae, Asteraceae, aster family

Sonchus asper—prickly sowthistle

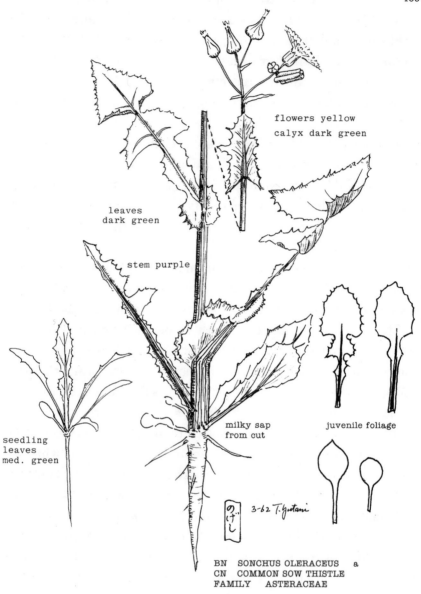

flowers yellow
calyx dark green

leaves
dark green

stem purple

seedling
leaves
med. green

milky sap
from cut

juvenile foliage

3-62 T. Gutani

BN   SONCHUS OLERACEUS   a
CN   COMMON SOW THISTLE
FAMILY   ASTERACEAE

Sowthistles, *Sonchus* spp., are plants in the lettuce tribe that are often mistaken for dandelions, which they somewhat resemble in the rosette stage because of their sharply pointed, backward-facing leaf lobes; but they are easy to tell apart from dandelions if one remembers a few simple differences. In the rosette stage, the leaves of sowthistles are a darker, grayer green than those of dandelions, and they are generally larger. Even more revealing, the sowthistle does not retain its rosette form for its entire life, and never flowers in that stage—before blooming, the plant grows a central stem, which is hollow (the term *sonchus* derives from the Greek word for "hollow"), then produces a cluster of yellow ray flowers that somewhat resembles a groundsel cluster, and subsequently forms a puffball of achenes with pappi, as does the dandelion. These are carried on the wind to their new homes.

The mature sowthistle grows 1 to 3 feet tall and produces numerous flower heads and seemingly innumerable seeds. The leaves clasp the stems and grow smaller as the stem elongates. Although usually classified as an annual, the sowthistle has a very long, sturdy taproot and will regenerate from fragments left in the ground. It often winters over in mild climates. For these reasons, it is probably best thought of as a short-lived perennial. It is sometimes described as an annual that tends to perennate. Like the dandelion, and all members of the lettuce tribe, it has sticky white latex sap.

Two species of sowthistle are commonly found in the Bay Area: *Sonchus oleraceus,* the common sowthistle, and *Sonchus asper,* the prickly or spiny sowthistle. They hybridize freely, and there are many intermediate forms that are difficult to assign to one species or another. Gardeners with a strong bent for taxonomy will enjoy struggling with the question of how to categorize individual specimens that show intermediate characteristics; but for practical purposes such as control, any sowthistle may be regarded as simply a *sowthistle.*

Sowthistles that may definitely be assigned to *Sonchus oleraceus,* the common sowthistle, will have leaves that are a dull grayish-green in color, with pointed, backward-facing lobes, and a terminal lobe that is larger and more rounded than the lower ones. The leaves of the rosette and those lower down the stems of the elongated plant have petioles; those higher up clasp the stem and have pointed auricles at their bases.

The leaves of the prickly sowthistle, *Sonchus asper,* have pointed lobes that terminate in sharp prickles, are more succulent than those of the common sowthistle, and are shinier green, often with very attractive magenta markings. They have a smaller, more acute terminal lobe, and the stem-clasping auricles are rounded rather than pointed. The most colorful of the magenta-tinted forms are a dazzling sight, well worth leaving in appropriate areas in the garden at least until they begin flowering. It might be worthwhile for innovative nursery growers to consider selecting seed from the most colorful and slow-bolting of these sowthistles and growing crops to sell as winter ornamentals—they would be an interesting alternative, or supplement, to the commonly sold "flowering" cabbages and kales. It would, however, be appropriate to include a warning about their weediness in advertising text and nursery labels.

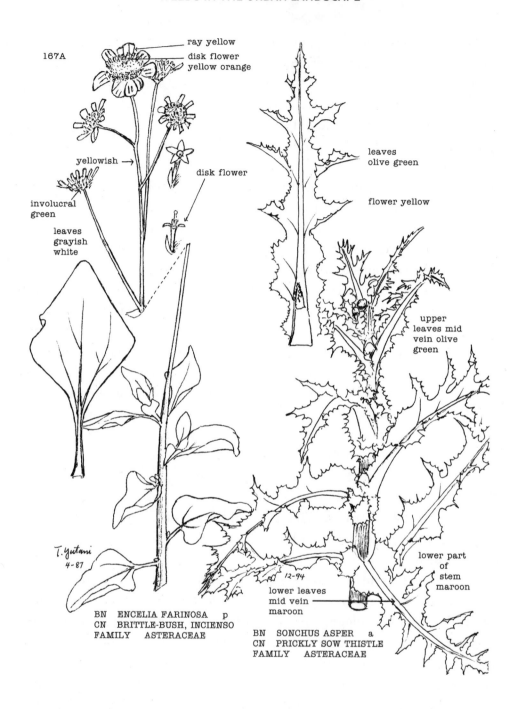

167A

ray yellow

disk flower
yellow orange

yellowish →

involucral
green

leaves
grayish
white

disk flower

leaves
olive green

flower yellow

upper
leaves mid
vein olive
green

lower part
of
stem
maroon

lower leaves
mid vein
maroon

T. Yutani
4-87

12-94

BN ENCELIA FARINOSA   p
CN BRITTLE-BUSH, INCIENSO
FAMILY   ASTERACEAE

BN SONCHUS ASPER   a
CN PRICKLY SOW THISTLE
FAMILY   ASTERACEAE

Sowthistles are ancient weeds in Europe and the Middle East, and there is a rich body of tradition and folklore associated with them. Their leaves were used as potherbs or in salads and were considered to be strengthening. The legendary hero Theseus ate a meal of sowthistle before taking on the bull of Marathon. In rural areas of Europe today the leaves are still used as food for rabbits, fowl, and, of course, pigs, but are probably seldom eaten by people. The ancient Roman encyclopedist Pliny recommends sowthistle for nursing mothers, probably associating its milky sap with lactation. Other traditional medicinal uses are for bronchial congestion, inflammation, hemorrhoids, deafness, and gout.

There are other sowthistles of note that are not commonly found in urban gardens, the most common probably being *Sonchus arvensis,* the perennial sowthistle, which spreads by rhizomes and is a common agricultural weed. A nursery in the Bay Area has recently introduced a sowthistle from the Canary Islands, *Sonchus palmensis,* for use as an ornamental. This forms a large rosette (18 inches across) of sharply lobed leaves, surmounted by 3- or 4-foot-tall spectacular yellow flower heads. It would be wise to consider this a potential weed and to watch it carefully.

There is a weed in Hawaii, *Emilia sonchifolia,* known commonly as Flora's paintbrush or red pualele, that is a dead ringer for a sowthistle with red flowers (also orange, pink, lilac, and white). This is a pan-tropical weed that probably originated in South Asia and is not a true sowthistle, but is closely related to groundsel. It has many medicinal uses, and is listed as an ornamental annual in some British seed catalogs.

TRUE THISTLES

Cirsium vulgare—bull thistle—Asteraceae, Compositae, daisy family

Silybum marianum—milk thistle—Asteraceae

Carduus pycnocephalus—Italian thistle—Asteraceae

Cynara cardunculus—cardoon, wild artichoke—Asteraceae

Various spiny herbaceous plants are referred to by the name *thistle,* but for the sake of botanical accuracy, only those belonging to the aster family *(Asteraceae,* or *Compositae),* tribe *Cardueae* (the thistle tribe), should be so designated. This is a group of annual or perennial composites with spiny leaves, bristly or thorny receptacles, and resinous rather than milky sap. Almost eighty genera with twenty-five hundred species are assigned to this tribe. They are native to temperate regions of Europe and Asia, with a few also occurring in Australia, tropical Africa, and North America. The genera containing most of the weedy thistles are *Carduus, Carthamus, Cnicus, Cirsium, Cynara,* and *Silybum.* Some of them are strikingly attractive plants with beautiful flowers and might be tolerated in some parts of the landscape as long as they are not allowed to go to seed.

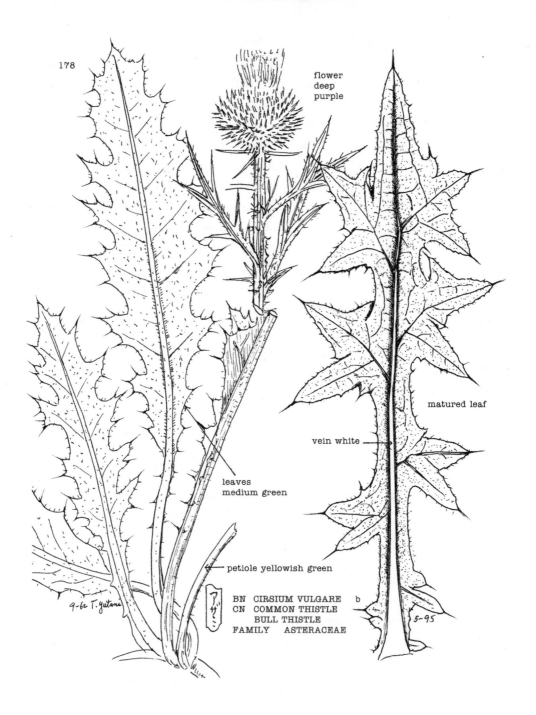

178

flower
deep
purple

matured leaf

vein white

leaves
medium green

petiole yellowish green

9-62 T. Yutani

BN CIRSIUM VULGARE   b
CN COMMON THISTLE
    BULL THISTLE
FAMILY   ASTERACEAE

5-95

The bull thistle, *Cirsium vulgare,* is perhaps the most attractive weedy thistle found in the Bay Area. This biennial begins its life cycle as a seedling rosette of dull green leaves covered with short, silvery hairs. They are narrowly oval to lanceolate, and entire or almost so. As the plant develops, the leaves become deeply lobed, develop spiny tips, and turn a darker green. Emerging from the rosette stage (theoretically in its second year), the bull thistle develops branching flower stems, each branch tipped with an inflorescence consisting of a globular receptacle, about an inch in diameter and covered with thorns, capped with reddish-purple disk flowers. Each of the flowers develops into an elongated yellowish achene with a silvery pappus.

A 5- or 6-foot-tall bull thistle in full bloom can be a glorious sight, but as soon as the purple flowers begin to develop achenes, it is time to remove it from the garden. A single plant can produce thousands of viable seeds, so one glorious specimen bull thistle can become the basis for an infestation covering many acres. This plant is classified as a noxious weed in nine states of the United States, as well as in many other countries.

Another strikingly attractive member of the thistle tribe is the milk thistle, *Silybum marianum,* also known as blessed milk thistle or Marian thistle. This is a herbaceous annual or biennial with shiny, light green leaves marked with creamy white along the veins, their lobes tipped with yellow spines. These leaves are thick and succulent, and on a large plant (6 feet or more), they can be 8 to 10 inches long.

Every milk thistle begins as a rosette of very crispy leaves, then elongates, sending up leafy stems, each of which is capped with a single inflorescence consisting of a receptacle covered with long, sharp spines and capped with reddish to purple ray flowers. This flower cluster is larger than that of the bull thistle, perhaps up to 3 inches in diameter, and can resemble a small artichoke.

Milk thistle grows in moist soil, often on roadsides and on the banks of ditches and streams, as well as in cultivated fields. It is frequently found in meadows and pastures, where it causes great concern to farmers and cattle ranchers because it can poison livestock with the large amounts of potassium nitrate it tends to accumulate in its leaf tissue.

Despite its poisonous nature, this plant has been used medicinally for two thousand years or more, mostly to treat liver disorders such as hepatitis, jaundice, and cirrhosis, as well as gall bladder afflictions. The extract of the seeds contains a flavonoid complex known as silymarin, which is claimed to be the efficacious ingredient. The Mayo Clinic has a website that evaluates medical claims made for various plant materials and gives milk thistle a grade of B—it seems to have some efficacy, they think, but the studies that have been done on humans have not been well designed, and so they decline to recommend it. Traditionally, a decoction of the seeds has also been used as a tonic, a stimulant, a diaphoretic, an emetic, and an emmenagogue. In large doses it is strongly emetic, capable of causing vomiting with very little pain. It has been used for purifying the blood, inducing lactation in nursing mothers, and curing vertigo, plague sores, rabies, and liver ailments.

The name Marian thistle refers to the virgin Mary, who, when nursing Jesus (so legend has it), accidentally allowed a few drops of her milk to fall on one of the leaves of this plant, which had up to then been solid green in color. Since that miraculous event, all milk thistle leaves have been variegated.

Like the artichoke, milk thistle was frequently cultivated for food until relatively recent times. The receptacle was peeled, then steamed or boiled, and served as a vegetable. The stalks were also peeled and eaten, as well as the small, tender side shoots, which were often used raw in salads. The plant was also cultivated as an ornamental, a use recommended by William Robinson in his book *The Wild Garden*. This suggestion will no doubt resonate with many contemporary gardeners who like to think of their gardens (and themselves) as wild—but, for reasons already mentioned, the use of weeds as garden plants has to be undertaken with a great deal of caution. The boundary between a garden *with* weeds and a garden *of* weeds can be pretty tenuous.

The Italian thistle, *Carduus pycnocephalus,* is a scruffy plant that does not have any of the potentially troublesome attractiveness of the bull and milk thistles. The rosette consists of a ring of lobed, spine-tipped leaves to 5 inches long, with faint white markings that often cause it to be confused with the milk thistle. These markings, however, are far less distinct than those of the Marian thistle, and the leaves are hairy—heavily woolly underneath, cobwebby on the upper surface—very unlike the smooth, succulent, shiny leaves of its cousin. When the Italian thistle elongates and produces branching stems, forming a mature plant generally less than 2 feet tall, the leaves become more deeply lobed, the markings even less distinct, and spiny, leafy appendages ("wings") grow along the length of the stems between the leaves. The branch tips sprout clusters of three or more small purple thistle flowers, each less than an inch in diameter. These produce the usual achenes with pappi, which enable the plant to spread aggressively.

Italian thistles are usually more prolific and aggressive on rough, disturbed ground than in more stable situations. They are found on roadsides, in pastures, along ditches and stream banks, and in swales on hillsides. On stable ground, they tend to eventually be outcompeted by weedy grasses, a process that can be accelerated by mowing, perhaps coupled with seeding of some of the more desirable grass species.

The artichoke thistle, or wild cardoon, *Cynara cardunculus,* is a striking plant, very large (up to 5 feet tall) and silvery gray with deeply cleft leaves that are covered with white woolly hairs beneath, sparser cobwebby hairs on the surface, and tipped at the apex and lobe ends with prominent spines. The very large (3 or 4 inches across), globe-like flower clusters consist of a receptacle composed of many spine-tipped bracts arranged in several series, which encase the slender purple flowers. Unlike artichokes, cardoon flower heads are surrounded at the base by inch-long spines. They grow in cymes on stout stems, usually one head per branch. The stems, like the leaves, are covered with cobwebby hairs.

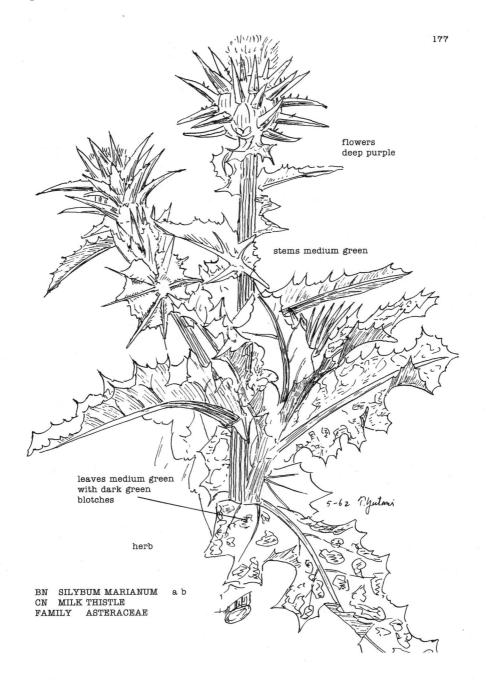

177

flowers
deep purple

stems medium green

leaves medium green
with dark green
blotches

5-62 T. Yutani

herb

BN   SILYBUM MARIANUM   a b
CN   MILK THISTLE
FAMILY   ASTERACEAE

Artichoke thistles are mostly found in rural areas, especially on grazing lands throughout California (most prominently in the coastal mountains), but they occasionally show up in urban environments, mostly in semiwild areas. Many originated as seedling escapees from fields of artichokes, *Cynara scolymus,* which generally revert to the wild spiny form from which the artichoke was derived (artichokes are kept true to type, and spineless, by vegetative propagation). Others originated as seedlings of cultivated cardoon.

Artichokes originated in the Mediterranean Basin and were domesticated in very early times. They were grown by the ancient Greeks and Romans, and during the fifteenth century they spread throughout the Mediterranean area. They were introduced to the New World by Spanish and French colonizers. Cardoon became a pest fairly rapidly. Charles Darwin describes it growing in Argentina in his 1839 book *The Voyage of the Beagle.* In Banda Oriental province, near Buenos Aires, he says, "Very many (probably several hundred) square miles are covered by one mass of these prickly plants, and are impenetrable by man or beast. Over the undulating plains, where these great beds occur, nothing can now live—I doubt whether any case is on record of an invasion on so grand a scale of one plant over the aborigines."

The artichoke thistle can be used as food by stripping the lobes from the midribs of the leaves, then cooking them. This vegetable, known as cardoon, is popular in Italian, Spanish, and other Mediterranean cuisines. Most cardoon sold commercially consists no doubt of artichoke midribs, but the wild form is fairly identical; the wild chokes, on the other hand, are too small and spiny to be a desirable food item.

As indicated by Darwin, the artichoke thistle impedes grazing by competing with desirable forage plants, and by physically excluding cattle from areas where it grows in dense stands. By the 1930s this plant had infested over 150,000 acres in California. Containment and eradication efforts have since reduced this number, but in some areas it is still considered too persistent and widespread to eradicate, and containment is the best that can be hoped for. Control strategies employ various combinations of physical and chemical approaches. Seed banks will persist for about five years, so a really effective program must be carried out for at least this long. Biological controls are problematic because of the plant's close relationship to cultivated artichokes; but in 1994 a fly that parasitizes the seeds was discovered in California (a creature native to the Mediterranean) living among wild artichoke thistles. This fly shows great promise as a control agent, since cultivated artichokes are not grown from seed.

WHITE CUDWEED

Pseudognaphalium luteoalbum—white cudweed—Asteraceae, Compositae, daisy family

White cudweed, sometimes known as cotton batting plant, is an attractive winter annual with silvery foliage and yellow and white flowers, the sort of

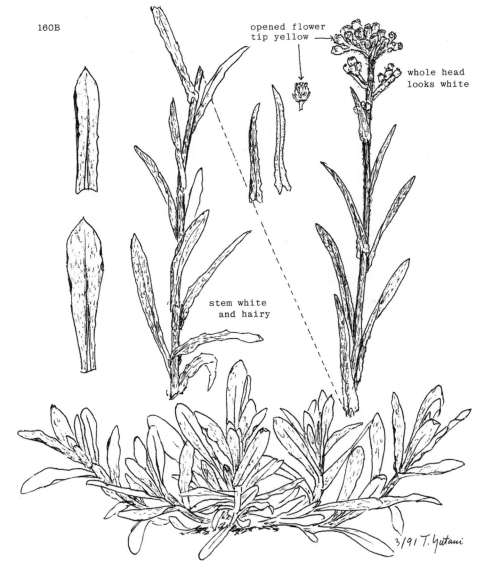

160B

opened flower
tip yellow

whole head
looks white

stem white
and hairy

3/91 T. Yutani

BN   PSEUDOGNAPHALIUM LUTEO-ALBUM
CN   WHITE CUDWEED
FAMILY   ASTERACEAE

plant gardeners value for softening bright colors in flower borders, or creating "white gardens." When it appears, it is all too easy to allow it to serve such a purpose and leave it, but watch out: a single plant will quickly produce myriad offspring. Be prepared to pay for such a gift with some extra weeding time.

White cudweed is an erect, sparsely branching plant that grows from about ½ to 1½ feet. Leaves appear first as a rosette; they are 1 to 2 inches long, narrow, wider at the tip than the base (spatulate), covered with woolly hairs on both surfaces, but with more beneath than above. They are alternate and clasp the stems. Flowers are in a dense cluster at the tips of the stems and in the leaf axils. They are yellow, but surrounded by woolly white bracts, hence the name *luteoalbum,* Latin for "yellow-white." Flowers turn a light brown when mature. The plant grows from a short taproot or fibrous root system.

Because of its dense hairs, white cudweed is very drought tolerant and often keeps growing and blooming throughout the summer; it can sometimes live well into a second year. It is native to Eurasia. Cudweed is found throughout coastal California and in the Central Valley. In urban areas it grows in various weedy haunts, but more often than not in dry situations with full sun.

Mrs. Grieve mentions another cudweed, *Gnaphalium uliginosum,* which grows in marshy areas in England and the rest of Europe and is also known as cotton plant or March everlasting. Medicinally, this has been used as an astringent and as a gargle for quinsy, a severe throat inflammation. Various cudweeds have also long been used in dried flower arrangements, so are sometimes referred to as everlastings or live-forevers.

YARROW

Achillea millefolium—yarrow, milfoil—Asteraceae, Compositae, aster family

Yarrow is a common weed of pastures, roadsides, and hedges in Eurasia and North America. *The Jepson Manual* describes it as a "circumboreal . . . highly variable polyploid complex . . .." In rural areas, it is mostly a pasture weed; in cities and suburbs, it tends to confine itself to lawns, sometimes escaping into other areas, such as sidewalk cracks.

Unmowed, yarrow plants can grow more than 3 feet tall. The leaves are about 3 or 4 inches long, gray-green in color, alternate, narrow but deeply lobed, and thus divided into many very fine segments crowded onto the midrib (hence, *milfoil,* "thousand-leaved"), giving them a feathery appearance. The leaves have a characteristic sweetly pungent aroma when bruised. Leaves and stems are covered with short, fine hairs.

Yarrow is perennial, growing from a crown with thick, sturdy, fibrous roots and spreading by short rhizomes to form clumps. The flower heads are clustered in umbels atop the stems. They are tiny, daisylike disk and ray structures, usually white, sometimes pale yellow or pinkish. The fruit is an achene. Although unmowed yarrow blooms atop tall stalks, yarrow in lawns is capable of producing flowers on very short stems.

In Europe, yarrow was widely used as a medicinal herb, principally to stop bleeding. The Trojan War hero Achilles is said to have used it to heal his wounded men, hence the genus name *Achillea*. Many of its common names reflect this use: soldier's woundwort, knight's milfoil, herbe militaris, nosebleed, carpenter's weed, bloodwort, staunchweed, sanguinary. Other common names refer to its status as a dark-side herb, used in witches' brews and for divination: devil's nettle, devil's plaything, bad man's plaything. It was also reputed to have the power to induce dreams revealing to women the identities of their future husbands. In the Orkneys, yarrow tea was considered a cure for melancholy. The plant was also used as snuff, to clear sinuses, and was known as old man's pepperweed. In the seventeenth century, it was used as an ingredient in salads. Its pungent flavor gave it the name *field hop* in Sweden, where it was used as a hop substitute in beer. Linnaeus thought beer brewed with this herb was more intoxicating than that made with hops.

Other medicinal uses for yarrow: the tea was given for colds and flu, to allay fevers and induce sweating; a decoction was taken internally for bleeding piles and kidney disorders; it was reputed to prevent baldness, if the hair was washed with water infused with the herb. Culpeper recommended it for cramps, Parkinson for ague. Although considered medicinally potent since ancient times, yarrow was removed from the British Pharmacopoeia in 1781.

Cultivars of yarrow have been developed in many colors for garden use. It is a sturdy, drought-tolerant perennial, well suited to summer dry climates.

See illustration of yarrow on p. 57.

WILD MUSTARDS

Hirschfeldia incana—shortpod mustard—Brassicaceae, Cruciferae, mustard family

Sisymbrium officinale—hedge mustard—Brassicaceae

The two weedy mustards described here can be easily distinguished from other common weeds in the mustard family by their relatively short siliques that grow close to, and nearly parallel to, the flower stem—they are said to be *adpressed*.

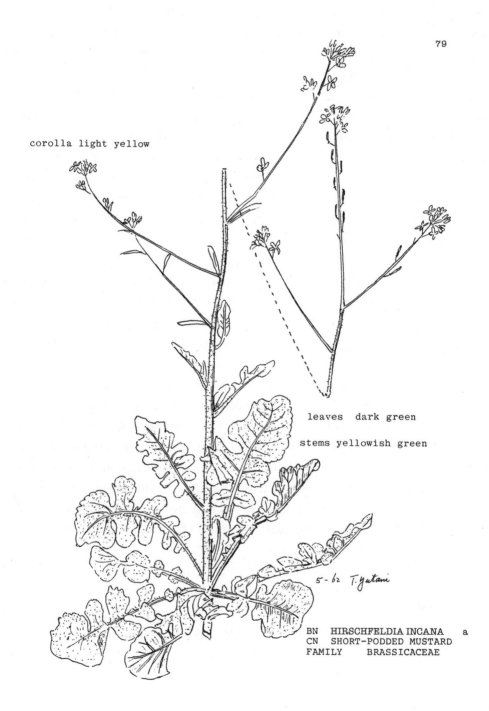

79

corolla light yellow

leaves   dark green

stems yellowish green

5- 62 T. yutani

BN   HIRSCHFELDIA INCANA   a
CN   SHORT-PODDED MUSTARD
FAMILY   BRASSICACEAE

Shortpod mustard, *Hirschfeldia incana,* is a biennial or short-lived perennial with deeply lobed, petioled leaves, hairy on top, woolly and almost white beneath. The leaves form a rosette, which persists even after the plant branches and flowers. The first to emerge have only slightly wavy margins, but they become more incised as they develop. The terminal lobe is the largest and is somewhat bulbous. These leaves can be easily confused with those of the wild radish, *Raphanus raphanistrum,* but the latter are larger, darker green, not woolly beneath, and have a terminal lobe more exaggeratedly bulbous than that of the shortpod mustard leaf. Upper stems of shortpod mustard have few leaves—these are smaller and less deeply lobed than the basal leaves, and they clasp the stems.

Once the plants bloom, there is no confusing them. Shortpod mustard develops short racemes of bright yellow flowers on bent or curving stems; radish flowers are lavender, purple, white, or very light yellow—never bright yellow. The bent stems of the shortpod mustard form a sort of tumbleweed late in the season; this dies back and sometimes breaks off, but a new basal rosette sprouts from the root.

The fruits are short (½ to ¾ inch) siliques that are closely pressed against the stems (adpressed); they contain reddish-brown, honeycombed, irregularly shaped seeds—their irregularity is a good identifying characteristic.

This plant has a deep, woody taproot and tends to grow in hot, dry areas, often in compacted soil. It remains green and flowers throughout the summer. By fall it is often a mass of dried-out stems, with a green rosette at the base that allows it to regenerate for at least another year.

Shortpod mustard can be controlled with herbicides, or by digging out all or most of the root. It can be suppressed, and seed production minimized, by mowing. Long-term control can be achieved by loosening and possibly amending the soil, and growing taller, shrubbier plants well suited to local conditions.

Hedge mustard, *Sisymbrium officinale* (a.k.a. wireweed, tumbleweed, tumble mustard), has short, adpressed siliques that closely resemble those of shortpod mustard, but the rest of the plant is very different. Shortly after germination, a rosette forms, but even here the difference is readily apparent. Rather than the rounded lobes of the shortpod mustard leaf, hedge mustard leaves have sharply pointed lobes, with the ones behind the terminal lobe often pointing backward toward the base at more or less a 45-degree angle—think of the wings of the F-86 Sabre jet, the famous 1950s fighter plane. The foliage is dull green and somewhat rough to the touch.

Being mostly an annual (sometimes biennial), hedge mustard quickly leaves the rosette stage and grows into a branching plant, producing much smaller leaves toward the tips of the stems, a distinctive characteristic of mustard family plants (wide variability in the shapes of the leaves is also characteristic). The stems tend to curve upward, reminding one of a candelabra. Small clusters of tiny yellow flowers appear at their tips and, also in characteristic mustard fashion, continue to develop while the tightly adpressed (clinging closely to the stems) siliques form behind them. Larger, multiply branched plants may break loose from their roots after they die in the fall and become "tumbleweeds."

Hedge mustard occurs in most California counties and in every state of the United States except Arizona. Like many Eurasian weeds, it is widespread throughout the temperate regions of the world.

Hedge mustard has been widely used in traditional European herbal medicine as a diuretic, expectorant, tonic, and laxative. Mustard oil rubbed on the chest can help relieve muscle tension in the chest and ease breathing—writing this, I think of the dreaded mustard plasters of my asthmatic childhood (diapers soaked in mustard oil). The ancient Greeks believed that hedge mustard was an antidote for all poisons. In traditional medicine it was also used to soothe sore throats, so was sometimes known as singer's plant.

Charlemagne lists *Sisymbrium* in his *Capitularies* as a plant that should be grown in medicinal herb gardens—this could be hedge mustard, tumble mustard, or London rocket.

Hedge mustard has a number of culinary uses, particularly in northern Europe, and especially in Germany, Denmark, and Norway. The leaves, particularly the young ones, have been used as potherbs and in salads, and the seeds ground into mustard paste for use as a condiment, much like the black or white mustard seeds from which the condiment is more often made.

MORE MUSTARDS

Brassica rapa—yellow mustard—Brassicaceae, Cruciferae, mustard or cabbage family

Sisymbrium irio—London rocket—Brassicaceae

Sisymbrium altissimum—tumble mustard

The following three mustards all share a characteristic that makes them easy to distinguish from shortpod and hedge mustard: they have long, narrow siliques on long pedicels and do not adhere closely to the stems they grow from; they are not adpressed. They also differ in other ways.

Yellow mustard, *Brassica rapa,* also known as field mustard, rape mustard, or turnip mustard, is a vigorous annual that is abundant in rural districts, where it is often sown as a cover crop in orchards and vineyards, producing broad expanses of bright yellow spring flowers, a very attractive seasonal feature in the landscape.

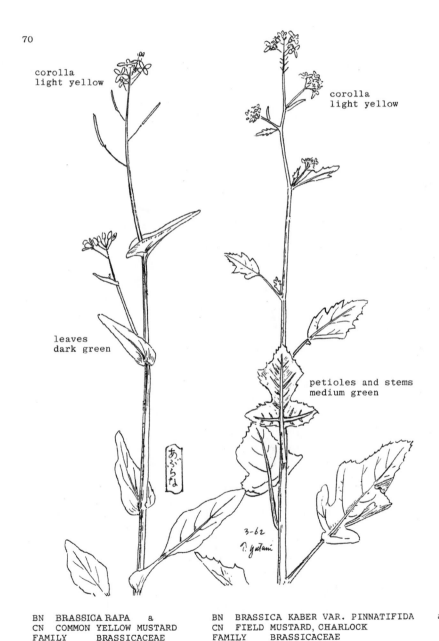

70

corolla
light yellow

corolla
light yellow

leaves
dark green

petioles and stems
medium green

3-62

BN   BRASSICA RAPA   a
CN   COMMON YELLOW MUSTARD
FAMILY   BRASSICACEAE

BN   BRASSICA KABER VAR. PINNATIFIDA   a
CN   FIELD MUSTARD, CHARLOCK
FAMILY   BRASSICACEAE

Yellow mustard has become a marketing icon for the Napa Valley in much the same way sunflowers have for Tuscany and Provence. In urban areas, it is far less common than some other mustards, such as shortpod and hedge mustard.

The leaves and stems of yellow mustard are smooth, blue-gray, often overlaid with a whitish bloom. They are narrow, pointed, lobed or entire (there is often much variation on the same plant), and most clasp the stems with earlike projections known as auricles. The plants branch freely, growing to a

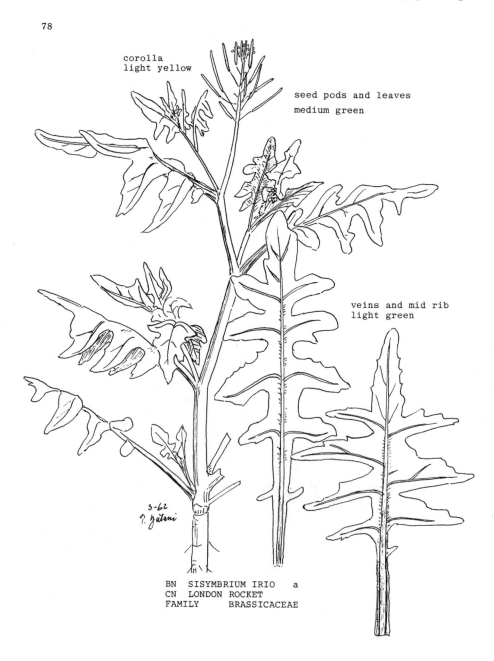

78

corolla
light yellow

seed pods and leaves
medium green

veins and mid rib
light green

3-62
7. yutani

BN   SISYMBRIUM IRIO   a
CN   LONDON ROCKET
FAMILY   BRASSICACEAE

height of about 2 feet. The four-petaled flowers are bright yellow, ½ inch or less across, and occur in short, terminal clusters. As the older flowers fade (new ones always forming in front of them), cylindrical siliques about 1½ inches long form, held to the stems by pedicels about half their length, and facing upward. The whole plant has a light, graceful, and succulent aspect.

Although annual, yellow mustard has a sturdy, fleshy taproot, which has enabled the development of many cultivars of turnips from this wild parent. It is also the parent of many varieties of mustard greens, of bok choy and other Chinese cabbages, and of a broccoli-like vegetable developed in Italy, rapini, or broccoli raab. Most of the culinary cultivars have, to some degree, the hot, pungent flavor and aroma of the parent plant. Wild mustard has traditionally been eaten as a potherb and salad green, and it has been used medicinally in much the same way as hedge mustard.

Some varieties of this plant are used for experiments, as they are fast growing and require little care. These have become known as Fast Plants, a trademark name registered for the variety developed at the University of Wisconsin. They grow quickly, maturing in about forty days—less in the case of some genetically modified varieties. Some of them have even been sent into orbit to test their ability to germinate in a gravity-free environment.

Yellow mustard occurs in all states of the United States, in most of Canada, and in Greenland. In California it is found throughout the state below 5,000 feet of elevation.

London rocket, or rocket mustard, *Sisymbrium irio,* closely resembles yellow mustard, differing from that plant in its shorter stature (up to 15 inches) and greener leaves that lack the whitish bloom found on the yellow mustard; the leaves of London rocket are narrower and more deeply incised. The siliques are narrower and longer, also on pedicels and pointing upward. The plant is less widespread than yellow mustard, both in California and the rest of the United States, and is absent from Canada. It is not, to my knowledge, grown as a cover crop, and is generally regarded as a fairly troublesome weed in agricultural areas, especially in the desert. It is more likely to be found in the city than yellow mustard and is fond of growing in sidewalk cracks.

London rocket derives its name from its sudden appearance in vast quantities after the Great Fire of London in the seventeenth century. It has been used in folk medicine in much the same manner as other mustards. In the Near East, it is still used to treat rheumatism and coughs and bronchial ailments and to heal wounds. The Bedouin use it as a tobacco substitute.

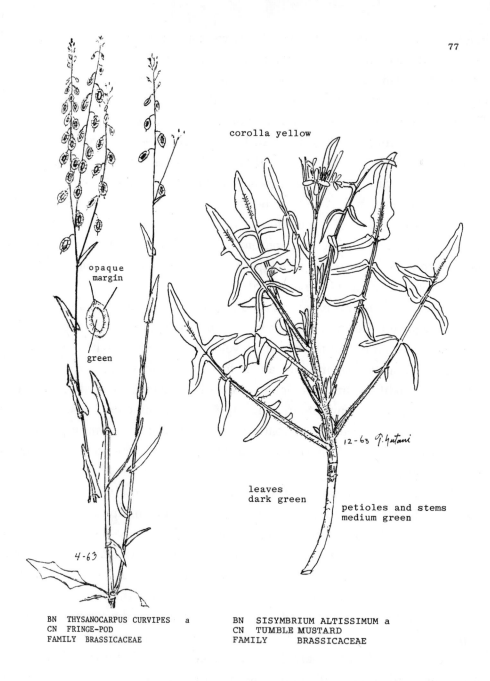

corolla yellow

opaque
margin

green

12-63 P. Yutani

leaves
dark green

petioles and stems
medium green

4-63

BN THYSANOCARPUS CURVIPES a
CN FRINGE-POD
FAMILY BRASSICACEAE

BN SISYMBRIUM ALTISSIMUM a
CN TUMBLE MUSTARD
FAMILY BRASSICACEAE

Tumble mustard, *Sisymbrium altissimum,* also known as Jim Hill mustard or tall rocket, looks like a larger version of London rocket, growing to a height of 3 feet or more. It has even narrower leaf lobes, which are threadlike on the upper leaves, and flower petals that extend noticeably beyond the sepals. It is much branched and, like shortpod mustard, forms a tumbleweed when the plant dries and detaches from its roots. Tumble mustard is widespread in California, is found in all states of the United States except Alabama, and grows in most of the provinces and territories of Canada.

JOINTED CHARLOCK, WILD RADISH

Raphanus raphanistrum—wild radish, jointed charlock—Brassicaceae, Cruciferae, mustard family

Raphanus sativum—wild radish

The wild radish is a tall (to 4 feet), bushy weed that closely resembles the mustards, but has several key features that make it easy to distinguish from them. The two species listed above form the large array of wild radishes that grow abundantly in urban and rural areas throughout most of the temperate world.

Jointed charlock, *Raphanus raphanistrum,* is the truly wild form of the radish, one of three species native to the Near East and the Mediterranean, any or all of which may be the ancestor of the cultivated radish, *Raphanus sativus.* It has deeply lobed, roughly hairy leaves, somewhat similar to those of shortpod mustard, but with a more bulbous terminal lobe. Once the plant flowers, there is no mistaking it from the mustard: all mustard flowers are bright yellow; wild radishes come in an array of colors, from pure to off-white, through various shades of lavender, and occasionally a reddish hue or a very light yellow—never the bright yellow of mustard. Perhaps the most common color of wild radish is off-white with lavender veins.

The fruit is also easy to distinguish from that of the mustards, being a comparatively fat (about ¼ inch) silique with a pointed tip—mustard siliques have blunt tips. These fruits are about 1½ to 3 inches long, and contain seeds about ¹⁄₁₆ inch in diameter, significantly larger than the minute seeds of mustard. Their presence is indicated by a bulge in the silique, giving the fruit a wavy or "jointed" appearance. The fruits do not dehisce, as do mustard siliques, but break open transversely at the joints in order to release the seeds.

The wild radish grows from a stout, somewhat woody taproot that resembles some forms of the culinary radish but is tough and hot. It is classified as a winter annual, but due to its stout root it often survives the summer, and may form a new rosette and live a second year.

The cultivated radish, *Raphanus sativum,* often escapes from farm fields and joins the weedy radish population. It can be distinguished from *R. raphanistrum* by its smooth, nonjointed (or sometimes shallowly jointed) siliques; however, it freely hybridizes with other wild and escaped radishes, making the two species difficult to tell apart. No need to fret about this—their behavior as weeds and the control options for them are virtually the same.

Radishes have been cultivated as a culinary crop since ancient Egyptian times. They are mainly grown as cool-season crops, since they flower early and quickly form woody roots in warm weather. There are two main types: the smaller spring radishes, eaten raw by themselves or in salads; and the larger winter radishes, planted in fall and harvested in the winter, when they have developed a large, cylindrical root, often a foot or longer. The Japanese version,

72

seed pods
yellowish green

leaves &
young stems
dark green

corolla white
to violet
leaves and stems
dark green

lower ½
of stem
dark brown

5-67

3-62 T. Yutani

herb

BN CARDARIA DRABA   p
CN HOARY CRESS
FAMILY   BRASSICACEAE

BN RAPHANUS SATIVUS   ab
CN WILD RADISH
FAMILY   BRASSICACEAE

known as daikon, is often served grated or pickled as a condiment with meals, and is sometimes cooked. Radishes contain an enzyme known as diastase, which helps digest starches, so they are popular as a condiment with rice in the Far East, with bread and breakfast cereals in Europe, and with bean- and tortilla-based Mexican cuisine.

Radishes have a tangy, spicy flavor, which is present in the pods and seeds as well as the roots. There are varieties grown in Europe especially for their succulent pods, which are eaten raw or pickled. A variety known as Muenchen bier is often eaten raw with beer in Germany, and the pods of a wild species known as rat-tailed radishes are eaten in Java. Radish seeds are sometimes sprinkled on salad to add spice and crunch. The leaves are also eaten, cooked or in salads.

In Oaxaca, Mexico, at Christmas time, a festival known as La Noche de Rábanos is celebrated on December 23. Locals carve radishes into the form of saints, animals, and popular figures and display them in the town square. Entire nativity scenes are made from radishes.

Medicinally, radishes have been used to treat gallstones and gravel, and as an antiscorbutic, since they contain a good deal of vitamin C.

SHEPHERD'S PURSE

Capsella bursa-pastoris—shepherd's purse—Brassicaceae, Cruciferae, mustard or cabbage family

Shepherd's purse is a winter annual that resembles bittercress *(Cardamine oligosperma)* in size, shape, and general appearance, but with key differences in the leaves and fruit. The plant first appears as a rosette, a ring of lanceolate leaves that are deeply lobed and pointed at the end and anchored by a slender taproot. Unlike the rounded lobes of bittercress, shepherd's purse lobes are sharply pointed and angled toward the fronts of the leaves. The rosette leaves have petioles; as the plant elongates, leaves that form on the upper stem have few or no lobes and usually clasp the stems.

Mature plants may be tiny, or as tall as 2 feet, depending on soil, moisture, and exposure. Flowers are white and very small, less than ⅛ inch across, almost indistinguishable from bittercress flowers. The development of the inflorescence follows the typical mustard family pattern, with new flowers forming at the tops of the elongating racemes as the older flowers lower down the stems develop into fruits. Unlike the long, slender siliques of bittercress, shepherd's purse fruits are triangular siliculas—the plant is named after their resemblance to the triangular purses, made from sheep scrota, that shepherds in Europe traditionally carried on their belts.

The seeds contain a mucilaginous substance, which becomes sticky when wet. Some botanists have theorized that this mucilage traps insects, whose decaying bodies can be used by the emerging seedling for nutrients, a phenomenon that is described as either protocarnivorous or paracarnivorous. The

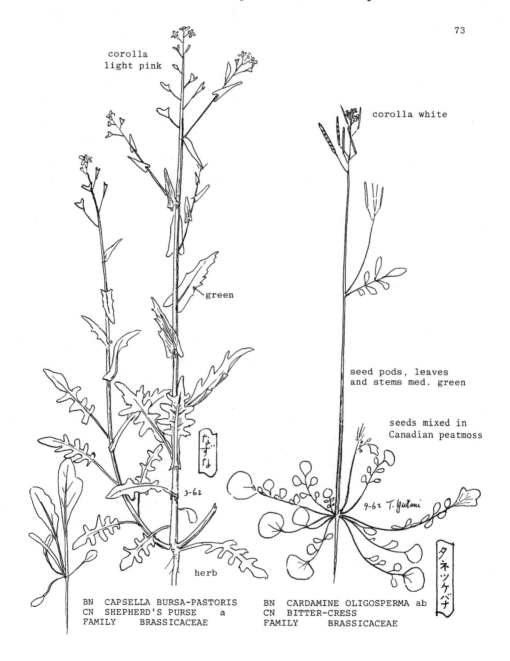

corolla
light pink

corolla white

73

green

seed pods, leaves
and stems med. green

seeds mixed in
Canadian peatmoss

3-62

9-62 T. Yutani

herb

タネツケバナ

```
BN  CAPSELLA BURSA-PASTORIS      BN  CARDAMINE OLIGOSPERMA ab
CN  SHEPHERD'S PURSE      a      CN  BITTER-CRESS
FAMILY    BRASSICACEAE           FAMILY      BRASSICACEAE
```

plant is basically a winter annual (spring annual in colder climates) but is capable of many generations a year and can flower and set seed almost continuously under ideal conditions.

Shepherd's purse probably originated in the Near East, but it spread throughout the agricultural regions of the Northern Hemisphere in ancient times. In Britain, it is known as an archaeophyte, a plant that did not originate in a particular location, but that has been naturalized there for hundreds or thousands of years (in England, plants that were introduced before 1492 qualify). It now grows widely throughout the temperate regions of the world, especially in colder climates.

As would be expected of a plant that has been a familiar in human habitats since ancient times, shepherd's purse has a variety of culinary and medicinal uses. Leaves have been cooked as a potherb and eaten raw in salads. The plant was sometimes fed to animals, although it developed a reputation for tainting the flavor of milk and for darkening egg yolks. Medicinally, shepherd's purse has been used as an astringent and a diuretic, an antiscorbutic and a stimulant. Its astringent properties have rendered it especially useful in treating diarrhea, and teas made from the plant have been used to stop internal and external bleeding—shepherd's purse was widely used for this purpose in Germany during World War I. The seed has long been a popular ingredient in birdseed mixes. It has also been used as a constituent of cosmetics.

Other common names for shepherd's purse are shepherd's bag, shepherd's scrip, shepherd's pouch, witches' pouches, rattle pouches, case weed, pickpocket, pick purse, blind weed, pepper and salt, poor man's parmacettie, sanguinary, mother's heart, and clappedepouch.

FUMITORY

Fumaria officinalis—fumitory, fumiter—Papaveraceae, poppy family

Alack, 'tis he ...
Crowned with rank fumiter and furrow weeds,
With hardocks, hemlock, nettles, cuckoo flow'rs,
Darnel, and all the idle weeds that grow
In our sustaining corn.

—Shakespeare, *King Lear*, act 4, scene 4

Fumitory is a tender, herbaceous vining annual, native to Europe; it shows up in late winter and persists until the ground dries out in late spring or early summer. It is a lush plant during the wet season, when it forms a dense ground cover and scrambles through taller herbaceous plantings and low shrubbery. Its leaves are smooth, yellow to blue-green, alternate, long-stalked and finely dissected, about an inch in diameter; they somewhat resemble those of maidenhair ferns or columbines. The stems are up to 3 feet long. The flowers are about ⅛ to ¼ inch long, tubular, on long racemes. They have four petals—the outer two are keeled and free, light pink in color; the inner two are fused, with a purplish tip. In the Bay Area, they bloom from March into late May or early June, but somewhat later right along the outer coast.

The root, as might be expected for a plant that produces so much top growth, is thick and sturdy.

Fumitory tends to grow in moist, somewhat shady locations. It may be found scrambling through shrubs and growing in cracks in rock walls, near bodies of water, and in dappled shade at the bottoms of slopes. It likes soil that is moist, but not boggy.

The name *fumitory* derives from the Latin *fumus terrae,* smoke of the earth, reflecting an ancient belief that the plant emerged from the ground like smoke from a furnace, without sprouting from seed.

KNOTWEEDS

Polygonum aviculare—common or prostrate knotweed—Polygonaceae, buckwheat family

Persicaria capitata (Polygonum capitatum)—rose carpet knotweed—Polygonaceae

Knotweed, *Polygonum aviculare,* is one of our oldest weeds—there is evidence from fossil pollen that it grew at the foot of glaciers during the last ice age. It is a summer annual with a deep taproot and long stems with swollen leaf nodes (the "knots"), which produce alternate, entire, narrowly lanceolate to elliptic leaves ½ to 1½ inches long, blue-green in color, with short petioles that are covered by the papery sheaths that wrap the swollen nodes. The slender, tough stems branch extensively and often change direction at the nodes, producing a zigzag effect. This plant occurs in both upright and sprawling forms; the latter produce a dense mat, usually about a foot across, but which can reach 2 feet or more. The upright form will grow to about a foot high and across.

The flowers, which grow in the leaf axils, either singly or in clusters of two to five, are tiny and surrounded by five greenish-white to pinkish sepals. They produce an abundance of very small, red-brown to black three-sided achenes (very characteristic of this family), which can literally cover the ground when the plant is removed after flowering.

This weed can grow in sun or shade, poor soil or rich, but is mostly found in dry, compacted soils. The prostrate version, with its sturdy, deep taproot and sprawling stems, is perfectly adapted to sidewalk cracks, anchoring its taproot in the relatively cool and moist soil beneath the sidewalk and sprawling its stems over the concrete pavement, giving it maximum exposure to light. It can establish itself as a weed in compacted, sparsely watered lawns, taking advantage of circumstances that challenge grasses. Although regarded as a summer annual, knotweed can be found year round in mild climates. Some tends to overwinter and become perennial; and the seeds, which usually germinate in the warm soil of late spring, sometimes germinate early during mild spells in winter, or where the soil warms early from heat accumulated by concrete exposed to sunlight, and so produce an early spring crop.

Knotweed is native to Eurasia. It is also known as knotgrass, centinode, ninety-knot, allseed, bird's or sparrow's tongue (from the shape of the leaves), armstrong (from the difficulty of pulling it out), and by names referring to the domestic animals that eat it: cowgrass, hogweed, pigweed, pig rush, swynel grass, and swinegrass. It was eaten mixed with farmed grains during the Iron Age, as evidenced by the analysis of the stomach contents of the Tollund man. Knotweed has a number of traditional medicinal uses, but has been used especially as an astringent. It has also been used to treat diarrhea, bleeding piles, wounds, and internal bleeding. The juice of the plant can be squirted up the nose to stop nosebleeds. Knotweed has also been used as a diuretic for expelling stones and killing worms. In *A Midsummer Night's Dream,* Shakespeare refers to the plant as "hindering knotgrass," reflecting the popular belief that a decoction of this plant is useful for stunting the growth of children and young domestic animals. We shudder at such an idea, but to people with very limited food resources, slowing the growth of offspring and animals might have seemed worth considering.

The word *Polygonum* comes from Greek and means "many knees or joints," a reference to the swollen nodes. *Aviculare* refers to birds, many of which are fond of knotgrass seed.

Rose carpet knotweed, *Persicaria capitata,* is a common ground cover that is widely grown in California and is capable of freely reseeding itself and becoming a weed where it is not wanted. It is very vigorous, needs little water, and forms a low mat that hugs the ground. It has the same knots on its stems as the weedier knotweed, *P. aviculare,* but its leaves are broadly oval, usually less than an inch across, and green when young, developing pinkish overtones as they mature. Roots develop at the knots, firmly anchoring the ground cover. Where this plant is not desired, it should be removed as soon as it appears; but consider—there are not many other herbaceous ground covers that are as tough, vigorous, and drought tolerant as rose carpet knotweed.

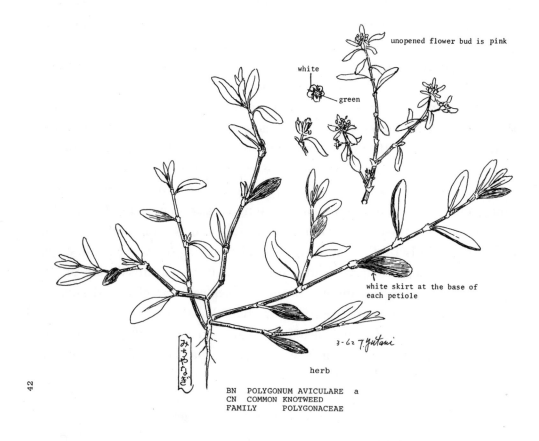

unopened flower bud is pink

white

green

white skirt at the base of each petiole

3-62 T.Yutani

herb

BN   POLYGONUM AVICULARE   a
CN   COMMON KNOTWEED
FAMILY   POLYGONACEAE

DOCKS

Rumex crispus—curly dock—Polygonaceae, buckwheat family

Rumex conglomeratus—cluster dock, green dock

Rumex pulcher—fiddle dock

These three docks are perennial, growing from a stout, dense taproot that often branches. If removed from the ground, they are capable of regenerating from the smallest root fragments, which are likely to be left, since they are very brittle. Their yellow-pigmented interior can be used to produce a dye.

Due to their love of water and their rosette-forming habit, the docks often appear in lawns and can be very persistent; a mowed plant merely reverts to the rosette stage.

Curly dock, *Rumex crispus*, also known as yellow dock and sour dock, is one of the classic Mediterranean weeds that is most at home in wet soil, where large colonies can often be seen. In winter, the whole plant takes on an attractive mahogany red appearance, due to the masses of reddish fruits it sets, as well as to reddish coloration that develops in the leaves during cold weather. The other two docks also grow in wet ground and have a similar winter look. All three, however, are very drought tolerant and can easily establish themselves, and persist, in dry ground.

The leaves of curly dock are thick, bluish-green, fairly narrow and pointed, 4 to 12 inches long with prominently wavy (crisped) margins. At first they grow in a rosette; later in the growing season, the plant produces a stout, branching central stem, which can become 2 to 5 feet tall. A narrow, dense, panicle, 4 to 20 inches long, consisting of tiny, greenish flowers (about ⅛ inch diameter), develops at the tip of the central stem. As these flowers mature, they produce a mass of brownish red, triangular achenes that persist through most of the winter. These clusters are often used in dried flower arrangements. The seed can be viable for up to eighty years, so flower arrangers—and weeders—should be careful about how they dispose of the fruit clusters—they should go into a hot compost pile if possible.

Cluster dock, *Rumex conglomeratus,* also known as slender dock or green dock, is difficult to distinguish from curly dock in its vegetative phase—its leaf margins are also crisped, although somewhat less prominently than those of curly dock. The inflorescence is different: less dense and massive, more slender and branching. It is at least as common in the Bay Area as *R. crispus.*

Fiddle dock, *Rumex pulcher,* is far less common than the other two and is easily distinguished from them by its broader leaves, most of whose margins are strongly indented at the middle of the leaf blade, reminding one of the shape of a violin body. This plant also has a noticeably zigzag pattern to its branching.

The leaves of the wild docks can be eaten, and two species especially esteemed for their leaves are often grown in gardens—*Rumex acetosa,* known as common or garden sorrel, and *R. scutatus,* French sorrel. In their wild forms, these are native to southern Europe, western Asia, and North Africa—the greater

Mediterranean region. The leaves have a sour flavor, produced by binoxalate of potash, a salt that can accumulate in the body and become somewhat toxic. Docks have sometimes been implicated in livestock poisoning. Humans, who eat far less greenery than cattle, are less likely to experience toxic effects. Still, it might be prudent to avoid eating the wild docks and stick with French sorrel, which is the least sour garden dock and has a distinctly lemony flavor.

46

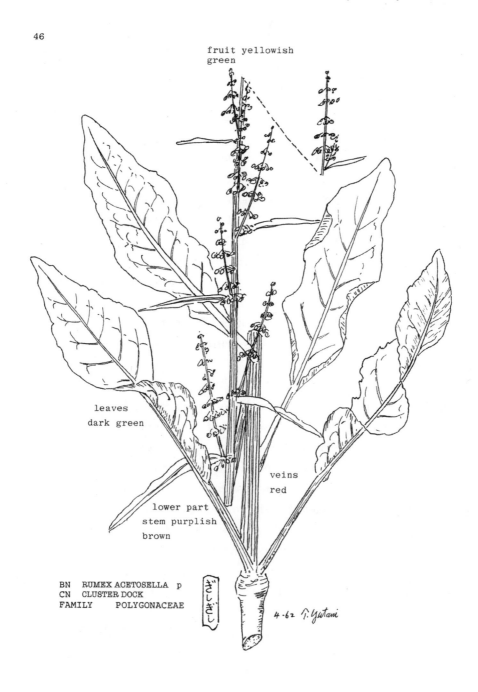

fruit yellowish
green

leaves
dark green

veins
red

lower part
stem purplish
brown

BN   RUMEX ACETOSELLA p
CN   CLUSTER DOCK
FAMILY   POLYGONACEAE

4-62 T. Yutani

Dock root has been used medicinally as a laxative, an alterative, and a mild tonic. It is astringent, and so it has been used for treating wounds, piles, and bleeding from the lungs. Dock has also been used to treat blood diseases, scurvy, scrofula, jaundice, and nettle stings. The active ingredient is a compound known as rumicin. Dock root medications are administered as extracts, tinctures, or syrups.

SHEEP SORREL

Rumex acetosella—sheep sorrel, sour dock—Polygonaceae, buckwheat family

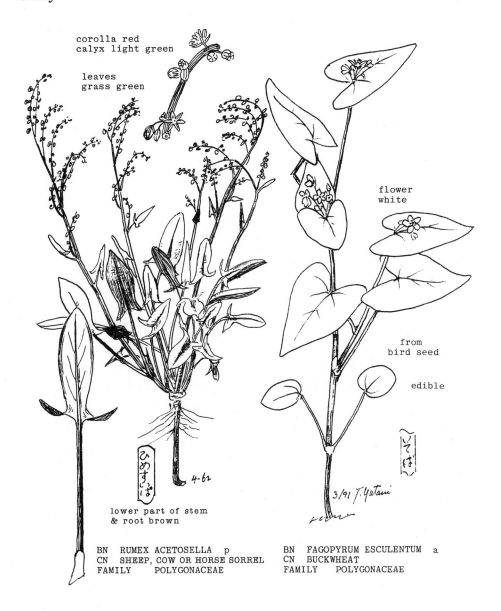

corolla red
calyx light green

leaves
grass green

flower
white

from
bird seed

edible

4-62

3/91 T. Yatani

lower part of stem
& root brown

BN   RUMEX ACETOSELLA p
CN   SHEEP, COW OR HORSE SORREL
FAMILY   POLYGONACEAE

BN   FAGOPYRUM ESCULENTUM a
CN   BUCKWHEAT
FAMILY   POLYGONACEAE

Sheep sorrel, a close cousin of curly dock, is a low-growing perennial that spreads aggressively by its fleshy, whitish rhizomes. Native throughout Europe and Asia, it has traveled to most other temperate and subtropical regions of the world. It grows in meadows and pastures, in open grasslands, in crop fields, and along roadsides, often in poor, gravelly soil. It does not often invade urban gardens, but if it does, it can spread aggressively and be very difficult to eradicate.

Sheep sorrel grows somewhat upright on numerous wiry, mostly unbranched stems that are 6 inches to a foot high—it has been reported to grow as tall as 2 feet under the right conditions (I have never seen it this tall). The leaves are alternate, 1 or 2 inches long, shaped like a spearhead (hastate), with a narrow tip, somewhat bulbed-out center, and two curved and pointed appendages at the base. Petioles are as long, or longer than, the rest of the leaf.

The flowers of sheep sorrel are tiny and greenish, on slender terminal panicles. They resemble miniature curly dock flower heads. Unlike curly dock, however, sheep sorrel has unisexual flowers, with male and female growing in separate clusters. The fruits are tiny triangular achenes, mahogany red in color.

Recognizing this plant when the infestation begins and digging it out completely is key to controlling it. Rototilling it is a bad mistake.

MALLOWS

Malva parviflora—cheeseweed, small mallow—Malvaceae, mallow family

Malva nicaeensis—bull mallow

Cheeseweed, or small mallow, *Malva parviflora,* is a sturdy winter annual or short-lived perennial that grows from a substantial taproot. It will thrive in sun or shade, dry or moist soil, and it is well adapted to compacted areas. In open ground, it grows from 1 to 3 feet tall; mowed repeatedly, it becomes almost prostrate, and so is able to live as a persistent weed in lawns, especially dry, compacted lawns.

Cheeseweed has roundish leaves arranged alternately on the stems; they are somewhat kidney shaped, with indentations on either side of the petioles. They are 1 to 3 inches wide, dark green and rough on both surfaces, and toothed at the margins, with 6 or 7 shallow lobes. The leaves are palmately veined and have a red spot where the blade meets the petiole. Petioles are more than twice as long as the blades.

The flowers of the small mallow are about ½ inch across, pinkish and five-petaled, with the apex of the petals notched—they resemble hollyhock blossoms, but are smaller. They grow in clusters in the leaf axils. Each flower has a calyx at the base that is almost as wide as the flower itself. The fruit is a roundish capsule about ½ inch across, with a small ridge running around the edge, green when young, brown at maturity. To some observers, the fruits resemble Edam cheeses; hence the name *cheeseweed* or *cheeses*.

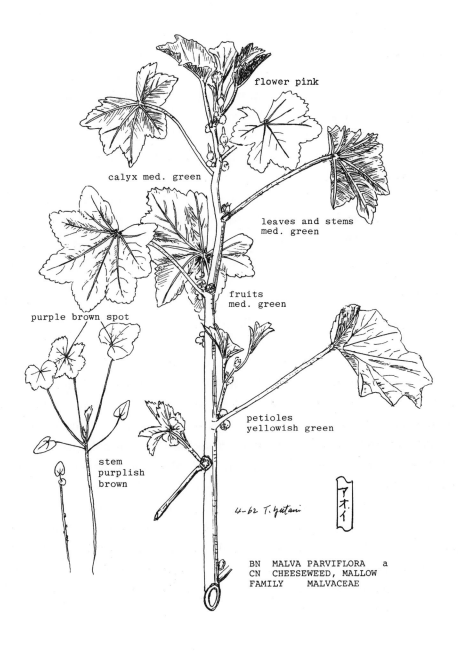

flower pink

calyx med. green

leaves and stems
med. green

fruits
med. green

purple brown spot

petioles
yellowish green

stem
purplish
brown

4-62 T. Yutani

アオイ

BN   MALVA PARVIFLORA   a
CN   CHEESEWEED, MALLOW
FAMILY   MALVACEAE

Cheeseweed is sometimes planted as a cover crop in orchards. In the city, it is invariably regarded as a weed. Poultry farmers dislike it because chickens that eat it lay eggs with pink-tinged whites. Traditionally, cheeseweed leaves have been used as soup or salad greens. A few often turn up in baby salad mixes.

Bull mallow, *Malva nicaeensis,* is almost as common as cheeseweed in the Bay Area, and resembles it closely; when young and not in flower, the two are very difficult to tell apart. All other things being equal, however, the bull mallow is a larger plant, sometimes growing as high as 6 feet. The leaves are quite similar, with the red spot at the base of the blade; but they tend often to be conspicuously creased along the veins (this sometimes occurs with cheeseweed, also). The flowers, however, are larger, about an inch across, with the petals growing noticeably beyond the rim of the calyx, and often striped pink and white, like some hollyhocks. Bull mallow, like cheeseweed, can grow and persist in lawns. The seed capsules are similar to those of cheeseweed, but without a ridge around their margins.

The mallow family contains a number of culinary plants and garden ornamentals. Okra, or gumbo, produces mucilaginous pods that become crisp when fried or dried, but thicken soups and stews when they are boiled; they are a key ingredient in gumbo, a seafood or meat stew. Cotton is in the mallow family, as are the many ornamental hibiscus; an annual hibiscus known as flor de Jamaica is grown for flowers that are used to produce a red, citrusy tea. Hollyhocks and abutilons are also mallow family members, as are tree mallows, some of which are garden-worthy California natives.

Mallows have a long history of medicinal uses, due to a soothing mucilage that is extracted from the roots. All members of the family contain this substance, but the mallow most often cultivated and used for medicinal purpose is *Althaea officinalis,* the marsh mallow. Mrs. Grieve has a good deal to say about this plant. It can be used as a demulcent, a kind of mucus substitute, for soothing bronchial tissues dried out by coughs and colds. Poultices can be made from it for skin inflammations, muscle aches, bruises, and sprains; it can be taken internally for urinary and intestinal tract disorders, as well as for bronchial ailments. The dried roots can be powdered and reconstituted with water to produce a gummy substance, then boiled in wine or milk to make a cough medicine. The flowers can be boiled in water or oil, and the mixture used as a gargle for sore throats. In France, marsh mallow flowers have been incorporated into a cold remedy known as *tisane de quatre fleurs.*

The marshmallows sold in grocery stores, well known to lovers of s'mores, contain no mallow mucilage—they are merely sugar and some other vegetable gum.

NETTLES

Urtica urens—dwarf nettle—Urticaceae, nettle family

Urtica dioicia ssp. *holosericea*—creek nettle

Dwarf nettle, also known as stinging or burning nettle, and, oddly enough, great nettle, is a winter annual native to Europe that has long been naturalized in the southern coast range and along the Southern California coast and is now seen with increasing frequency in the Bay Area. It is usually 1 or 2 feet tall, branching and compact, anchored by a sturdy taproot. It grows mostly in moist locations, and is an especially troublesome weed in irrigated crops. It rarely invades gardens, but needs to be recognized when it does.

The leaves of the dwarf nettle are ovate, opposite on the stem, ½ to 2 inches long, bright medium green, coarsely dentate, and covered with tiny, sharp bristles capable of penetrating the skin of anyone who touches them and injecting formic acid, which causes skin irritation, and sometimes blisters. The plant produces many clusters, about ½ inch across, of tiny, greenish-white flowers in its leaf nodes. These are either male or female, with only one kind generally (but not always) occurring on any given plant. Fruits are achenes, enclosed in the calyx segments that remain after the petals have dropped.

Once identified visually (hopefully), this plant needs to be handled with leather gloves. It can be pulled fairly easily, then taken home, cooked and eaten—the bristles are softened and the formic acid neutralized in the cooking process, the result being a tasty green. Nettles have long been tolerated in cottage gardens in Europe because of their edibility.

Another ancient use for nettles was making thread from the fibers of the mature stems, a practice in northern Europe that preceded the introduction of flax and hemp, essentially southern European plants, in the Middle Ages. A variety of fabrics, coarse and fine, were woven from nettle fibers. This was still the case in Scotland in the sixteenth and seventeenth centuries. Mrs. Grieve quotes a Scots poet named Campbell, who tells us: "In Scotland, I have eaten nettles, I have slept in nettle sheets, and I have dined off a nettle tablecloth. The young and tender nettle is an excellent potherb. The stalks of the old nettle are as good as flax for making cloth. I have heard my mother say that she thought nettle cloth more durable than any other species of linen."

The practice of growing nettle for fiber was revived in Germany and Austria when cotton was in short supply. During the World Wars, nettle fiber was sometimes mixed with ramie, a fiber derived from a tropical member of the nettle family, and used in the manufacture of gas masks.

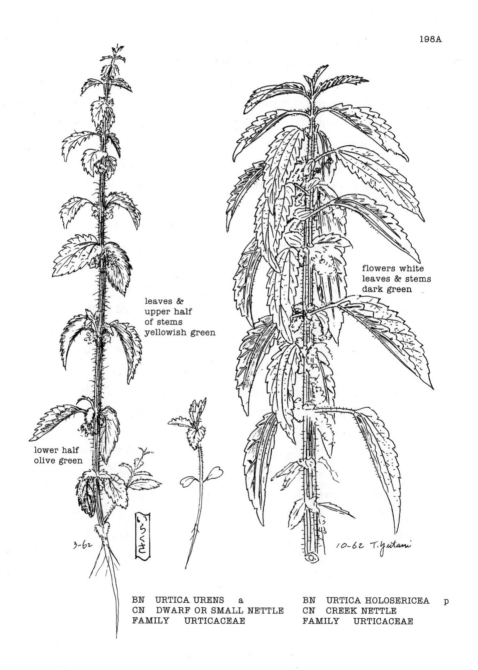

198A

leaves &
upper half
of stems
yellowish green

lower half
olive green

flowers white
leaves & stems
dark green

3-62

10-62 T. Yutani

BN URTICA URENS   a
CN DWARF OR SMALL NETTLE
FAMILY URTICACEAE

BN URTICA HOLOSERICEA   p
CN CREEK NETTLE
FAMILY URTICACEAE

Nettle has also been esteemed as a medicinal herb, valued as an internal and external astringent, and used for treating bronchial ailments, as well as any number of more dubious purposes, including weight loss, hair growth, and kidney problems. Flogging with nettles was once considered a remedy for chronic rheumatism and loss of muscle power. The plant does contain a lot of vitamin C, so was an effective antiscorbutic.

Nettle once was widely grown (or gathered) as fodder for farm animals, including chickens—it was said to significantly increase egg production. Most animals will not eat the fresh plant because of the stinging, but drying it makes it palatable. It was also used for curdling milk in cheesemaking (as a rennet substitute), for manufacturing nettle beer (often in combination with dandelions and ginger), and for making a beautiful and permanent green dye. Mixed with alum, it produces a yellow dye, which was used by Russian peasants for dyeing yarn and coloring Easter eggs.

The creek nettle, *Urtica dioicia* ssp. *holosericea*, is a subspecies native to California of the European great nettle *(Urtica dioicia)*. The creek nettle often occurs along stream banks; on the Point Reyes peninsula, it can be found in great abundance along certain trails. This plant grows from 4 to 10 feet tall and has coarsely toothed leaves 3 to 5 inches long that are bristly above, gray pubescent below. It has the same stinging properties as the dwarf nettle.

A long-standing popular remedy for nettle stings is to rub the afflicted area with crushed curly dock plants. One wonders if plantain, often used as a remedy for poison oak, might not be just as effective.

JERUSALEM PELLITORY

Parietaria judaica—Jerusalem pellitory—Urticaceae, nettle family

When I first encountered this plant growing in deep shade in a garden I was caring for, I asked myself, "Is this a weed, or something that was planted?" It was not bad looking, and it was thriving in an area where most other plants are challenged; it seemed that it might be a good idea to keep it, and see what happened. What happened, of course, was it dropped a huge amount of seed and began traveling around the garden, dominating shaded areas, but doing pretty well in full sun, also. I now keep it on my A-list—the weeds I try to squelch upon their first appearance.

Jerusalem pellitory, also known as pellitory of the wall (Latin *parietaria,* "of the wall," from *paries,* "wall"), is a decumbent to erect plant that grows between

6 and 30 inches tall. The stems are hairy and often red; the leaves, placed alternately on the stems, are 1 to 3 inches long, oval or lanceolate, with a long, tapering tip and smooth margins. They are conspicuously five-nerved (i.e., with five prominent, nearly parallel veins). The petalless flowers are tiny, clustered tightly in the leaf axils, and light green or sometimes whitish due to their papery white anthers. The fruit is a black drupe, about a millimeter across.

The plant has a fibrous root system growing from a very sturdy crown, which is hard to dig out completely when it attains a significant size. The roots prefer shade—the plant will grow in full sun if the root is shaded—so it thrives in cracks and crevices in rocks and walls, along house foundations, in the midst of ruined buildings. It is a very abundant plant in Italy, a country with lots of stone buildings and pavement, and plenty of ruins.

Medicinally, pellitory is a diuretic, laxative, refrigerant, and slight demulcent. It can be used for bladder stones, gravel, and dropsy; as cough medicine; as a gargle for sore gums and teeth; and as a remedy for earaches, piles, skin disorders, gout, and fistula. Old herbals sometimes refer to it as *lichwort*.

In his book *The Greek Plant World in Myth, Art, and Literature*, Hellmut Baumann tells us a story about pellitory taken from Pliny the Elder. According to Pliny, "When the Acropolis of Athens was being built, a slave fell from the top of the Parthenon. Athena made it known to Pericles in a dream that the pellitory, a plant growing in abundance on the Acropolis, would effectively heal his wounds." Baumann also cites Dioscorides, who "called the plant helixine, and cited its cooling and astringent properties for all manners of inflammations."

NIGHTSHADES

Solanum americanum—American black nightshade, white nightshade—Solanaceae, nightshade family

Solanum nigrum—European black nightshade

Robbins's *Weeds of California* lists more than a dozen weedy solanums that grow in California, a number of which are native. I'll discuss the two most likely to be found as weeds in the Bay Area, and probably in most other West Coast urban environments.

American black nightshade, *Solanum americanum,* is a branching annual or herbaceous perennial that grows from 1½ to 3 feet tall. Its stems are somewhat woody, often tinged purple. Leaves are alternate, firm in texture, smooth, more or less triangular in outline, with somewhat wavy, sparsely toothed margins.

The flowers are white, with five-united petals; five yellow stamens project from the center, closely surrounding a beak-like pistil. The petals are surrounded at the base by a calyx of five separate sepals, which reflex at maturity. These flowers grow in short clusters, then produce shiny black berries. The roots are fibrous.

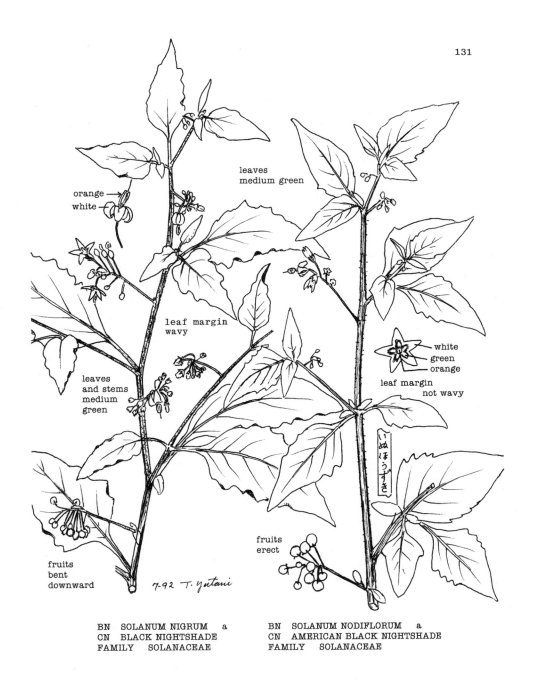

131

leaves
medium green

orange →
white →

leaf margin
wavy

leaves
and stems
medium
green

white
green
orange

leaf margin
not wavy

fruits
erect

fruits
bent
downward

7-92 T. Yatani

BN   SOLANUM NIGRUM   a
CN   BLACK NIGHTSHADE
FAMILY   SOLANACEAE

BN   SOLANUM NODIFLORUM   a
CN   AMERICAN BLACK NIGHTSHADE
FAMILY   SOLANACEAE

This species, native to California and elsewhere in North America, occurs mostly near the coast, and tends to grow in moist, shady places, although it by no means confines itself entirely to these situations. Uncontrolled, it can be a troublesome weed in gardens.

American black nightshade is often confused with European black nightshade, *S. nigrum,* which can be distinguished from the North American weed by thinner, less firm leaves, smaller, umbel-like flower clusters, berries that are dull rather than shiny, and a calyx of united sepals that do not reflex at maturity. It is thought to confine itself entirely to gardens.

S. americanum can also be confused with *S. Douglasii,* a native nightshade that has been implicated in livestock poisonings. The latter can be distinguished by the minute hairs that cover its leaves, as well as by larger flowers and berries. It is not listed by Ertter and Naumovich as growing in the Bay Area.

All members of the nightshade family have some poisonous part, but many have edible portions. Nightshades commonly encountered in grocery stores include tomatoes, peppers, eggplant (fruit is edible, foliage poisonous), and potatoes, with poisonous foliage and edible tubers. I have personally observed people of Mien ethnicity (Laotian) gathering the leaves of *S. americanum* to eat; they know to avoid the berries. The poisonous properties of the nightshades make many of them very useful as narcotics, the most famous of which is *Atropa belladonna,* commonly called belladonna, or deadly nightshade. This is still grown commercially and can be used as a narcotic in very small doses, as can a number of other nightshades. It was also employed by women in earlier times to dilate their pupils, thus enhancing their seductiveness (the term *bella donna* is Italian for "beautiful lady").

European black nightshade, *Solanum nigrum,* confined to gardens here, is a fairly common weed throughout Europe. There is some dispute as to how toxic the berries really are; they have been known to cause death when ingested green, but seem to have no ill effect on adults when ripe. I would recommend being extremely cautious about eating any part of any wild nightshade.

European black nightshade is an annual that used to be grown in gardens more widely than it is now; it is still sold in nursery catalogs, labeled as wonder berry or garden huckleberry. It bears small black fruits that are edible when fully ripe and cooked; however, ingesting unripe berries or leaves can cause violent illness or death.

Medicinally, black nightshade has been used to induce sleep. In Bohemia, placing the leaves in the cradles of infants for this purpose was once a widespread tradition. Bruised leaves have also been applied to external wounds and sores as an analgesic; the juice has been used to treat earache, gout, and ringworms, and mixed with vinegar as a gargle for sore throats or mouth ulcers. Again, I would not recommend experimenting with nightshades—the line between effective medicine and deadly poison can be very fine.

Another useful species of solanum is *S. indigoferum,* a tropical species cultivated for indigo, the ubiquitous dark blue dye used to color denim and various other cloths.

PETTY SPURGE

Euphorbia peplus—petty spurge—Euphorbiaceae, spurge family

Petty spurge, *Euphorbia peplus,* is a pretty little winter annual, native to Europe, that often appears in abundance in the shadier areas of gardens during the winter and spring, standing out due to its chartreuse-green color. It can grow in full sun and tolerate some drying, but is most prolific in moist soil in the shade. Petty spurge often forms dense colonies under greenhouse benches.

This plant is upright and somewhat branching, capable of reaching 8 inches in height under some conditions, but usually growing to 6 inches or less. The leaves are opposite, with petioles, rounded or oval and wider at the end than the base (obovate), about ¼ to ½ inch long. They diminish in size as they approach the tip of the stem. The flowers are in small terminal clusters enclosed by a ring of pointed bracts; each cluster consists of several staminate and one pistillate flower. These are tiny and yellow to chartreuse in color. Three-celled capsules, bearing one seed per cell, develop as the flowers fade.

Like other euphorbias, *E. peplus* has dense, milky sap in its stems that can irritate the skin, so care, and perhaps gloves, are advised when weeding—a fairly easy job, as the roots are fibrous and the stems sturdy and easy to grasp. The sap has constituents that are emetic and purgative, and has sometimes been used medicinally in the Mediterranean region; however, it is *Euphorbia resinifera,* official spurge, that is most commonly employed as medicine. This is a succulent plant resembling a cactus that grows on the slopes of the Atlas Mountains in Morocco, and whose sap has been collected, dried into cakes, and sold throughout Europe and the Near East since ancient times; Pliny and Dioscorides discuss the medicinal uses of this resin. Despite its efficacy, euphorbia can be toxic and is seldom used in medicine today, except in very minute doses by homeopaths.

Another euphorbia with medicinal uses is the pantropical *E. pilulifera,* Queensland asthma weed, a bronchial dilator that is also fairly toxic, known to kill small animals in fairly large doses. Yet another, *E. ipecacuanha,* a South American tropical vine, is the source of ipecac, used to induce vomiting after other poisons are ingested, and is still sold in drug stores without a prescription. Be cautious, however, if you choose to use ipecac—instructions for dealing with poisoning often say *not* to induce vomiting, as damage to the esophagus from highly caustic or acidic materials may occur.

Some spurge family members produce high-quality oils with a number of uses. The fruits of the candlenut tree, *Aleurites moluccana,* which is very common in Hawaii (it was brought there from the South Pacific by Polynesian settlers), can be burned whole for illumination. The seeds of *Aleurites cordata,* another South Pacific tree, produce tung oil, widely used in varnishes and for polishing furniture. *Euphorbia lathyrus,* caper spurge, is still often planted as a gopher repellent, with uncertain effect; its ability to become a weed is far more certain.

See illustration of spotted spurge on p. 57.

PIGWEEDS

Amaranthus deflexus—pigweed, low amaranth—Amaranthaceae, pigweed family

Amaranthus blitoides—prostrate pigweed

Pigweed is a name that has been applied to a number of weeds that are eaten by hogs; however, the movement to semistandardize common names proposes to restrict this designation to several species of *Amaranthus,* a convention I shall observe here.

Amaranthaceae is a family that is widespread throughout tropical, subtropical, and temperate regions north and south of the equator. Most members are herbs or shrubs, rarely climbers. They are characterized by smooth-margined (entire) leaves without stipules, opposite or alternate on the stems, and small flowers surrounded by bracts, sometimes solitary, more often in spikes growing in the leaf axils or at the ends of stems. Members of this family, especially those in the genus *Amaranthus,* have long been grown by people for food and ornament, mostly in Central and South America, but also in Asia and Africa. Some of these, the so-called grain amaranths, produce highly nutritious seeds that are ground into meal or cooked whole; others are grown for their leaves, which are spinachlike and can be eaten cooked or raw. The best-known ornamental amaranth is *Amaranthus caudatus,* love-lies-bleeding, which grows to about 2 feet tall and produces dense crimson flower spikes. In ancient Greece, this flower, or something very similar, was sacred to Artemis of Ephesus, and symbolized immortality (the word *amaranthos* means "unwithering," a reference to the long-lasting flowers).

Low amaranth, *Amaranthus deflexus,* usually called simply pigweed, is a low-growing, sprawling, somewhat ascending plant with a long central taproot. It sometimes spreads to 3 feet wide, but more typically about a foot to 18 inches. The leaves are alternate, entire, more or less oval, with petioles sometimes as long as the leaf blade. Flowers are small and greenish, usually growing in dense terminal cymes about an inch long or more, but sometimes in short heads in the leaf axils. The fruit is a fleshy, three- to five-lobed structure known as an *urticle.* Unlike the fruits of most other amaranths, it does not dehisce.

Prostrate pigweed, *Amaranthus blitoides,* is probably the second-most common urban pigweed. It resembles *Amaranthus deflexus* in most respects, but differs by producing flowers only in small axillary spikes, and by its fruit, a dehiscent urticle. It grows under the same conditions as low amaranth and is also esteemed by pigs.

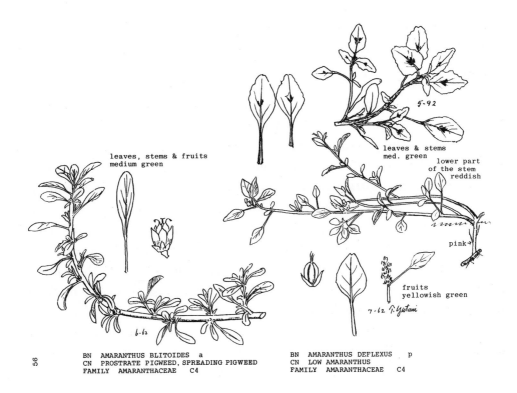

leaves, stems & fruits
medium green

leaves & stems
med. green

lower part
of the stem
reddish

5-92

pink→

fruits
yellowish green

7-62 *T. Yutani*

6-62

56

BN   AMARANTHUS BLITOIDES   a
CN   PROSTRATE PIGWEED, SPREADING PIGWEED
FAMILY   AMARANTHACEAE   C4

BN   AMARANTHUS DEFLEXUS   p
CN   LOW AMARANTHUS
FAMILY   AMARANTHACEAE   C4

Pigweeds thrive in poor, dry ground, like heat, and are very much at home in sidewalk cracks. They are summer annuals, germinating in late spring, thriving throughout the warmer months, often overwintering in mild climates. They are native to Europe, among the "classic" weeds that coevolved with grain agriculture.

I have been able to find no evidence of medicinal uses for the amaranths; their health-promoting properties are related to their food value, which is mostly based on high levels of high-quality proteins in the grain amaranths. Recently, however, the presence an antioxidant known as *squalene* has promoted interest in these plants as possible anticarcinogens—research into this is now being conducted. Squalene is also present in shark oil, and the Japanese Pharmacopoeia has long recognized shark oil–derived squalene as a health-promoting substance and more or less of a cure-all. Whether or not amaranth proves to be therapeutic for cancer, its growing popularity as a source of nutritious grains and greens is well deserved.

PLANTAINS

Plantago lanceolata—buckhorn plantain, ribgrass—Plantaginaceae, plantain family

Plantago major—common or broad-leaved plantain

Plantago coronopus—saltmarsh plantain

We have already encountered the buckhorn plantain, *Plantago lanceolata* (a.k.a. ribgrass), as an indicator species used to trace the spread of grain agriculture in Europe during Neolithic times. Other common names given to this plant are English plantain, snake plantain, black plantain, ribwort, ribble grass, black jack, jack straw, lamb's tongue, hen plant, wendles, kemps, cocks, quinquenervia, and costa canina. It is a herbaceous perennial, growing upright to about a foot high (2½ feet is possible, but occurs rarely). The leaves are about 3 to 12 inches long, an inch wide, lanceolate, entire, and dark green, with five to seven prominent ribs that appear to be parallel (hence the name *quinquenervia,* Latin for "five nerves"), making it possible to mistake this plant for a monocot—it is not. The plant is stemless, with the leaves emerging from a sturdy crown growing atop short, thick, fibrous roots.

The flowers of ribgrass are greenish-brown, crowded into a narrow, somewhat conical spike about 1 to 3 inches long, at the top of an 8- to 32-inch stem. A large, somewhat isolated plant, with its cluster of upright leaves accented

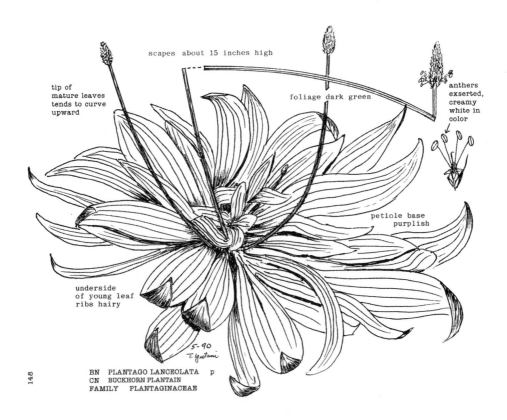

scapes about 15 inches high

tip of
mature leaves
tends to curve
upward

foliage dark green

anthers
exserted,
creamy
white in
color

petiole base
purplish

underside
of young leaf
ribs hairy

5-90
T. Yutani

BN   PLANTAGO LANCEOLATA   p
CN   BUCKHORN PLANTAIN
FAMILY   PLANTAGINACEAE

148

by tall, narrow flower spikes, it can be seen as an elegant form in an open landscape, an exclamation point of a sort. It is tempting to use it as a container plant; however, it would no doubt spread from the container into areas where it would be less welcome. Buckhorn plantain can be found in any number of habitats, sunny or shady. It will grow in rich or poor soil. It is frequently found in lawns, as it adapts well to mowing because of its basal growing point. This plantain tends to grow in drier areas of the lawn, with the moist parts often dominated by its cousin, the common plantain. Ribgrass spreads entirely by seed, of which it produces a great abundance.

Buckhorn plantain has the same medicinal properties as the common plantain; I'll discuss these later. The sticky mucilage exuded by seeds soaked in water has been used for a variety of purposes, including stiffening muslin, and as a hair lotion. It was cultivated in England as a forage crop for sheep cattle and horses, but once farmers realized that it crowded out other desirable vegetation, and that sheep didn't seem to like its bitter flavor, this practice tended to die out.

The common plantain, *Plantago major,* also known as the broad-leaved plantain or dooryard plantain, somewhat resembles ribgrass due to its basal growth habit, prominently nerved leaves, and narrow flower spike, but differs in several easily recognized ways. The leaves, instead of being long, narrow, and upright, are broadly ovate and tend to form a flattish rosette, which makes it supremely well adapted to lawns, especially heavily watered lawns. In open ground, common plantains can be as tall as a foot, with the leaves somewhat ascending; in often-mowed lawns, they lie very flat. The broad, thick roots send many fibrous branches deep into the soil, so the plant will persist in areas that experience seasonal drying.

The inflorescence of the common plantain is, like that of the buckhorn plantain, a narrow spike of brownish flowers on a stalk, but the stalk is shorter than that of its cousin (a foot, at most), and about half its length is covered by the flowers. After blooming, they produce tiny capsules that split across the middle, the top falling away like a lid.

Besides lawns, the common plantain can be found in fields and meadows, on roadsides, and on the banks of ditches and streams. The first step for controlling it and checking its spread is to create drier conditions: improve drainage and water less frequently, decreasing the total amount of water applied, if possible, and allowing the soil to dry between irrigations. These actions need to be followed by dealing with the plants themselves: digging them out, using herbicides, or both.

The genus name *Plantago* was taken from the ancient Roman common name for this plant, a word referring to the *planta,* the sole of the foot—the Romans perceived the long, prominent leaf veins as tarsals and metatarsals. The Native Americans who encountered English settlers during the seventeenth and eighteenth centuries referred to the plant as white man's foot or Englishman's foot, a reference either to the appearance of the leaves or to the tendency of the plant to seemingly germinate wherever white people walked.

The number of common names for the plantains and the variety of allusions they engender point to a very long familiarity with them in Europe, and to their status in the culture of the region, mostly as medicinal herbs. They are mucilaginous and astringent; they have been used to sooth inflamed skin, treat malignant ulcers, stop bleeding, and draw poisons from wounds. Plantain, especially the common plantain, is still highly regarded for treating poison oak and ivy, and for nettle stings. In Scotland, it was called *slanlus,* Gaelic for "plant of healing." The Anglo-Saxons called it *weybroed,* "way bread," and regarded it as one of their nine sacred herbs. Pliny cites plantain as a cure for rabies; Erasmus mentions it as a remedy for spider bites—he

151A

leaves and petiole
light green

BN   PLANTAGO MAJOR   p
CN   COMMON PLANTAIN
FAMILY   PLANTAGINACEAE

tells the story in his *Colloquia* of a toad who cured himself by eating a plantain leaf after being bitten. In the United States, plantain was regarded as a cure for snakebite.

According to Mrs. Grieve, decoctions of plantain entered into almost every old remedy. It was often boiled with docks, comfrey, and a variety of flowers. Decoctions of plantain were used for kidney disorders and for diarrhea and piles. It was also taken as a diuretic; it was used for expelling worms, as a cough medicine, as a cure for epilepsy, jaundice, convulsions, dropsy, and gout, as well as for reducing fever. Chaucer refers to the medicinal properties of the plant at least once, Shakespeare several times.

Another exotic, found mostly in areas immediately adjacent to salt water, but also in salty soil away from the sea, is the saltmarsh plantain, *Plantago coronopus*. This is an annual that grows as a rosette of long, narrow leaves with many deeply incised, narrow lobes—these might remind one of the horns of a deer. In England, saltmarsh plantain is referred to as the buck's horn, whereas the English call our buckhorn plantain ribgrass or ribwort. This plant is also known in England as cornu cervinum (Latin for "buck's horn"), buckshorne, hartshorne, herba stella (because of its starlike rosette), or herb ivy. In Europe, it has about the same medicinal uses as the other plantains. In Italy, it was sometimes grown in gardens as a salad herb, a use cited also for buckhorn and common plantain in England.

Although it seemingly does not occur in California, another European plantain, *Plantago psyllium,* psyllium or fleaseed, is a source of a product often sold in health food stores here—the dried husks commonly called psyllium. Soaked in water, these quickly produce a mucilaginous drink that provides fiber and acts more or less as a stool softener. This plant was often used in southern Europe and North Africa for the same medicinal purposes as *P. major* was in more northerly regions.

There are several plantains native to California. They occur in wild lands and do not invade the horticultural realm, although some might possibly be grown there by adventurous gardeners.

SHARP-POINTED TOADFLAX

Kickxia elatine—sharp-pointed toadflax, Fluellin—Plantaginaceae, plantain family

The name Fluellin, a rather common Welsh name that is more often spelled Llewellyn, indicates the European origin of sharp-pointed toadflax and of a closely related plant, *Veronica chamaedrys,* commonly called germander speedwell, or Fluellin the male. Readers of Shakespeare might recognize the name as belonging to a character in *Henry V* named Captain Fluellin, who, just before the battle of Agincourt, discourses with other soldiers on why he has another plant—not Fluellin—stuck in the band of his hat.

Sharp-pointed toadflax is hardly confined to Wales—it is widespread throughout most of Europe and Asia and has introduced itself on other continents where Europeans have settled.

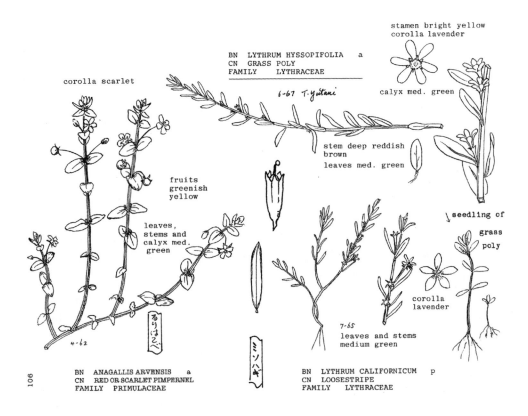

stamen bright yellow
corolla lavender

BN   LYTHRUM HYSSOPIFOLIA   a
CN   GRASS POLY
FAMILY   LYTHRACEAE

corolla scarlet

6-67 T. yutani

calyx med. green

stem deep reddish
brown
leaves med. green

fruits
greenish
yellow

leaves,
stems and
calyx med.
green

seedling of

grass

poly

corolla
lavender

7-65
leaves and stems
medium green

4-62

106

BN   ANAGALLIS ARVENSIS   a
CN   RED OR SCARLET PIMPERNEL
FAMILY   PRIMULACEAE

BN   LYTHRUM CALIFORNICUM   p
CN   LOOSESTRIPE
FAMILY   LYTHRACEAE

Fluellin is a very adaptable plant that can grow in sun or shade, rich or poor soils, but prefers sunny, dryish areas with lean soils. It is an annual that spreads by seed, a mass of sprawling stems to 18 inches long that grow from a long, slender taproot. The leaves are ½ to 1 inch long, oval or triangular with a sharp tip, sometimes with pointed lobes at the base (hastate—like a spear point), gray-green and hairy, with smooth margins. They grow alternately along the stems.

Flowers are short and chunky, about ½ inch long and wide, tubular with two prominent lips, spurred, yellowish on top, purplish below. The fruit is a roundish capsule containing many rough-surfaced seeds.

There seem to be few medicinal uses for this plant other than as a vulnerary, used to stanch bleeding wounds and help them heal. An alternate name, sharpleaf cancerwort, seems to indicate some uses in folk medicine for treating tumors.

Fluellin is rare in the more urbanized parts of the Bay Area, but has been making some inroads. In recent years, I have encountered it at Merritt College atop the East Bay hills and at Mountain View Cemetery in Oakland.

PURSLANE

Portulaca oleracea—purslane—Portulacaceae, purslane family

Purslane, also known as pursley, pursley duckweed, or, to Spanish speakers, *verdolaga,* is a summer annual weed that seldom sprouts before June in the Bay Area but can be seen thriving well into autumn. It tends to be a weed mostly of well-cultivated, moist soil in full sun, so can be a problem in crops and in vegetable gardens and annual beds. It is native to Europe but thought by some botanists to have originated in India.

Purslane is a prostrate, mat-forming, semisucculent plant whose fleshy stems are often a reddish color; it can grow to a foot or more. It is anchored by a short taproot, which soon branches. Leaves grow alternately on the stems, sometimes in clusters; they are thick, entire, wedge shaped with blunt tips (cuneate), shiny green, but sometimes tinged with red. The flowers are sessile, growing in the leaf nodes, about ⅛ to ¼ inch across, five-petaled and bright yellow, rather attractive. The fruit is a capsule with a "lid"—the top half breaks off, allowing numerous seeds to fall out.

Although Americans tend to regard purslane mostly as a weed, it has long been esteemed—and cultivated—in Europe as a salad green and potherb. The thick stems of plants gone to seed were often pickled in salt and vinegar for use as winter salads. Both Gerard and John Evelyn, a seventeenth-century writer and garden designer, recommended purslane salads and regarded them

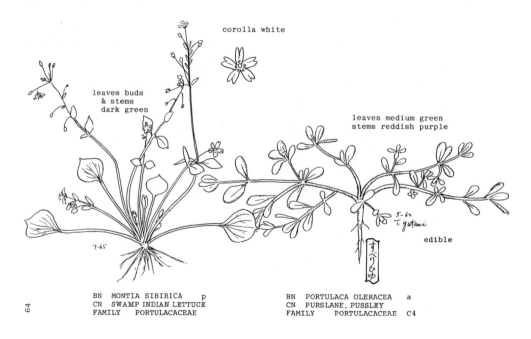

corolla white

leaves buds
& stems
dark green

leaves medium green
stems reddish purple

7-65

5-62
T. yutani

edible

BN MONTIA SIBIRICA   p
CN SWAMP INDIAN LETTUCE
FAMILY   PORTULACACEAE

BN PORTULACA OLERACEA   a
CN PURSLANE, PUSSLEY
FAMILY   PORTULACACEAE C4

64

as "cooling" and as stimulating to the appetite. A golden-leaved variety was especially esteemed for culinary use; Mrs. Grieve lists it as *Portulaca sativa*, but finding no other references to this species, my guess is that it is simply a yellow-leaved form of *P. oleracea*.

In France, purslane is mixed with sorrel to make a soup known as *bonne femme*. On the West Coast, it often appears in Hispanic grocery stores as *verdolaga*.

Purslane has a number of traditional medicinal uses. The juice is used for strangury, a painful urinary disorder. Taken with honey, it relieves dry coughs, shortness of breath, and immoderate thirst. Poultices of the plant can be applied externally for inflammation and sores and to stop bleeding. Mrs. Grieve cites an unidentified herbalist as saying that purslane could be used to "cool heat in the liver" and was excellent for "hot agues" and all headaches "proceeding from the heat, want of sleep, or the frenzy." Other practices recommended by the old herbalists are applying the bruised herb to the forehead to alleviate fever and to the eyes to relieve inflammation. Purslane was also used to treat mouth sores and swollen gums and to tighten loose teeth. The seeds, bruised and boiled in wine, were given to children to expel worms.

Here are some close relatives of purslane and some of their uses: miner's lettuce, *Claytonia perfoliata*, native to western North America, is used as a salad green; *Lewisia rediviva*, bitterroot, is a plant of rocky outcrops in the western mountains, whose root Native Americans used for food on long journeys; and *Portulaca grandiflora*, the moss rose, is a South American native with bright, attractive flowers in many colors, cultivars of which are used as summer annuals in gardens. Another lewisia, *L. cotyledon*, a rosette-forming succulent native to high mountains in Northern California and southern Oregon, has been selected and hybridized to be grown in gardens for its attractive flowers; much of this work has been done in England, and English cultivars are often sold in nurseries in the United States.

SCARLET PIMPERNEL

Anagallis arvensis—scarlet pimpernel—Primulaceae, primrose family

They seek him here, they seek him there,
Those Frenchies seek him everywhere.
Is he in heaven, or is he in hell?
That damned elusive Pimpernel!

These words are spoken in the movie version of *The Scarlet Pimpernel,* a film based on a French novel about a dashing English nobleman who, known only as the Scarlet Pimpernel, a code name that refers to the eponymous common weed, saves condemned French aristocrats from the guillotine. Our hero reveals himself at critical times by showing his ring, on which is depicted the small (¼ inch), orange-red, five-petaled flower that graces this pretty little weed, making it a prime candidate for consideration as a welcome volunteer in some gardens, rather than simply a weed. Other attractive features of the plant are its smooth, shiny, semisucculent leaves, which are broadly ovate with entire margins and set opposite one another on long, sprawling, squarish-looking (actually five-sided) stems growing from a crown attached to a cluster of fibrous roots.

Scarlet pimpernel is a winter annual that blooms from mid through late spring, sometimes persisting into summer. The flowers are followed by globular fruits about ⅛ inch in diameter, which open by the detachment of a "lid" consisting of the upper third of the fruit, thus allowing the seed to spill out. Fruit and seed are very abundant, and wise gardeners will not allow their love for the flowers to prevent them from pulling these weeds aggressively once the fruits begin to show.

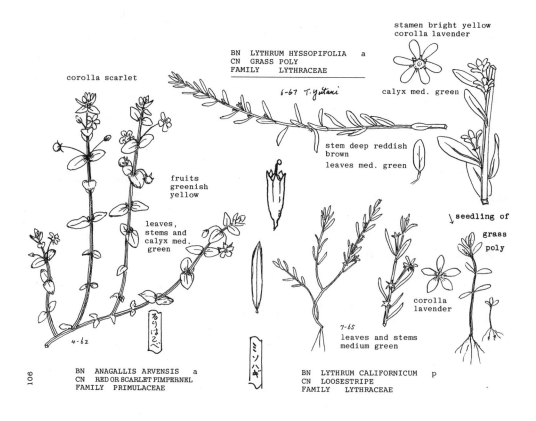

corolla scarlet

BN   LYTHRUM HYSSOPIFOLIA   a
CN   GRASS POLY
FAMILY   LYTHRACEAE

6-67 T. Yutani

stamen bright yellow
corolla lavender

calyx med. green

stem deep reddish
brown
leaves med. green

fruits
greenish
yellow

leaves,
stems and
calyx med.
green

seedling of

grass
poly

corolla
lavender

7-65
leaves and stems
medium green

4-62

106

BN   ANAGALLIS ARVENSIS   a
CN   RED OR SCARLET PIMPERNEL
FAMILY   PRIMULACEAE

BN   LYTHRUM CALIFORNICUM   p
CN   LOOSESTRIPE
FAMILY   LYTHRACEAE

Scarlet pimpernel has been referred to by a number of other common names. The flowers characteristically close on cloudy days and near sunset, hence the names shepherd's barometer, shepherd's clock, and poor man's weather glass. It has also been known as adder's eyes (the flowers have a bluish spot in the middle); red chickweed; eyebright, indicating either a medicinal use or the resemblance of the flower to eyes; and bipinella, perhaps referring to the opposite placement of the leaves.

Red chickweed is native to Europe and the Near East, where it has been used for a number of curative purposes: for liver disorders and rabies and as a diuretic, diaphoretic, and expectorant. According to seventeenth-century herbalist Gerard, Shakespeare's contemporary, it "prevents witchcraft, as Mother Bumby doth affirm."

The reference to Mother Bumby is intriguing, and crops up a number of times in Gerard's *Herball,* casual references that seem to assume that his readers would know who she was. He and other educated pharmacists apparently depended a good deal on advice from country herbwives, who were most likely illiterate but were the recipients of empirical knowledge about potent plants.

Scarlet pimpernel was sometimes eaten as a salad green in France and Germany, but has also been reported as poisonous to livestock, as well as to people who consume too much of the decoction when using the plant medicinally, so it should be approached with caution.

A close relative, *Anagallis linifolia,* blue pimpernel, is a perennial with a blue flower that has traditionally been grown in English cottage gardens. Seed is still available from some catalogs.

THE SPEEDWELLS

Veronica persica—bird's eye speedwell—Plantaginaceae, plantain family

Veronica arvensis—corn speedwell

Veronica serphyllifolia—thyme-leaf speedwell

The three species named above are all low-growing, spreading herbs that are common in lawns and adjacent bare ground. Two are annual, one perennial; although these three resemble each other, there are key features that make them fairly easy to distinguish.

Bird's eye speedwell, *Veronica persica,* is a low-growing annual with trailing stems about 3 to 6 inches long. Opposite pairs of roundish leaves about ¼ to ½ inch wide, with toothed edges and fine hairs, grow along these stems, which are also somewhat pubescent. The whole plant forms a sort of loose tuft, usually no taller than 6 inches. The flowers, which grow in loose racemes originating in the leaf axils, are four-petaled, about ¼ inch across, deep blue with a white eye. Small as it is, this flower is a good deal larger than those of the other two weedy species of speedwell. The fruit is a small capsule.

Bird's eye speedwell will thrive in sun or shade as long as it gets adequate moisture. It is most often found in lawns or on their margins, filling in bare spots, arguably providing a pleasing variation in color and texture to an otherwise uniform sward of turf grass. A lawn with a sprinkling (I emphasize *sprinkling*) of bird's eye speedwell, English daisy, and dandelions (not to mention white clover) can be quite beautiful, resembling the flowery meads that were considered ideal lawns in the Middle Ages. The small stature and fibrous roots of bird's eye speedwell make it fairly easy to control where it is not wanted.

Corn speedwell, *V. arvensis*, also a fibrous-rooted winter annual, has more or less the same growth habit as bird's eye speedwell: it is spreading but erect, usually growing 3 to 6 inches tall, although it can reach a foot in good soil. It, too, inhabits lawns, but also grows in nurseries and garden beds, crop fields and pastures, in meadows and on roadsides, and in any number of other disturbed habitats. It likes moisture but can withstand some drought.

Corn speedwell has leaves similar to those of its bird's eye cousin, but smaller—generally no more than ¼ inch across. Flowers are tiny, ⅛ inch or less, blue-violet, growing singly and sessile in the leaf nodes. Its tiny flowers

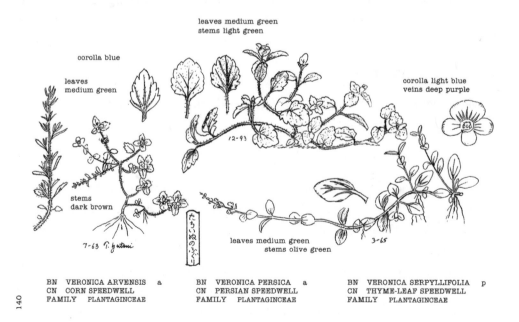

leaves medium green
stems light green

corolla blue

leaves
medium green

corolla light blue
veins deep purple

stems
dark brown

12-93

7-63 P. yutani

leaves medium green
stems olive green

3-65

BN VERONICA ARVENSIS a
CN CORN SPEEDWELL
FAMILY PLANTAGINCEAE

BN VERONICA PERSICA a
CN PERSIAN SPEEDWELL
FAMILY PLANTAGINCEAE

BN VERONICA SERPYLLIFOLIA p
CN THYME-LEAF SPEEDWELL
FAMILY PLANTAGINCEAE

140

do not make it as attractive as bird's eye speedwell in lawns, but it can still be tolerated to some extent in healthy and vigorous turf.

Perhaps the peskiest of the speedwells is *V. serphyllifolia,* thyme-leaf speedwell, a prostrate, mat-forming perennial that roots at the nodes and is quite capable of becoming predominant in compacted or otherwise unhealthy lawns. As the grass thins, it can fill every available bare spot. This weed can be readily distinguished from its less aggressive cousins by its rooting habit, its smooth, oval leaves that are only sparsely toothed, or sometimes entire, and by its flowers, about the size of the corn speedwell blooms, but very pale blue with darker veins, and growing in short racemes that arise from the mat. Keeping lawns uncompacted, well aerated, and growing vigorously is the key to preventing invasions of this weed and minimizing its impact if it does appear.

The speedwells are native to Europe, and, as their name implies, have a long history of medicinal uses. The principal plant used medicinally is *V. officinalis,* common speedwell, which is native in much of Europe, but also widely naturalized in the eastern United States. It has astringent and bitter qualities, making it useful for stopping bleeding and treating wounds, as well as for skin diseases, coughs, and other bronchial ailments. It is also considered diaphoretic, tonic, alterative, and expectorant. Another speedwell used for similar purposes in England is *V. chamaedrys,* germander speedwell, also known as Fluellin the male, Paul's betony, eye of Christ, angel eyes, and cat's eyes, references to the white spot in the middle of the flowers. The name Fluellin is simply a corruption of the Welsh name Llewellyn, an indication of the widespread use of this plant in Wales; it is also a name applied to a number of other plants growing in Britain, including *V. officinalis.* Two other common names for this plant, farewell and goodbye, refer to the tendency of the flowers to lose their petals when touched only lightly; Mrs. Grieve speculates that this tendency may also be the origin of the name *speedwell;* I think it is more likely that it refers to the healing properties of these plants.

MULLEIN

Verbascum thapsus—mullein, common mullein—Scrophulariaceae, figwort family

In California, mullein is a weed mostly found in dry, gravelly ground in rural areas. It grows in places such as dry streambeds, abandoned pastures and corrals, and semi-arid grasslands. In urban areas, it is sometimes grown in gardens, from which it can escape and colonize bare ground elsewhere. It has a long history of use for healing and other purposes in Europe, and has acquired many common names that refer to these uses, as well as to the physical characteristics of the plant. In England, it is known as great mullein, white mullein, torches, our lady's flannel, velvet dock, candlewick plant, rag paper, bullocks' lungwort, Aaron's rod, shepherd's club, clot, cuddy's lungs, feltwort, and hag's taper (see Mrs. Grieve for even more names). The name *mullein* came into English from Anglo-Saxon *moleyn* or Old French *malen* (or both); these two names seem to have come from the Latin *malandrium*, "leprosy," a word that was later understood to indicate diseases in general; so *mullein* refers to the medicinal value of the plant.

Mullein is native throughout Eurasia and North Africa and has become widespread in North America. Its most recognizable characteristic is its leaves, 10 to 20 inches long, alternate, oval with somewhat wavy margins, and covered top and bottom with dense, soft, silvery hairs that form a woolly mat. The plant is a true biennial in cold-winter climates that support such a habit of growth: the leaves form a rosette the first year, send up a flower stalk the second, forming an unbranching, upright plant that can be as tall as 7 feet. The stems of mullein sprout progressively smaller leaves as they reach their ultimate height; they end in flower spikes about a foot long. These tend to branch into three segments at their peaks. The spikes are densely covered with flowers of an attractive sulfur-yellow color, which open a few at a time, and in random order. These are about ½ to ¾ inch long, with five petals forming two lobes. The fruit is a globular capsule about ¼ inch across, filled with many seeds.

The soft, silvery leaves of mullein and its sulfur-yellow flowers make it very attractive to landscape gardeners, and its medicinal properties established it as an essential cottage garden plant even before cottage gardening became merely a style. It is not grown as much as it used to be, since there are closely related verbascums that have just as beautiful flowers and bloom less randomly; but *V. thapsus* seed is still sold, gardeners still grow it, and it sometimes appears unbidden. If it seems to serve a visual or other purpose, there is no reason not to leave it—it is fairly easy to remove excess seedlings. I find the rosettes that volunteer in cracks in stone walls especially attractive.

The hairs of mullein, which cover the stems as well as the leaves, have long been used as tinder, and before cotton became abundant, mullein was made into candlewicks (hence the common name candlewick plant). The whole stalk was sometimes dipped in tallow and used as a crude candle or torch, a habit often attributed to witches (hence, hag's taper or hedge taper, the Anglo-Saxon word *hage* meaning both "witch" and "hedge"). Throughout Europe and Asia,

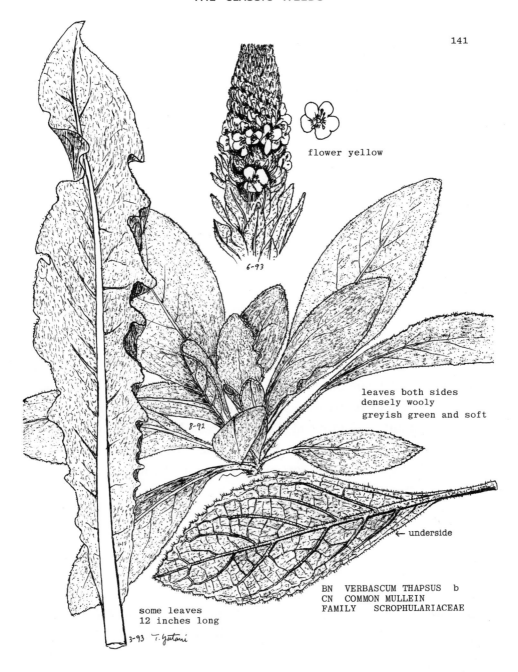

flower yellow

leaves both sides
densely wooly
greyish green and soft

← underside

BN   VERBASCUM THAPSUS   b
CN   COMMON MULLEIN
FAMILY   SCROPHULARIACEAE

some leaves
12 inches long

3-93 T. Yatani

mullein was thought to be capable of driving away witches and evil spirits.
Homer tells us that Odysseus took some mullein with him on his visit to Circe,
to protect himself from her spell; his companions, unfortunately, apparently
neglected to do this.

Medicinally, mullein is demulcent, emollient, and astringent, thus useful for
coughs and other bronchial ailments, including bleeding lungs. A decoction of
the leaves is mucilaginous and can be taken as a cough medicine and to soothe

irritated throat and lung membranes. The dried leaves are sometimes smoked for these purposes. Fresh leaves can be used as poultices to stop bleeding and soothe rashes and sores. Mullein taken internally is effective against diarrhea due to its astringent properties; its emollient nature also enables it to soothe inflamed bowels. It has also been used to treat ringworm, earaches, migraine headaches, toothaches, cramps, convulsions, gout, warts, and epilepsy.

Mullein is also slightly narcotic for people, perhaps more so for fish, as indicated by its long-standing use as fish poison in some European and Asian cultures. It has also been employed as a dye, imparting a yellow hue to hair (Roman women used it for this purpose), greenish to cloth.

YELLOW OXALIS

Oxalis corniculata—yellow oxalis, creeping wood sorrel—Oxalidaceae, sorrel family

Yellow oxalis is a creeping perennial that roots at the nodes and spreads as well by rhizomes. It can form a mat 2 feet or more in diameter. It also reproduces freely and abundantly from seed. Wood sorrel grows in sun or shade, but has a special affinity for moist soil in shaded areas. It is especially troublesome in lawns, where it resembles clover, but has none of the benefits; in containers, its rhizomes entwine with the root of the other plants, making it difficult to extract.

The leaves of the yellow oxalis are bright green and trifoliate, hairy beneath, sometimes an inch or more in length (usually less), on long, slender petioles. The leaflets resemble those of clover, but are heart shaped rather than oval. They lack the chevron markings of white clover, and the plant lacks clover's nitrogen-fixing ability.

The flowers of yellow oxalis, which bloom nearly year round, make it quite easy to distinguish from the clovers. They are regular, with five bright yellow petals, about ¼ inch in diameter. These flowers produce angled, pointed seed capsules, about ½ inch long and much narrower, that resemble the horns of short-horned cattle, or the gold charm known as a *corno* that is sometimes worn by Italian men to ward off the evil eye. The capsules dehisce, propelling their seeds some distance.

Its reproductive triple threat—rhizomatous roots, stolons, and abundant seed production—make this weed very hard to eradicate, especially in ground kept constantly moist. It is an especially troublesome pest in nurseries. It needs

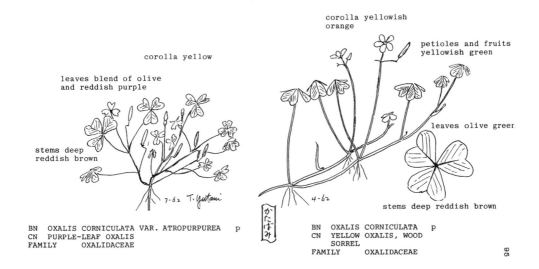

corolla yellowish
orange

corolla yellow

leaves blend of olive
and reddish purple

petioles and fruits
yellowish green

leaves olive green

stems deep
reddish brown

7-62 T. Yustani

4-62

stems deep reddish brown

BN   OXALIS CORNICULATA VAR. ATROPURPUREA   p
CN   PURPLE-LEAF OXALIS
FAMILY   OXALIDACEAE

BN   OXALIS CORNICULATA   p
CN   YELLOW OXALIS, WOOD
      SORREL
FAMILY   OXALIDACEAE

95

to be dealt with when it first appears, with consistent follow-up. Sometimes it is tolerated in lawns—maybe people think, or pretend, it is clover—but if the variety *O. corniculata* var. *atropurpurea* shows up, its purple leaves quickly give the game away, indicating that something is amiss with the lawn. It is best to remove it as soon as it appears, and overseed the lawn with clover to give it some competition if *(when)* it recurs.

Creeping wood sorrel is native to Europe, where it is sometimes known as clover sorrel, or sour grass. Mrs. Grieve does not list it as a medicinal plant, but she has a good deal to say about a close relative, *Oxalis acetosella,* a woodland plant with white flowers on long stems. This oxalis is also known as wood sour, sour trefoil, stickwort, fairy bells, hallelujah, cuckowes meat, three-leaved grass, and stubwort. All the sorrels contain binoxalate of potash, an acid-forming substance. The leaves of this plant, and perhaps other species of oxalis, are used medicinally, as a diuretic, astringent, antiscorbutic, and refrigerant. Oxalis tea is given for high fevers, and in Russia a cooling drink, somewhat resembling lemonade, is made from the leaves. Oxalis has also been used to treat hemorrhaging and for urinary disorders, as a blood cleanser, as a stomach toner, to treat wounds, to stanch bleeding, and to reduce mouth ulcers. It was once popular as a potherb in England, but fell into disuse when French sorrel, *Rumex scutatus* (which has similar properties, but is in the buckwheat family), was introduced.

The names hallelujah and cuckowes meat are explained by someone Mrs. Grieve refers to as an "old writer"; I quote him or her here: "The apothecaries and herbalists call it Alleyluya and Paniscuculi, or Cuckowes meat, because either the Cuckoo feedeth thereon, or by reason when it springeth forth and flowereth (when) the Cuckoo singeth most, at which time also, Alleyluya was wont to be sung in Churches."

This was, of course, spring. Mrs. Grieve tells us that the wood sorrel flowers between Easter and Whitsuntide.

ANNUAL BLUEGRASS, TOAD RUSH

Poa annua—annual bluegrass—Poaceae, Gramineae, grass family

Juncus bufonius—toad rush—Juncaceae, rush family

Annual bluegrass is a low-growing annual weed that flowers and sets seed continuously during the cooler parts of the year. It grows mostly in lawns and along their margins. It tends to die out in the summer except in the most heavily irrigated lawns and can leave brown patches in turf grass that can easily be mistaken for fungal damage. Annual bluegrass can grow almost anywhere there is abundant moisture, even in compacted soils. A European native, it has spread widely throughout the cool coastal areas of California, but it is fairly

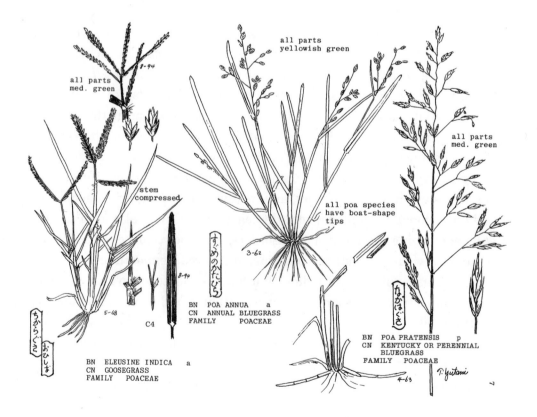

rare in the dry interior sections. It is present in most of the rest of the United States and at high altitudes in tropical America.

Annual bluegrass grows in small tufts, seldom higher or wider than 3 or 4 inches, although it can reach 6 inches or more in loose, rich soil. Like the perennial bluegrass grown for turf, it has narrow, linear leaves that are folded along the prominent midrib, with a somewhat rounded tip, causing it to be described as "boat shaped"; once you have seen enough bluegrass leaves to internalize this concept, you'll never fail to recognize it. These leaves are yellow-green, somewhat lighter than those of the turf bluegrass, making its presence in lawns fairly noticeable.

Annual bluegrass in turf can also be readily recognized by its inflorescences, short panicles of very small, awn-less spikelets that are constantly in flower, even in the most closely mowed putting greens (which are mowed to ⅛ inch or less). The flowers give a tan or whitish overlay to the light green blades.

The roots of annual bluegrass are fibrous and dense, usually no more than 2 inches deep, but adhering tightly to the soil in which they grow. It is nearly impossible to pull them out without also removing a substantial clump of top-soil. Eradicating it completely from lawns is also nearly impossible, something that golf course managers have discovered after much fruitless and costly effort

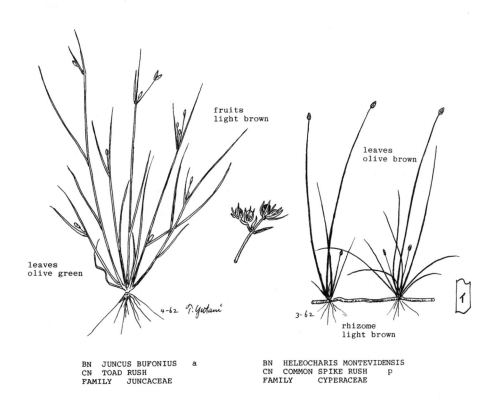

fruits
light brown

leaves
olive brown

leaves
olive green

4-62 T. Yutani

3-62

rhizome
light brown

BN   JUNCUS BUFONIUS   a
CN   TOAD RUSH
FAMILY   JUNCACEAE

BN   HELEOCHARIS MONTEVIDENSIS
CN   COMMON SPIKE RUSH   p
FAMILY   CYPERACEAE

34

(home gardeners, on the other hand, tend to ignore it). Managing lawns to favor the perennial grasses, allowing them to fill in and provide little space for weeds to germinate, is the best strategy. Avoiding compaction is paramount. The soil in lawns tends to compact and resist infiltration due to mowing and foot traffic (not to mention the practice of parking cars on lawns). A common response to grass stressed by lack of water infiltration is to irrigate even more, creating runoff, since compacted soil absorbs water only in its top few inches, and slowly. This is not enough to favor strong growth of perennial grasses but creates ideal conditions for annual bluegrass. Periodic aerating and top-dressing, and deeper, less frequent watering, will reverse these conditions, favoring the perennials and allowing a more desirable balance to be established.

According to an article in *California Agriculture* magazine, many golf course managers have discovered that, whatever its appearance, mowed annual bluegrass makes about as good a putting surface as any other fine-bladed grass, and they see no need to eradicate it totally. Furthermore, they are finding that perennial strains are developing, which die out less easily.

Annual bluegrass usually enters turf as an impurity in lawn seed, as does another small plant with which it is often confused, toad rush, *Juncus bufonius*. Toad rush is a low-growing annual with fibrous roots, about the size of annual bluegrass, and a flower head that somewhat resembles that of annual bluegrass: a branching panicle of greenish or brownish flowers consisting of glumelike segments with pointed tips. The flowers of annual bluegrass have no awns, so this feature distinguishes them, as does a color difference: annual bluegrass is light green, toad rush dark green, or sometimes bronzy. Its stems are round in cross section and wiry; the leaves are stiff, narrow, and pointed. The presence of toad rush in lawns generally indicates that they are being overwatered, since this weed likes wet ground—it can, however, withstand considerable drying out.

Toad rush is native to most of the temperate Northern Hemisphere (Europe, America, Asia), including California, where it is represented by a variety designated *Juncus bufonius* var. *occidentalis*. The weed found in lawns, however, might well have come from Europe.

SELF-HEAL

Prunella vulgaris—self-heal—Lamiaceae, Labiatae, mint family

Self-heal, also known as all-heal, hook-heal, slough-heal, heart-of-the-earth, and brunella in Europe, sometimes as blue-curls in North America, is a mat-forming herb that grows ubiquitously in Europe and other regions in which Europeans have settled. It loves moist soil in sun or shade and thrives especially well in turf, where it forms solid mats that tend to displace the grasses. Mowed, it hugs the ground closely; unmowed, the ends of the stems tend to ascend, growing to a height of 4 to 10 inches.

As with many other mint family plants, the leaves are placed opposite one another on square stems—in the case of prunella, hairy square stems. These leaves are oval or oblong, rounded at the base, sometimes slightly toothed, about 1 to 3 inches long, on short petioles. They are mostly green, but, when mature, can acquire a bronzy cast, making this plant hard to ignore when it invades lawns.

The flowers grow on a dense spike that forms on short stems. They are typical of the mint family, the five petals grouped into two lips (hence the family name—*labium* is Latin for "lip"); the calyx is purplish, the corolla bluish, violet, or lavender, sometimes with tones of magenta. It flowers in late spring, giving color to the lawns it invades; if only it could be kept from forming such solid mats.

Prunella spreads by seeds and by forming roots at every node that touches the ground. It is a weed mainly of lawns, to a lesser extent of meadows and pastures; but it can escape and grow along roadsides and invade garden beds. Effective control requires early intervention, and possibly some use of herbicides.

There is a variety of self-heal that is native to North America, *P. vulgaris* var. *lanceolata*. It grows mostly in the mountains of the West, including the Sierra Nevada and the San Bernardino mountains, but also occurs in places on the Atlantic coast. Not having the same weedy qualities as its European cousin, and possessing larger flowers, it is sometimes grown as a garden perennial. It can be seen on the planted roof of the California Academy of Sciences in Golden Gate Park in San Francisco.

Medicinally, self-heal has been used to stanch bleeding, as a tonic, and as a wound treatment *(vulnerary)*—it has been especially esteemed for this last purpose since the Middle Ages or earlier. Self-heal has also been used to stop internal bleeding, and for mouth ulcers. The name *Prunella* is a Latinized German word—*brunellen*—referring to a disease known in Germany as *die Breue,* an inflammation of the mouth. The herbalist Cole *(The Art of Simpling)* explains that this condition was quite common among encamped soldiers and produced inflammation and swelling in the throat as well as the mouth. Self-heal was considered the best cure for this condition, along with bugle *(Ajuga reptans),* a relative that it closely resembles. Bugle, or carpet bugle, is a fairly popular ground cover, growing vigorously with adequate water, but lacking the invasive potential of self-heal.

125

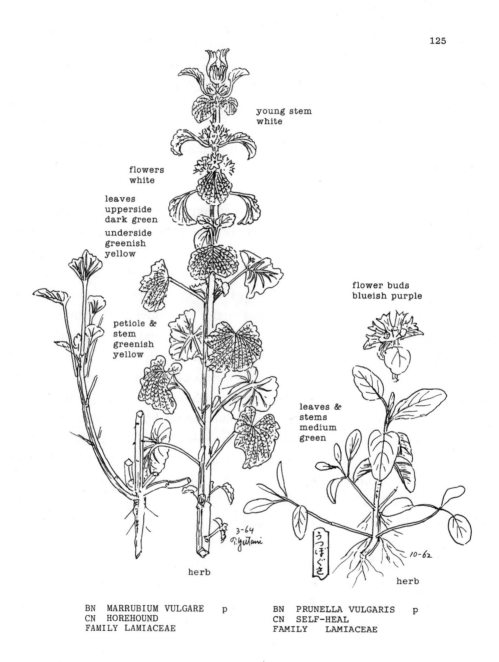

young stem
white

flowers
white

leaves
upperside
dark green

underside
greenish
yellow

flower buds
blueish purple

petiole &
stem
greenish
yellow

leaves &
stems
medium
green

3-64
P. yutani

10-62

herb

herb

BN MARRUBIUM VULGARE   p
CN HOREHOUND
FAMILY LAMIACEAE

BN PRUNELLA VULGARIS   p
CN SELF-HEAL
FAMILY LAMIACEAE

DEAD NETTLES

Lamium amplexicaule—dead nettle, henbit—Lamiaceae, Labiatae, mint family

Lamium purpureum—red dead nettle

The dead nettles are weeds in the mint family that are native to Europe. Both are winter annuals that sometimes turn perennial; both like fairly moist conditions and are somewhat shade tolerant. They are typical mint family herbs (*Lamium* is considered the type genus of this family), with opposite leaves and square stems. The name *dead nettle* refers to a perceived resemblance of the leaves to those of nettles, but without the stinging quality (thus, "dead") of nettles. Neither is particularly abundant in urban areas; but neither are they uncommon.

Henbit, or dead nettle, *Lamium amplexicaule,* is an upright plant that grows from 6 to 18 inches tall. The leaves are about an inch wide, light green in color, coarsely toothed, hairy, with prominent netted veins. They are more or less kidney shaped, without petioles, so an opposite pair somewhat resembles a single orbicular (stem-surrounding) leaf. Flowers are slender, tubular, about ½ to ¾ inch long, in clusters in the upper leaf axils. The stems are ascending, but often parallel to the ground for some distance from the crown; where they touch the ground, they may form fibrous roots. When growing in areas that retain some moisture in the summer, henbit plants may live a second or even a third year.

Red dead nettle, *Lamium purpureum,* differs from henbit by producing stems that hug the ground, although they sometimes generate ascending side branches that grow as tall as a foot. The leaves are more or less heart shaped, usually no more than ½ inch across, palmately veined, toothed, with petioles, hairs, and, quite often, reddish coloration. Flowers are small and purple and white; they grow in whorls in the leaf nodes. The stems root at the nodes, often allowing this plant, like its cousin, henbit, to become a short-lived perennial. In winter and spring, red dead nettle can be quite abundant in low, moisture-retaining ground, forming an attractive ground cover. Selective weeding might be a good option in these areas.

In rural areas, red dead nettle often forms a solid ground cover in orchards, meadows, pastures, and fallow crop lands. In the city, it likes moist situations, sunny or semishady. It is a pretty plant that can serve quite well as an attractive, though short-lived, ground cover in areas where gardeners see no need to plant a more permanent one.

The genus *Lamium* also includes a number of perennial, herbaceous herbs that are planted as small-scale ground covers in ornamental gardens. There are several cultivars with white or yellow variegations on the leaves, which stand out in shady areas. These live longer than the weedy dead nettles and are not nearly as invasive.

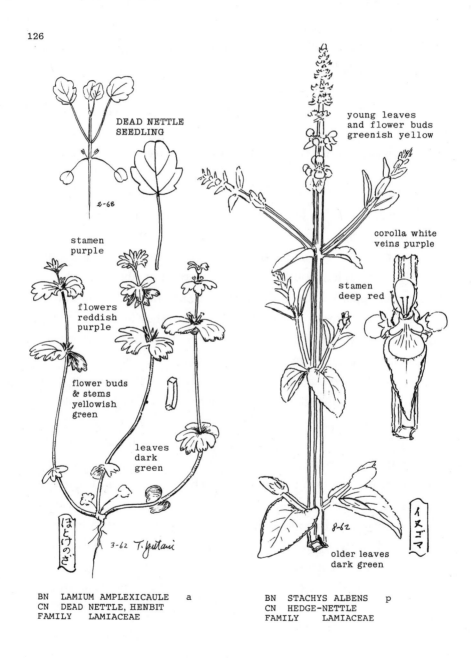

126

DEAD NETTLE
SEEDLING

2-68

stamen
purple

flowers
reddish
purple

flower buds
& stems
yellowish
green

leaves
dark
green

3-62 T. Jritani

young leaves
and flower buds
greenish yellow

corolla white
veins purple

stamen
deep red

8-62

older leaves
dark green

BN   LAMIUM AMPLEXICAULE   a
CN   DEAD NETTLE, HENBIT
FAMILY   LAMIACEAE

BN   STACHYS ALBENS   p
CN   HEDGE-NETTLE
FAMILY   LAMIACEAE

MARIJUANA, OR HEMP

Cannabis sativa—hemp, marijuana—Cannabinaceae, hemp family

Hemp, a native of Central Asia, has been grown since ancient times as a fiber plant. It was used for making rope and cordage, for weaving sturdy cloth (canvas—note the word's similarity to *cannabis*), and many other uses. The plant contains a resin that has narcotic properties, and varieties high in resin have been selected since Greek and Roman times. The ancient Greek historian Herodotus recounts the use of this drug by the Scythians, Central Asian nomads whom the Greeks encountered in the Black Sea region. He writes as follows:

> Now, there is a plant growing in their country called cannabis, which closely resembles flax, except that cannabis is thicker-stemmed and taller. . . . It grows wild, but is also cultivated, and the Thracians use it, as well as flax, for making clothes. . . . Anyone unfamiliar with cannabis would suppose the clothes to be linen. Anyway, the Scythians take cannabis seeds, crawl in under their felt blankets, and throw the seeds on the glowing stones. The seeds then emit dense smoke and stones, much more than any vapor bath in Greece. The Scythians shriek with delight at the fumes. This is their equivalent of a bath, since they never wash their bodies with water.

Cannabis is also a fairly popular recreational drug in the United States, more so in many other countries; in most states it is still illegal to grow, sell, or consume. Recently, however, various medicinal benefits attributed to this plant have made its cultivation and sale to patients with prescriptions legal in several states, including California. State law conflicts with federal law, however, and the outcome of this conflict has yet to be resolved.

Growing cannabis for any reason has been illegal in the United States since the 1930s, but this law was relaxed during World War II, when the main fiber then used for rope and cordage, called Manila hemp, became unavailable after the conquest of the Philippines by Japan. Midwestern farmers were given licenses to grow hemp, and it became widespread throughout the region. It is no longer grown there, but is a fairly common roadside weed. It is much less common in California, despite the presence of illegal and semilegal plantings of narcotic cannabis—these are not allowed to go to seed, as unfertilized female plants produce the most resin. The occasional plants found in urban areas probably originate mostly from the discarded seeds of narcotic or medicinal marijuana that has not been grown with the care required to produce first-rate sinsemilla.

111A

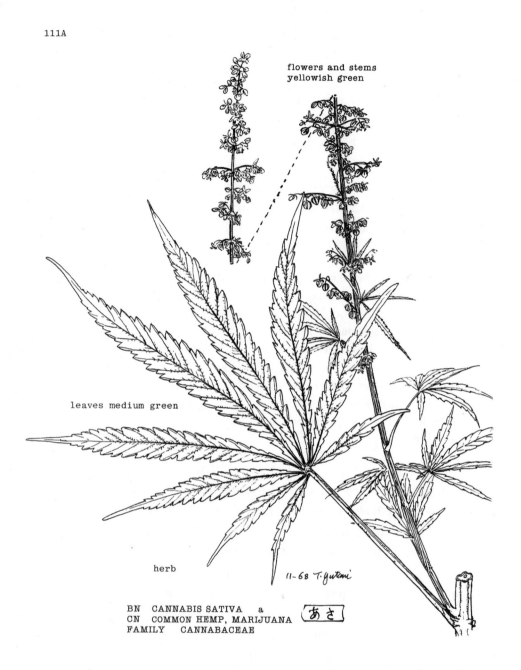

flowers and stems
yellowish green

leaves medium green

herb

11-68 T. Gutani

BN   CANNABIS SATIVA   a
CN   COMMON HEMP, MARIJUANA   あさ
FAMILY   CANNABACEAE

Hemp plants are easily recognized by their compound palmate leaves, alternate above, compound below; deep green on the upper surface, lighter below. Leaflets are lanceolate and pointed, with serrated edges, about 3 to 5 inches long. Plants grow anywhere from 3 to 16 inches tall.

Hemp is dioecious, with male and female flowers on different plants. Staminate flowers are on narrow, loose panicles growing in the leaf axils; the pistillate flowers, the ones that produce the most resin, are in erect, leafy spikes, also axillary. They are both greenish in color. Marijuana growers usually try to eliminate the male plants to minimize pollination; fiber plants are allowed to go to seed.

Hemp has long been used openly as a narcotic and medicinal drug in the Near East and Africa, as well as India and Southeast Asia, but there is no clear evidence I know of that it was used as a narcotic in Europe before modern times. In the nineteenth century Romantics in Europe and America (including Louisa May Alcott) discovered this drug, mostly in its compressed form called *hashish* in the Middle East. Marijuana and the far more addictive opiate drugs entered American bohemian culture during the early twentieth century, after first becoming popular among jazz musicians. All of these drugs were outlawed in 1937, except as prescribed medicine (the federal government acknowledges the medicinal efficacy of the opiates, but not of marijuana, which remains entirely illegal under federal law). In the last decade or so, several states have legalized cannabis for medicinal use, and a few for recreational use, although under federal law it is still not legal.

Cannabis has acquired many picturesque common names from recreational users: weed, pot, boo, muggles, grass, skank, dope, and others too numerous to mention.

6

THE GREEN AND GOLDEN
HILLS OF CALIFORNIA

*T*he mythic view of early Spanish-speaking California is of a timeless, unspoiled landscape, first settled by benevolent padres who built missions where they converted willing Indians to Christianity and taught them useful trades; then by rancheros who grazed their cattle on the green and golden hills that had been awaiting their arrival for many centuries. It was a bucolic land, inhabited by happy, industrious people whose peaceful activities were interrupted only by horse races, bear hunts, fandangos, and feasting on the endless supply of beef that the green and golden land produced. Anglos who embrace this myth often look back with some sense of wistful regret at their own arrival onto this scene; but then, it was all ordained by Divine Providence.

This myth was taught to me as history many decades ago when I was in the fourth grade in Riverside, California, and we all embraced it; some of us know better by now. I have already outlined the disastrous effect on the native population of the arrival of Spanish, then English speakers during this period, due to European diseases, enslavement, wanton killing, and decimation of the resources upon which the Native Californians depended. These resources included native grasses, mostly perennial, many of which provided edible grain. These perennial grasses were displaced by the European annual grasses that invaded the hills soon after cattle grazing began; the green and golden grasses had not been there all along. They provide ample nutrition for cattle and sheep, but very little for humans. They still cover most of the open ground in the foothill areas surrounding the Central Valley and the coastal valleys. The valley bottoms, now consisting of farmland, pasture, and urban development, were originally covered with a large assortment of broad-leaved herbaceous plants rather than grasses. John Muir and others described the Central Valley in spring as one vast carpet of wildflowers.

The hills, too, had their wildflowers, and still do, but the green and golden grasses have taken their toll, allowing only highly competitive natives such as California poppies, buttercups, and clarkias to compete with them. There are still some extensive wildflower displays in areas such as serpentine barrens, whose soils limit the growth of the European annuals; native perennial bunch grasses thrive in these places as well. Unfortunately, in recent years, another human activity has been posing a threat to these native grasslands—nitrates generated by automobile traffic are being deposited by rainfall, enriching the soil enough to make the green and golden grasses more competitive. In the Bay Area, Edgewood County Park in San Mateo, adjacent to the I-280 freeway, has, in a few years, been changed from a breathtakingly diverse assemblage of native wildflowers and bunch grasses to just another hillside blanket of wild oats and ripgut brome, with only sparse wildflower growth.

But, despite tragedies like Edgewood Park, California's green and golden foothills are a glorious sight: bright expanses of tall green grasses in the spring, undulating in the wind, then turning golden or buff in the summer, contrasting with the evergreen oaks and laurels in the canyons and the trees and shrubs growing on the upper slopes of the hills. The whole scene still says "California" to most viewers, residents and visitors alike.

GRASSES

Wild Oats

Avena fatua—wild oats—Poaceae, Gramineae, grass family

The golden portion of the "green and golden hills" of California consists mostly of wild oats and ripgut brome, two grasses that have become identified with the "classic" California landscape, but that, in reality, are native to the Near East and the Mediterranean, and were introduced (inadvertently) into California by Hispanic settlers only about 250 years ago. Yet, if one thinks of the California landscape not as a purely natural, but also a cultural environment, these grasses are as much a part of this landscape as palm and eucalyptus trees.

Oats are thought to have originated as a weed in wheat; this original "weed" was *Avena sativa,* a diploid plant that is now grown as our cultivated oat, the grain that we feed to horses and use to make oatmeal. This weed was recognized early on as a valuable grain crop and came to be grown deliberately, especially in cooler regions where it tended to outcompete the wheat in the

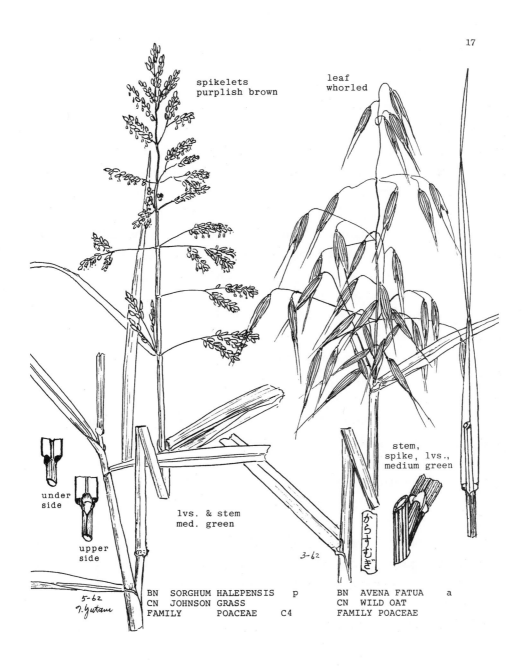

17

spikelets
purplish brown

leaf
whorled

under
side

upper
side

lvs. & stem
med. green

stem,
spike, lvs.,
medium green

3-62

5-62
T. Yutani

BN SORGHUM HALEPENSIS p
CN JOHNSON GRASS
FAMILY   POACEAE   C4

BN AVENA FATUA   a
CN WILD OAT
FAMILY POACEAE

fields it invaded (the same is true of rye). At some point in its career, however, *Avena sativa*'s chromosomes multiplied, and it evolved into a distinct species, *Avena fatua*, with decidedly weedy characteristics, and with grains less desirable than those of its parents. It became not only an invader of crop lands, but also one of the predominant grasses growing on fallow and uncultivated lands.

The USDA PLANTS Database describes the wild oat as a parent of the cultivated oat. Edgar Anderson, however, points out that whereas a polyploid plant could have arisen from a diploid ancestor, the laws of genetics would preclude the opposite—there is no way for a plant with fewer chromosomes to evolve from one with more. Therefore, the weed could well have evolved from the crop plant (or its ancestor), but the crop plant could not have come from the weed. If there was a common ancestor for both these plants, it has not yet been identified.

The wild oat is a tall grass, generally growing 2 or 3 feet high, but capable of reaching twice that height (or more) in rich, moist soil. It has leaves that are usually fairly smooth, but sometimes a little hairy. They are placed alternately on the stems. This grass is most readily identified by its inflorescence, consisting of several spikelets, each of which dangles from its individual pedicel, thus allowing it to move freely in the breeze. The outer layer of the spikelet consists of two papery glumes, which remain on the stem once the grain has ripened and dropped; beneath the glumes are two lemmas, each tipped with a short, straight awn that becomes twisted as the spikelet ages.

In North America, the wild oat is very widely distributed, growing as far north as Alaska and some of the Arctic islands in the north of Canada. It generally prefers drier, leaner soils, but has a very wide range of tolerances, but shade is not one of them. It grows in many types of soil, from very sandy to heavy adobe clays.

Oats have many traditional medicinal uses, including some stimulant properties—they contain an alkaloid that stimulates the motor ganglia. Eating oats has long been known to excite horses; hence the expression "feeling his oats." Wild oat has also been used as a nervine and as an antispasmodic and has traditionally been administered for these purposes in the form of a gruel. Oatmeal pastes and poultices have been used as an emollient, to soothe inflamed tissue; they have sometimes been taken internally as an antidote to acid poisoning, or even administered as an enema to soothe inflamed intestinal tissue. Oats have also been used as diuretics and refrigerants.

The wild oat has food value for animals and humans and can be made into flour and meals; but the cultivated oat, *Avena sativa,* is better for this purpose, as it has a much plumper grain. This oat sometimes escapes from grain fields and becomes a weed, but usually does not persist for long. It can be readily distinguished from the wild oat by its somewhat larger grain and straight awns, or sometimes no awns. Cultivated and wild oats also can hybridize, forming intermediate varieties that are more difficult to identify.

There are two other species of wild oat which are not as abundant as *Avena fatua* and are difficult to distinguish without a key. These are the slender oat, *Avena barbata,* and the animated oat, *Avena sterilis.* The slender oat is quite common and can usually be distinguished by its smaller, more slender and delicate spikelets, especially if there are specimens of *Avena fatua* growing nearby. *Avena sterilis,* the animated oat, has an awn that twists visibly in response to changes in humidity and moisture.

Ripgut and Spanish Brome

Bromus diandrus—ripgut brome—Poaceae, Gramineae, grass family

Bromus madritensis—Spanish brome

Ripgut brome is the second-most abundant annual grass in the "green and golden" hills of California, the first being the wild oat. Ripgut is a grass of medium height, about 1½ to 2½ feet tall. It is widespread at lower elevations throughout the American West.

The leaves of ripgut brome are light to medium green and hairy all over. The inflorescence consists of a loose panicle with individual spikelets on long pedicels, which allow them to droop, much like wild oats (the term *brome* comes from a Greek word that means "oat"). The spikelet consists of multiple florets, each with a bristle (awn) that is much longer than the base of the floret. These awns are 1½ to 2 inches long and are stiff and rough textured. The fruit, known as a grain, is covered with rough, backward-facing bristles, which can cause it to lodge in the hooves, nose, and eyes of grazing animals. Although the young plants are good forage for grazers, the bristles on the grains and the long, stiff awns of mature spikelets can cause external and internal injury to livestock.

Fields of ripgut brome can be a glorious sight, especially in late spring and early summer, the season known to some Native Californians as the "season of turning from green to gold." The slender, long-awned spikelets, dangling from long pedicels, vibrate in the wind; the mass of plants ripples in graceful, wave-like motions, while the long awns and hairy leaves reflect the sunlight in ever-changing patterns of light and shadow. This same effect can be produced by one of our more common long-awned native grasses, *Nasella pulchra,* the purple needlegrass, which, ironically, is much less abundant than it used to be because most of its habitat has been taken over by exotic annuals such as ripgut brome.

Spanish brome closely resembles ripgut, but is a generally smaller plant, about 1 to 1½ feet tall, and the awns are shorter, about equal in length to the rest of the floret. Like ripgut, several florets are assembled into a spikelet on a pedicel, and these are loosely assembled into a head.

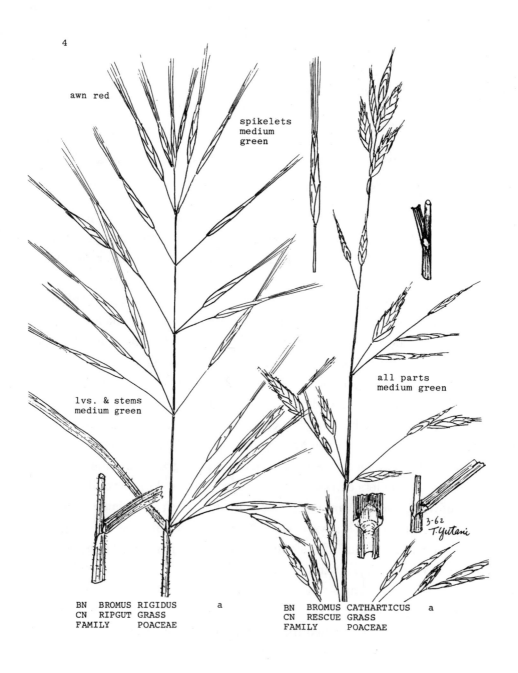

4

awn red

spikelets
medium
green

all parts
medium green

lvs. & stems
medium green

3-62
T. Yutani

BN   BROMUS RIGIDUS   a
CN   RIPGUT GRASS
FAMILY   POACEAE

BN   BROMUS CATHARTICUS   a
CN   RESCUE GRASS
FAMILY   POACEAE

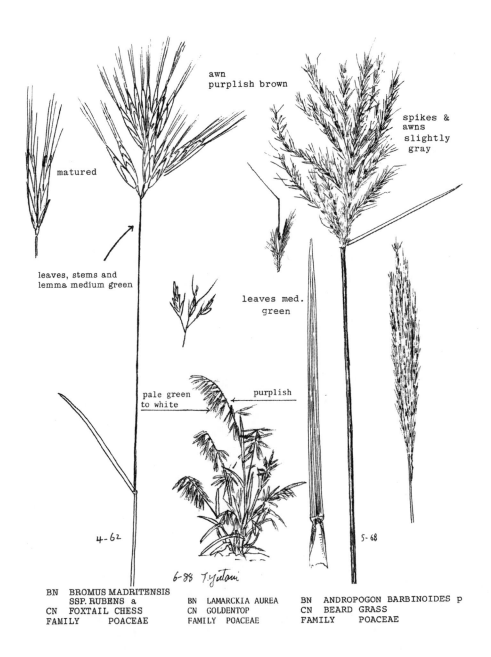

awn
purplish brown

spikes &
awns
slightly
gray

matured

leaves, stems and
lemma medium green

leaves med.
green

pale green
to white

purplish

4-62

5-68

6-88 T.Yutani

BN BROMUS MADRITENSIS
    SSP. RUBENS a
CN FOXTAIL CHESS
FAMILY   POACEAE

BN LAMARCKIA AUREA
CN GOLDENTOP
FAMILY POACEAE

BN ANDROPOGON BARBINOIDES p
CN BEARD GRASS
FAMILY   POACEAE

Spanish brome does not form the same kind of extensive stands as do ripgut and wild oats, since it is often outcompeted by these taller grasses. It is more likely to be found in mixed stands of shorter grasses, or mixed with broad-leaved weeds.

A subspecies known as red brome—*Bromus madritensis* ssp. *rubens*—has bushier heads consisting of more densely packed spikelets, which tend to turn a reddish color as the grass dies out. This reddening does not definitively indicate the subspecies, however. The typical Spanish brome can also exhibit this trait, as can ripgut brome. Reddish coloration in plants is often caused by soil conditions and weather and is not always, in itself, a reliable way to identify them.

Spanish brome is also known as compact brome and foxtail chess.

Soft Chess

Bromus hordeaceus—soft chess—Poaceae, Gramineae, grass family

Soft chess grows at low elevations throughout most of California and is fairly common, if not abundant, in urban areas. It is a winter annual with fibrous roots. In stature and size—6 inches to 3 feet tall, depending on soil, moisture, and exposure—it resembles many other bromes. It can be distinguished from them most readily by an abundance of soft hairs on the leaves, sheaths, and flowers.

The spikelets are small, ½ to ¾ inch long, with short awns (less than 10 cm), flattened in cross section, though less so than many other bromes, and covered with fine, downy hairs. One can often confirm identification of this grass simply by stroking the panicle, a pleasant experience akin to stroking a cat's tail. These hairs often make the flower spike glisten in the sunlight, and

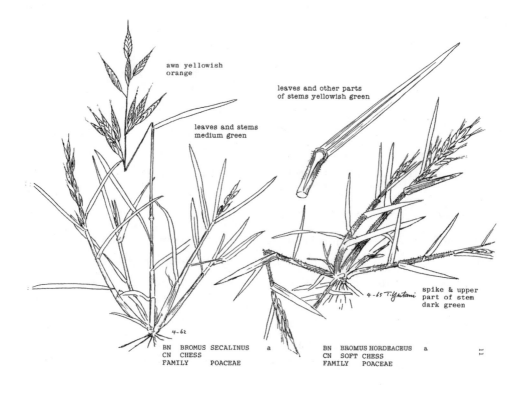

awn yellowish orange

leaves and other parts of stems yellowish green

leaves and stems medium green

spike & upper part of stem dark green

4-65 T. Yutani

4-62

BN   BROMUS SECALINUS   a
CN   CHESS
FAMILY   POACEAE

BN   BROMUS HORDEACEUS   a
CN   SOFT CHESS
FAMILY   POACEAE

since this is one of the less aggressively spreading weedy annual grasses, it is an excellent candidate for allowing to reseed as a winter ground cover.

Ranchers in valley and foothill rangelands consider soft chess to be a valuable forage plant, with very nutritious seed heads, and often sow it in seed mixtures of pasture grasses and forbs. It was introduced from Europe and occurs throughout most of the United States (including Alaska and Hawaii) and Canada, and even in Greenland.

Foxtail Barley

Hordeum jubatum ssp. *jubatum*—foxtail barley, hare barley—Poaceae, Gramineae, grass family

Foxtail barley, *Hordeum jubatum,* also known as hare barley, wild barley, farmer's foxtail, or mouse barley, is a winter annual native to the Mediterranean and the third-most abundant nonnative annual grass in California (after wild oats and ripgut brome). This grass can grow up to 2 feet tall, but more commonly reaches a foot or so. Its leaves are flat and smooth, 1 to 5 inches long.

Flower stems each bear a terminal spike about 2 inches long, often partially enclosed by the upper leaf sheath, and consisting of densely packed spikelets arranged in groups of three around the stem of the inflorescence. Each spikelet is enclosed by two narrow glumes, resembling awns; the true awns, of course, grow from the lemmas. These are about twice as long as the rest of the fruit and are covered with small barbs. Viewed from top to bottom, the spikelets are in three ranks along the axis of the spike.

Foxtail barley is often confused with red brome; keeping the details of the structure of the inflorescence in mind will help distinguish them. Red brome has shorter awns, and the spikelets are not arranged in distinct vertical ranks.

Roots of hare barley are fibrous, but sturdy and extensive enough to allow the plant to stay green in California well into the dry season. Mowing it in June and then watching it resprout, and even produce flowers, is not an uncommon experience. In agricultural areas, it is considered an especially troublesome weed in alfalfa, and it can infest other crops as well. Foxtail barley also grows along roadways and ditch banks, in meadows and pastures, and in hillside grasslands. In urban areas, it can show up almost anywhere, generally preferring full sun. It is widely distributed throughout the United States, but shows its true winter annual character best in California.

The bristly awns of wild barley enable it to be carried in the fur of animals and the clothing of humans, and the sharp tips of the spikelets can penetrate clothing and skin and cause injury to livestock, especially by piercing their mouths or eyes. Sheep have been blinded or choked by foxtails.

There are other barleys in California, weedy and native; hare barley is the most ubiquitous, and the only one commonly seen in urban areas. *H. vulgare,* the barley grown as a grain crop, is sometimes included in seed mixes designed to provide quick cover for burned-over and eroded areas. It sometimes escapes and becomes a roadside weed, but it generally does not persist for long. It can

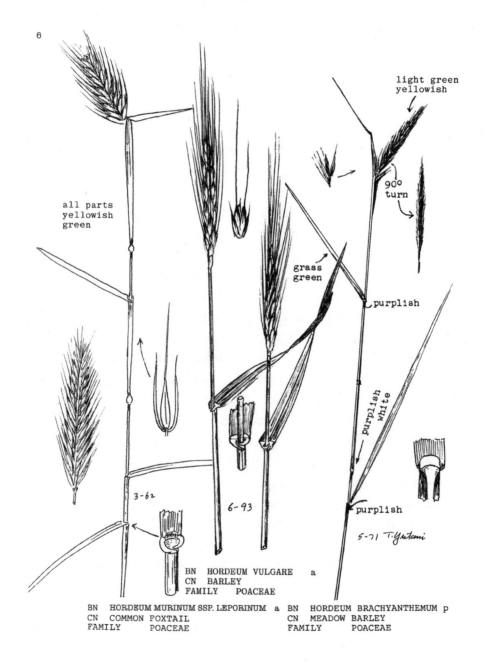

BN   HORDEUM VULGARE   a
CN   BARLEY
FAMILY   POACEAE

BN   HORDEUM MURINUM SSP. LEPORINUM   a   BN   HORDEUM BRACHYANTHEMUM p
CN   COMMON FOXTAIL   CN   MEADOW BARLEY
FAMILY   POACEAE   FAMILY   POACEAE

be recognized by its height (3 to 4 feet) and its large spikes with very long awns. *H. brachyantherum,* a graceful perennial native to California, is sometimes planted in gardens, sometimes volunteers; its very narrow flower spikes consisting of densely packed, short-awned spikelets make it fairly easy to recognize. If it comes unbidden to your garden and does well, you might consider keeping it.

Hordeum murinum ssp. *leporinum,* hare barley (a.k.a. squirreltail barley, tickle grass, flickertail, and skunk grass), is an introduced perennial species that is far less common than common foxtail; it confines itself mostly to rural areas. It can be distinguished from common foxtail by its longer awns, approaching the length of those of the cultivated barley. It can be distinguished from the latter by its lower stature and more spreading habit. It is sometimes sold as a garden grass by mail-order nurseries and seed catalogs. Hare barley is attractive, but, if planted, may have more invasive potential than its purveyors—and their customers—suspect.

Italian Ryegrass

Lolium multiflorum—Italian ryegrass—Poaceae, Gramineae, grass family

Italian, or annual, ryegrass is one of the more common winter annual grasses in coastal California, and it is easily recognizable by two distinctive characteristics: the shiny undersides of its leaves, which distinguish it from other annual grasses even before it blooms, and its distinctive inflorescence.

Like many other annual grasses, Italian ryegrass grows from 1 to 3 feet tall and forms upright clumps. Leaves are apple green, dull and prominently veined above, glossy with less conspicuous veins on the underside. Roots are fibrous.

The inflorescence is an elongated spike, generally about 6 inches long, but sometimes as much as a foot. It consists of short-awned spikelets, about ½ to 1 inch long, which are sessile on the main stem. They are arranged alternately on opposite sides of the rachis and point upward at about a 60-degree angle, forming a structure reminiscent of a fish bone. The weight of the spikelets often causes the spikes to droop and nod.

Italian ryegrass is native to Europe, and it is found in all fifty states of the United States and most of Canada. It even grows in Greenland. It is widely planted for pasture and silage and often used as a cover crop and for erosion control. Italian ryegrass is a problematic competitor of native vegetation because of its allelopathic characteristics and its tolerance for a wide range of habitats, including wetlands. Although it is often recommended as a "nurse crop" for revegetation projects, restoration workers avoid using it, preferring less aggressive, early-blooming grasses such as *Vulpia myuros;* sometimes they forgo nurse crops altogether and simply plant the grasses they hope will predominate.

Italian ryegrass is sometimes used to overseed lawns consisting primarily of warm-season grasses such as Bermuda, which tend to turn brown in the winter. The ryegrass produces some green color, often patchy, in the lawn. In

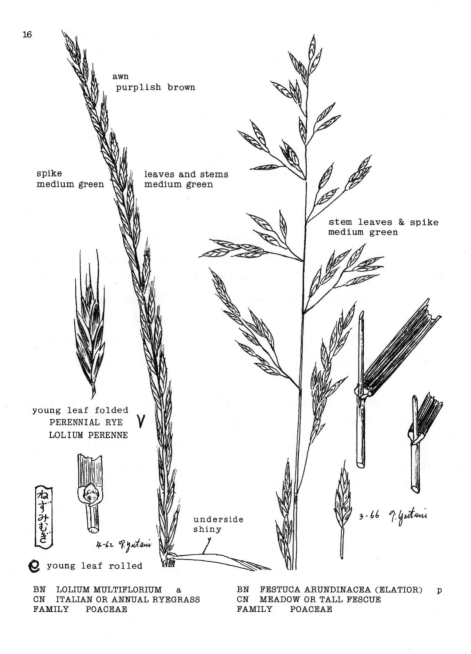

16

awn
purplish brown

spike
medium green

leaves and stems
medium green

stem leaves & spike
medium green

young leaf folded
PERENNIAL RYE
LOLIUM PERENNE

underside
shiny

young leaf rolled

4-62 T. Yutani

3-66 T. Yutani

BN   LOLIUM MULTIFLORIUM   a
CN   ITALIAN OR ANNUAL RYEGRASS
FAMILY   POACEAE

BN   FESTUCA ARUNDINACEA (ELATIOR)   p
CN   MEADOW OR TALL FESCUE
FAMILY   POACEAE

summer, of course, it dies, so gardeners who overseed often end up with partially brown lawns year round. Overseeding with perennial ryegrass might be a better choice—this would eliminate the brown patches of dead annual ryegrass that often appear in overseeded Bermuda grass lawns in summer.

Perennial ryegrass, *Lolium perenne,* closely resembles annual ryegrass. The spikelets of the perennial are shorter than those of annual ryegrass, and they lack awns; the whole plant is somewhat smaller. The two can also be told apart by cutting through the base of the emerging leaves: in annual ryegrass, the leaves in this "bud" look rolled; in the perennial, folded. Perennial ryegrass is the source of all the ryegrass lawn cultivars, and it can escape from lawns and form localized weed populations near turf that is not mowed often enough to prevent flowering.

Rescue Grass

Bromus catharticus—rescue grass, Shraeder's grass—Poaceae, Gramineae, grass family

Rescue grass is a South American native that has been widely planted for forage in the warmer parts of the United States, particularly the Southeast, as well as in other warm temperate and subtropical parts of the world. It has become widely naturalized in these and adjacent areas—in other words, it has become a weed. If my personal observations are valid, rescue grass populations have been increasing conspicuously in the San Francisco Bay Area since about the 1990s, and it is becoming a component of the flora of the green and golden hills.

Rescue grass is a short-lived perennial (annual in cold-winter areas) with a fibrous root system, smooth or slightly hairy leaves, and large (to 1 inch), compressed, noticeably flattened, hairy spikelets with very short (⅛ inch or less) awns, or sometimes no awns. They are on pedicels about 2 inches long and arranged in large (to 8 inches), open panicles, which often droop with the weight of the spikelets. Rescue grass grows in full sun, in almost any soil. The roots sprout from a sturdy crown and anchor the plant firmly, making it difficult to pull.

The name *rescue* grass is a corruption of "fescue," apparently indicating an early misidentification of this plant. It can be a strikingly attractive grass, but because of its perennial nature, tenacious roots, and prodigious self-sowing capacity, it should probably be considered a less desirable urban weed than, say, *Bromus hordeaceus* or *Vulpia myuros,* both of which can have considerable ornamental value in the right places.

See illustration of rescue grass on p. 164.

Rattail Fescue, Zorro Fescue

Vulpia myuros—rattail or zorro fescue—Poaceae, Gramineae, grass family

This slender, graceful annual grass usually grows to about a foot tall, but can sometimes reach 2 feet. It has narrow, bright green, smooth leaves that are less than ¹⁄₁₆ inch wide. The inflorescence consists of a peduncle about 8 inches long,

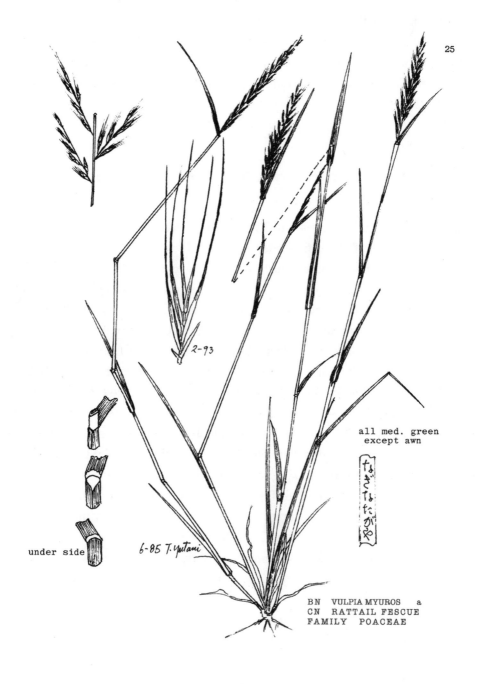

25

2-93

all med. green
except awn

under side

6-85 T. Yutani

BN VULPIA MYUROS a
CN RATTAIL FESCUE
FAMILY POACEAE

with very slender, awned spikelets on short pedicels, growing at close intervals along the stem. These spikelets are no longer than ⅜ inch. They tend to bloom early and persist throughout the growing season, and even into the summer, hanging on well after the plant has dried out.

Rattail, in my opinion, has great aesthetic value as a winter ground cover for areas that go brown in the summer. Since it is relatively short in stature and keeps its flowers, it looks good even when dried out, and can be retained for as long as it does not present an undue fire hazard. It is most attractive in solid stands, so selective weeding of broad-leaved weeds and taller grasses is in order. If this is done throughout the season, and the zorro fescue is allowed to remain and drop its seed, it will eventually become dominant without frequent weeding. When this happens, introducing some wildflowers might be worth a try.

Rattail fescue grows in full sun and part shade. It is widely naturalized throughout the United States. It was originally classified as a fescue, hence its common name.

FORBS

A forb is a herbaceous plant that is not a grass or other monocot. A number of these are often deliberately planted along with annual grasses in rangelands and pastures. In other situations, they are usually considered weeds. They include the filarees, plants in the geranium family that germinate after the first autumn rains, even rains that are too light to germinate substantial quantities of grass seed; so they are the earliest dependable source of pasturage for cattle that can be grown without irrigation. They also include a number of cloverlike legumes: perennial clovers (genus *Trifolium*), bur clovers and medics (genus *Medicago*), vetches (genus *Vicia*), sweet clover (genus *Melilotus*), and birdsfoot trefoil (genus *Lotus*) All these are nitrogen fixers, and so help fertilize the grasses—and they are highly nutritious. They tend to spread from pastures and seeded rangelands into uncultivated grasslands, and so have become naturalized throughout the green and golden hills.

The Filarees

Erodium moschatum—whitestem filaree—Geraniaceae, geranium family

Erodium cicutarium—redstem filaree

Erodium botrys—broadleaf filaree

These three herbs are all members of the geranium family, with beaked fruits similar to those of geraniums—but the beaks are longer. Geraniums have commonly been referred to as cranesbills, filarees, as storksbills. An older, currently little-used common name for these plants is pinweed (or pin grass, or pin clover), again referring to the beaked fruit. The word *filaree* comes from the Spanish *alfileria,* meaning "little pin," again a reference to the fruit.

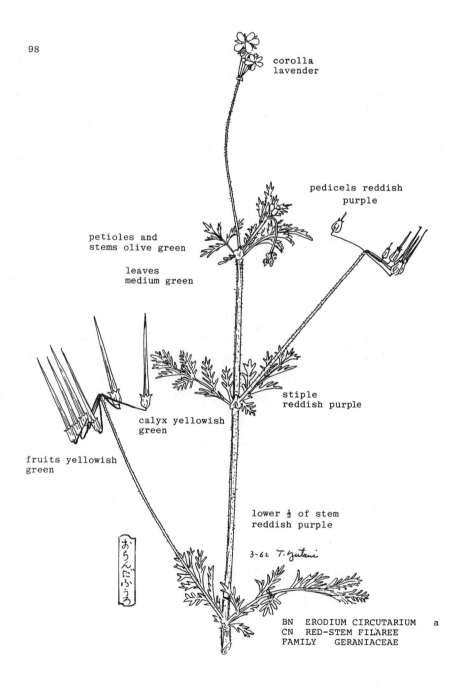

98

corolla
lavender

pedicels reddish
purple

petioles and
stems olive green

leaves
medium green

stiple
reddish purple

calyx yellowish
green

fruits yellowish
green

lower ½ of stem
reddish purple

3-62 T. Yutani

BN   ERODIUM CIRCUTARIUM   a
CN   RED-STEM FILAREE
FAMILY   GERANIACEAE

Blackwood acacia (*Acacia melanoxylon*)

Tree of heaven (*Ailanthus altissima*)
in the Arkansas Ozarks

Acanthus (*Acanthus mollis*)

Acanthus at Mountain View Cemetary, Oakland, CA

Yarrow (*Achillea millefolium*)

A flowery mede—minus the grass

Wild onion (*Allium triquetrum*)

Neapolitan onion (*allium neapolitanum*) with Pride of Madeira (*Echium candicans*)

Red brome (*Bromus madritensis ssp. rubens*)

"That!" grass (*Ehrharta erecta*)

Giant reed (*Arundo donax*) at Mountain View Cemetery

Jubata grass (*Cortaderia jubata*), Mills College, Oakland, CA

Italian arum (*Arum italicum*)

Italian thistle rosettes (*Carduus pycnocephalus*)

Mature Italian thistle

Bittercress (cardamine oligosperma),
Mountain View Cemetery

Swinecress rosette (*Coronopus didymus*), Mountain View Cemetery

Red valerian (*Centranthus ruber*)

Miner's lettuce (*Claytonia perfoliata*)

French broom (*Cytisus monspessulanus*)

Field horsetail (*Equisetum arvense*)

Western bracken fern (*Pteridium aquilinum ssp. pubescens*)

Mexican fleabane (*Erigeron karvinskianus*) in the author's garden

Dove's foot geranium (*Geranium molle*)

Prickly lettuce rosette (*Lactuca serriola*)

Mature prickly lettuce

Red dead nettle (*Lamium purpureum*)

Wild cucumber (*Marah fabaceus*)

False garlic (*Nothoscordum inodoratum*)

Periwinkle (*Vinca major*)

"Labrador" violet, European dog violet (*Viola riviniana*)

Calla-lily (*Zantedeschia aethiopica*) with prickly
lettuce rosettes, Mountain View Cemetery

The fruit, formed from a five-parted pistil, contains five seeds in five united carpels, which form the cone-shaped base; extending from this is the remnant of the style, developed as a twisted, hairy tail with a thin outer covering. This cover falls away at maturity, exposing the twisted tail, which coils tightly when wet, then uncoils as it dries, driving the fruit into the ground like an auger bit.

All three of these filarees are winter annuals that germinate with the earliest and lightest autumn rains, then grow very quickly; for this reason, dairy farmers and cattle ranchers consider them valuable forage, since they mature well before most grasses. Filarees are planted deliberately in pasture lands and are only considered weeds when they escape into crop lands, to roadsides, and into gardens and planted landscapes.

In addition to filaree, various other broad-leaved herbaceous plants, especially legumes, are sown into pastures to supplement the forage provided by grasses—these are known collectively as *forbs*.

The most common filaree found in urban environments is the whitestem filaree, *Erodium moschatum*. This plant begins its vegetative life as a tiny rosette, a circle of leaves that lie flat on the ground, growing directly from the root crown. This rosette typically grows to 6 to 8 inches in diameter before beginning to elongate. The leaves are dark green, hairy, compound pinnate with rather coarse serrations on the leaflets. Stem coloration is typically lighter green than the leaves, but can be reddish if soil and weather conditions are right (red coloration in many plants typically occurs during colder weather).

Later in the spring, beginning in late February or March in coastal California, the filaree plants begin to grow out of their rosette form, developing ascending, branching stems that terminate in clusters of five-petaled pink flowers typical of the geranium family, about ¼ inch in diameter. These are followed by the beaked fruits, about an inch long.

Redstem filaree very much resembles its white-stemmed cousin but is a somewhat smaller plant (although the sizes of individual plants overlap a good deal), with leaflets that have finer and more deeply cut teeth on their edges. Reddish coloration of the stems is more common than on whitestem filaree, but is by no means universal, so positive identification cannot be made on the basis of stem color alone. The flowers of *E. cicutarium* tend to be more magenta than pink, and often have darker mottling. The fruits are somewhat longer and more slender than those of the whitestem.

Redstem filaree is one of the earliest weeds to be introduced to California. Its pollen is found in the oldest adobe bricks, and it may have arrived before the first Hispano-American colonists. It was most likely present on the Great

Plains and in Intermountain areas well before then. The Blackfoot, Shoshone, and Cahuilla Indians were all known to have gathered and eaten the leaves of redstem filaree, raw or cooked—it reportedly tastes like spinach. Quail, ground squirrels, and kangaroo rats have also been observed feeding upon it. Medicinally, it has been used as a diuretic.

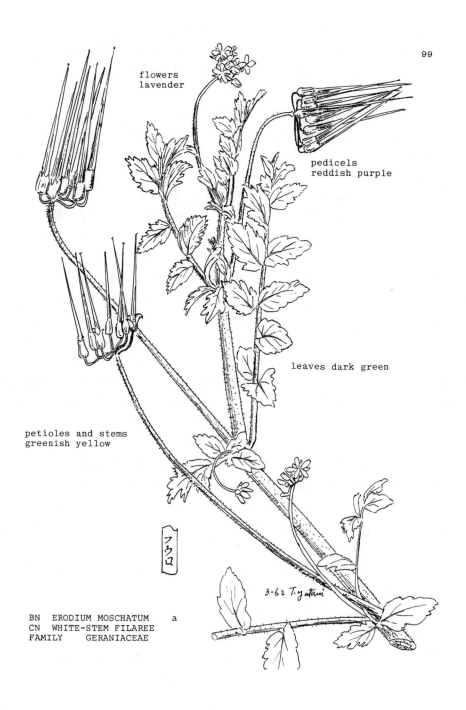

99

flowers
lavender

pedicels
reddish purple

leaves dark green

petioles and stems
greenish yellow

3-62 T.yutani

BN   ERODIUM MOSCHATUM   a
CN   WHITE-STEM FILAREE
FAMILY   GERANIACEAE

Broadleaf filaree, *Erodium botrys,* is seldom found in urban gardens, growing mostly in pasture lands and adjacent wild lands. It differs from the other two in having simple lobed leaves rather than compound pinnate, and much longer beaked fruits, typically 4 to 5 inches in length.

See illustration of broadleaf filaree on p. 72.

Clovers, Sweet Clovers, Bur Clovers

Trifolium repens—white clover—Fabaceae, Leguminosae, pea or bean family

Trifolium pratense—red clover, meadow clover

Trifolium hirtum—rose clover, hykon clover

Melilotus indica—yellow sweet clover—Fabaceae

Medicago lupulina—black medic—Fabaceae

Medicago polymorpha—bur clover

Medicago arabica—spotted bur clover, spotted medic

Medicago sativa—alfalfa

Lotus corniculatus—birdsfoot trefoil—Fabaceae

The seven legumes presented here are the most common clovers and cloverlike plants that grow in the green and golden hills, often planted there deliberately, and invade gardens elsewhere. All of these species are grown by ranchers and dairy farmers as forage, since they are highly nutritious and provide the added bonus of fixing nitrogen in the soil, thus increasing the nutrients available to grasses. When they establish themselves in other areas, they often become weeds.

White clover, *Trifolium repens*, also known as white Dutch clover, is perhaps the best known of this group, the plant known simply as clover to many, and the source of the elusive four-leaved clover. It is a perennial, with an extensive rhizomatous root system and above-ground stolons that root at the nodes. It produces petioled leaves with three leaflets (rarely, four), each about ¾ inch long, with small serrations and a slight depression at the tip. Leaves are bright green, with a whitish, chevron-shaped marking at the middle of each leaflet, a characteristic that distinguishes this clover from most others.

The flowers of white clover are about ⅜ inch long, white to pale pink, in globular clusters at the ends of long stems (6 inches or so). The clusters are about an inch across. Several flushes of bloom occur between April and December. The height of an unmowed patch of clover is about a foot.

In urban areas, clover is usually found in lawns, where it may or may not be regarded as a weed. Whenever it spreads beyond the lawn, it definitely becomes weedy, growing aggressively and forming solid mats. If it invades other ground covers, your choice is either to eradicate it or to allow it to become the prevailing ground cover—not such a bad option, in some cases. Once it shows up, you need to decide quickly—its extensive rhizomes make it nearly impossible to dig out once it has spread extensively, and any herbicide used will damage the ground cover the clover has invaded.

Clover was once considered a beneficial component of a lawn, since it fixes nitrogen, often does well in parts of the lawn where the grass struggles, and provides contrasting color and texture that, arguably, make the lawn more interesting and beautiful. The invention of "weed and feed" fertilizers after World War II, products that combined chemical fertilizers with preemergent and selective postemergent herbicides, gave the lawn industry a strong incentive to promote the notion that the only acceptable lawn was a closely mowed sward of fine-textured grass, preferably of a single type. Today, as more and more people seek to avoid, or at least moderate, the use of pesticides and chemical fertilizers, clover is once again becoming a respectable component of lawns, as are small, scattered quantities of other flowering broad-leaved plants such as dandelions and English daisies. "Meadow lawns," unmowed (or infrequently mowed) turf consisting of grasses such as hard fescue and an abundance of low-growing, flowering perennials (including bulbs), are becoming quite the thing in some gardening circles, and make a good deal of sense, since they require much less labor and water than a lawn that is mowed weekly. Meadow lawns reflect the medieval ideal of the lawn, the "flowery mede," which consisted mostly of grasses and weeds harvested as turf from meadows and cow pastures, but often incorporated larger flowering plants, such as lilies and roses.

White clover alone makes a perfectly lovely lawn, but after a while it will inevitably become as infested with grasses as grass lawns will with white clover. So—why fight it? Plant both from the start. About 10 percent (maybe less) white clover seed mixed with the grass seed will produce a stand of clover distributed fairly uniformly throughout the lawn, avoiding the clumpiness that often occurs when clover invades the lawn as a weed. If you mow such a lawn, leave the clippings—their nutrients, along with the nitrogen fixed in the soil by the clover, should eliminate the need for fertilizer.

Medicinally, a fluid extract of clover has been used as an alterative and antispasmodic, to suppress coughs and ease other bronchial ailments. It was also once applied as a poultice to cancerous growths. White clover attracts bees, a fact often cited by weed and feed sellers as a reason to keep it out of lawns where children may run barefoot (are these bees any more of a hazard than the chemicals in weed and feed?). Clover honey is regarded by many as particularly delectable.

Red clover, *Trifolium pratense* (also known as trefoil, purple clover, or meadow clover), a plant very similar to white clover, sometimes appears in lawns, although it is seldom planted, as it is shorter lived, albeit still perennial. It can be distinguished from white clover by its somewhat larger leaflets, which are pointed at the apex, and its reddish-purple and white flower clusters. Like white clover, red clover has whitish chevrons on the leaflets.

Trifolium repens and *T. pratense,* along with a smaller species, *T. dubium,* lesser trefoil, are three of the four species of clovers known in Ireland as shamrocks; they are widely grown there as pot plants for distribution on Saint Patrick's Day. (The fourth is black medic, *Medicago lupulina,* an annual). Many myths are associated with shamrocks, such as that they grow only in Ireland; the reality is that all four species are widely distributed throughout Europe and elsewhere and are often considered weeds. It is also claimed that shamrocks never flower. They became associated with Saint Patrick by eighteenth-century

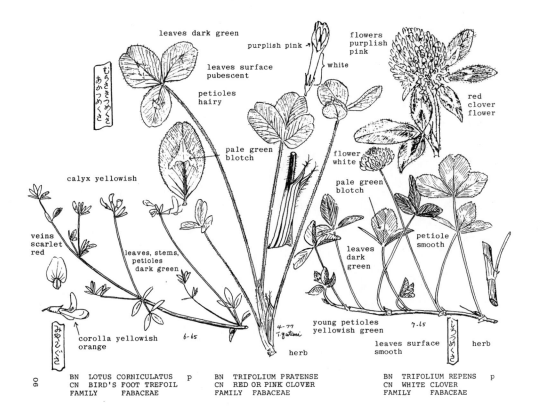

BN LOTUS CORNICULATUS   p
CN BIRD'S FOOT TREFOIL
FAMILY   FABACEAE

BN TRIFOLIUM PRATENSE
CN RED OR PINK CLOVER
FAMILY FABACEAE

BN TRIFOLIUM REPENS   p
CN WHITE CLOVER
FAMILY   FABACEAE

Irish churchmen, who liked to claim that he used shamrocks as a teaching aid to illustrate the concept of the Trinity. This is a plausible notion, but one not validated by the historical record. Shamrocks have a more ancient connection with Irish religion, however; the Druids venerated them, considering their occasional four-lobed leaves as a good-luck charm. Some of the shamrocks grown in Ireland are shipped here and sold on Saint Patrick's Day. The seeds of these weeds are sold through catalogs and to tourists in Ireland—for a hefty price. Most of the "shamrocks" sold by American nurseries are a type of oxalis.

Rose clover, or hykon clover, *Trifolium hirtum,* is an annual that is often seeded on lean, dry, hillside soil in cattle-raising areas, as well as along road shoulders. It forms an ascending or erect plant, as tall as 2 feet (usually less). Leaves are trifoliate, gray-green, and hairy, with a lighter chevron marking. Flowers are pink with white tips, in dense, global clusters. This can be a very attractive plant when it blooms in May and June, and there is no reason not to sow it in marginal areas as competition for less attractive weeds. In urban parts of the Bay Area, it generally confines itself to road shoulders and uncultivated areas in hill neighborhoods.

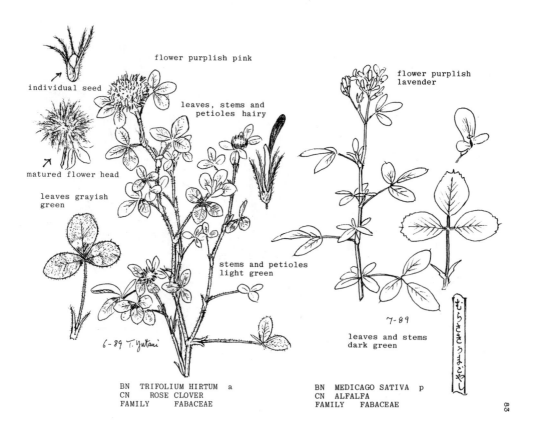

individual seed

flower purplish pink

leaves, stems and petioles hairy

flower purplish lavender

matured flower head

leaves grayish green

stems and petioles light green

6-89 T. Yutani

7-89

leaves and stems dark green

むらさきうまごやし

BN   TRIFOLIUM HIRTUM   a
CN   ROSE CLOVER
FAMILY   FABACEAE

BN   MEDICAGO SATIVA   p
CN   ALFALFA
FAMILY   FABACEAE

83

There are a number of annual cloverlike plants known as bur clover, or medic, that are sown for pasture and grow as weeds elsewhere; three of these inhabit the Bay Area. The most common is *Medicago polymorpha,* bur clover.

Bur clover is a sprawling, ground-hugging plant, sometimes somewhat upright, with stems about 1½ feet long (sometimes up to 2 feet) that grow from a deep central taproot. These bear trifoliate leaves that are hairless or nearly so, each leaflet notched at the end and minutely toothed. Leaflets are more or less an inch long, on somewhat longer petioles that have conspicuously toothed

82

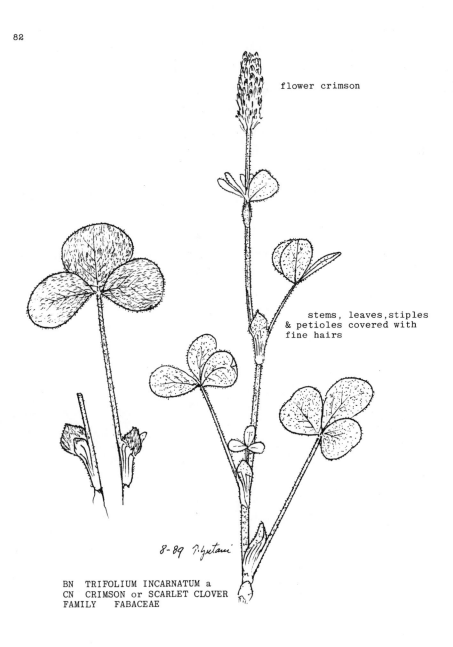

flower crimson

stems, leaves, stiples
& petioles covered with
fine hairs

8-89 T.Yutani

BN TRIFOLIUM INCARNATUM a
CN CRIMSON or SCARLET CLOVER
FAMILY FABACEAE

stipules at their bases—an important identifying characteristic. These leaves lack the chevron markings of many of the trifoliums. Tiny (about ³⁄₁₆ inch long) yellow flowers clustered at the ends of short stems develop in the leaf axils; these are the typical keel-and-wing legume flowers, with three to five per cluster. Flowers are followed by a bur-like fruit, coiled pods about ³⁄₁₆ inch in diameter or less, with double rows of prickles on their edges. They adhere readily to fur and clothing, aiding in their movement to new locations.

While bur clover does fix nitrogen, it can be a troublesome weed in lawns. Because it is annual, it dies in summer, leaving brown patches. It is best to pull it when it first appears; the stems can be gathered and grasped in one hand, allowing the taproot to be extracted with a slow, steady pull—a very satisfying weeding experience. Ignore it, and it will produce fruits all along its many stems, each of which will release a quantity of seeds. Allow these to germinate, and you will have a dense mass of seedlings, very tedious to remove, instead of a few widely scattered plants that can be yanked out easily.

Besides infesting lawns, bur clover thrives along roadsides, in garden beds, and in most other disturbed locations, sunny or shady. It does fine in poor, dry, even compacted, soils, due to its deep taproot and ability to fix nitrogen. It is native to Eurasia.

Spotted medic, or spotted bur clover, *Medicago arabica,* is nearly identical to bur clover, except for a reddish-brown spot on each leaflet. It produces the same sort of fringed stipules and burred fruits, and is just as problematic as a weed, although, arguably, somewhat more attractive.

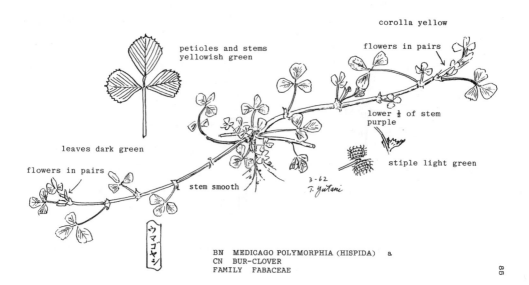

corolla yellow

petioles and stems
yellowish green

flowers in pairs

lower ½ of stem
purple

leaves dark green

flowers in pairs

stiple light green

stem smooth

3-62
T. Yutani

BN   MEDICAGO POLYMORPHIA (HISPIDA)   a
CN   BUR-CLOVER
FAMILY   FABACEAE

85

Black medic is less common than bur clover, and it is sometimes hard to tell them apart. The most important distinguishing characteristics are the leaves, which have a grayish cast and are covered with fine hairs (as are the stems), and have much smaller and less ragged stipules at the base of the petioles; and the flowers and fruits. Individual flowers are like those of bur clover, but even tinier; these grow in dense heads at the tips of 1- to 3-inch stalks, with many flowers per head. They are followed by clusters of small black fruits, which look like tiny balls or pebbles; upon closer examination, these turn out to be spiral pods, tiny versions of the bur clover fruit, but lacking bristles and with only one seed per pod. The plant produces lots of these, however, and can be as troublesome a weed as bur clover.

Alfalfa, *Medicago sativa,* a perennial grown for hay, sometimes escapes from fields and appears as a weed in various places. It is upright, growing to about 1½ to 2 feet tall, with clusters of blue flowers. Alfalfa is sometimes consumed by humans in the form of sprouts, but caution is in order here—along with other medics, it is known to contain the amino acid L-canavanine, which can cause abnormal blood cell counts, spleen enlargement, or recurrence of lupus in those who once had the disease under control. Seeds and sprouts contain more of this substance than leaves or roots. Bur clover and black medic have also been suspected of causing bloating in cattle when consumed in excessive quantities; nonetheless, they are still widely grown as forbs and are considered highly nutritious.

Medicago, or "medic," seems to indicate medicinal uses for this group of plants, but, in fact, does not. Green Deane, the proprietor of the website Eat the Weeds (www.eattheweeds.com), reports that the term comes through Latin from the ancient Greeks, who obtained alfalfa from the Medes, inhabitants of ancient Persia, and referred to it by a term that can be translated as "Median grass." Mrs. Grieve does not mention medic or bur clover at all. In the case of black medic, the specific epithet *lupulina,* Latin for "little wolf," seems to refer to the resemblance of the flower clusters to hops, or *Humulus lupulus*—the wolf reference in the hop vine's name probably refers to its habit of climbing on a tree known as the willow wolf in Germany. Deane neglects to explain the association of this tree with wolves.

Yellow sweet clover, *Melilotus indica,* is a cloverlike winter annual that is erect and branching, growing to a height of about 1½ to 3 feet from a sturdy taproot. Also known as yellow melilot, melilot trefoil, king's clover, plaster clover, sweet lucerne, wild laburnum, and hart's tree, this plant has a long history as a forage and medicinal plant throughout Europe. It is native to Europe and temperate Asia.

The leaves of yellow sweet clover are trifoliate, with wedge-shaped, oblance-olate or obovate leaflets that measure an inch or so, and are toothed. The pedicel of the central leaflet is slightly longer than the other two. The foliage has a sweet, new-mown-hay scent, which intensifies when it is dried. The flowers are tiny yellow pea flowers, on racemes that can be as long as 4 inches (usually less)—they produce an abundance of nectar, so melilot is highly regarded as a honey plant.

Yellow sweet clover is commonly planted as a forage or cover crop in California, and it frequently escapes and establishes itself as a weed along roadsides, on hillsides, and in fallow fields; it is also often seen in the city. Melilot likes full sun, tolerates dry soil, and often stays green and blooms throughout the summer. It can be a fairly pleasant weed in areas where weeds are tolerated.

Melilot has a long history of use as a medicinal herb. Gerard discusses it in great detail, and it was listed in the German Pharmacopoeia until fairly recently, if not still. It is aromatic, emollient, and carminative; it can be used in poultices to soothe abrasions and skin inflammations, as eye drops to improve

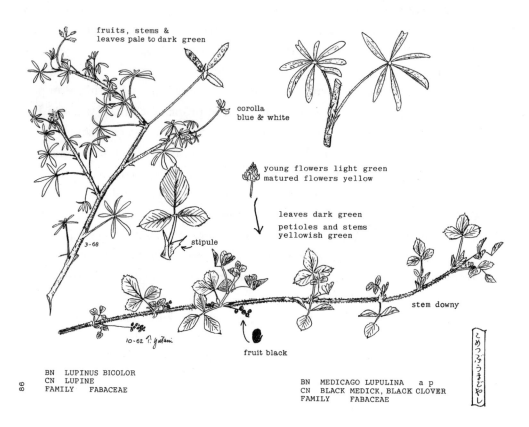

fruits, stems &
leaves pale to dark green

corolla
blue & white

young flowers light green
matured flowers yellow

leaves dark green
petioles and stems
yellowish green

stipule

3-68

10-62 T. Yutani

stem downy

fruit black

BN LUPINUS BICOLOR
CN LUPINE
FAMILY FABACEAE

86

BN MEDICAGO LUPULINA   a p
CN BLACK MEDICK, BLACK CLOVER
FAMILY   FABACEAE

blurry vision, for earaches and headaches, and as a digestive. The seventeenth-century herbalist Culpeper says that a distillate of this herb can be used for washing the head, in order to cure apoplexy and the loss of the senses. As a culinary herb, the leaves are mixed into a green Swiss cheese called *schabziger,* imparting nuances of new-mown hay to its flavor.

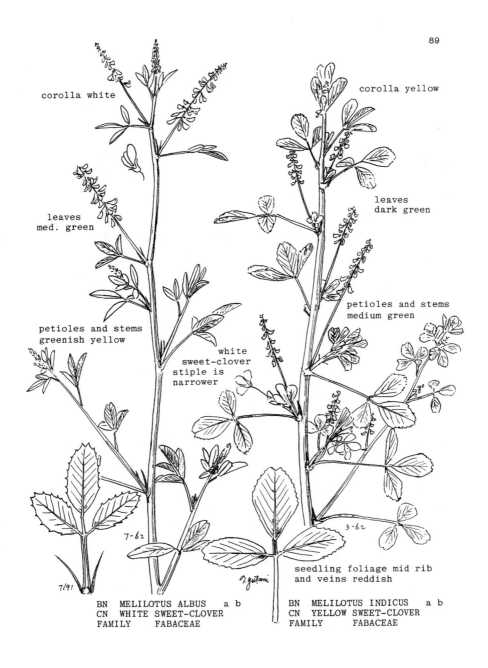

89

corolla white

corolla yellow

leaves
dark green

leaves
med. green

petioles and stems
medium green

petioles and stems
greenish yellow

white
sweet-clover
stiple is
narrower

seedling foliage mid rib
and veins reddish

7-62

3-62

7/91

BN   MELILOTUS ALBUS   a b
CN   WHITE SWEET-CLOVER
FAMILY   FABACEAE

BN   MELILOTUS INDICUS   a b
CN   YELLOW SWEET-CLOVER
FAMILY   FABACEAE

White melilot, *Melilotus albus,* very similar to yellow sweet clover, but larger (to 6 feet), with white flowers, and sometimes perennial, is also grown as a forage crop, and is commonly seen along rural roadsides; it seldom appears in urban areas. Another yellow sweet clover, *Melilotus officinalis,* is, as its name implies, the one most highly regarded for medicinal uses and most often listed in pharmacopeias; it is somewhat shorter than *M. indica* and has slightly larger flowers and ovate leaflets. It occasionally shows up as a weed.

A legume that somewhat resembles the bur clovers is *Lotus corniculatus,* birdsfoot trefoil, sometimes called bacon and eggs, or ground honeysuckle. This is a perennial plant with procumbent to ascending stems 5 to 12 inches long, growing from a long taproot. It often forms a dense mound. The leaves are bright green, smooth, trifoliate with narrowly ovate or obovate leaflets about ¼ to ½ inch long, subtended by two leaflet-like stipules. The pea flowers are about ½ inch long, bright yellow, the banner petals sometimes reddish, in three- to six-flowered umbels. It can be quite attractive in the right place in a garden; you may want to keep it long enough to see if it becomes too much of a pest.

Birdsfoot trefoil seed is often included in pasture mixes, as well as "wild-flower" mixes sown along roadsides. It tolerates drought and poor, rocky soils, and it can become quite lush and dense in gardens. There is a cultivated form, Pleniflorus, with double gold and copper flowers.

Birdsfoot trefoil is native to Europe and grows in America as an introduction or a weed; there are also a number of native members of the genus *Lotus* in California and other parts of the West. These are not often found in urban areas and are not at all invasive.

See illustration of birdsfoot trefoil on p. 90.

Vetch

Vicia sativa—common vetch, spring vetch—Fabaceae, Leguminosae, pea family

Vicia sativa ssp. *nigra*—narrow-leaved vetch

Vicia faba—fava bean, horse bean

Common vetch, *Vicia sativa,* the "tares" of the King James Bible, has long been a serious weed of grain fields, and still is in the Sacramento–San Joaquin Delta; it is not a significant pest elsewhere in rural California, and is highly regarded as a nutritious forage for cattle and sheep, and often planted as such. In urban areas, it can be a significant garden weed that often clambers over low ground cover and shrubs.

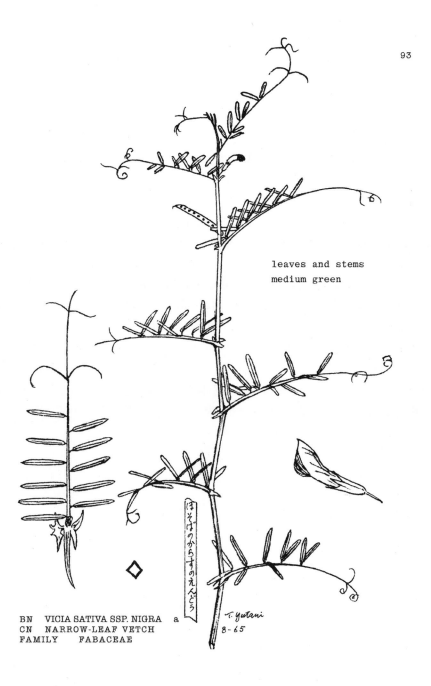

leaves and stems
medium green

BN   VICIA SATIVA SSP. NIGRA   a
CN   NARROW-LEAF VETCH
FAMILY   FABACEAE

T. Yutani
8-65

Vetch is a vining winter annual with sprawling, 2-foot stems that grow from a taproot. Its leaves are alternate and pinnately compound, with seven pairs of narrowly oval or obovate (wider at the tips than the bases), smooth-margined leaflets and a terminal tendril. Except for the tendril, these leaves could belong to any number of leguminous plants. Leaflets are an inch or less in length, the whole leaf 2 or 3 inches long.

Vetch flowers are inch-long keel-and-wing flowers typical of the pea family, short-stalked, growing singly or in pairs in the leaf axils. They are usually some shade of purple or magenta, although sometimes white. Some color variations can be quite beautiful, and gardeners often let them grow for a while in spring, pulling them out when the seed pods begin to form. These pods are typical legume fruits, like peas, about 1½ to 3 inches long, and hairy. The seeds have been reported as poisonous, but the plant is considered good cattle food by many ranchers.

Vetch can be found growing in all sorts of uncultivated ground, usually in sun, but sometimes in the shade. It has even been known to invade lawns.

Narrow-leaved vetch, *Vicia sativa* ssp. *nigra,* has smaller leaves and flowers than common vetch, with narrower leaflets. It is a little darker green, sometimes with a purplish cast. The flowers, too, are smaller, and mostly a particularly lovely shade of purple-magenta. This is definitely one weed worth tolerating, and even allowing to reseed (a little), if you can tolerate it at all.

The fava bean or horse bean, *Vicia faba,* is an upright vetch with rounded leaves that is grown in the winter as a cover or forage crop and is sometimes planted by gardeners as a cool-season vegetable. It occasionally escapes from plantings, but does not tend to be a serious weed. Like most legumes, it fixes nitrogen, as do the other vetches.

7

OTHER INVASIVE GRASSES AND GRASSLIKE PLANTS

CRABGRASS

Digitaria sanguinialis—hairy crabgrass—Poaceae, Gramineae, grass family

Digitaria ischaemum—smooth crabgrass

Crabgrass, the nemesis and sworn enemy of lawn purists throughout the world, is actually not very abundant in the urban Bay Area where I live. Where it does occur, it creeps through desirable lawn grasses and roots at the nodes on its prostrate stems, much like Bermuda grass, which is often misidentified as crabgrass. True crabgrass is a summer annual that grows especially well in the heat of late summer, so in cool-summer areas it does not have a marked competitive advantage over cool-season grasses. Still, it can be troublesome in any lawn where it does become established.

The most common crabgrass species is the hairy crabgrass. It germinates in late spring, from seed that has been dropped the previous season, and forms a clump of pale green leaves, 2 to 5 inches long unmowed, somewhat hairy on the surface of the blades and along the margins. Flower stems can grow to 3 feet. These are decumbent, spreading along the ground before they ascend. Where the nodes touch bare soil, they root.

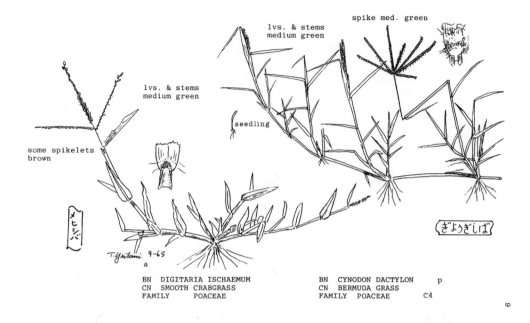

spike med. green

lvs. & stems
medium green

lvs. & stems
medium green

seedling

some spikelets
brown

メヒシバ

T. Yutami 9-65
a

(ぎょうぎしば)

BN DIGITARIA ISCHAEMUM   BN   CYNODON DACTYLON   p
CN SMOOTH CRABGRASS   CN   BERMUDA GRASS
FAMILY   POACEAE   FAMILY POACEAE   C4

At the ends of the flower stems, four to eight branches form; these bear the spikelets, tiny grains growing in pairs along one side of each branch. These inflorescences resemble those of Bermuda grass, adding to the confusion caused by the creeping habit of both plants. Crabgrass, however, is annual, dying out in the winter and leaving dead patches among the green cool-season grasses that we grow intentionally in lawns. Winter or early spring is a good time to address these dead areas, by cleaning them out and overseeding with desirable grasses that germinate well in the cool winter months; this should be done before late February, as crabgrass can begin germinating then in mild-winter climates. Alternatively, or in addition, short-term preemergent herbicides can be applied just before the crabgrass is expected to germinate. This is the approach usually taken by the larger commercial maintenance organizations, which often apply them in the form of "weed and feed" fertilizers, with a high level of nitrogen. They also contain postemergent herbicides selective for broad-leaved weeds, including clover, a beneficial addition to any lawn. I think that following cultural practices that favor the growth of desirable grasses and allow them to compete well with weeds is the best overall defense against crabgrass and other interlopers.

Smooth crabgrass is very similar to hairy crabgrass, but smaller, with smooth leaves. It is far less common and can be controlled by the same strategies used on the hairy crabgrass.

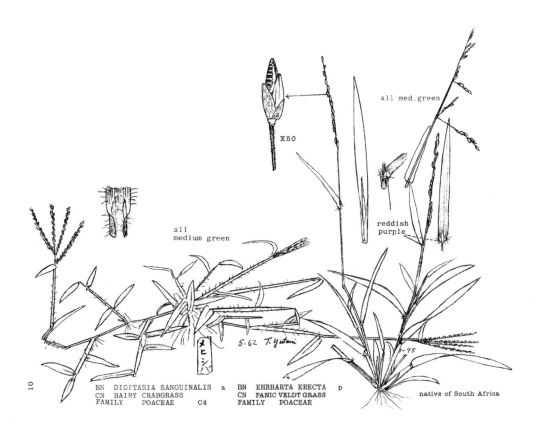

X50

all med.green

all
medium green

reddish
purple

5-62 T. Yutani

10

4-95

BN   DIGITARIA SANGUINALIS   a
CN   HAIRY CRABGRASS
FAMILY   POACEAE   C4

BN   EHRHARTA ERECTA   p
CN   PANIC VELDT GRASS
FAMILY   POACEAE

native of South Africa

In some places, especially in the southeastern United States, crabgrass is often planted as a late-season forage crop, or for hay, due to its abundant growth in late summer. It often escapes from these hay fields and colonizes roadsides, ditch banks, pastures and meadows, orchards and vineyards, vegetable gardens and truck farms. Although mostly a lawn weed in urban areas, it can easily escape and invade other parts of home gardens and public parks.

THAT! GRASS

Ehrharta erecta—panic veldt grass—Poaceae, Gramineae, grass family

I once cotaught a weeds class at Merritt College in Oakland with my late colleague, Jane Andrews, a former junior high school English teacher who later in her life had developed an enthusiasm for all things horticultural, including weeds. When she would try to describe panic veldt grass to students, she often had difficulty finding terms that provoked recognition. After a period of halting, shifting descriptions that were greeted with puzzled expressions, someone in the class would invariably shout out, "Oh! *That* grass!" That! grass is what I have called it ever since; the term is still in wide use around the Merritt College horticulture department. However, the more widely recognized names are panic veldt grass and ehrharta grass—so it would be best to use these any place other than Merritt.

The term *panic* in the name does not refer to the feeling that comes to an experienced gardener upon the first appearance of ehrharta grass in a planted area, although it might well; it refers to the tiny, round grains that develop on the flower panicles and resemble those of panic grass (genus *Panicum*). Veldt, of course, refers to its South African origin.

Panic veldt grass is a fairly recent introduction to California's weed flora. The 1970 edition of Robbins's *Weeds of California* (the last edition published, unfortunately) does not even list it, although other records indicate it has been in California since the 1930s. It is now hugely abundant, a fast-spreading and ubiquitous weed in gardens and wild areas. It has become a solid ground cover in many creek canyons, crowding out native vegetation. It will grow anywhere, but persists best as a perennial in moist, shaded areas. It will sometimes actually die in the summer when it establishes itself in hot, dry ground; but, since it sets prolific seed, it will inevitably return in the winter.

Ehrharta grass is a medium-sized clumping perennial with fibrous roots. Its leaves are an almost chartreuse green, 2 to 5 inches long, broad at the base and tapering to a sharp point. New seedlings appear as more or less rosettes; they can be recognized easily by their chartreuse color and by slightly wavy leaf margins—this waviness disappears as they mature. Panic veldt grass has no rhizomes, but can tiller, producing clumps of crowns.

Ehrharta flower stalks grow to about 10 to 18 inches, ending in a narrow panicle of tiny grains. Flowering continues throughout the season, and seed production is prodigious: when it grows in cracks in concrete, the pavement beneath the plants is sometimes literally covered with grains.

Even though panic veldt grass should be on every conscientious gardener's A-list of weeds that must be relentlessly suppressed, some of its characteristics can actually be regarded as virtues. A. S. Hitchcock, in his *Manual of the Grasses of the United States,* opines somewhat naively that it "shows considerable (competitive) ability, and may become of value in replacing some of the troublesome weeds." I have observed that it is often the only plant that will grow in the most deeply shaded areas of some lawns; one might grudgingly accept it there as an alternative preferable to dry ground, assuming it can be contained, probably a rash assumption. It would be nice if plant breeders could do something with it—make it deeper green and less clumping, and lower its capacity to set so much seed, but still retain the qualities that make it one of the toughest and most shade-tolerant of grasses.

See illustration of panic veldt grass on p. 191.

TALL FESCUE, FINE FESCUE

Festuca arundinacea—tall fescue—Poaceae, Gramineae, grass family

Festuca rubra—fine fescue, creeping red fescue

Tall fescue is a large, robust perennial grass that has become a serious ecological weed in the Great Plains states, where it crowds out native and other grasses favored as forage, while itself providing very little nutrition to grazing animals. It is sometimes used for turf areas that need to withstand a lot of foot traffic with minimal maintenance, such as school playing fields, but its broad leaves and clumping habit make it less desirable for ornamental lawns or professional-quality sports turf. When it occurs in lawns, it stands out from the finer-bladed grasses and is usually regarded as a weed.

A breeding revolution that occurred in the later twentieth century, however, changed the status of tall fescue as a turf grass. Forms were developed that not only had narrower blades, but tillered more freely, enabling them to grow as less clumpy, more continuous turf. These were more disease resistant and drought tolerant than other cool-season turf grasses, and heat resistant enough to be grown in some areas, such as Southern California, where previously only warm-season grasses such as Bermuda could be used for turf. Turf-type tall fescues are now the predominant lawn grasses in California and many other parts of the United States. There are even dwarf varieties.

I think it is safe to say that most of the tall fescue that occurs as a weed in urban areas escaped from fescue lawns that had gone to seed, a common occurrence during rainy springs when mowing sometimes has to be delayed for several weeks. The seedlings produce plants up to 4 feet tall (in bloom; about a foot shorter without the flowers), with dark green, stiff, flat, glossy, narrow leaves that are conspicuously ribbed on the upper surface. The inflorescence is a spreading panicle, 4 to 12 inches long, which can be erect or nodding. The spikelets are short and fairly wide, consisting of three to ten flowers, awn-less or with minute awns. Roots are tough and fibrous, difficult to extract from the ground even when the plants are small.

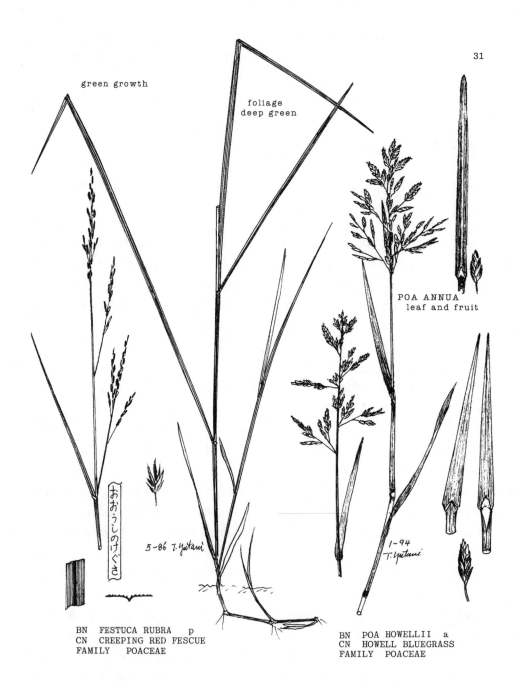

green growth

foliage
deep green

POA ANNUA
leaf and fruit

おおうしのけぐさ

5-86 T. Yutani

1-94
T. Yutani

BN   FESTUCA RUBRA   p
CN   CREEPING RED FESCUE
FAMILY   POACEAE

BN   POA HOWELLII   a
CN   HOWELL BLUEGRASS
FAMILY   POACEAE

The first generation of seedlings to escape the lawn usually has leaves as narrow as its parents; as time goes by, however, it tends to revert to the more typically wide-bladed wild type. When these seed themselves into lawns, they again become a weed, all too easy to distinguish from the highly selected turf fescues from which they may have originated.

Fine fescues, very narrow-bladed grasses originating mostly from *Festuca rubra,* are grown for turf in shady areas. These can also withstand considerable sun, and are more drought resistant than the turf-type tall fescues, so have recently become popular for unmowed or seldom-mowed turf, or, combined with bulbs and low-growing perennials, as the predominant vegetation in meadow gardens. When these escape from lawns, they can become problematic weeds in other parts of the garden.

Other fescues are used in ornamental borders and mixed plantings, most commonly the low blue-green, clumping varieties of *F. rubra,* creeping red fescue, and some other species of fescue, as well as the more bluish forms of *F. californica,* a taller native grass that is often found in the wild growing in the shade of oaks and other foothill woodland plants. California fescue grown in landscape plantings is quite capable of producing abundant seedlings, tenaciously rooted and difficult to dig out.

See illustration of tall fescue on p. 170.

RABBIT'S FOOT GRASS

Polypogon monspeliensis—rabbit's foot grass, beard grass—Poaceae, Gramineae, grass family

Rabbit's foot grass is a winter annual that occurs mostly in very moist to wet ground, in meadows, pastures, irrigation ditches, or seasonally swampy or over-irrigated crop lands. In urban areas, it is most often found in low-lying lawns and street gutters. It is native to Europe—probably southern Europe, as its specific epithet indicates (*monspeliensis* is Latin for "at Montpelier," a city in southern France). Rabbit's foot grass has smooth leaves, 2 to 8 inches long, growing from stems that are often bent sharply at the lower joints.

The inflorescence of rabbit's foot grass makes it very easy to distinguish from other grasses. It is a short, dense, spikelike panicle, 1 to 3 inches long, consisting of densely packed spikelets with straight, slender awns growing from the glumes; these are very soft to the touch and give the spike its rabbit foot–like look and feel. When young, these spikes are green; mature, they have a buff or amber color.

As an impurity in hay, rabbit's foot grass can reduce its value on the market; as an urban weed, it can be very pleasant in appearance and to the touch, and it is not much of a threat except in overwatered areas, where its presence can be regarded as a call to action.

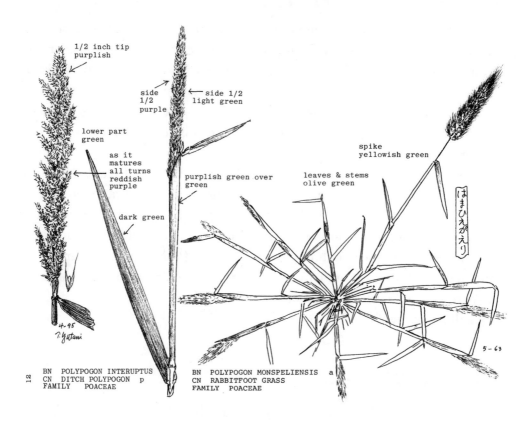

1/2 inch tip
purplish

side
1/2
purple

side 1/2
light green

lower part
green

as it
matures
all turns
reddish
purple

purplish green over
green

leaves & stems
olive green

spike
yellowish green

dark green

4-95
T.Yatani

5-63

BN POLYPOGON INTERUPTUS
CN DITCH POLYPOGON p
FAMILY POACEAE

BN POLYPOGON MONSPELIENSIS a
CN RABBITFOOT GRASS
FAMILY POACEAE

はまびえがえり

12

ORCHARD GRASS

Dactylis glomerata—orchard grass, cocksfoot—Poaceae, Gramineae, grass family

Orchard grass is widely grown as a pasture grass and a cover crop in orchards; like many other pasture grasses and forbs, it frequently escapes to colonize roadsides, farm fields, meadows, woodland edges, and other disturbed habitats. It is not particularly common in urban areas, but occurs frequently enough that it is worth learning to recognize.

A perennial that forms tufted clumps with sturdy fibrous roots, orchard grass can be difficult to eradicate once established, especially in lawns, where it is not unknown. In marginal areas, there may be no need to control it, since it is more attractive than many other weeds and gives them some competition.

Cocksfoot can be recognized easily by its inflorescence, a panicle consisting of clusters of short-awned, densely packed spikelets atop a culm 2 to 4 feet tall. When young, all the clusters closely adhere to one another, appearing as a single spike; as the panicle matures, the lowest cluster separates from the rest, standing out like a thumb, or the spur on a rooster's foot—hence, cocksfoot, the common name for this grass in England. The other panicles then commence to separate from the initial clump, forming discrete clusters at the ends of short branches off the main stem.

The leaves of orchard grass have a somewhat rough surface and are ⅛ to ½ inch wide.

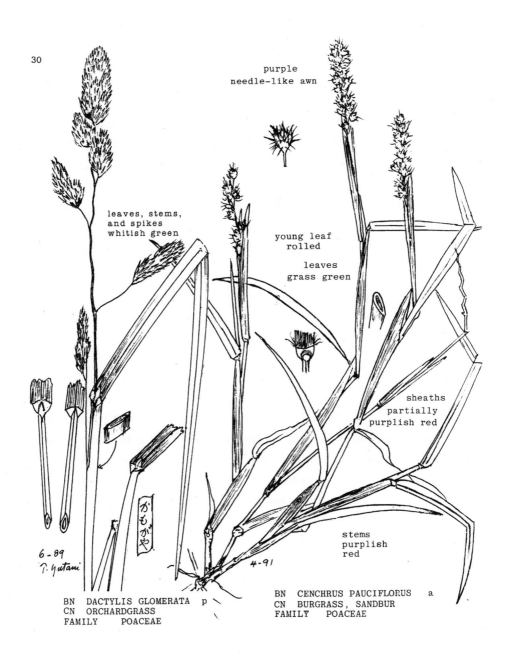

30

purple
needle-like awn

leaves, stems,
and spikes
whitish green

young leaf
rolled

leaves
grass green

sheaths
partially
purplish red

stems
purplish
red

6-89
T. Yutani

4-91

BN   DACTYLIS GLOMERATA   p
CN   ORCHARDGRASS
FAMILY   POACEAE

BN   CENCHRUS PAUCIFLORUS   a
CN   BURGRASS, SANDBUR
FAMILY   POACEAE

This grass likes full sun and is not particular about soil. It does better in ground that retains some moisture throughout the summer.

A variegated form of cockscomb with white margins, dubbed Variegata by horticulturists, is sometimes cultivated in landscape borders.

SMILO GRASS

Stipa miliacea—smilo grass, San Diego grass—Poaceae, Gramineae, grass family

Smilo is a stout perennial Mediterranean grass that is sometimes grown for pasture. Once rare or unknown in the Bay Area, it is becoming increasingly common. It is a large, clumping grass, growing 2 to 5 feet high, with shiny, light green foliage. Leaf blades are narrow, about ¼ to ⅓ inch wide. The spikelets are round, tiny, with short awns, growing in loose panicles 4 to 12 inches long. Smilo, with its delicate, airy panicles and foliage, is a very attractive plant, which would look good in gardens and containers. Many of our horticultural grasses have a tendency to self-sow freely, and this one may not be any more invasive than a number of others we accept as garden plants; however, its spread as a weed has been slowly but steadily increasing in recent years.

SUBTROPICAL GRASSES

Cynodon dactylon—Bermuda grass—Poaceae, Gramineae, grass family

Pennisetum clandestinum—Kikuyu grass—Poaceae

Paspalum dilatatum—dallis grass—Poaceae

The relatively mild winters of lowland and coastal California and the Pacific Northwest permit the cultivation of many plants native to parts of the world closer to the equator; this includes some grasses used in lawns, others grown for pasture. They tend to be perennial and to spread through aggressive rhizome and stolon growth, and so travel easily well beyond their intended boundaries, becoming ecological as well as garden weeds. Two of the most aggressive lawn grasses are Bermuda grass, *Cynodon dactylon,* and Kikuyu grass, *Pennisetum clandestinum.*

Bermuda grass, sometimes called devil grass, even crabgrass, is not native to Bermuda—it was simply established there for some time before it entered the United States. Its original home is the savannahs of East Africa, but it has

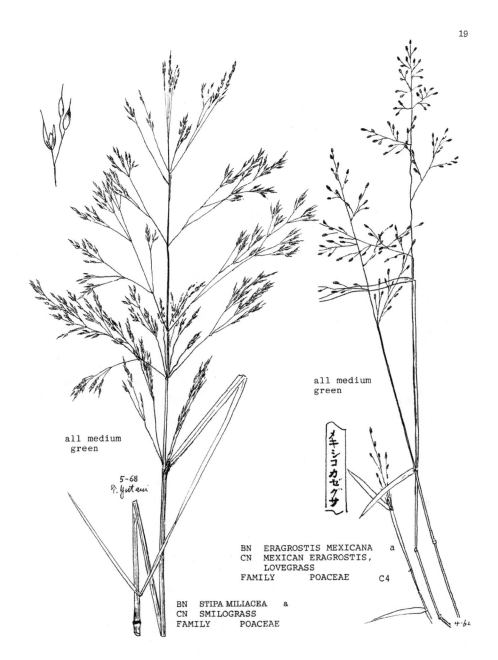

all medium
green

all medium
green

5-68
F. yutani

BN   ERAGROSTIS MEXICANA   a
CN   MEXICAN ERAGROSTIS,
      LOVEGRASS
FAMILY   POACEAE   C4

BN   STIPA MILIACEA   a
CN   SMILOGRASS
FAMILY   POACEAE

naturalized in warmer, drier areas all over the world (including the Arabian Peninsula), from about 45 degrees north latitude to 45 south. It has been grown as a pasture grass in the southeastern United States and was adopted there and in the warmer parts of the West as a turf grass, since it performs much better in the hot summers of these regions than do the cool-season lawn grasses such as bluegrass (since the introduction of Bermuda grass, the Mason-Dixon Line has sometimes been referred to as the Bluegrass Line). Since the development of the turf-type tall fescue lawn grasses, which perform well in hotter- and cooler-summer areas, Bermuda grass has come to be regarded increasingly as a weed in turf as well as elsewhere.

Bermuda grass creeps and forms mats, spreading by both stolons and rhizomes. The stolons are thin and wiry, and they grow roots wherever a node touches the ground. The leaves are less than an inch long, ⅛ inch wide, smooth or slightly hairy, green with a slightly grayish cast. The inflorescence forms atop a culm that is sometimes jointed, and produces leaves at the nodes that are 1 to 4 inches long. The culms are 4 to 18 inches high and form clusters of four or five shorter, upward-angling branches at their tips. These branches produce two alternate rows of small, flattened spikelets along one side—just like crabgrass.

Although it blends well visually with cool-season lawn grasses, Bermuda grass's tendency to turn brown in winter is objectionable to many lawn owners. There are two traditional ways to address this problem: use a green dye on the brown lawn, which seldom looks natural; or overseed with annual ryegrass, which turns brown in summer, and for a time is not completely hidden by the regreening Bermuda grass. I think a better idea is to overseed Bermuda lawns with perennial ryegrass or other perennial cool-season turf grasses, and let them establish their own territorial and seasonal balance.

Even where Bermuda grass is considered a desirable turf component, it creates a weed problem by readily spreading beyond the boundaries of the lawn, both by vegetative growth and from seed (the seed can remain viable for many years). Frequent mowing will minimize seed production, but can also form new colonies, since any piece of stolon with a node is capable of producing a new plant (Bermuda grass lawns are usually established by sowing stolon pieces, not seed). There are herbicides, such as DSMA and MSMA, that are selective for warm-season grasses and can be used to control infestations in cool-season turf or broad-leaved ground covers; but these are, unfortunately, arsenic based. This plant has become resistant to a number of other herbicides, and mechanical control is difficult and labor intensive. Robbins points out that Bermuda grass does not do well in dense shade, which suggests the use of smother crops for control.

Devil grass has been used for erosion control along stream and canal banks in the Central and Imperial Valleys of California and so has become a major crop weed in these regions. Although extremely drought tolerant, it does just fine in wet ground and tolerates high salt levels. According to Robbins, Bermuda grass that had been immersed in salt water for over two years when the Salton Sea rose resprouted and flourished when the water finally subsided.

Bermuda grass has been used medicinally in India for centuries: as a diuretic, as a pain killer for ailments such as toothache, and as a treatment for dysentery. Hindus regard it as sacred to Ganesha. Recent studies in India have indicated serum glucose–lowering and antidiabetic effects, as well as antimicrobial and antiviral properties. The only reference I have found to it in European herbal texts is by Pliny, who reports its use as a diuretic by the Romans. In South Africa, it has been used to give acidity to indigenous beers.

See illustration of Bermuda grass on p. 190.

Kikuyu grass, *Pennisetum clandestinum,* is another warm-season grass that spreads by stolons and rhizomes. Also native to East Africa, it is sometimes confused with Bermuda grass, but there are significant differences. The leaves of Kikuyu grass are longer and wider than those of Bermuda grass, and bright green rather than gray-green. The stolons are much thicker, less wiry, and somewhat flattened. In contrast to Bermuda grass's long-stemmed inflorescences, Kikuyu grass has inconspicuous flowers that are hidden in the leaf nodes. Like Bermuda, Kikuyu grass makes a dense, drought-tolerant turf that is nearly impenetrable to weeds; like Bermuda, Kikuyu readily travels well beyond the boundaries intended for it and can infest cool-season lawns by starting from pieces of rhizome deposited by lawn mowers.

In Africa, Kikuyu grass grows at higher elevations than Bermuda, so it is better adapted to cooler climates. This gives it an advantage over Bermuda

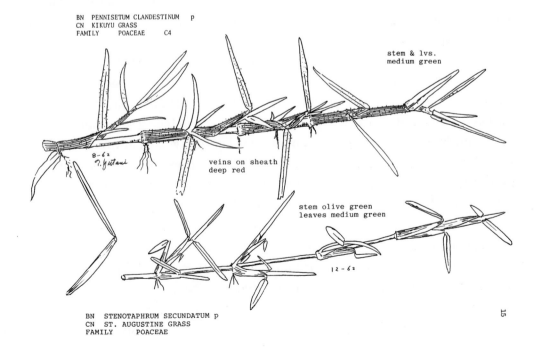

BN PENNISETUM CLANDESTINUM p
CN KIKUYU GRASS
FAMILY POACEAE C4

stem & lvs.
medium green

veins on sheath
deep red

stem olive green
leaves medium green

BN STENOTAPHRUM SECUNDATUM p
CN ST. AUGUSTINE GRASS
FAMILY POACEAE

grass in the cool coastal areas of California, where it does not turn nearly as brown in winter as the latter; it also makes it a more aggressive weed in these locations. Growing outside of lawns, Kikuyu can form thickets of billowy stems and leaves 2 feet high or higher; it especially loves to invade sand dunes.

Even so, Kikuyu grass is often the turf grass of choice in large parks, where its toughness and drought tolerance provide an acceptable offset to the extra labor required to keep it from spreading. Extra mowing labor is often needed as well: because of its thick stolons, which can build up in layers, it becomes very deep and dense after several years, often capable of stopping power mowers in their tracks; so this mat has to be reduced with a special mower known as a verticutter, which leaves nothing but a mass of brown stubble behind once the masses of mowed stems are raked up; this stubble, however, produces fresh, dense, green grass in a matter of weeks.

Eradicating large infestations of Kikuyu is a formidable task, as all the rhizomes and stolons must be either physically removed or killed with herbicides. Even translocated herbicides sometimes leave small parts of an extensive system of rhizomes intact, so follow-up inspections and applications are needed. Vigilance in spotting regrowth is extremely important.

Dallis grass is a robust perennial, a South American native that has been widely planted as a pasture grass in the warmer parts of the country. It often escapes and becomes a weed of roadsides, stream and ditch banks, and lawns. In the Bay Area, it is a widespread lawn weed, forming clumps of broad-bladed, dark green leaves that contrast annoyingly with the lighter-colored, finer-textured lawn grasses.

Dallis grass spreads by rhizomes, which are thick and knobby, often having the appearance of segmented insect bodies. Unmowed, this grass has leaves on stems that can grow 1½ to 2 feet high in open ground; in mowed lawns, crowns form at ground level. The leaves are dark green, pointed, sessile, and smooth, 2 to 6 inches long. Flower stems often develop in lawns that are not mowed weekly, and produce spikelets that dangle in pairs from the side branches that grow alternately along the tops of the culms. The flower stems tend to resist being mowed, guaranteeing a generous supply of seed that can be spread (often by the mowers) into virgin areas of the lawn. These spikelets are one flowered, ovate, and hairy.

The antidote for a lawn that is marred or dominated by dallis grass is early recognition and quick action. Nonselective herbicides work, as long as you don't mind browning out some of the adjacent lawn grasses. Even so, some of the rhizomes may survive. Thorough digging of all the rhizomes when the clump is small is the best strategy. In lawns where limited availability of labor precludes this, the best strategy is to watch vigilantly for new clumps at the edges of infestations and to go after these.

A lawn of solid dallis grass would still function as a lawn, and it would be drought tolerant to boot; but this grass is pretty much outside the boundaries of most people's idea of what is acceptable in a lawn.

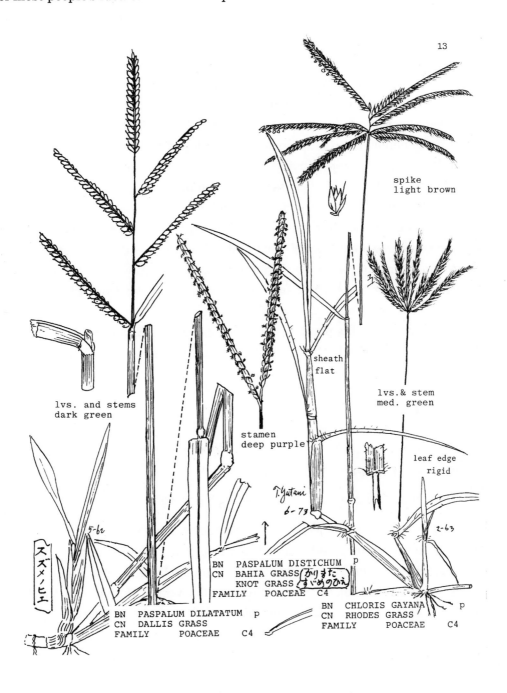

13

spike
light brown

sheath
flat

lvs. & stem
med. green

lvs. and stems
dark green

stamen
deep purple

leaf edge
rigid

T. Yutani
6-73

5-62

2-63

スズメノヒエ

BN   PASPALUM DISTICHUM   p
CN   BAHIA GRASS かりまた
      KNOT GRASS すじめのひえ
FAMILY   POACEAE   C4

BN   PASPALUM DILATATUM   p
CN   DALLIS GRASS
FAMILY   POACEAE   C4

BN   CHLORIS GAYANA   p
CN   RHODES GRASS
FAMILY   POACEAE   C4

QUAKING GRASS

Briza maxima, B. minor—quaking grass—Poaceae, Gramineae, grass family

The quaking grasses, *Briza maxima* and *B. minor,* also known as rattlesnake grass, are two small, pretty winter annual grasses that are sometimes included in wildflower mixes. When these are sown along roadsides, they often establish themselves in adjoining grasslands.

The most notable feature of these species is their flower spikelets, which are broad, flattened, more or less heart shaped, without awns. These chunky little appendages are grouped into panicles and dangle from threadlike pedicels, which enables them to quiver with a rustling sound in the slightest breeze; hence, the common name rattlesnake grass. When dry, the light-colored, vibrating spikelets shimmer, producing a very pleasant effect. Although they are officially weeds, the quaking grasses are much tolerated, even planted as components of "wildflower" or erosion control mixes.

The main difference in the two species is the size of the spikelets. Those of *Briza maxima* are about ½ inch long and not quite as wide; those of *B. minor* about ⅛ inch long and wide. The larger quaking grass grows 1 to 2 feet tall and has leaves as long as 6 inches; small quaking grass grows from 4 to 16 inches tall, with leaves no longer than 4 inches.

A third species of this plant, *Briza media,* resembles *B. maxima* but is perennial. This is, perhaps, a better choice for use in gardens.

WILD ONIONS

Allium triquetrum—wild onion—Alliaceae, onion family

Allium neapolitanum—Neapolitan onion

Nothoscordum inodorum—false garlic—Alliaceae

Onions, garlic, chives, and leeks, as well as the various "wild onions" that grow in woods and meadows and are sometimes planted as ornamentals, used to be classified as members of either the lily family (Liliaceae) or the amaryllis family (Amaryllidaceae), but were split out into a family of their own, the Alliaceae, when a massive revision of the enormous lily family and the closely allied Amaryllidaceae was completed in the late 1990s. These plants are monocots, with long, narrow, entire leaves, and flowers in clusters atop a stalk known as a scape. Many have long histories as cultivated plants, grown for culinary, medicinal, and ornamental purposes. Some are weeds.

Allium triquetrum, the wild onion (it could be called the three-cornered onion), is a Mediterranean allium that spreads aggressively in urban gardens and open spaces, especially in moist locations. Growing from a bulb, it forms a plant about a foot tall, consisting of upright, linear leaves about ⅜ inch wide, with a prominent midrib; the lower portions of these leaves are somewhat triangular in cross section. The flower scape, a little taller than the leaves, is also three-sided, and it is capped by an umbel of drooping, pure white, bell-shaped flowers with green markings. Leaves and bulbs are onion scented, with some garlicky overtones. They can be eaten, if you find them palatable.

These wild onions are very attractive when they first appear in the garden, and you might be tempted to leave them—do not succumb to this temptation. Growing from bulbs, these weedy onions are perennial—and the bulbs produce many offsets. The flowers engender oval, three-lobed seed capsules, which release multitudes of black, wrinkled, readily germinating seeds. Once *Allium triquetrum* has entered a garden, it will most likely always be there; if it is not dealt with quickly and firmly, it will take over. Intervening early and often will keep it to a manageable level. A translocated herbicide such as Roundup can be helpful in reducing severe infestations, but it will not control the offsets— patient, persistent digging is always required.

The Neapolitan onion is an attractive allium that is often planted as an ornamental but tends to spread freely and move from garden to garden. It is not nearly the menace *Allium triquetrum* is, and it is worth learning to distinguish it from the three-cornered onion. Neapolitan onion is a taller, more graceful plant, with a long, sometimes slightly curving flower stem, round in profile. The individual flowers that form the umbel are open, on longer pedicels, and face upward. These mix very nicely with blue flowering plants that bloom at about the same time (mid-March on the California coast), such as Spanish bluebells *(Endymion hispanicum)* and pride of Madeira *(Echium fastuosum).* Both these plants can also spread quite freely.

Perhaps the most menacing wild onion is false garlic, a plant with narrower and darker green leaves than *A. triquetrum* and *A. neapolitanum,* no fragrance, and clusters of dull white flowers with greenish bases and reddish ribs on the outsides of the petals. These blooms are fairly small and generally brownish in appearance. This plant spreads just as aggressively as *A. triquetrum* but has none of its virtues. In the Bay Area, it is believed to have originated as an escapee from the UC Botanical Garden at Berkeley; it has also appeared in

Marin and Fresno Counties and in Southern California, perhaps moved from Berkeley in plant and seed exchanges.

Some of the alliums grown as ornamentals also have a potential to become weeds. The late Wayne Roderick, former head of the Regional Parks Botanic Garden in Tilden Regional Park in Berkeley, reported that *Allium unifolium* and *A. hyalinum,* both California natives, had become pests in his garden. Bulbous

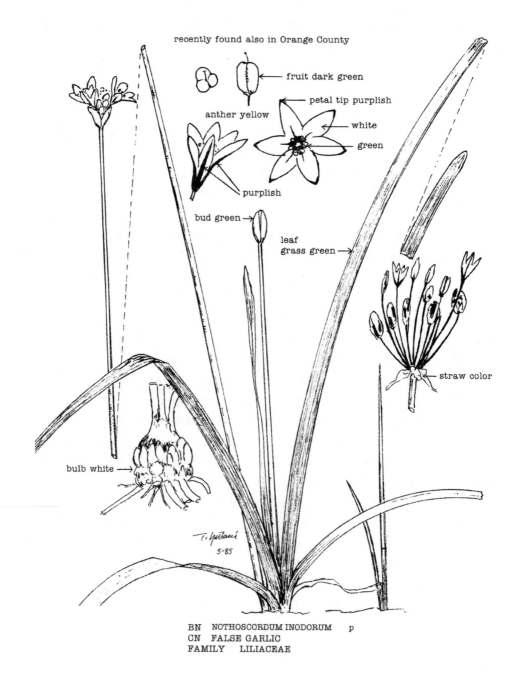

recently found also in Orange County

fruit dark green

petal tip purplish

anther yellow

white

green

purplish

bud green

leaf grass green

straw color

bulb white

T. Yutani
5-85

BN   NOTHOSCORDUM INODORUM   p
CN   FALSE GARLIC
FAMILY   LILIACEAE

plants in general need to be watched—they are supremely well adapted to the long dry season of the West Coast, and they have a tendency to produce offsets.

The common cultivated onion, *Allium cepa,* and its cousin, garlic, *A. sativum,* have been used since ancient times in Europe to flavor soups, stews, and bland porridges, and for a number of medicinal purposes. Onion and garlic are both regarded as effective antiseptics and antibiotics. Onion has also been used as a diuretic, and as a cough and cold medication. Roasted onions have been applied to the body to cure earaches and shrink tumors, and macerated onion soaked in gin has been administered as a cure for gravel and dropsy.

8

OTHER BROAD-LEAVED WEEDS

BRASS BUTTONS

Cotula australis—Australian or southern brass buttons—Asteraceae, Compositae, aster family

Cotula coronopifolia—common brass buttons

Australian brass buttons is a small, delicate winter annual that forms mounds 2 to 5 inches high and wide. It likes moist, cool conditions, so it is most abundant during the winter months. It is very much at home in concrete cracks, as well as in compacted soil, where it sometimes forms a continuous, not unattractive ground cover.

The leaves of this plant are simple, 1 to 1½ inches long, and very finely divided into filament-like lobes (*pinnate/pinnatifid* is the technical term). The flower heads are about ⅛ inch across, composed entirely of tiny, closely set disk flowers, very pale yellow in a brownish receptacle. Roots are fibrous. Southern brass buttons sometimes invades bare areas of lawns, but provides no significant competition to vigorous, healthy grass. It will grow in sun or shade.

Less common in urban areas than Australian brass buttons is common brass buttons, *Cotula coronopifolia,* a larger perennial that grows in wet, swampy areas, including salt marshes. It can invade lawns that are overwatered or poorly drained. This plant has somewhat succulent leaves that grow alternately on stems about a foot long that sprawl over the ground. The shape of the leaves is quite variable: they can be linear, lanceolate, or oblong; the edges are entire, or coarsely toothed, or deeply lobed. The flower heads are round, a compact cluster of disk flowers about ¼ inch across, on long stalks. Their color is a bright yellow—gold, the color of a metal brass button. They can bloom throughout the year in mild climates.

Brass buttons is native to South Africa and was possibly introduced elsewhere as an ornamental. The California Invasive Plant Council (Cal-IPC) rates it as a "limited" threat to native wetlands. It grows in a number of states other than California: Oregon, Arizona, Utah, New Mexico, and Texas in the West; on the East Coast it is found in Florida, North Carolina, and Maine.

A few other species of cotula are sold in the nursery trade as ornamentals. So far, these do not seem to be invasive.

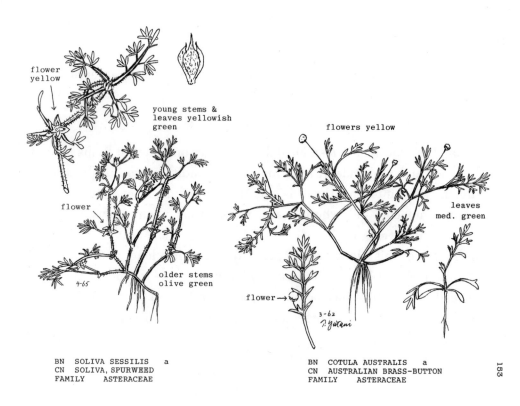

flower yellow

young stems & leaves yellowish green

flower

older stems olive green

4-65

flowers yellow

leaves med. green

flower →

3-62

P. Yutani

BN SOLIVA SESSILIS   a
CN SOLIVA, SPURWEED
FAMILY   ASTERACEAE

BN COTULA AUSTRALIS   a
CN AUSTRALIAN BRASS-BUTTON
FAMILY   ASTERACEAE

153

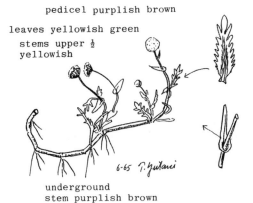

ray yellowish orange
disk sandy yellow

flower no rays
disk yellow

pedicel purplish brown

leaves yellowish green
stems upper ½
yellowish

leaves
& stems
yellowish
green

6-65 T. Yutani

underground
stem purplish brown

BN   COTULA CORONOPIFOLIA p
CN   AUSTRALIAN BRASS BUTTONS
FAMILY   ASTERACEAE

BN   BAERIA CALIFORNICA   a
CN   GOLD FIELDS
FAMILY   ASTERACEAE

FLEABANES

Conyza bonariensis—flax-leaved fleabane—Asteraceae, Compositae, aster family

Conyza canadensis—horseweed, Canadian fleabane

Flax-leaved fleabane, also known as asthma weed, hairy horseweed, wavy-leaf fleabane, and hairy fleabane, is a South American native that is widely distributed in the warmer regions of the United States. In California, it is found mostly in the coastal counties from San Francisco Bay to the Mexican border. Worldwide, it grows in most tropical and subtropical regions, and has even become a not-too-common weed in southern England.

Conyza bonariensis is an annual or biennial herbaceous plant, from 1 to 3 feet tall, erect and often much branched. The leaves are 1 to 3 inches long, linear to lanceolate, grayish-green and hairy, entire to lobed. Rosette leaves usually have three sharp-pointed lobes at their tips.

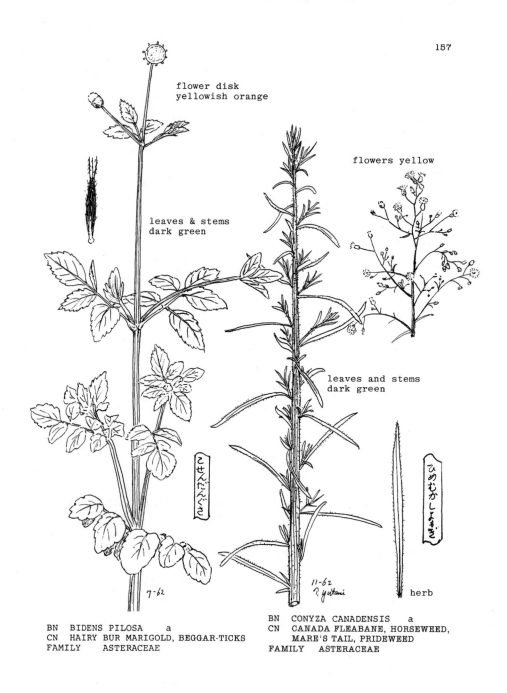

flower disk
yellowish orange

flowers yellow

leaves & stems
dark green

leaves and stems
dark green

こせんだんぐさ

ひめむかしよもぎ

7-62

11-62
P. yutani

herb

BN   BIDENS PILOSA   a
CN   HAIRY BUR MARIGOLD, BEGGAR-TICKS
FAMILY   ASTERACEAE

BN   CONYZA CANADENSIS   a
CN   CANADA FLEABANE, HORSEWEED,
     MARE'S TAIL, PRIDEWEED
FAMILY   ASTERACEAE

Flax-leaved fleabane germinates in spring, at first forming a rosette, but quickly assuming an upright, branching habit. Flowering takes place throughout the summer, when clusters of greenish-yellow inflorescences form at the tips of the branches. These consist of yellow disk flowers enclosed by purple-tipped bracts. They open fully when the fruits have developed, revealing clusters of achenes with pappi that present the same whitish or light tan puffball appearance as the mature flower heads of dandelions or groundsel.

A close cousin of the flax-leaved fleabane, which sometimes grows along with it in mixed stands, is *Conyza canadensis,* commonly known as horseweed. It is very similar to flax-leaved fleabane but is a taller, greener, less hairy plant that forms a very large, dense flower head at the tips of the branches. It is native to most of North and Central America.

In urban gardens, these weeds can easily be controlled by digging them out, preferably before they set viable seed. Learning to recognize them in their pre-flowering stage is beneficial. Herbicides may also be useful, but *C. bonariensis* has shown some signs of developing resistance to glyphosate.

The name *asthma weed* seems to indicate use of this plant as a bronchial dilator, but I have been unable to find definitive information about this. There are other plants known as asthma weed, notably *Euphorbia pilulifera,* Queensland asthma weed, and *Lobelia inflata,* Indian tobacco, a North American plant that an untrained eye might possibly confuse with flax-leaved fleabane. *Parietaria judaica,* Jerusalem pellitory, and marijuana, *Cannabis sativa,* are also sometimes known as asthma weed. The fleabane referred to in the old European herbals is *Inula (Pulicaria) dysenterica,* a European wildflower (or weed) with hairy gray leaves and striking yellow flowers. It has astringent properties and was also burned to drive away fleas—it is closely related to *Conyza.* Gerard reported that "fleabane bound to the forehead is a great helpe to cure one of the frensie." It was also hung by doors to drive away demons.

I have been able to find no information on traditional uses of fleabane in the Americas.

Research done recently in Tanzania and Pakistan has indicated antibacterial and antifungal properties for *Conyza bonariensis.* In Tanzania, the crushed plant is sometimes applied to a mother's nipples to induce reluctant babies to suckle.

See illustration of flax-leaved fleabane on p. 153.

SOLIVA

Soliva sessilis—soliva—Asteraceae, Compositae, aster family

Soliva, a fairly recent immigrant from Chile, has become an increasingly common lawn weed, aggressively colonizing turf that has become sparse due to compaction. It is a prostrate winter annual, a tuft 1 to 2 inches tall, 2 to 4 inches in diameter, with many stems growing from a central crown atop a long taproot. Soliva seeds itself aggressively and can form solid mats where the grass is too thin to shade it out. It also grows in compacted bare ground beyond the lawn, in sun or shade.

The leaves of soliva are soft and finely dissected, compound pinnate on long petioles, the pinnae divided into deep, linear lobes. Stems and leaves are very finely hairy, and the stems tend to be somewhat sinuous. The flower heads are about ¼ inch across, greenish, surrounded by six petallike bracts. They are sessile, growing in the leaf nodes.

It is the fruit of this plant that makes it really interesting, suggesting names like "ouch weed" to some. Although the foliage is seductively soft, unwary lawn loungers leaning on their palms often receive a sudden jolt in the heels of their hands—the ripe fruit is a sharply pointed achene, the point formed by the hardened style. These can very easily pierce the skin.

Although patches of this weed do not look at all bad when the plants are young and fresh, they do dry out by summer or early autumn, leaving bare spots in lawns. Controlling this weed is best done by good lawn culture practices that favor the vigorous growth of turf grasses.

See illustration of soliva on p. 153.

TARWEEDS

Madia sativa—coast madia, Chilean tarweed—Asteraceae, Compositae, sunflower family

Madia elegans—common madia

Hemizonia spp.—hayfield tarweed—Asteraceae

The tarweeds are a group of sticky, aromatic composites that include a few perennials but are mostly summer annuals, and mostly native to California. Most of these are in the genus *Madia*.

The most common of the true tarweeds is the coast madia, which is native to Chile as well as California. This is a tall, branching plant that may reach 6 feet but is more commonly found in the 1- to 4-foot range. Leaves are narrowly ovate to lanceolate, up to 6 inches long, entire, tapering to a pointed tip. They are opposite and sessile on the stout stems, hairy, and sticky, with a strong, resinous odor. The stems as well as the leaves bear resin glands. The flowers

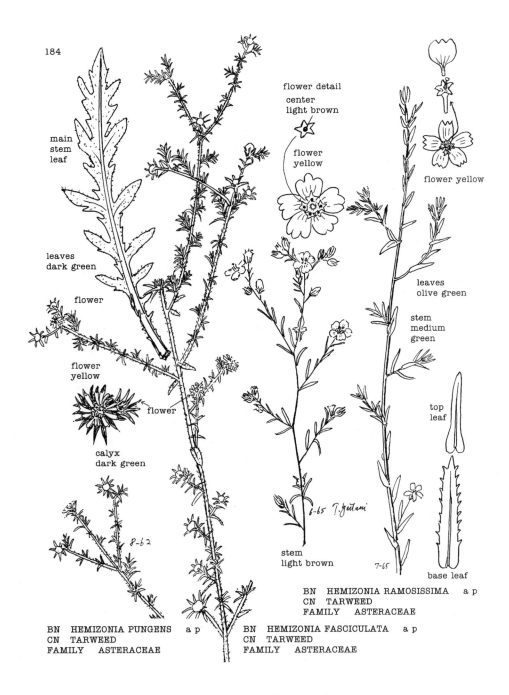

184

main
stem
leaf

leaves
dark green

flower

flower
yellow

flower

calyx
dark green

8-62

flower detail
center
light brown

flower
yellow

6-65 T.Yutani

stem
light brown

7-65

flower yellow

leaves
olive green

stem
medium
green

top
leaf

base leaf

BN   HEMIZONIA RAMOSISSIMA   a p
CN   TARWEED
FAMILY   ASTERACEAE

BN   HEMIZONIA PUNGENS   a p
CN   TARWEED
FAMILY   ASTERACEAE

BN   HEMIZONIA FASCICULATA   a p
CN   TARWEED
FAMILY   ASTERACEAE

are in broad or narrow clusters at the stem tips, consisting of dark yellow rays surrounding a central disk. The rays are three-lobed at their tips.

Chilean tarweed grows in sunny open fields, along roadsides, and in neglected pastures. It thrives in poor, rocky soil. It is mostly a weed of rural areas and the fringes of urban development, and it is unlikely to become a pest in city gardens.

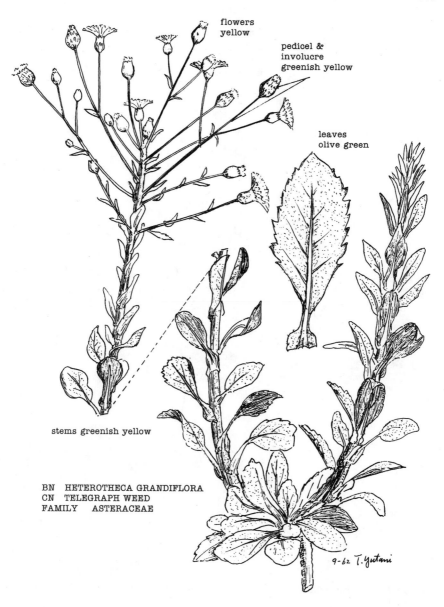

flowers
yellow

pedicel &
involucre
greenish yellow

leaves
olive green

stems greenish yellow

BN   HETEROTHECA GRANDIFLORA
CN   TELEGRAPH WEED
FAMILY   ASTERACEAE

9-62 T. Yutani

A tarweed even less likely to be found in the city, but one worth looking for, is the common madia, with large, showy inflorescences somewhat resembling gaillardias—the yellow tips of the rays have red bases. The leaves are fairly similar to those of the coast madia, perhaps not as long. The whole plant is smaller, reaching a height of about 2 feet. This madia is sometimes grown as an ornamental; it is especially suited to dry gardens.

HAYFIELD TARWEEDS

The hemizonias, or hayfield tarweeds, are smaller sticky yellow-flowered composites, generally shorter than the madias, with narrow, lobed leaves. Like the madias, they are mostly rural weeds, but they can often be found in undeveloped urban areas.

TELEGRAPH PLANT

> *Heterotheca subaxillaris* spp.—telegraph plant, telegraph weed, camphorweed—Asteraceae, Compositae, aster family

In the city, telegraph weed most often appears in open fields, vacant lots, and along roadways; it seldom invades well-maintained gardens. Camphorweed is a tall, erect summer annual that grows about as high as coast tarweed—from 2 to 4 feet, usually; sometimes as tall as 6 feet. It has gray-green leaves covered with dense hairs top and bottom, slightly toothed, oval and petioled below, lanceolate and sessile higher up on the plant. The basal leaves are often lobed. These are sticky and fragrant, with a camphor odor. The plant tends to be single-stemmed and narrow, suggesting a telegraph pole.

Flowers of telegraph weed are in somewhat flat-topped clusters at the tips of the stems, each head consisting of about thirty narrow, yellow ray flowers surrounding a central disk. The tips of the rays often curl outward. Like the other tarweeds, camphorweed has a stout taproot, and its hairs and resin make it extremely drought tolerant—so it can be expected to persist throughout the summer.

DODDER

> *Cuscuta* spp.—dodder, love vine, hairweed, devil's hair—Convolvulaceae, morning glory family

The dodders are a group of parasitic annuals that grow in crop and grain fields, in meadows and pastures, in forests and grasslands, even in salt marshes. In wild lands, they are mostly native, part of the vegetation, and not considered weedy. In crop lands and pastures, they are definitely problematic. In the East Bay, eight species are represented; all except one are native, according to Ertter and Naumovich. They are easily recognized by their yellow or orange color and their slender, threadlike, leafless stems, which clamber vine-like over the vegetation they infest. New plants have roots, but these soon wither; the plants then proceed to penetrate the living tissues of their hosts with specialized structures known as *haustoria*—knobby, wartlike stem appendages. The flowers are small (¼ to ½ inch), fleshy, bell shaped, mostly white, in branched clusters. These produce globular, papery seed capsules, each bearing one to four seeds.

There are species of dodder associated with specific crops. Some, such as alfalfa dodder, produce seed that mimics that of the crop, making it difficult to separate. Badly infested fields sometimes need to be burned and replanted. In the Bay Area, *Cuscuta salina* can often be seen in salt marshes, growing on pickleweed *(Salicornia)*.

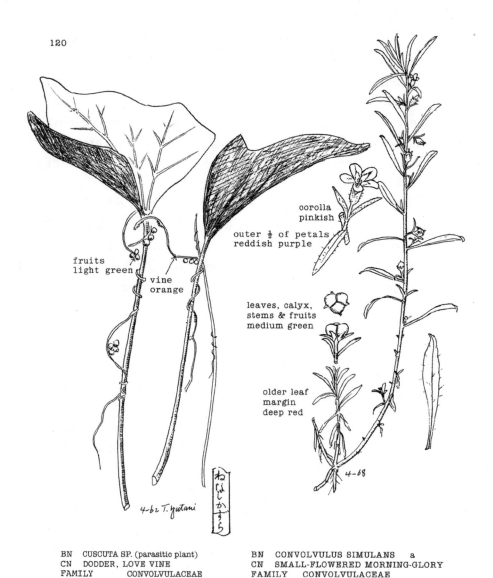

120

fruits
light green

vine
orange

corolla
pinkish

outer ½ of petals
reddish purple

leaves, calyx,
stems & fruits
medium green

older leaf
margin
deep red

4-68

4-62 T. yutani

BN   CUSCUTA SP. (parasitic plant)
CN   DODDER, LOVE VINE
FAMILY   CONVOLVULACEAE

BN   CONVOLVULUS SIMULANS   a
CN   SMALL-FLOWERED MORNING-GLORY
FAMILY   CONVOLVULACEAE

FIREWEEDS, OR WILLOW HERBS

Epilobium angustifolium—fireweed—Onagraceae, evening primrose family

Epilobium ciliatum—fireweed, willow herb

Epilobium brachycarpum—panicled willow herb

The evening primrose family (not to be confused with the Primulaceae, the primrose family) is a widespread group of plants whose members occur on all continents except Antarctica, with the greatest diversity in the western United States and Mexico, where all known genera occur. It consists mostly of herbaceous annuals and perennials, and some woody shrubs. It contains a number of popular ornamentals, including evening primroses, fuchsias, and clarkias (godetia), as well as California fuchsia *(Epilobium californicum),* an often-cultivated California native subshrub with some weedy tendencies.

Three species of *Epilobium* occur as weedy plants in California. *Epilobium angustifolium,* fireweed, or rose bay willow herb, is a tall perennial (up to 2 feet) with slender, pointed, willowlike leaves and clusters of attractive, deep pink to magenta flowers. It grows in a number of open locations in our mountains, including roadsides, gravel bars, scree slopes, and meadows. It is especially abundant after wildfires—that is how it got its name. This fireweed is usually not found in lowland areas unless it is planted, which it often is, since it makes a lovely, undemanding addition to a mixed flower bed.

Fireweed's range is circumboreal—it is native to northern Europe and Asia as well as North America.

Epilobium ciliatum, also called fireweed, sometimes willow herb, is a herbaceous perennial with narrowly lanceolate, sharply pointed, shiny, often reddish leaves (hence, *fireweed*) that form rosettes when young. Several of these may be clustered on a single crown. These rosettes elongate to form a branching plant that reaches a height of 12 to 18 inches in the flowering stage. Flowers are in terminal racemes of long, narrow, four-petaled blossoms, rose-pink to magenta, sometimes white. They are followed by dehiscent capsules, which split open and release fruits with tufts of silky hairs attached, somewhat resembling milkweed fruits (the hairs enable wind dispersal).

Fireweed grows mostly in moist areas, in sun or shade. It is not unattractive and mixes well with some herbaceous ornamentals grown as bulb cover. Colonies of fireweed often occur under greenhouse benches. If it becomes too abundant in a garden and needs to be controlled, keep in mind that it is perennial, and the entire crown needs to be dug out.

Willow herb is native to most of North America, as well as to eastern Asia and southern South America. It has been introduced into Australasia, Europe, and western Asia.

Epilobium brachycarpum, panicled willow herb, is somewhat similar to *E. ciliatum,* but is annual, with smaller, narrower leaves and longer branches.

115

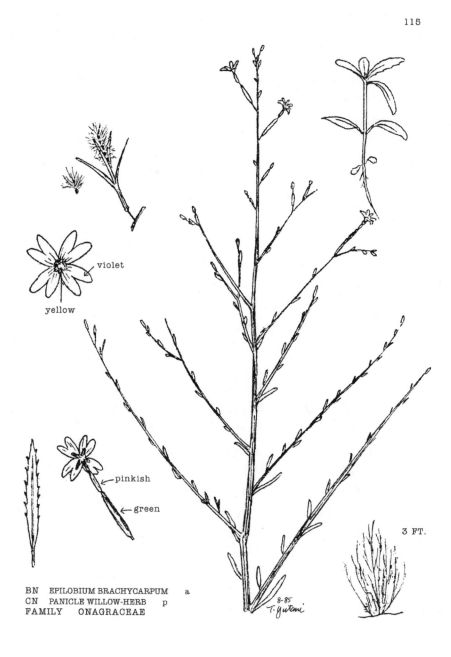

violet

yellow

pinkish

green

3 FT.

BN   EPILOBIUM BRACHYCARPUM   a
CN   PANICLE WILLOW-HERB   p
FAMILY   ONAGRACEAE

8-85
T. Yutani

The mature plants are 1 to 3 feet tall. The leaves of panicled willow herb are smaller than those of fireweed, less glossy, entire when young, minutely toothed at maturity. The flowers are small (¼ inch across), light pink to magenta, and borne singly or in small clusters at the ends of stems (the reference to panicles in the name of the plant presumably refers to the complex branching of the entire plant, not to the flower clusters). Flowers are followed by four-celled, dehiscent capsules, which release fruits covered with tufted silky hairs very similar to those of *E. ciliatum*.

Unlike its fireweed cousins, panicled willow herb grows in dry situations, such as open woodlands, grasslands, and roadsides. It blooms throughout the summer, and many see it as an attractive flowering plant along roadsides, a virtual wildflower. Panicled willow herb is native to California and most of the rest of the western United States. In cultivated gardens, it can be an unwanted weed. Since it is annual and grows from a taproot that does not regenerate, it is easy to pull out.

This plant is also known as field willow herb, tall annual willow herb, annual fireweed, and summer cottonweed.

JIMSON WEED

Datura stramonium—jimson weed, thornapple, tolguacha—Solanaceae, nightshade family

Jimson weed is an upright, shrubby, herbaceous annual that grows from 1 to 5 feet tall and has spread throughout the warmer regions of the world. Its place of origin is disputed: when it was found growing near Jamestown, Virginia, the first British colony in North America, the English apparently knew it and assumed it came from the Old World; some Europeans thought it had been brought there from the Americas. *The Jepson Manual* says it is probably native to Mexico; other botanists think it originated in Central Asia. In *Weeds of California,* Robbins describes this plant as a "rank-smelling annual," the scent exuding from both the flowers and the leaves. The leaves are alternate along the stems, smooth and thin, more or less triangular or deltoid, 3 to 8 inches long, the margins unevenly toothed. The flowers are funnel shaped, 4 or 5 inches long, white or purplish, and emerge singly from the leaf axils. They produce a hard, prickly, oval capsule about 2 inches long that splits into four segments to release many flattened dark brown to black seeds with wrinkled and pitted surfaces. All parts of the plant are toxic, the seeds being the most so.

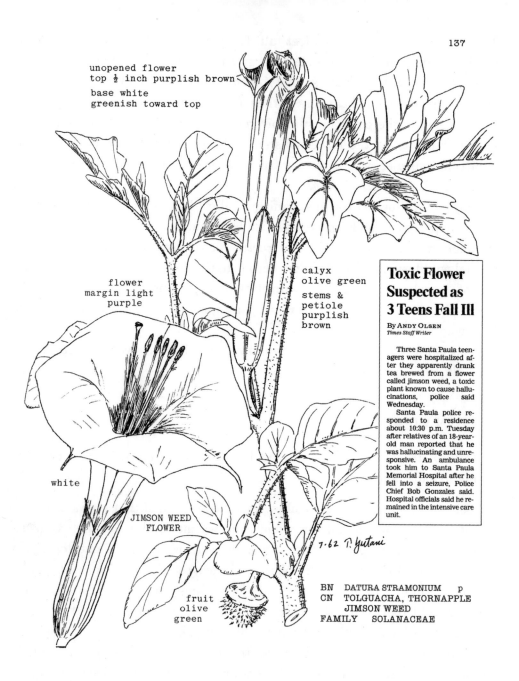

unopened flower
top ½ inch purplish brown
base white
greenish toward top

calyx
olive green

stems &
petiole
purplish
brown

flower
margin light
purple

white

JIMSON WEED
FLOWER

fruit
olive
green

7·62 P. Yutani

Toxic Flower Suspected as 3 Teens Fall Ill

By ANDY OLSEN
Times Staff Writer

Three Santa Paula teenagers were hospitalized after they apparently drank tea brewed from a flower called jimson weed, a toxic plant known to cause hallucinations, police said Wednesday.

Santa Paula police responded to a residence about 10:30 p.m. Tuesday after relatives of an 18-year-old man reported that he was hallucinating and unresponsive. An ambulance took him to Santa Paula Memorial Hospital after he fell into a seizure, Police Chief Bob Gonzales said. Hospital officials said he remained in the intensive care unit.

BN   DATURA STRAMONIUM   p
CN   TOLGUACHA, THORNAPPLE
     JIMSON WEED
FAMILY   SOLANACEAE

Jimson weed is not abundant in the San Francisco Bay Area, but it can be found in a number of locations along the East Bay hills and flatlands. Despite its rarity, it has generated a high level of concern due to the tendency that has arisen to experiment with ingesting the seeds of this weed, the most toxic part, to produce the hallucinogenic effects so vividly described in Carlos Castaneda's *Don Juan* books that were so popular a few decades ago. (This concern is reflected in the newspaper clipping that Tom Yutani has added to his illustration of the weed). Although Castaneda seems to have survived his ingestions of this plant none the worse for the wear, the dose that is psychoactive is very close to the amount that is fatally poisonous, and deaths have occurred.

Nearly all the Native American groups in Central and Southern California used tolguacha in coming-of-age ceremonies to produce visions and commune with deities; it was also used by tribes outside of California, including the East Coast Algonquin. The Navajo, the Cherokee, and the inhabitants of Marie-Galante, a Caribbean island, also used *Datura* to induce hallucinations. In California, it was most popular in the south, especially among the Gabrieleño, Luiseño, and Diegueño groups; but it was also used by the Ohlone and other groups who lived around San Francisco Bay.

The active ingredients in jimson weed are atropine and hyoscyamine, the same constituents found in belladonna. Thornapple has traditionally been used by Ayurvedic practitioners in India for controlling asthma symptoms—it is smoked in cigarettes or pipes. During the late eighteenth century, James Anderson, the physician general of the East India Company, discovered this and popularized it in Europe. Other medicinal uses had been established there well before this. John Gerard and Nicholas Culpeper, early seventeenth-century herbalists, both describe this herb and list its medicinal uses. Gerard's *Herball* of 1597 states: "[T]he juice of Thornapple, boiled with hog's grease, cureth all inflammations whatsoever, all manner of burnings and scaldings, as well of fire, water, boiling lead, gunpowder, as that which comes by lightning and that in very short time, as myself have found in daily practice, to my great credit and profit."

In the American Southwest, Zuni medicine men once used jimson weed as an analgesic to render patients unconscious while bones were being set; in China, it was used as a surgical anesthetic. According to Wade Davis's book *The Serpent and the Rainbow,* this plant, called "zombie cucumber" in Haiti, is used by voodoo priests there to concoct a potion that can turn unsuspecting imbibers into zombies.

A contemporary account of the activities of British soldiers sent to Jamestown to quell an insurrection that became known as Bacon's Rebellion tells the following story about an encounter with jimson weed by some of these troops:

> The James-Town Weed (which resembles the Thorny Apple of Peru, and I take to be the plant so call'd) is supposed to be one of the greatest coolers in the world. This being an early plant, was gather'd very young for a boil'd salad, by some of the soldiers sent thither to quell the rebellion

of Bacon (1676); and some of them ate plentifully of it, the effect of which was a very pleasant comedy, for they turned natural fools upon it for several days: one would blow up a feather in the air; another would dart straws at it with much fury; and another, stark naked, was sitting up in a corner like a monkey, grinning and making mows [grimaces] at them; a fourth would fondly kiss and paw his companions, and sneer in their faces with a countenance more antic than any in a Dutch droll.

In this frantic condition they were confined, lest they should, in their folly, destroy themselves—though it was observed that all their actions were full of innocence and good nature. Indeed, they were not very cleanly; for they would have wallowed in their own excrements, if they had not been prevented. A thousand such simple tricks they played, and after eleven days returned themselves again, not remembering anything that had passed.

Mrs. Grieve reports that thornapple leaves were, at the time she wrote, official in all pharmacopeias. Atropine is used as an antidote for nerve poisons and is still an essential component in the kits of combat medics.

These are some other common names for jimson weed: mad apple, stinkwort, loco weed, hell's bells, devil's trumpet, pricklyburr, and devil's cucumber.

RUSSIAN THISTLE

Salsola tragus—Russian thistle, tumbleweed, wind witch—Chenopodiaceae, goosefoot family

The Russian thistle, the "tumbling tumbleweed" so familiar to all Americans who watch Western movies, is even more directly familiar to dwellers of the wide open spaces of the American West, where its prolific growth competes with grasses and forbs used as forage by cattle and sheep. This annual plant forms a rounded bush about 2 feet across; when it dies and dries out, it breaks off at the base and rolls along the ground, driven by the wind, scattering its seeds, which can number fifty thousand per plant. The Russian thistle is also a host to the beet leafhopper, a carrier of the virus that causes curly top disease in sugar beets, as well as blights of spinach, tomatoes, beans, and some other crops.

This weed first appeared in 1874 in Scotland, South Dakota, and is thought to have come in a shipment of flax seed ordered from Russia—the plant is native to the dry plains (steppes) in the southeast of that country, and to western Siberia. By 1895, it had spread to sixteen states, and from Ontario to Labrador in eastern Canada. It now grows in the drier interior valleys of California, especially Southern California.

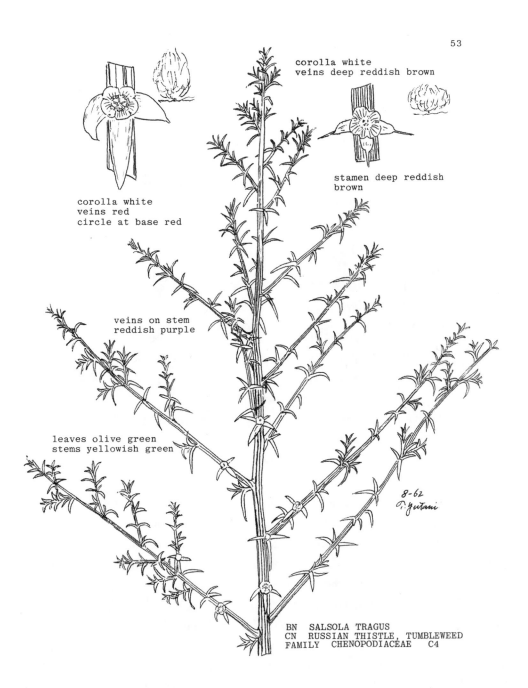

corolla white
veins deep reddish brown

corolla white
veins red
circle at base red

stamen deep reddish
brown

veins on stem
reddish purple

leaves olive green
stems yellowish green

8-62
P. Yutani

BN   SALSOLA TRAGUS
CN   RUSSIAN THISTLE, TUMBLEWEED
FAMILY CHENOPODIACEAE   C4

When the tumbleweed first germinates in spring, it forms a more or less prostrate plant with upturned stem ends; in very poor soil, it will remain this way to maturity. In better soils, it quickly develops into a 1½- to 2-foot bush, with its branch ends incurved. These stems are ridged, pale green to reddish. The young leaves are long, soft, threadlike, sessile (no petioles), and alternate, an inch or more in length; as these mature, they become much shorter, stiff, and scalelike, with spiny tips. The small, greenish flowers form in the upper leaf axils, producing papery seed capsules. Seeds are distributed almost entirely by the mature, detached, windblown plants, the tumbleweeds.

The Russian thistle is not common in the Bay Area; when it is found, it is most likely to appear in or near rail yards, probably moved from drier regions by trains.

The plant is said to be edible in its very young, succulent stage; it may be used in salads or as a cooked green.

SMILAX ASPARAGUS

Asparagus asparagoides—smilax asparagus, bridal creeper—Asparaga-ceae, asparagus family

Bridal creeper is a shiny, bright green, rampant vine that is also grown in the florist trade for its ornamental foliage. It is often found in older gardens, where it persists due to its large, fleshy root. Birds love the berries, so it often spreads by seed into areas where it was not formerly present.

An attractive plant, bridal creeper is grown in coastal California as foliage for floral bouquets; it probably spread from flower farms into the surrounding landscape. It is now established as a weed near the immediate coast from the Bay Area south. It is native to tropical and southern Africa.

Bridal creeper's tuberous root makes this plant well adapted to poor, dry, even rocky soils. If it receives no irrigation, the tops die back, but the roots remain alive, ready to resprout during the next rainy season. It then forms a mass of twining stems, which can grow as long as 20 feet and form a mat about 4 inches deep. When they encounter trees or shrubs, the stems climb, often engulfing the plants that support them.

The "leaves" of bridal creeper (actually phylloclades, flattened stems that resemble and function as leaves) are sickle shaped, bright, shiny green, entire, about an inch long and ½ inch wide. They have conspicuous parallel veins and pointed tips. The flowers are small (about ¼ inch across), six-petaled, white or greenish-yellow with orange stamens, growing singly or in pairs. They produce shiny berries about ⅜ inch across, red at first, then turning blue.

Smilax asparagus tolerates a variety of soils and water regimens, but usually looks best in part shade with regular irrigation (assuming you actually want to grow it). If you want to control it (a better idea), letting it dry out and then removing the roots completely is the most effective way. Cutting back the top growth before it flowers will help check its spread from seed and may eventually starve the root.

Besides gardens, bridal creeper also invades riparian woodlands along the central and south coast of California. Its extent is considerably more limited than that of pests such as Cape ivy, English and Algerian ivy, and French broom. Cal-IPC rates it as a "moderate" pest.

A cultivar of this plant, myrtifolius, known according to *The Sunset Western Garden Book* as baby smilax, has smaller leaves and grows more gracefully than the species. If you like smilax and want some in your garden, this one might be easier to keep in bounds.

HYSSOP LOOSESTRIFE

Lythrum hyssopifolium—hyssop loosestrife, grass poly—Lythraceae, loosestrife family

Hyssop loosestrife is a usually prostrate but sometimes erect, sprawling, mat-forming weed that grows in wet to very wet situations. In rural areas, this native of Europe occurs in farm fields, especially where water accumulates; in the city, it is not very abundant, growing mostly on the margins of shallow, standing water and in overwatered lawns. It can be recognized by its angled stems and its pale green, smooth, linear to oblong leaves, which are about ¼ to ½ inch long, set alternately, and sessile, on angled stems. They somewhat resemble the leaves of hyssop *(Hyssopis officinalis),* a mint family herb sometimes grown in gardens for its dark blue flowers and medicinal properties.

The flowers of hyssop loosestrife grow in the axils and are solitary and sessile. They are whitish to pale purple, with five to six petals that form a tube about ⅙ inch long—the stamens are enclosed within this tube. The fruit is a two-celled capsule.

Hyssop loosestrife is not a particularly troublesome weed, except perhaps in areas that cannot be dried out; if you try to grow a bog garden, you may have to deal with it. A close relative, purple loosestrife, a large perennial (to 6 feet) with magenta to purple flowers, has long been a staple in perennial borders in England, but has become a serious ecological weed in the eastern half of the United States, where it infests wetlands. It does not seem to be much of a problem in California, perhaps because we have less extensive and more isolated wetlands, perhaps because it never really caught on as a garden plant here. Hopefully, it will remain unfashionable.

See illustration of hyssop loosestrife on p. 140, where it is labelled "grass polly," an alternative common name.

EPAZOTE

Dysphania (Chenopodium) ambrosioides—epazote, Mexican tea—Chenopodiaceae, goosefoot family

Another goosefoot weed often found in the Bay Area, especially close to saltwater marshes and along the bay shoreline, is *Dysphania ambrosioides,* epazote

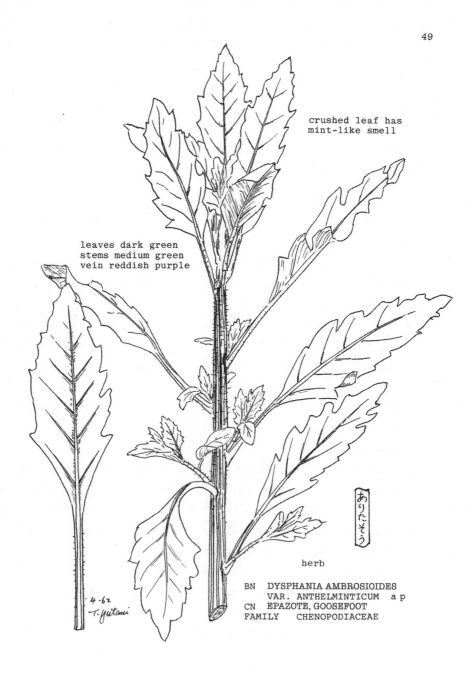

49

crushed leaf has
mint-like smell

leaves dark green
stems medium green
vein reddish purple

herb

BN DYSPHANIA AMBROSIOIDES
    VAR. ANTHELMINTICUM a p
CN EPAZOTE, GOOSEFOOT
FAMILY   CHENOPODIACEAE

4-62
T. Yutani

or Mexican tea, sometimes also known as wormseed, Jerusalem tea, Spanish tea, or strong-scented pigweed. This species, introduced from tropical America and naturalized along the Atlantic seaboard as well as in California, somewhat resembles lamb's quarters, but there are differences that make them fairly easy to tell apart. Epazote leaves have a strong, somewhat camphor-like aroma and are more serrated than those of lamb's quarters. They are glandular and hairy and grow on ridged stems, which are more often than not covered with minute hairs. The flowers are small and greenish, similar to those of lamb's quarters, densely clustered on spikes or panicles growing in the leaf axils.

Epazote is used as a culinary herb in southern Mexico and Central America, mostly to flavor black beans, but also sometimes in enchiladas, quesadillas, and a number of other dishes. It is also eaten as a leaf vegetable. The plant has a number of medicinal uses, some of which are indicated by its other common names: wormseed, Jesuit tea, Mexican tea, herba Sanctae Mariae. It is considered carminative, an antidote to flatulence, hence its use in bean dishes. It has also been employed to kill intestinal worms and has been listed as official for this purpose in the United States Pharmacopeia. Other reported uses are to induce menses and to alleviate menstrual pain; as a cure for malaria, hysteria, catarrh, asthma, even cancer; as an antispasmodic; and to induce abortion. Epazote contains terpenes, compounds that are insecticidal; a proprietary mixture of some of these is currently used in a product called Requiem. There is enough demand for epazote leaves in the herbal trade that it is grown commercially on a small scale.

SWINE CRESS

Coronopus didymus—swine cress—Brassicaceae, Cruciferae, mustard family

Swine cress, also known as wart cress, is a prostrate, spreading weed with numerous branches whose stems can grow from 6 inches to 2 feet. Plants usually grow no higher than 6 inches but can sometimes reach a foot or more. Swine cress is a winter annual, but it has a short, sturdy taproot that enables it to grow well into the summer. The entire plant has a disagreeable, skunk-like odor that is easily recognizable, especially in warm weather. It grows in a wide variety of habitats, in sun or shade, and thrives in difficult areas such as hard, compacted soil and sidewalk cracks. It recovers well from mowing, and so it can invade lawns, especially those that have become neglected.

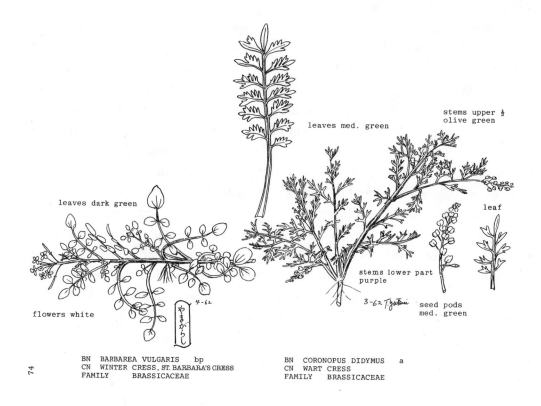

leaves med. green

stems upper ½
olive green

leaves dark green

leaf

stems lower part
purple

3-62 T.Gustavus

seed pods
med. green

flowers white

4-62

やまがらし

BN   BARBAREA VULGARIS   bp
CN   WINTER CRESS, ST. BARBARA'S CRESS
FAMILY   BRASSICACEAE

BN   CORONOPUS DIDYMUS   a
CN   WART CRESS
FAMILY   BRASSICACEAE

74

The leaves of swine cress are ½ to 1 inch long and deeply divided into narrow, toothed segments, occasionally entire. When very young, it can be easily confused with various other low-growing weeds, such as pineapple weed, soliva, even Australian brass buttons; as it matures, differences become readily apparent (not the least of which is its odor). The flowers are very small, less than ¹⁄₁₆ inch in diameter, greenish-white, with the four equal petals. These are clustered in short racemes, which, in the manner typical of the mustard family, continue to elongate and flower at their tips, as the spent flowers give way to siliculas about ⅛ inch in diameter, deeply wrinkled and segmented—they appear to consist of two lobes.

Swine cress is native to South America but has spread widely throughout the world. Control is not particularly difficult: hoeing or digging, with some follow-up to eliminate the next crop of seedlings, will keep it in check.

BRISTLY MALLOW

Modiola caroliniana—bristly mallow—Malvaceae, mallow family

Bristly mallow is a perennial native to the southeastern United States that somewhat resembles a prostrate, mat-forming cheeseweed. It occurs most often in lawns but sometimes spreads to other areas of the garden. This plant grows from a strong taproot and forms secondary roots wherever the nodes of the long stems, which measure 6 to 18 inches, touch the ground. The stems are pubescent, bearing alternate, palmate leaves about 1 to 1½ inches across, rounded with rounded (crenate) lobes. The flowers are small—less than ½ inch across, brick red, with five petals and two or three narrow bracts at their bases. They grow singly in the leaf axils. The flowers are succeeded by round, somewhat flattened fruits consisting of fifteen to thirty carpels with bristles on their edges.

Bristly mallow likes sun or part shade and is not particular about soil, but it thrives in ground drier than grass needs. The key to keeping it under control in lawns is to make sure sprinkler coverage is as even as possible, then to water deeply and not too often, a practice that will tend to favor grasses over many of the broad-leaved weeds.

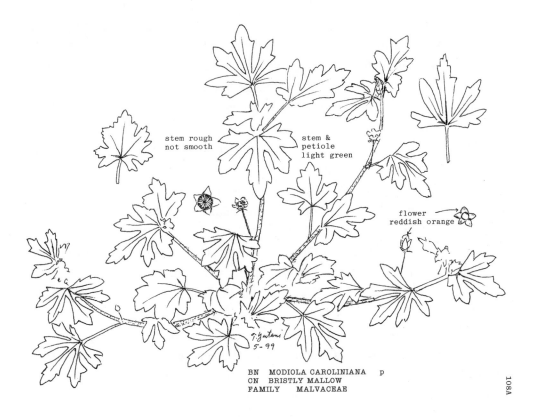

stem rough
not smooth

stem &
petiole
light green

flower
reddish orange

r. gutani
5-99

BN   MODIOLA CAROLINIANA   p
CN   BRISTLY MALLOW
FAMILY   MALVACEAE

108A

NONFLOWERING WEEDS

Equisetum arvense—field horsetail—Equisetaceae, horsetail family

Equisetum hyemale—scouring rush

Pteridium aquilinum var. *pubescens*—western bracken fern—Dennstaedtiaceae, bracken fern family

The phyla of plants that do not reproduce from seed-bearing fruits generated by flowers, but instead from spores consisting of a hard coating around a few cells of the parent plant, have been known traditionally as cryptogams, plants whose male and female parts are hidden. At some time, some botanists decided that these sexual reproductive organs didn't really exist, that cryptogams reproduced only clonally, from the tiny spores that contain cellular material identical to that of their parents. If this were so, they would evolve much more slowly than seed plants, changing only when genetic mutations caused by cosmic rays or some other external stimulus produced an alteration; and these alterations could be passed on only to the direct clonal offspring of their parents. But the notion of the hidden organs never disappeared completely, and during the twentieth century, these were discovered, present on a small, inconspicuous juvenile form of the plant (the gametophyte) that until then had not been recognized as an infant fern. The gametophyte of a fern is a tiny, leafy structure, generated from the spores. It grows in moist ground and produces gametes of both sexes, which usually swim about in the film of water coating the bottom of the tiny plant and unite with opposite sex gametes of the same plant; but some of them manage to swim to other plants, so fern evolution does occur, albeit very slowly. The united gametes remain attached to the thallus, where they grow into a full spore-bearing plant, a sporophyte, with leaves, stems, roots, and vascular tubes.

The cryptogams—algae, mosses, liverworts, club mosses, horsetails, and ferns—developed much earlier than the conifers and flowering plants, and they dominated the world's vegetation during the Paleozoic era. There were forests of treelike club mosses, horsetails, and ferns, with understories consisting of smaller members of these phyla, as well as mosses. Various reptiles lived in these forests and the swamps among which they grew, but no dinosaurs—they did not appear until the Mesozoic era, when conifers dominated the woodlands. Today, the cryptogams are much fewer in numbers of plants and species than the flowering plants, generally growing only in swampy areas or very moist forests. The horsetails, formerly consisting of a number of families, have been reduced to a single genus, *Equisetum,* of the family Equisetaceae, in the order Equisetales, class Equisetopsida, phylum Equisetophyta.

Where, as François Villon might have asked, are the giant horsetails of yesteryear? The giants are long gone, and the remaining horsetails have been backed into a virtual evolutionary corner; but, amazingly, at least two of them appear frequently in gardens as fairly pesky weeds.

33

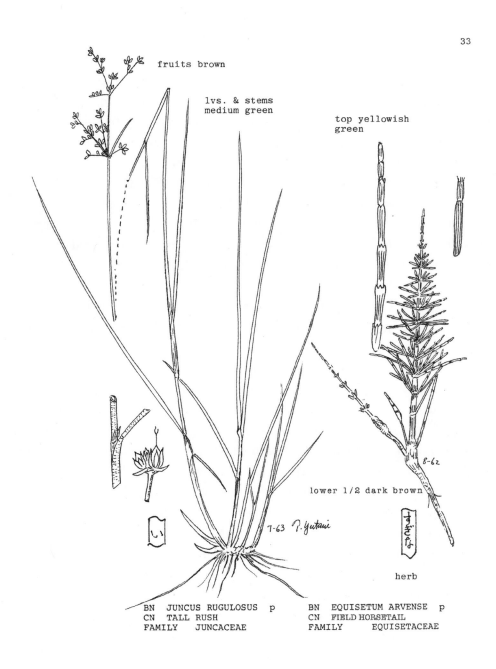

fruits brown

lvs. & stems
medium green

top yellowish
green

lower 1/2 dark brown

7-63 P. Yutani

8-62

herb

BN   JUNCUS RUGULOSUS   p
CN   TALL RUSH
FAMILY   JUNCACEAE

BN   EQUISETUM ARVENSE   p
CN   FIELD HORSETAIL
FAMILY   EQUISETACEAE

The equisetum that produces most of the unwanted infestations in the Bay Area is the field horsetail, a native of the arctic and the temperate Northern Hemisphere. In cultivated ground, it usually appears in soil that has been kept way too wet for way too long, but, due to its tough, silica-bearing stems and extensive rhizome system, it will persist long after the soil has dried out. This horsetail consists of long, slender, hollow stems, gray-green in color, ridged, and with somewhat raised horizontal rings of buds, which sprout whorls of slender, jointed, linear, leaflike branches. Atop each stem a conical structure appears, on which masses of pale green to yellow spores develop. Underground rhizomes spread aggressively, especially in areas with high water tables. If the high water is due to excessive irrigation, it can easily be lowered by irrigating less frequently; if it occurs naturally, an elaborate and expensive drainage system may be needed. In such areas, planting moisture-loving bog plants able to coexist with the horsetails might be a better idea than trying to drain the soil. Spraying herbicides into standing water is never a good idea and is usually illegal.

The scouring rush, although far less common in California than field horsetail, is nevertheless worth knowing. Native to all parts of the temperate Northern Hemisphere, it has one variety that is native specifically to California, *E. hyemale* var. *californicum*. This plant can easily be distinguished from the field horsetail by its lack of long, whorled branches (although it can produce a few every now and then); instead, the branches are much smaller and form a jagged, close-set ring around the nodes. The conical fruiting bodies develop atop some of the stems; sterile stems grow a cluster of dense, short, whorled branches at their tips, configured in a conical shape similar to that of the strobili, the fruiting bodies. Scouring rush seldom appears in horticultural plantings, but it can be troublesome when it does. Due to its high silica content, this horsetail has a long history of use for cleaning pots and pans and removing oxidation from the surface of metal, hence its common name. In England, it is also known as pewterwort, bottle brush, shave grass, Dutch rushes, and paddock pipes. It was formerly used a great deal by cabinetmakers, whitesmiths (tradesmen who finish and polish the ironwork that blacksmiths forge), and tinsmiths. It is used as reindeer fodder by Sami (Lapp) herdsmen in the north of Scandinavia and Russia (although in cattle-raising country it is thought to be poisonous to livestock). It has even been eaten sometimes out of desperation by humans, even those who thought it toxic to their livestock. Medicinally, scouring rush has been employed as a diuretic, an astringent, and a vulnerary. Ashes of the burned stems have been used to reduce stomach acidity and to treat internal bleeding.

The western bracken fern, *Pteridium aquilinum* var. *pubescens,* is a variety native to western North America of a species that grows over the entire temperate Northern Hemisphere. It occurs mostly in clearings in woodlands, which subsequently become occupied by dense growths of a single kind of plant; these growths are known as *brakes* (hence, *bracken*). Bracken fern often invades land recently cleared by logging, as well as pastures and crop lands adjacent to woodlands. Unlike many ferns, bracken likes full sun and will tolerate considerable drought.

Bracken fern has a rhizomatous root system that enables it to grow in solid masses over extensive areas. Leaf stalks arise from these rhizomes, beginning as fiddleheads, tightly coiled stems that straighten as they grow. They branch into a compound pinnate frond, gray-green and leathery on top, covered with brown spore cases on their undersides. The leafy parts are broadly triangular, divided into many narrow pinnae, with the terminal lobe larger than the ones below it; but since the lower lobes grow on stalks that are longest at the base, the whole frond has, overall, a triangular appearance. Fronds grow from 1½ to 6 feet tall. They are poisonous and thus a danger to livestock. Poisoning in horses and sheep seems to be cumulative, and symptoms may not appear until well after the initial feeding.

When bracken fern gets into gardens, it can be quite troublesome due to its extensive rhizomatous root system, although it might well be considered a wild garden plant on the edges of larger properties.

The fiddleheads, or fiddlenecks, of bracken fern, as well as many others, can be cooked and eaten like asparagus, and are considered a delicacy by many; however, they are suspected of causing stomach cancer. Although the evidence for this is somewhat mixed, it is probably best to avoid eating them.

A similar species, the Australian brake fern, *Pteris tremula,* is sometimes grown as a ground cover in shady areas; it has fronds that are lacier than those of *P. aquilinum* and somewhat grayish in color. It spreads freely and can become an aggressive weed.

Another brake fern that grows in clearings in wet forests in Hawaii and on other Pacific islands is *Dicranopteris emarginata,* the false staghorn fern, or *uluhe* in Hawaiian. Its fronds grow atop stems that reach 10 to 15 feet in length; they consist of palmate clusters of long, pointed leaflets, pinnate with narrow, deeply incised lobes on their margins. These can cover large areas in forested lava flows, often growing on banks created by slides. Native Hawaiians used the bitter juice of the *uluhe* stems and leaves as a laxative and an emetic, that is, to induce vomiting.

9

GARDEN ESCAPEES AND WILD-LAND INVADERS

INTRODUCTION

The weeds I have discussed so far all share the common characteristics described by Herbert Baker in his list "The Ideal (?) Weed" (see the bibliography for the source of this list). These include quick germination, rapid growth, abundant seed production, and ability to compete successfully with slower-growing species, especially in disturbed ground. Most of the weeds I have discussed so far tend to confine themselves mostly or entirely to frequently disturbed habitats—farm fields, pastures, roadsides, vacant lots—and will not colonize stable wild environments; they may establish themselves along trails or in campsites, but they cannot move much beyond these regularly disturbed areas. There is another group of weeds, however, that can easily plant themselves in any breaks in normally stable plant communities, form colonies that resist the reestablishment of native species, and move from there into the surrounding wild lands. These have been designated as invasive exotics, or ecological weeds.

Most of these invasive exotics are, or once were, horticultural plants, fast-growing, robust, versatile (all adjectives that should remind us of Dr. Baker's list) ornamentals, beautiful plants that perform wonderfully in gardens with minimal input from gardeners—until it becomes apparent that they perform too wonderfully and need to be controlled or eliminated. But, by the time they have been removed from gardens, they have often established themselves in adjacent wild areas, where they are extremely difficult to control and nearly impossible to eradicate. This is not for lack of trying, however. Impressively large sums of public and private money are being spent on the effort; armies of volunteers periodically descend on wild areas to cut broom, dig out Cape ivy, and plant natives. If these efforts are supported by intelligent strategies and regular follow-up, they are often successful. Researchers are continuously working on the problem, and their articles appear regularly in publications such as *California Agriculture,* as well as in journals dedicated to the control of invasive exotics and the restoration of wild lands. There is an extensive bureaucracy that deals with the problem of invasive exotics. In California, there are county-based Weed Management Areas (some of them covering multiple counties) that address significant weed problems, including invasive exotics—these are state funded. The California Invasive Plant Council (Cal-IPC, formerly the California Exotic Pest Plant Council), an independent nonprofit organization, works with land managers, researchers, policy makers, and concerned citizens to deal with the problem of invasive plants on many levels. They issue publications, organize educational programs, coordinate weed mapping efforts, provide training for weed workers, and advocate policies. Their excellent publication *The Weed Workers' Handbook* is essential reading for anyone wishing to learn more about invasive exotics or to get involved with restoration work. It can be downloaded for free from their website.

Much is made of the enormous financial losses caused by weeds, but, ironically and perversely, it seems that our responses to the problem actually generate economic activity that at least partly offsets these losses. There is a small but growing group of private companies that contract with public agencies to control these exotics and restore wild lands; others provide training to weed workers and concerned citizens. Manufacturers of tools, equipment, herbicides, and weed barriers also benefit from the necessity for weed control. This is all ultimately paid for by consumers and taxpayers, most of whom would probably rather spend their money in other ways; so preventing the introduction of new exotics is probably the most cost-effective strategy in the long run. Herbert Baker's list needs to be more widely distributed and understood.

ACANTHUS, BEAR'S BREECHES

Acanthus mollis—acanthus, bear's breeches—Acanthaceae, acanthus family

Acanthus is a very attractive ornamental that grows in sun or shade from an extensive system of large, spreading rhizomes and roots. It can always be counted on to move beyond the area where it is desired—a shame, since its foot-long (sometimes 2-foot-long), very dark green, deeply lobed, shiny leaves are quite striking, as are its spikes of flowers, which can reach 4 or 5 feet and are covered with hooded blossoms, whitish, rose, or purple in color, and surrounded by spiny green or purplish bracts that persist when the flowers have faded. Without summer irrigation, the leaves of this plant dry up and crumble, but the flower spikes persist. Occasional watering can keep them green all summer but also encourages the spread of the rhizomes. These are almost impossible to dig out completely, especially when they intertwine with roots of adjacent trees and shrubs. Once established in a garden, acanthus is nearly impossible to eliminate completely. Keep this in mind before planting it someplace new.

Acanthus is native to the Mediterranean Basin and was well known to the Greeks and Romans. It is the leaf represented on the capitals of Corinthian columns, and it sometimes appears as decoration on other parts of classical buildings.

AFRICAN CORN FLAG, MONTBRETIA

Chasmanthe floribunda—African corn flag—Iridaceae, iris family

Crocosmia × *crocosmiiflora*—montbretia, crocosmia—Iridaceae

The Cape region of South Africa, which has a Mediterranean climate similar to that of California, is rich in bulbous monocots, mostly in the iris family; many of these are grown as ornamentals here. Being well adapted to our summer-dry environment, they tend to naturalize in gardens, coming back in increasing numbers year after year, allowing gardeners to forgo the laborious digging, storing, and replanting of bulbs such as tulips, which come from cold-winter areas and need winter chill (in California, often done in refrigerators). Some of these South African plants are a little too vigorous, capable of dominating gardens and even moving into the wild if left unchecked. By far the most rampant is the African corn flag, *Chasmanthe floribunda*.

African corn flag has leaves 2 to 3 feet long and 1 to 2 inches wide that are bright green and pointed at the tips. A small cluster of these leaves grows from an underground corm; the corms produce offsets, which develop into new corms; so the plant tends to grow in large clusters. The corms sprout in the fall, after the first substantial rains, and the leaves remain green throughout the winter.

The flowers bloom in late winter, beginning usually in February (sometimes even January), continuing until April or May. They are slim and tubular, slightly curved, orange with yellow stripes, about 3 inches long. They grow opposite one another on stems that emerge from the leaf clusters. Round seed capsules follow, green at first, then black; if allowed to ripen, these split open and drop their seeds, which produce an abundance of new plants, adding to the ample numbers produced by corms and their offsets.

Corn flags can provide a lush, colorful display in winter, usually the best time of year for gardens dominated by them. When the leaves die back, they are unsightly and need to be removed, an often laborious process that is best begun while they are still green, before the capsules have opened and scattered their seeds. This can be done in stages, allowing the still-green leaves to persist until they have dried out. Once this process is complete, gardeners often find that many of the plants they count on for summer bloom have suffered or even died, smothered by the rank growth of corn flag. It is best, therefore, to keep the clusters small by digging out a substantial number of corms every year and removing unwanted seedlings as they occur. Although eliminating the entire population of corn flags from a garden where they have naturalized would be a substantial job, it is well worth considering.

Chasmanthe is frost tender and will only naturalize in the coastal areas at elevations of 150 feet or less. They are common on the central coast and in the San Francisco Bay Area.

Often confused with *Chasmanthe floribunda* is another South African bulb, the montbretia, *Crocosmia* × *crocosmiiflora.* The flowers are similar, usually orange, sometimes yellow or red, with a short tube and six petals, placed alternately on the flower stalks (which are shorter than those of *Chasmanthe,* as are the leaves). They bloom in late spring and summer rather than winter. Montbretias were popular garden plants in the early part of the twentieth century, and many variations were selected, resulting in yellow and red strains as well as orange. Once montbretias went out of favor, they were found mostly where they had naturalized in older gardens, often spreading, but not nearly as invasive as *Chasmanthe.* The red and yellow forms seem to be making a comeback, as are red and yellow corn flags, and the corms can be quite expensive.

Sometimes, a form of crocosmia with blooms on only one side of the spike is found in older gardens. This is probably *Crocosmia masoniorum,* one of the species involved in the montbretia hybrid.

Other South African iris family bulbs grown in California gardens include those in the genera *Freesia, Ixia, Sparaxis, Gladiolus* (there are a number of species grown, some winter blooming, as well as the taller, more garishly colored hybrids), *Watsonia,* and *Babiana.* These all naturalize readily but seldom become truly weedy.

BERMUDA BUTTERCUP

Oxalis pes-caprae—Bermuda buttercup, sour grass, English weed—Oxalidaceae, sorrel family

> I hate it, I hate it, I can't get rid of it, I WANT IT TO DIE.
>
> —Tia Foss, on hortiplex.gardenweb.com

Bermuda buttercup is a herbaceous perennial from South Africa that grows from bulbs and produces bright yellow, five-petaled flowers on long stems in the fall and winter. The three-lobed leaves, which resemble clover, have somewhat heart-shaped leaflets that some say resemble goats' hoof prints, hence the specific epithet *pes-caprae.* The leaves are often spotted and have petioles up to a foot in length. They grow from a fleshy, translucent taproot, which sprouts from a small, brown bulb.

This plant is attractive and easy to grow, and it spreads rapidly, making it an ideal winter ground cover in mild-winter climates. As warm weather sets in, it obligingly shrivels and virtually disappears, giving way to summer-blooming annuals and perennials. For these reasons, the plant was sent from its South African home to gardens in many warm temperate parts of the world. Its first stopping place was Bermuda. Soon after it was planted, it quickly became apparent that this "too good to be true" plant was an aggressive invader, spreading both by fleshy, translucent rhizomes and bulblets that form on the taproot emerging from the bulb, as well as on the rhizomes.

Bermuda buttercup sets no seed but spreads entirely by vegetative means. Oddly, in its native South Africa, it does produce viable seed and is not particularly weedy. The version that has become a worldwide pest apparently stems from a genetic mutation (perhaps occurring in Bermuda?) that made the plant sterile, so it compensated by developing the ability to reproduce aggressively from bulbs and underground stems. In California, Bermuda buttercup was first found in a walnut grove in San Juan Capistrano in 1928; it has since spread throughout the coastal zone, appearing in orchards, vegetable fields, and ornamental plantings. One tiny bulblet, spread by moving soil, or by mud on the soles of shoes or garden tools or farm implements, or possibly by birds or burrowing animals, can start an infestation that can cover acres.

Completely eradicating Bermuda buttercup anywhere it grows is nearly impossible, but preventing new infestations and reducing populations in already infested areas is quite feasible. As with all integrated pest management approaches, setting a threshold is important, and the threshold must be realistic in terms of how much time is available to devote to the project. Herbicides work—they will kill entire plants, including their rhizomes and any bulblets still attached to these rhizomes; but those that have detached will not be affected. Digging out crowns, rhizomes, and bulblets is effective, but the limiting factor is time and patience. Simply removing the tops of the plants will not prevent new growth from the roots, but repeated cutting will eventually starve the plant (although probably not before it has put out some bulblets). New infestations spread fairly slowly—the tops die back in summer—so digging out newly emerged plants at the edges of established colonies can contain, and perhaps reduce, the infestation. Closely observing the landscape and digging out the beginnings of new colonies while the plants are young is perhaps the most effective way of keeping this weed from spreading.

Mulching established colonies, especially sheet mulching, can be very effective, although new growth will appear at the edges and in gaps in the mulch—but digging this out is easier than engaging in the nearly hopeless task of eradicating an entire colony by digging. Tall, woody ground covers such as juniper can also suppress Bermuda buttercup—it will scramble through the shrubs in order to seek sunlight, but this growth can easily be removed, and the rhizomes beneath will eventually starve.

Many people regard this plant as an attractive winter ground cover, more attractive than many of the annual winter weeds that it can outcompete, so there are good arguments for leaving it alone in certain areas. Cal-IPC lists its impact on wild lands as moderate, with the caveat that, in coastal areas, its impact may become more severe in the future. Anyone wishing to grow native wildflowers in urban zones will find Bermuda buttercup a serious competitor. It can also be a major pest in herbaceous ornamental plantings and vegetable gardens.

In the United States, *Oxalis pes-caprae* is found only in California, Arizona, and Florida. Worldwide, it grows in the Mediterranean Basin and has

become a widespread pasture weed in southern Australia, where it sometimes poisons sheep who eat too much of it; oxalic acid, the compound that
gives this and other sorrels their sour taste, can be toxic in large quantities. But, no worries, as Australians might say—the tiny amount ingested by
chewing on the stems of "sour grass," as many children are wont to do, is little
cause for concern.

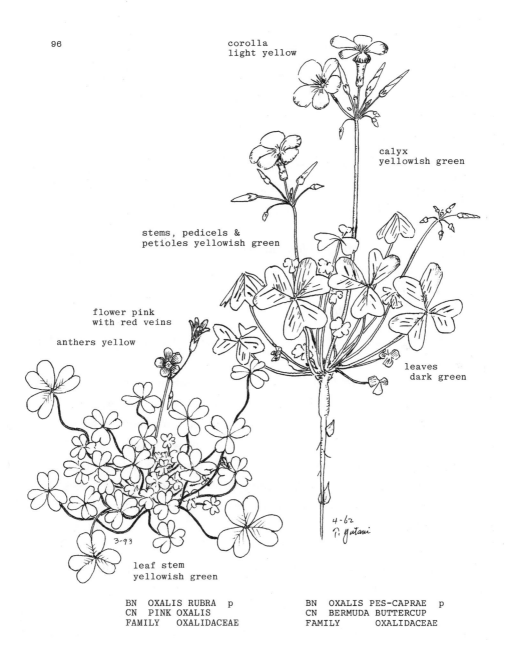

96

corolla
light yellow

calyx
yellowish green

stems, pedicels &
petioles yellowish green

flower pink
with red veins

anthers yellow

leaves
dark green

leaf stem
yellowish green

3-93

4-62
T. gutani

BN   OXALIS RUBRA   p
CN   PINK OXALIS
FAMILY   OXALIDACEAE

BN   OXALIS PES-CAPRAE   p
CN   BERMUDA BUTTERCUP
FAMILY   OXALIDACEAE

BLACKBERRIES

Rubus armeniacus—Himalayan blackberry, Himalaya berry—Rosaceae, rose family.

Rubus lacinatus—cutleaf blackberry

Rubus unifolius var. *inermis*—thornless elm-leaf blackberry

Rubus ursinus—native California blackberry

The Ballad of Barbara Allen, a folk song from the English-Scottish borderlands, mentions two plants in the rose family that are often regarded as weeds. I quote the last two stanzas from one of many versions:

Barbr'y Allen was buried in the old churchyard,
Sweet William was buried beside her,
Out of Sweet William's grave there grew a rose,
From Barbr'y Ann's, a briar.

They grew and grew in the old churchyard,
'Til they could grow no higher;
In the end they formed a true lovers' knot,
And the rose grew out the briar.

Briar is a generic term referring to any thorny vine or shrub, including blackberries and roses; a more specific term referring to blackberries is *bramble* (sometimes spelled brambel or brymbl), a Middle English word meaning "prickly." Blackberries are widespread throughout the temperate Northern Hemisphere, and in Europe and Asia they have been used as food and medicine for millennia. More than forty species grow in Britain alone: in the wild, in hedges, on formerly cultivated ground, even in gardens. They often become weedy pests, but their many uses have assured their continuing proximity to dwellings. Most blackberries grown today (as well as their close cousins, the raspberries) are complex hybrids of wild species and later selections, including some derived from crosses with the raspberries.

The Himalayan blackberry is one of these cultivars, introduced into California and the Pacific Northwest as a crop plant in the late nineteenth century. It is native to Europe, where it also tends to be invasive; how it came to be identified with the Himalayas is a mystery. This bramble yields large, juicy, delicious fruits that are still highly regarded today; however, shortly after its introduction, Himalaya berry began to appear, and proliferate, in pastures and crop lands, along roadsides, and in backyards, sometimes forming dense, impenetrable thickets composed of stout, arching canes with large, often reddish recurved thorns—these canes can extend up to 10 feet. They can layer (form new roots) where they touch the ground, which enables them ultimately to extend to 40 feet or more. Thickets of Himalaya berry occur up and down the Pacific coast, from wetter areas of Southern California to British Columbia. Some people treasure their favorite patches (usually well outside their own gardens), where they go in July and August to harvest the ripe berries.

Himalaya berry leaves are palmately compound, borne alternately on the canes, with five leaflets when mature (newly emerged leaves have three; two more develop from lobes that form on the outer two). Each leaflet is 4 to 5 inches long and broad, rough and somewhat prickly on top, serrated on the edges, woolly white beneath. The flowers are in terminal panicles and are five-petaled, generally white but sometimes light pink, with many yellow stamens and pistils. These closely resemble the flowers of many wild roses (roses and blackberries are closely related), measuring about 1 to 1½ inches across. The roundish, shiny, dark purple fruits that follow consist of an aggregation of drupelets, formed from many pistils in a single flower measuring about ½ inch across.

Seedling blackberries have a stout taproot, which soon begins to produce many short rhizomes, from which new crowns form. New crowns also form when the tips of the canes touch the ground and self-layer. The juicy, prolific berries are attractive to birds, which can spread this plant far and wide. In gardens, the roots and rhizomes of Himalaya berry can easily intertwine with the roots of ornamentals, making it nearly impossible to dig out completely. Herbicides work, but often require repeated applications, due to the plant's extensive rhizomes. Gardeners are well advised to learn to recognize Himalaya berry seedlings and to dig them out early. Continuing vigilance is needed, as even small root fragments are capable of regenerating.

The bark and especially the root of the blackberry contain considerable tannin, so it has been used traditionally as an astringent and tonic, to treat wounds, to facilitate digestion, and to alleviate diarrhea. The ancient Greeks regarded blackberry as a cure for gout, and the English used it as a remedy for burns and scalds. In rural England, passing back and forth through the arch formed by a layered cane was formerly (maybe even recently, in some areas) believed to cure hernias in children (Mrs. Grieve reports that the passing of children through holes in the earth, rocks, and trees was once an established rite in rural parts of England, meant to keep them healthy or cure their ailments). Very young shoots of the plant were once eaten as a salad and were reputed to have the ability to tighten loose teeth, perhaps due to shrinkage of gum tissue by tannin. A black dye can be made from the leaves of brambles boiled with lye—this is sometimes used to color hair.

An old name for blackberry, scaldhead, may refer to a scalp disease of children that was sometimes attributed to consumption of overripe fruit; or it may refer to the use of the leaves as a remedy for burns and scalds (Gerard, the seventeenth-century herbalist, suggests adding a little alum). Creeping under a bramble bush was sometimes regarded as a charm against rheumatism, blackheads, boils, and other afflictions, and blackberries were once thought to give protection against evil runes (spells) if gathered at the right phase of the moon.

Another species of weedy blackberry often found along streams is the cutleaf blackberry, an escaped cultivated berry of European origin. It has deeply and finely cut leaflets, somewhat shorter canes, and smaller flowers than Himalaya berries. Also sometimes found in riparian areas is the thornless elm-leaf blackberry, easily recognized by its thorn-free canes.

There is a native species of blackberry that sometimes intermingles with the escaped exotics: *Rubus ursinus.* It has very slender, flexible stems that scramble through other vegetation. These canes can be 15 feet long and are covered with short, fine prickles rather than stout, recurved thorns. The leaves have three rather than five leaflets; their undersides are woolly or smooth to slightly fuzzy. This berry seldom invades gardens. *R. ursinus* has been crossed with other blackberries to produce boysenberries, loganberries, and youngberries.

Two upright, shrubby California natives in the genus *Rubus* grow in the woodlands of California and the Pacific Northwest: they are the thimbleberry, *R. parviflorus,* with palmate leaves, and the salmonberry, *R. spectabilis,* with a trifoliate leaf. Both have light red berries that are edible, but not as tasty as blackberries or raspberries. They are excellent ornamental plants for shady, relatively moist gardens.

BROOM AND GORSE

Genista monspessulana—French broom—Fabaceae, Leguminosae, pea family

Cytisus scoparius—Scotch broom—Fabaceae

Spartium junceum—Spanish broom—Fabaceae

Ulex europaeus—gorse—Fabaceae

The eleventh-century Count of Anjou, Fulk III, the Black, also known as Fulk Nerra, spent his life fighting wars with his neighbors, expanding his land holdings in and beyond his home region in central-western France. When Fulk rode off to his wars, he wore in his bonnet or helmet a sprig of *planta genista,* a type of broom, a group of leguminous shrubs native to much of Europe. Through aggressive campaigning and building of fortifications to defend and consolidate his gains, he was able to build a virtual empire that allowed him to rival the king of France in power and prestige. In the early twelfth century, one of his descendants inherited the English throne. This king, Henry I, took the surname Plantagenet, a reference to Fulk's broom sprig, which had become a symbol on the family coat of arms. The Plantagenets continued to rule England, and much of France, for the next two hundred years. The last of the line was Richard III, who offered his kingdom for a horse, but found no takers.

In the Middle Ages, *planta genista* was the Latin designation for a number of species of broom that grew along Europe's Atlantic coast, in the Mediterranean Basin, and in the Azores, Canary Islands, and Madeira. The Plantagenet broom was probably one of the Atlantic species, such as *Cytisus supinus* or *C. scoparius.* Another species of *planta genista* that grows in southern France and elsewhere in the Mediterranean region, *Genista monspessulana,* has become a major weed along the Pacific coast of North America, where it is known as French broom, although often called, mistakenly, Scotch broom.

French broom, an upright, rounded, or irregular shrub that grows from about 5 to 12 feet or more in height, has masses of bright yellow flowers that produce beautiful displays in coastal brush fields and chaparral where it has naturalized. It was introduced as an ornamental, escaped from cultivation, and spread aggressively—the weedy brooms now cover perhaps as many as half a million acres along the Pacific coast, from San Diego to Washington, and French broom is by far the most abundant.

The leaves of French broom, like those of many legumes, are trifoliate, with leaflets about ½ inch long, covered with silky fuzz above and beneath, growing alternately along stems that are angled rather than rounded. The flowers are the typical keeled, winged, and bannered legume blossoms, less than ½ inch long, growing in short terminal racemes. They are followed by dehiscent fruits, the typical bean-like legume, about an inch long. When these pods burst open, they propel the seeds as far as 12 feet. The masses of bright yellow blooms in the spring forewarn of a prodigious seed production capacity—researchers have counted more than 6,700 seeds in a single square meter plot. These are viable for about eight years.

Broom is anchored to the soil by a taproot and grows from a crown capable of resprouting. Cut just below ground level, this crown loses much of its regenerative capacity, although not all.

"Broom bashes" have become a popular activity among environmentalists and native plant lovers, and may well be having some effect in controlling the spread of this shrub, or even reducing the size of infestations in some areas. Broom is best bashed in winter and spring, when the ground is moist and the roots of at least the smaller plants can be extracted with reasonable ease. The most popular tool for this job is a weed wrench, a metal bar with an appendage that grasps the trunks of the shrubs, and can pry out the roots by lever action. Leaving the roots in the ground disturbs the soil less, so workers often opt to cut off the shrub close to the ground, and then peel back the bark to ground level to minimize resprouting, or brush partially diluted herbicide onto the stumps. Alternately, one can dig out the crown with a Pulaski, pick, or shovel and simply leave the remaining roots to rot in the ground. Young seedlings can be pulled, hoed, or sprayed with herbicide. An effective broom control project requires follow-up for at least eight years, removing additional seedlings and, hopefully, planting natives that can replace the broom.

Control of French broom is a massive undertaking in wild lands and urban fringe areas; but this plant can easily be kept out of urban gardens if one learns to recognize it. It is no longer sold in nurseries, and there is no reason to ever plant seeds or seedlings taken from the wild; there are a number of other brooms available that do not spread nearly as aggressively as French broom.

The second-most widespread weedy broom on the Pacific coast is Scotch broom, a plant native not only to Scotland but other parts of coastal northern Europe, as well as to the Mediterranean and the foothills of North Africa. It was brought to California during the nineteenth century and used primarily as a dune stabilizing plant on the northern coast. Scotch broom has spread up and down the Pacific shore, but infestations tend to be smaller and more isolated than those of French broom, with which it sometimes mixes. It has ridged green stems that produce only a few leaves, which it loses in the fall. The flowers are larger than those of French broom, and deeper yellow, sometimes tinged with red. The fruits have hairs only on their seams, unlike those of French broom, which are fuzzy all over.

Even less widespread, but still weedy, is the Spanish broom. This plant has bright yellow flowers, larger than those of French or Scotch broom, growing on bright green stems that are round in cross section. These often sprout a few tiny simple leaves that fall off at the onset of hot weather. Most of the year, its stems do all the photosynthesizing. Spanish broom is the most deeply rooted of these three brooms, with a taproot that descends as deep as 6 feet, making it difficult to pull out. In California, it does not form huge infestations and is often tolerated. In Italy, Spanish broom has become a rampant, aggressive spreader, much like French broom in California. French broom, however, is both native and well behaved in that country.

Other brooms that sometimes escape from cultivation are *Genista canariensis,* Canary Island broom, similar in appearance to *G. monspessulana* but with long, pointed, terminal racemes, and *G. × spachianus,* Easter broom, a horticultural hybrid. *Jepson* states that the wild population of French broom includes many hybrids with both these species.

Closely related to broom, but armed with stout spines, is gorse, *Ulex europaeus,* a dense shrub 2 to 4 feet tall with spiny stems, few scaly leaves, and clusters of showy yellow two-lipped flowers. Originally introduced as an ornamental, it has escaped and formed thickets along the Northern California coast from Marin to Humboldt Counties, sometimes spreading over adjoining farmland, pastures, and logged-out forest areas. It spreads both by seed and rhizomes. On the Big Island of Hawaii, it has covered vast areas on the slopes of Mauna Kea, almost completely excluding native vegetation.

CALLA LILY

Zantedeschia aethiopica—calla lily, common calla—Araceae, arum family

Although commonly called calla lily, these plants are not lilies at all, although the shape and size of the white flower bract makes them resemble the white lilies sold at Easter. This bract (spathe) encloses a pointed spike (spadix), which bears masses of tiny yellow flowers. The whole structure is 3 or 4 inches long, 1 or 2 inches wide, borne singly on a pithy stem 2 to 4 feet tall. They bloom from mid-spring well into summer.

Calla leaves are somewhat hastate, up to a foot long, on petioles that are about twice their length, pointed at the tips, with smooth, slightly wavy margins. The perennial root system produces tubers that look like very small potatoes and remain in the ground after the top dies back to produce new plants.

In California, callas grow year round in soil that remains moist in summer; they tend to die back to their tubers when the soil dries out. They can spread fairly freely around gardens but have limited ability to invade wild lands. They can sometimes be seen naturalized around ponds and seeps and on the edges of wetlands.

Cultivars of common callas have been developed, some of them dwarf; there are other species and hybrids, smaller than the common calla, with variously colored flowers. None of these are robust spreaders.

CAPE IVY

Delairea odorata—Cape ivy—Asteraceae, Compositae, sunflower family

Cape ivy, also known as German ivy, is a native of South Africa and Botswana (a former German colony) that was introduced into the United States in the 1850s as an ornamental and soon came to be used for erosion control as well. An attractive vine with shiny green leaves and showy racemes of yellow flowers, Cape ivy is also a rampant grower, spreading by underground rhizomes. It is ideally suited to cool, moist environments in coastal forests, especially gullies and canyons. It drapes itself over native trees and shrubs, robbing them of light and nutrients; it can virtually smother low-growing native vegetation. The rhizomes entwine with the roots of other plants, making it virtually impossible to remove without damaging or killing them.

Cape ivy sends out long stems that can grow to 20 feet. These climb by twining and produce leaves about three inches across, palmately veined and more or less heart shaped, with five to seven lobes; the margin between the points of the lobes is conspicuously curved. The leaves are shiny, smooth, bright green, and alternate on the stems. They are often confused with the leaves of the native wild cucumber, *Marah fabaceus;* these latter, however, are darker green with a rougher surface, and the plant climbs by tendrils, not by twining.

German ivy flowers are small, typical pig-snouted groundsel-like blossoms, very bright yellow, in showy panicles. They bloom in January and February and set seed shortly thereafter. In California, however, most of the seed seems to be sterile. No matter; the plant can reproduce with amazing speed and vigor from its purple, evil-scented rhizomes, or from stem fragments, leaf petioles, or self-layering; indeed, from any part of the plant except the leaf blade. The actual roots are shallow and fibrous, but the plant stores water in its rhizomes and

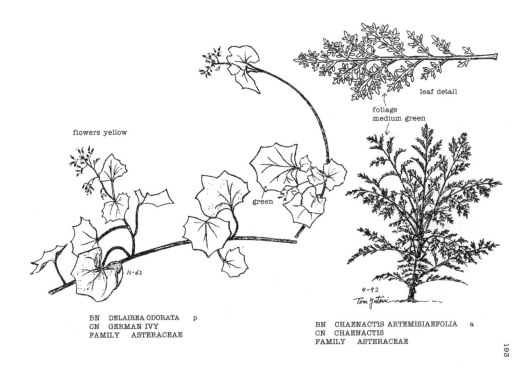

flowers yellow

green

11-62

foliage
medium green

leaf detail

4-92
Tom Yatani

BN   DELAIREA ODORATA   p
CN   GERMAN IVY
FAMILY   ASTERACEAE

BN   CHAENACTIS ARTEMISIAEFOLIA   a
CN   CHAENACTIS
FAMILY   ASTERACEAE

193

stems, so it is very drought tolerant. It may die back in the summer in some places but will almost certainly regenerate when the fall rains return.

Eradication efforts are often organized by managers of parks and wild lands, or by teams of volunteers. This requires a prodigious amount of hand labor, and frequent follow-up, to be even marginally successful. The first step in addressing an infestation is to isolate it, creating a zone of bare ground about a yard wide around the edge. Anything that resprouts in this zone must be dug out or sprayed. Once the isolation zone is established (it could take several months before all traces of the invader are removed), teams of volunteers can move in, cut back all stems to the base, grub out whatever rhizomes they can, and remove all this vegetation from the site. Resprouting can be dealt with by re-grubbing, spraying, or painting the bases of the cut stems with a 50 percent glyphosate solution.

Some restoration practitioners prefer to remove all low-growing vegetation, native and alien, from an eradication site in order to more fully access resprouting Cape ivy. This requires pruning low-growing branches on trees and shrubs to about breast height to facilitate access to the low growth. Areas subjected to these drastic treatments are vulnerable to erosion and colonization by other weeds, requiring even more labor before they can be replanted.

Debris needs to be dried out thoroughly, on plastic tarps, before being composted. This process can be hastened somewhat by spraying the piles with a weak solution of glyphosate.

Considering the amount of labor required to remove Cape ivy and the complexity of the task, it will probably remain a component of the wild vegetation of coastal California for far longer than most readers of this book will live. Its spread can be controlled, however. Removal of small outlying colonies should be given the highest priority, especially those found in the upper reaches of stream valleys, where fragments can wash downstream and establish new infestations. Devoting available labor to these smaller projects, and especially to follow-up labor, will undoubtedly do more in the long run to control the population of Cape ivy than squandering it on massive removal efforts that cannot be followed up with adequate monitoring and ongoing removal.

CASTOR BEAN

Ricinus communis—castor bean—Euphorbiaceae, spurge family

The castor bean is a subtropical perennial native to Asia and Africa that has been widely grown as an annual crop in temperate regions for its oil. In mild-winter areas such as coastal California, it sometimes escapes and becomes a weed in vacant lots, pastures and meadows, and riparian zones. It has not become widespread, as it is frost tender and often unable to survive winters except in the most consistently frost-free areas.

Castor bean is a large, attractive, shrub-like herbaceous perennial that grows from 4 to 15 feet tall and bears palmate leaves that usually measure about 6 inches across but sometimes reach a foot. Each leaf has five to twenty-two lobes and serrated margins. They are dark green, sometimes with reddish coloration along the veins. Both staminate and pistillate flowers grow on the same plant. They are small and greenish, clustered in racemes or panicles. These are followed by round, spiny, often reddish fruits. This attractive plant is often cultivated in gardens, where it tolerates a variety of soils and watering regimens, grows quickly to its maximum size, and functions well as screening or as an attractive specimen. Its seeds are poisonous if eaten, however, and sometimes cause skin irritations, so it should be planted with caution. It seeds freely, so it must be monitored in the garden and not allowed to escape.

In rural areas, castor bean has caused livestock and human poisoning. It has the potential for becoming an ecological weed in river floodplains, but so far it has not become a seriously threatening invader.

COTONEASTERS

Cotoneaster franchetii—cotoneaster—Rosaceae, rose family

Cotoneaster pannosa—cotoneaster

Cotoneasters (pronounced *kuhtonie aster,* not *cotton easter*) have proven to be very valuable woody landscape shrubs: they are evergreen, vigorous, long-lived, attractive in flower and fruit, and, despite their origin in China, a fairly wet country, they are remarkably drought tolerant. They can grow in many types of soil. Some species are low and spreading, useful as sturdy ground covers; others are tall, arching shrubs that grow to 10 feet or more and can be used as garden specimens, screening shrubs, or even small, multitrunked trees. Two of these latter, however, have a tendency to seed themselves very freely and become invasive pests in native shrublands and woodlands.

Cotoneaster franchetii and *Cotoneaster pannosa* are nearly identical, except for one feature: *C. franchetii* has orange-red berries, *C. pannosa* dark red. Both plants grow 10 feet tall or more, with a spread of 6 to 9 feet; both have gracefully arching branches. The leaves are alternate, about an inch long, elliptic to obovate with smooth margins, grayish-green when young, maturing to bright green above, white and fuzzy beneath. Cotoneasters bloom from winter through late spring, forming clusters of up to twenty white (sometimes tinged with pink), five-petaled flowers, about ½ inch across, resembling tiny wild roses. These are followed by fruits about ¼ to ⅓ inch in diameter, which resemble tiny apples: cotoneasters are members of the pome tribe of the rose family, along with apples, pears, and quinces. These fruits are very attractive to birds but are so abundant that enough are left to litter the ground even when the birds are done with them; thus, abundant seedlings emerge the following spring. Uncontrolled, a single shrub can easily produce a thicket under the right conditions. Bushes that are cut back can easily resprout from the stumps.

The best way to control the spread of these two cotoneaster species is not to plant them in the first place—there are other species of similar size and shape, such as *C. lacteus,* which resembles the two weedy ones somewhat, but has larger leaves; and *C. salignus,* the willow-leaved cotoneaster, with long, narrow, somewhat shiny, dark green leaves. These two do not produce a lot of seedlings. If you already have *C. franchetii* or *C. pannosa* in your garden and do not wish to remove it, you will have to work aggressively to weed out their offspring.

CREEPING BUTTERCUP

Ranunculus repens—creeping buttercup—Ranunculaceae, buttercup family

The creeping buttercup is a low-growing herbaceous perennial that roots at the nodes and likes wet soil. It is frequently found in lawns, especially in areas that remain moist, although it can withstand considerable drying once established. Unmowed, it will mound up to 18 inches, but in mowed lawns it forms mats the same height as the grass.

The leaves of the creeping buttercup are bright green, trifoliate, and covered with hairs. They have 6-inch petioles and can measure up to 4 inches across; on mowed plants, they are considerably smaller. Each leaflet has sharply pointed lobes. Foliage of this plant superficially resembles that of bristly mallow and is sometimes confused with it, but the mallow is darker green and likes drier soil. The flowers are quite different: the creeping buttercup has bright, shiny yellow flowers about ½ inch across, with five petals and fifty to eighty stamens (bristly mallow has a brick-red flower). They bloom in spring and early summer. The fruit is a flattened achene with a beveled margin and a short, recurved beak. Creeping buttercup likes moisture and tolerates considerable shade. Besides lawns, it may sometimes be seen growing in wet ground at the edges of lakes and ponds, where it develops ascending stems that can grow to 2 feet. The flowers can be attractive, but a lawn can become quickly dominated by this weed. Controlling it is difficult, as fibrous roots form at every stem node that contacts the ground. Herbicides can help eliminate small, scattered infestations if used carefully, but would probably kill more grass than weeds in a heavily infested lawn. The key to controlling this pest is early recognition and intervention, along with careful water management.

There is a double-flowered cultivated variety, Pleniflorus, that is sometimes grown as a ground cover or pond-edge plant in gardens; it sometimes escapes.

There are other buttercups in California, native and alien. The most common native is *Ranunculus californicus,* a native meadow flower that blooms in April and May. It is upright, with bright yellow flowers on long stems. It dies back after blooming, but reemerges from a perennial rootstock after the rains begin. It competes with weeds better than most wildflowers, so has some potential for moving into gardens, where it may well be welcome.

Of several alien buttercups that have shown up in scattered areas as pests in grain fields, meadows, and pastures and as invaders of wetlands, the spiny-footed crowfoot, *Ranunculus muricatus,* is probably the most common. This is a stout annual or short-lived perennial, growing 3 to 10 inches tall, with smooth, somewhat succulent, yellow-green foliage. It produces an egg-shaped, flat-sided achene, with many stout, curved spines on each side.

EUCALYPTS

Eucalyptus globulus—blue gum—Myrtaceae, myrtle family

Eucalyptus camaldulensis—river red gum

There are five hundred to seven hundred species of *Eucalyptus* in the world, depending on whom you ask. Most are native to Australia, a few to adjacent islands, including New Guinea and the Philippines. None are native to New Zealand, although this is a common belief, since a number of them have been planted there.

Eucalypts have been planted in California since the 1850s and are a familiar sight in the California landscape. They grow in all parts of the state, have often been depicted in landscape paintings, and are thought by many people to be native. Coming from generally dry climates, and well adapted to prolonged droughts, they grow readily in many parts of California where even native trees are absent, and, in moister areas, readily naturalize and become part of the landscape. Many native plant enthusiasts are emphatically opposed to planting these trees anywhere in California and want to eradicate them where they are already established. The California Invasive Plant Council (Cal-IPC) regards two species as ecological weeds: *Eucalyptus globulus,* to which they give a "moderate" rating, and *E. camaldulensis,* whose invasive potential they rate as "limited."

These two species are the most widespread eucalypts in California. They are huge trees, imposing in the landscape, but really too large for most urban settings (although that hasn't stopped people from planting them in cities), and very messy to boot, dropping large quantities of bark, which they shed regularly. They have been planted in rural areas as windbreaks and have been grown for timber and firewood. The first timber plantings were done in the 1870s and were relatively modest; during the first two decades of the twentieth century, many more were planted in huge land development schemes, touted to investors as fast-growing, high-quality hardwood timber that would thrive without irrigation in dry areas and sell for premium prices when harvested, creating instant wealth for their owners. Vast areas in the East Bay hills were soon covered with eucalyptus groves, creating dense forests in areas that were formerly grasslands or savannah.

Most of the trees planted were *Eucalyptus globulus,* and to a lesser extent *E. camaldulensis,* possibly the two worst choices for timber production. *E. globulus,* the Tasmanian blue gum, is native to Tasmania, one of the wettest areas of Australia, where it grows under temperate rain forest conditions. *E. camaldulensis,* the river red gum, is native to a drier region, the Murray River basin, but grows on the river's floodplain, where it is regularly inundated. These two trees will grow in some of the driest areas of California, but, without irrigation, do not get very large. Unfortunately, wood from both species warps and cracks when harvested at diameters smaller than 3 feet, as most of them were. Some did grow to a 3-foot diameter and produce harvestable timber, much of which was used for finish work in Bay Area houses. Known as gumwood trim, it is a very beautiful, fine-grained, light brown wood with a reddish cast. Some of the timber was used for railroad ties; a good deal more as firewood. Ultimately, most of the large hill plantations were abandoned and eventually sold to the East Bay Regional Park District or the East Bay Municipal Utility District, where they still survive, effectively crowding out native vegetation by dropping tons of shredded bark and leaf and twig litter and resprouting from stumps wherever they are cut. They are also a severe fire hazard—eucalypts contain large quantities of volatile oils, which makes them ignite readily and burn at a high temperature, a fact that became tragically apparent during the 1991 firestorm in the Oakland hills.

Since that fire, there has been a concerted effort to remove some of the groves, especially those close to densely inhabited areas, and replace them with native vegetation, an effort that has attracted some opposition from tree lovers—except for native tree lovers, some of whom advocate getting rid of every eucalypt in California. However, eradicating large stands even to a limited extent is immensely difficult and expensive: they resprout readily from the stumps and produce an abundance of seedlings, requiring follow-up spraying with herbicides, which engenders further public opposition. The market for the wood, even sold as firewood, is limited. Restoring native vegetation to areas covered in acres of eucalypts seems desirable, and removing strategic portions of these groves for fire control is necessary, but preventing the further spread of these trees is a much more realistic goal than attempting total eradication. Fortunately, limiting spread is not that difficult—as I said earlier, the red gum is regarded as only a limited threat to native vegetation by Cal-IPC; the blue gum is rated moderate, but mostly in coastal areas subject to fog drip.

Places to monitor are areas of native vegetation adjacent to planted groves—the seeds generally do not travel far.

Blue and red gums look alike at first glance: massive but graceful trees, considerably taller than wide, with long trunks and large, narrow-angled branches. Trees of both species can easily grow over 100 feet tall where they receive adequate water. The bark, when new, is light brown, or almost white; as it matures, it darkens and begins to detach, hanging in shreds from the trunk and eventually falling to the ground. The leaves are thick and leathery, dark green, entire, sickle shaped, 6 to 10 inches long. The flowers start out as clusters of woody buds, consisting of a receptacle covered by an operculum, a lid of sorts that drops off when the buds open. The flowers of the blue gum and red gum are white, consisting mostly of many stamens protruding from the receptacle. When they fade, woody seed capsules develop, and these are distinctive enough to provide a reasonably easy way to tell the two species apart. The capsules of the blue gum are large, about ¾ inch across; those of the red gum about ¼ inch. In bloom, the flowers of the blue gum are larger than those of the red—about an inch across, as compared to about ⅓ inch for the red gum. Seedlings of both have juvenile foliage that is distinct from the mature foliage: juvenile leaves are oval and covered with a white bloom.

Other species of eucalypts that occasionally turn up as weeds are *E. rudis,* the swamp, or flooded gum; *E. viminalis,* the manna gum, much like the red gum but with whiter bark; and *E. umbellata,* the forest red gum. All these trees, in limited quantities, have a place in the larger California landscape; none of them are particularly appropriate urban trees, except perhaps in large parks. Venerable specimens that are healthy should not be removed; but for new plantings, there are plenty of other choices: eucalypts that are stately and imposing, but not nearly as large; with bark that does not shred; with larger, more colorful flowers. There are even shrubby forms, the mallees, whose horticultural potential has not nearly been realized.

FEVERFEW

Tanacetum parthenium—feverfew—Asteraceae, Compositae, aster family

Feverfew is an easy to grow, freely spreading garden plant that does well in sun or part shade. It has long been grown in Europe, as well as in China and Japan, and is quite common in Bay Area gardens. It was a popular plant in Victorian gardens and is still fairly popular, despite its weedy tendencies.

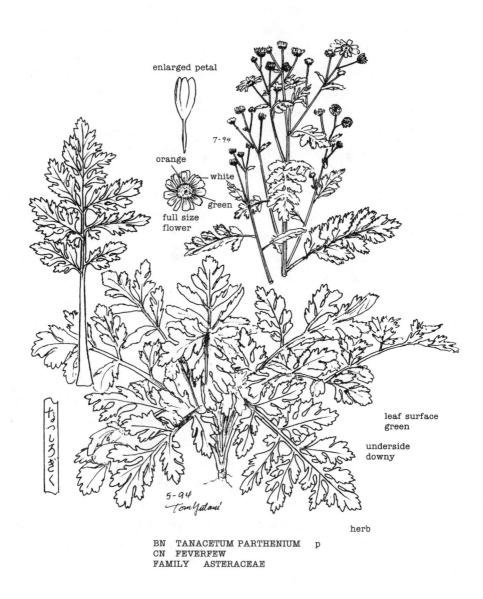

enlarged petal

7-94

orange

white

green

full size
flower

leaf surface
green

underside
downy

5-94

Tom Yatani

herb

BN   TANACETUM PARTHENIUM   p
CN   FEVERFEW
FAMILY   ASTERACEAE

Feverfew is an upright, bushy plant that is reported to grow as tall as 3 feet; but in my experience it generally stays well below 2 feet. It is pungently aromatic, producing an odor that many find objectionable but others consider a pleasantly medicinal scent (I identify with the latter group). The leaves are lobed and deeply incised, generally 1½ to 4 inches long and not quite as wide, with an overall oval shape, sharply pointed on the ends. Individual lobes are also deeply incised—the whole leaf has a jagged appearance. The color is usually light green, but there is some variation.

The inflorescences are small, usually no more than ¼ inch across; petals are white, the centers yellow. They grow in panicles, with a large terminal cluster at the apex and smaller clusters emerging from the leaf axils. The root system consists of fibrous roots emerging from a perennial crown.

If you like having feverfew in your garden at all, controlling it is simple: just root out the ones that grow where you don't want them and leave the rest. A single yank will usually do—there is no rhizome system, no bulblets. If you plant flower beds consisting entirely of attractive, freely spreading volunteers such as rose campion *(Lychnis coronaria),* red valerian *(Centranthus ruber),* forget-me-not *(Myosotis sylvatica),* love-in-a-mist *(Nigella damascena),* and sweet alyssum *(Lobularia maritima),* ignore some of the more attractive weeds such as scarlet pimpernel, fireweed, and any others you like that seem reasonably well behaved, and you will hardly need to weed at all.

There are cultivars of feverfew, which probably don't spread nearly as aggressively as their seedling parents. Some examples are Aureum, with chartreuse foliage (sometimes sold as Golden Feather), Golden Ball, with bright yellow flower heads and no rays, and Silver Ball, with fully double flowers whose white rays hide the golden centers.

Mrs. Grieve reports that feverfew grows in every hedgerow in England (I doubt that she actually verified that assertion, but I find it believable) and has long been used by country dwellers as a favored medicinal plant, primarily for lowering fever, but also for other purposes. Gerard reports it as a cure for ague, administered both as a drink and bound to the wrist; it was also employed as an aperient (gentle laxative), a carminative (facilitates farting), and an emmenagogue (induces menses). It was given to ease hysteria, calm nerves, and raise spirits. Decoctions with sugar or honey were given to suppress coughs and open bronchial passages, and a tincture was applied locally to treat insect and rat bites. When none of the forgoing ailments were present, it could be used as a general tonic to promote well-being.

FORGET-ME-NOT

Myosotis sylvatica—forget-me-not—Boraginaceae, borage family

The forget-me-not is a common garden annual that self-sows aggressively, usually becoming a weed even in the gardens where it is planted. It can be a good filler in borders and at the bases of shrubs, and it is an easy bulb cover. It takes proactive gardening to keep it confined to the areas where it is wanted.

The name *forget-me-not* refers to the plant's habit of spreading its burred fruit on the clothing of passersby, dogs, and gardeners. They are produced in abundance, and it often takes several days for the creature upon which they are bestowed to rid itself entirely of them. These fruits are small nutlets, produced four per bloom by the tiny (about ¼ inch), light blue (white at the center), five-petaled flowers. These blossoms grow on a single-sided cyme, the buds developing on a coiled stem tip; they open top to bottom along the curled stem as it uncoils. Plants grow upright, to about a foot tall.

Forget-me-nots are cool-season annuals that love shade and moisture. They may produce successive generations every year in well-watered gardens, especially near the coast. They have escaped into coastal forests—some trails on Mount Tamalpais are literally lined with blooming forget-me-nots. They do not travel very far from well-trodden paths, however, and so do not present much of an ecological threat—as weeds, they certainly do not belong in the same category as Cape ivy.

Forget-me-nots are European natives, and they were traditionally used to alleviate respiratory ailments—the plant was considered especially efficacious for afflictions of the left lower lung. There is a traditional belief that a decoction of the plant can be used to harden steel.

There are several close perennial relatives of forget-me-nots that may be grown in gardens—they are less evanescent than their annual cousin and do not seed prolifically but spread by underground rhizomes. One such is *Myosotis scorpioides,* the perennial forget-me-not, native to Europe, Asia, and North America, which has blue flowers with yellow eyes. *Omphalodes cappadocica,* a native of Turkey, produces sprays of bright blue, white-eyed flowers in spring. Blue-eyed Mary, *Omphalodes verna,* with heart-shaped leaves, forms a foliage mat 3 feet tall and wide and generates dark blue flowers with white eyes.

Other borage family members grown in gardens are borage itself *(Borago officinalis),* an annual used as a culinary herb, which can also spread itself easily around gardens where it is planted; various phacelias native to California, annual and perennial; and the western houndstongue, *Cynoglossum grande,* another native California woodland perennial that resembles forget-me-not and blooms in early spring.

GIANT REED

Arundo donax—giant reed, giant cane, river cane—Poaceae, Gramineae, grass family

Giant reed is a bamboo-like perennial grass that grows along streams and canals and on the margins of lakes, ponds, and wetlands. It can reach heights of 20 feet and spreads aggressively by rhizomes. The stems consist of jointed, woody culms, with long (a foot or more), pointed, entire leaves growing alternately along the stems and clasping them at the nodes. The plant blooms at the top of its culms, producing a feathery inflorescence that, however, does not set viable seed, at least in areas where it thrives as a weed. In Afghanistan and Iran, countries close to the plant's suspected place of origin, the river valleys of India, strains have been found that do produce viable seed. Perhaps the seed-bearing strains represent the species at its most primitive, and the ones with aggressive rhizomes are a later development, a response to a sterilizing genetic mutation, something we know is the case with *Oxalis pes-caprae.*

Arundo rhizomes produce long, tough, fibrous roots that penetrate deeply into the soil. The plant is capable of forming impenetrable thickets, which can spread for miles along riparian corridors, crowding out native trees and shrubs. It does not shade riverbanks as effectively as the cottonwoods and willows that would normally grow there, and so contributes to higher water temperatures, which can negatively affect aquatic life. The lack of diversity in these cane thickets often has a deleterious effect on populations of native insects, birds, and mammals.

Giant reed was probably first introduced into the United States in the Los Angeles area in the early 1800s, most likely planted to control erosion. It has now spread into suitable habitats throughout the southern half of the United States, but is most aggressive and abundant along rivers in Southern California, where it has formed monocultures along miles of streambed, often totally crowding out the native vegetation. It spreads not only by rhizome growth, but by fragments and virtual rafts of rhizomes that are dislodged by winter floods and carried downstream to establish new colonies.

Concerted attempts to eradicate giant reed and reestablish native riparian forest have been made along the Santa Ana River and other streams, attempts that have been somewhat successful, although at great cost. Roundup sprayed at relatively low concentrations has been effective, although the dead vegetation and rhizomes need to be removed, and repeat spraying is often needed, before other species can be planted.

Giant reed has long been considered a useful plant; it has been grown in the Mediterranean Basin since ancient times as a soil stabilizer, windbreak, and screening plant. The young, succulent stems can be eaten by cattle, a practice favored by ranchers who regard them as highly nutritious fodder. The hollow stems have been used to make flutes, pan pipes, and primitive pipe organs, and are still widely thought to be the only satisfactory material for woodwind reeds, although some musicians have lately become enamored with plastic reeds. It is still grown deliberately for this purpose—there is a small farm in Sonoma County at present. Whole canes have been used to make fishing rods, split canes for basketry, and the plant has a number of uses in folk medicine.

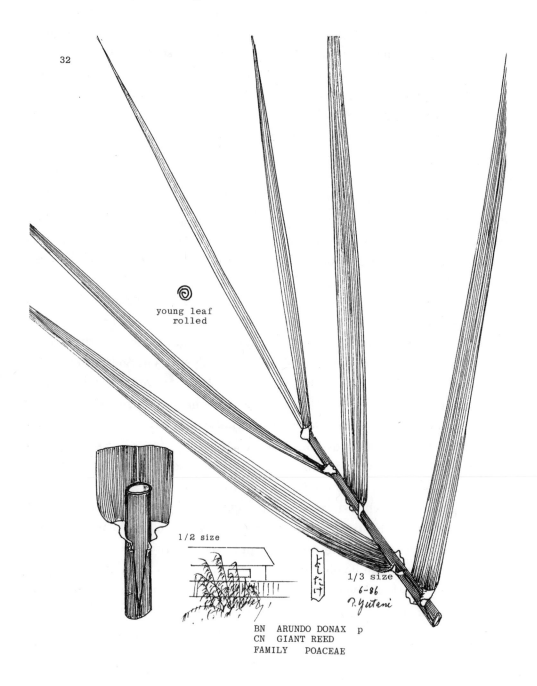

32

young leaf
rolled

1/2 size

1/3 size
6-86
T. Yutani

BN ARUNDO DONAX p
CN GIANT REED
FAMILY POACEAE

Arundo is still grown for erosion control, screening, and cattle forage in the southeastern United States, where its invasive potential appears to be lower than in California. This is possibly because bottomland forests there are denser and compete better with invasives.

Somewhat recently, this plant has come to the attention of companies wanting to produce biomass for fuel, paper pulp, or manufactured lumber. A Tacoma, Washington–based company known as Alex-Alt Biomass began contracting with public agencies in Southern California in 1997 to cut and haul away arundo. They signed a five-year contract with Riverside County to pay thirty dollars a ton for this material, money that the county has used to buy glyphosate to eradicate the regrowth and to reestablish native vegetation. At present, many areas formerly covered with giant reed seem to be well on their way to restoration of their riparian forests.

Right now, the attractiveness of river cane for use as biomass may be aiding in eradication efforts, but, of course, this cannot go on indefinitely. As with forests cut for timber, new plantations will have to be established if these industrial uses are going to be sustainable. This is already happening in places like Florida and Australia, where power companies are proposing establishment of giant reed plantations to produce fuel for generating electricity. Native plant groups and other environmentalists oppose these schemes, fearing that the spread of giant reed from these plantations cannot be contained, and that another ecological disaster could be the result.

Arundo donax can easily be mistaken for many bamboos, as well as for *Phragmites australis,* the common reed, a large grass that grows in temperate and tropical wetlands throughout the world, including California and much of the rest of the United States. Bamboo leaves, however, grow on side branches rather than the main stem. Common reed does not grow quite as tall as giant reed. It ranges from 6 feet to about 20 feet, while giant reed usually reaches at least 8 or 9 feet and can grow as tall as 30; but these ranges overlap considerably, so this size difference is not particularly helpful. However, common reed blooms reliably every year, while arundo flowers only every twenty to thirty years. Phragmites usually grows directly in the water, while giant reed grows mostly on stream edges and floodplains.

In the eastern United States, common reed is a major invader of wetlands, and planting it is prohibited in many states; the California Invasive Plant Council regards it only as occasionally problematic in this state, while it designates giant reed as highly invasive. The state of California has declared arundo a noxious weed.

The canebrakes described by the eighteenth-century American naturalist William Bartram in his *Travels,* and referred to frequently in early American songs, literature, and folklore, as well as in still-current place names, consist of neither giant reed nor phragmites, but of a number of species of *Arundinaria,* a genus of bamboo that grows in the eastern United States.

HARDING GRASS

Phalaris aquatica—Harding grass—Poaceae

Harding grass is a common invader of wet meadows and pastures. This perennial native of the Mediterranean Basin can form an erect tuft 3 feet tall, with the flower spikes reaching a height of 4 feet. It is a bunch grass, producing offsets on short rhizomes, creating clumps that can be very difficult to dig out; any roots or rhizomes left in the ground will regenerate. Perhaps originally introduced as a pasture grass, it is now considered an ecological weed that can compete aggressively with native grassland species. Although it likes wet ground, its sturdy root system enables it to tolerate considerable drought.

The leaves of Harding grass are gray-green and smooth and can grow to 15 inches long; the stems are hollow. Flowers are in densely crowded spikes 2 to 5 inches long, which taper to a point at the tips; they turn a light tan color when dry, then produce abundant seed, most of which is shed from May through September.

Harding grass grows slowly at first, so recognition of the clumps while young enables timely removal, which should greatly improve chances of checking its spread. Digging clumps out as completely as possible is the preferred method for removing it; any roots over 2 inches long can regenerate. Mowing the more established clumps several times throughout the growing season is also an option; this will keep it from flowering and will weaken the plant. Regrowth of mowed clumps can be prevented by heavy mulching; treating regrowth with herbicide can also be effective.

Harding grass may have been brought to California from Australia, where it is a valued forage grass because of its high-protein content. It does, however, contain quantities of DMT, a federally controlled hallucinogen (planting the grass is not illegal, however) that can affect sheep, sometimes fatally, with a condition known as staggers—it does not seem to bother cows and horses. It has been planted sometimes for postfire revegetation—not a good idea.

I have no illustration for Harding grass; I am providing one of *Phalaris canariensis,* a similar weed that does not pose a serious ecological threat.

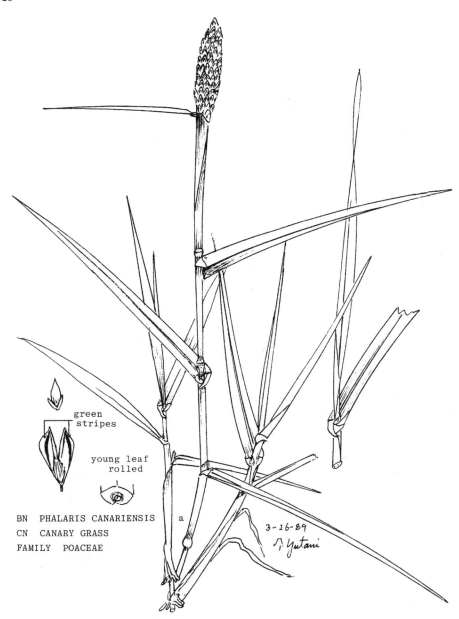

green
stripes

young leaf
rolled

BN   PHALARIS CANARIENSIS
CN   CANARY GRASS
FAMILY   POACEAE

a

3-16-89
T. Yutani

HELLEBORINE

Epipactis helleborine—wild orchid, broad-leaved helleborine—Orchidaceae, orchid family

Orchids are usually thought of as delicate hothouse flowers, needing very exacting care, and little regard is given to their potential as weeds. True, most orchids that are grown as ornamentals are from the tropics and unable to withstand cold; but tender they are not. Many of them have thick, succulent leaves that enable them to withstand prolonged drought, an occurrence quite common in most of the tropics. Most tropical forests are not rain forests but monsoon forests, and their plants are adapted to surviving many months of hot, dry weather, as well as to intensely rainy periods. Epiphytic orchids, those that attach themselves to the branches of trees and shrubs for support, get their water and nutrients directly from the air or from rain, through their aerial roots. In many tropical areas, such as Hawaii, these plants have become weeds, escaping from greenhouses where they are grown for the house plant trade and establishing themselves in forests where they are not native.

In the temperate zone, most orchids are terrestrial, growing in humus-rich soil in woodlands and by stream sides. These generally reproduce sparingly and do not move out of their native environments. There is at least one exception, however: *Epipactis helleborine,* a small terrestrial orchid native to European woodlands that found its way to America as a garden flower and has become a minor weed pest, traveling beyond where it has been planted and freely reproducing in shady areas and in woodlands.

Helleborine grows from a fleshy, branching rootstock, sending up stems that can reach as high as 3 feet (usually a foot or less in California). These are often tinged purple at the base and are covered with clasping, semisucculent leaves, ovate to lanceolate in shape, sharply pointed at the tips. The inflorescence is a terminal raceme with a green bract at its base, consisting of fifteen to thirty small (about ½ inch long) flowers. The flowers have the typical lipped appearance common to orchids; they are greenish, with some pinkish-purple highlights. In California gardens, this plant can spread freely but is not super-aggressive, and it is often regarded as a welcome addition to a woodland garden.

The fleshy rhizome of helleborine is able to persist in the soil for many years without producing top growth, so the plant is very tolerant to prolonged drought. It is aided by a symbiotic association with a fungus that attaches itself to the rhizome and provides it with nutrients from the soil.

Broad-leaved helleborine first appeared in the United States in 1879, when it was found in New York State. How it got there is not known, but it was adopted by members of garden clubs and was spread widely throughout the eastern United States. It has become a common and aggressive pest in and around Milwaukee, Wisconsin, where it was first discovered in Lake Park in 1930. Helleborine has spread throughout the surrounding counties, aggressively invading undisturbed habitats. Drier conditions in California make it likely that it will remain only a minor pest here.

INDIAN MOCK STRAWBERRY

Duchesnea indica—Indian mock strawberry—Rosaceae, rose family

Indian mock strawberry is a widely planted ground cover that tends to escape from the areas in which it is planted, spreading by seeds and stolons. It will readily colonize lawns, especially shady portions where the grass grows thinly. It can also escape into other ground covers and flower beds, and even into moist woodlands.

This plant looks like a strawberry: it has three-lobed leaves that are bumpy (rugose) on their top surface and hairy. The plant spreads by above-ground runners, bears a red fruit consisting of a reddish receptacle covered with dark red achenes, and has the five-petaled flowers with many stamens that are typical of the rose family. These are yellow, however, rather than the white or slightly pinkish color of strawberry flowers. The fruit is edible but has little or no flavor. It grows above the leaves rather than under them as many true strawberries do. It is grown only for its ornamental value.

Mock strawberry is perennial, with fibrous roots, which form everywhere a stem node touches the ground. It can escape from plantings quite easily and can be truly rampant in well-watered gardens, especially in shady areas. It is very susceptible to a rust fungus that forms orange pustules on the undersides of the leaves.

Given that it is disease prone and weedy, mock strawberry is a mediocre ground cover at best; so, why plant it? Why not plant real strawberries, which bear delicious fruit and do not spread as rampantly? The sand strawberry, *Fragaria chiloensis,* native to California as well as Chile, makes a fine ground cover in sunny areas, as long as it can be irrigated from time to time. Although somewhat drought tolerant due to its thick, dark green leaves, it needs moderate water to thrive. In shady areas that receive regular irrigation, consider the native woodland strawberry, *Fragaria vesca* var. *californica,* which sometimes appears spontaneously in gardens. It can be recognized by its thin, bright green, rugose leaves with serrated margins. It spreads by runners, as does the sand strawberry, and thrives in shade. Although native to summer-dry California, it will need some water to maintain a lush appearance year round.

The fruits of both these native strawberries are said to be edible and tasty, but I cannot confirm this, as I have never actually found one—they probably get eaten by birds as soon as they ripen. A better choice for easy-care fruiting strawberries is the European version of *Fragaria vesca,* the alpine, or, more accurately, woodland strawberry, long cultivated for its tiny fruits, which are sold in France as *fraises de bois* (birds probably eat these, too—but they flower and fruit a lot more prolifically than the native strawberries). This plant has leaves similar to those of its California cousin, but it does not spread by runners—the leaves are attached to 6-inch stems that emerge from a single crown. Woodland strawberries spread by producing short-stemmed offsets from the mother plant, as well as by seeding themselves fairly freely. They might be considered a weed, but with delicious fruit, and an intense flavor stronger than that of most larger strawberries (which are hybrids between *F. vesca* and an eastern American strawberry, *Fragaria virginiana*).

Fragaria vesca should be a welcome addition to any garden that is kept moderately moist, whether it is planted or appears spontaneously. Cultivars of the woodland strawberry include yellow- and white-fruited forms; the best red-fruited one is probably Rugen Improved. Plant a few, you'll soon have many; they are almost a weed, but not really. They would be a good companion for Labrador violets (so-called—more on these later) in ground cover under rhododendrons or other shade and moisture-loving plants. Just remember to weed out any mock strawberry that appears.

ITALIAN ARUM

Arum italicum—Italian arum—Araceae, arum family

The large arum family, represented most heavily in the tropics and subtropics, is the source of many ornamental house and garden plants, including philodendrons, caladiums, calla lilies, and a number of other tough, tolerant, tuberous-rooted perennials. In the tropics, they are mostly forest understory plants, and so they tolerate low light. Their tuberous roots make them highly drought resistant, although they also thrive with abundant water. In temperate woodlands in the eastern United States, the arum family is represented by skunk cabbage and jack-in-the-pulpit. A number of arums grow in Mediterranean woodlands, and so they are well adapted to dry shade in California; the most common of these is the Italian arum.

This attractive aroid has triangular leaves with wavy margins and, quite often, whitish variegation along the veins. They grow directly from the crown of a fleshy root, on petioles about as long as the leaf blades. The full height of the plant is generally about a foot, but sometimes up to 2 feet. The flower is calla-like, consisting of a white or greenish-white (sometimes purple-spotted) bract called a spathe, which half encloses a short, thick, fleshy spike, the spadix, which is covered with tiny yellow flowers. These are followed by orange-red fruits; this dense cluster of round fruits atop the bare stem reminds one of corn on the cob. After bloom, the leaves die to the ground, but the red berries remain.

Italian arum is ideally adapted to dry shade and so is an ideal plant to grow under live oaks. It does not spread much vegetatively but tends to volunteer from seeds, so it can become something of a pest in some situations. It is fairly easy to control where it is not wanted, as long as one digs out the entire root.

IVIES

Hedera canariensis—Algerian ivy—Araliaceae, aralia family

Hedera helix—English ivy

Ivy is one of the most widely planted ground covers in California, mostly due to its fast growth and wide spread. Both these attributes create maintenance problems by allowing it to grow far beyond its boundaries, climb trees, fences, and walls, and escape into the wild, where it can displace native vegetation. Planted in full sun on freeway embankments, it needs copious amounts of water; even if it gets it, the leaves will still burn in direct midday sun. In the shade, both species are quite drought tolerant and are best not watered at all, in order to minimize their rampant growth. In the wild, ivy is considered an ecological weed; more and more, it is coming to be regarded as a weed in gardens.

I mention Algerian ivy first because it is the more rampant of the two species. It is a perennial vine, native to North Africa and the Canary Islands. Stems grow from a sturdy crown sitting atop a branching taproot; they can grow 20 feet long, but since they branch and produce adventitious roots at the nodes, a plant from a single crown can spread as far as growing conditions are suitable. The stems are pinkish in color and produce alternate, broadly oval to palmately lobed leaves (three lobes per leaf) that are glossy, dark green, and 5 to 8 inches across. Recently planted ivy hugs the ground, but as it reaches its growth limits (often imposed only by continuous, laborious trimming at the desired boundaries), it begins to mound up, often reaching a height of 2 or 3 feet. This is ideal habitat for rats, who do not hesitate to seize any opportunities we offer them for food and shelter.

Ivy vines are actually the juvenile stage of the plant: after eight to ten years, the growth will turn shrubby, ascend to heights of 6 to 8 feet or more, grow oval leaves without lobes, and flower, producing 6-inch umbels of ¼-inch white blossoms that are ball shaped, with protruding stamens. The flowers give way to inky blue to black capsules, which split around the circumference, then split in half and release numerous seeds. Birds eat the fruits, aiding in the plant's spread.

Kept trimmed and mowed, ivy will remain in its juvenile stage indefinitely.

English ivy is a little smaller and better behaved than Algerian ivy, but not much. This plant is native to Europe, where it inhabits woodlands from the Mediterranean Basin to southern Scandinavia. English ivy also grows throughout temperate Asia. It can be distinguished from its Algerian cousin by its leaves, which are smaller (up to 4 inches across), less glossy, sometimes with a reddish tinge, and three- to five-lobed. In its mature stage, this ivy produces clusters of yellow flowers.

The adventitious roots of the ivies allow them to climb by attaching themselves to fences, walls, and tree bark. Ivy climbs trees readily, and it can harm them by retaining excess moisture around the crowns. It climbs walls just as readily, but tends to fall off after a time. The "ivy-covered walls" of eastern universities are mostly created by using two clinging non-ivy vines in the grape family: Boston ivy, *Parthenocissus tricuspidata,* and Virginia creeper, *P. quinquenervia.* These adhere by a sort of suction cup, which sticks more firmly than ivy roots, and does not damage masonry by penetrating it with its roots, as ivy does.

Ivy has many associations with ancient myth and legend and was, in ancient times, thought to prevent or cure drunkenness (Bacchus wore a crown of ivy), but it is no longer used medicinally. It was a pagan symbol of regeneration and renewal, so it was often used as a Christmas green (as referenced in the carol "The Holly and the Ivy"), despite opposition to this practice by an early council of the church, which objected to its pagan associations. Greek priests, however, presented wreaths of ivy to newlyweds, and the plant remained a symbol of fidelity throughout the ages in Europe. Poets were honored with wreaths of ivy, as well as with laurel.

Roman agricultural writers recommended ivy leaves as cattle food, despite the fact that cows do not seem to like them; sheep and deer will sometimes browse on ivy in the winter. The wood of the mature ivy stems is fine-grained and was used by wood turners in southern Europe to make wine cups, among other things (Homer's *Odyssey* mentions an ivy-wood cup)—but this wood is soft and porous, and the wine stains it red. Thin slices of ivy wood have also been used to filter wine.

JUBATA GRASS

Cortaderia jubata—jubata grass—Poaceae, Gramineae, grass family

Jubata grass is a close cousin of the widely planted ornamental known as pampas grass, *Cortaderia selloana,* and is sometimes confused with it. It probably arrived in California as an ornamental, perhaps mistaken for *C. selloana,* and quickly became established as an invasive exotic. It seeds prolifically and has spread rapidly over large areas, often crowding out native vegetation. It does well in serpentine soil, where it competes with some of the endemic species that have evolved to adapt to these nutrient-poor soils.

Jubata is a large, perennial grass from the eastern foothills of the Andes in Ecuador, Bolivia, and Peru. Its leaves are narrow, tapered, about 3 to 4 feet long, and finely serrated on the edges. These edges are extremely sharp and can produce deep cuts, much like paper cuts, in the fingers of the unwary. The flower clusters are large, terminal, plume-like panicles, usually white, sometimes pink, on stalks that grow as high as 8 feet. All flowers are female: the plant reproduces apomictically (i.e., without pollination). Flowers are followed by plumed fruits, which are easily carried great distances by the wind. Jubata grass is not rhizomatous but has large, very stout roots that anchor it firmly and make it difficult to dig out.

Jubata grass can grow nearly anywhere its seeds drop, but it is especially prone to invade areas of sandy soil or serpentine. It has formed vast colonies on the sand dunes near Monterey and along the Big Sur coast. In Oakland, it is a familiar sight around the Oakland Airport and on steep slopes in the East Bay hills. Organized efforts have been made to eradicate or check its spread on public lands, with varying degrees of success. Gardeners should not plant it but should learn to recognize it and intervene early and often when it appears. Clumps can be dug out with some effort, but, if done well, will not reappear. Seedlings will be a problem for many years; they should be dug out or sprayed as soon as they appear.

Pampas grass can also be somewhat invasive, but not nearly as much as jubata. To distinguish these two grasses, you should compare the relative lengths of the leaves and flower stalks. The leaves of jubata are 3 to 4 feet long, the flower stalks about twice that; so the plumes are held considerably above the tussock. Pampas grass has leaves that are 7 to 8 feet long, and the flower plumes are only a little higher than the tussock.

If you like the appearance of pampas grass but want to be sure you don't plant something that will become invasive, it is best to stick with the recently developed dwarf hybrids. These grow from 3 to 5 feet high (a more sensible size for most small gardens than their 8-foot-tall parents), do not set viable seed, and come with white- or yellow-margined leaves, as well as plain green ones.

KENILWORTH IVY

Cymbalaria muralis—Kenilworth ivy, ivy-leaved toadflax—Plantaginaceae, plantain family

Kenilworth ivy is a pleasant little annual vine, native to the Mediterranean Basin. It freely sows itself throughout gardens in which it is planted and often moves into other gardens. It has slender, trailing stems, sometimes reddish, that grow 2 or 3 feet long and form mats 2 or 3 inches high. It will grow in sun or deep shade and prefers moist soils. It is often planted, or volunteers, in crevices in rock walls, which can retain moisture long after more open soil has dried.

The leaves of Kenilworth ivy are about ¼ to ½ inch across, round and shallowly lobed, medium green, smooth, and palmately veined. The tiny flowers, resembling miniature snapdragons, grow singly on long pedicels in the leaf axils. They are bicolored, purple and white. The fruit is pinkish and warty.

Kenilworth ivy is a plant that needs little control; it can be a good ground cover under shrubs, often works well as a filler in flower borders, and can provide some competition to less desirable weeds. If it grows where other plants are preferred, it can easily be pulled out. It has naturalized in a number of coastal California counties but has not become a serious ecological threat.

LILY OF THE VALLEY VINE

Salpichroa origanifolia—lily of the valley vine—Solanaceae, nightshade family

Lily of the valley vine is an escaped ornamental, originating in South America, that has escaped from cultivation and established itself in the wild and in parks and gardens in various parts of California, from San Diego to Yolo

Counties. In the San Francisco Bay Area, it is fairly abundant, and I have seen it in Oakland. It is a perennial that grows from an extensive woody root system that puts out a lot of top growth and makes it difficult to eradicate.

The stems of this vine grow 1 or 2 feet long, but they branch freely, and the entire plant can become 5 feet wide. The leaves, alternate on the stem, are medium green, broadly oval with pointed tips, an inch or more in length—very much like oregano leaves. The flowers are bell shaped, white with protruding yellow stamens, with a green calyx on a purple stem, ¼ to ⅓ inch long. The fruit is an oblong yellowish-white berry ½ inch or less in length.

Covered with flowers and fruit, this can be a very attractive vining ground cover in a garden; but its propensity to escape means it should be grown with caution, if at all, especially near wild areas.

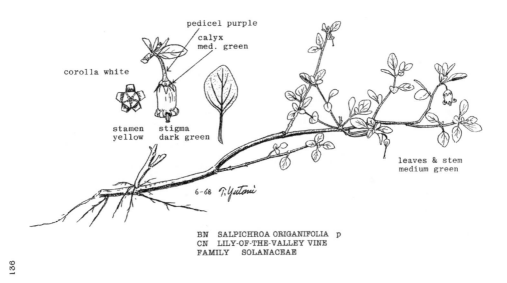

pedicel purple

calyx
med. green

corolla white

stamen   stigma
yellow   dark green

leaves & stem
medium green

6-68 T. Yatani

BN   SALPICHROA ORIGANIFOLIA p
CN   LILY-OF-THE-VALLEY VINE
FAMILY   SOLANACEAE

138

LIPPIA

Phyla nodiflora—lippia—Verbenaceae, verbena family

Lippia, also known as mat grass, frog fruit, and turkey tangle, is a prostrate, creeping perennial ground cover that spreads by rooting at the nodes of the above-ground stems. It forms a dense, flat mat no more than 2 inches tall. At one time, it became somewhat popular as a lawn substitute, since it requires no mowing and uses considerably less water than grass. However, it is susceptible to invasion by taller weeds, so it is seldom used for lawns anymore. It is mostly found in older, neglected gardens, from which it occasionally escapes.

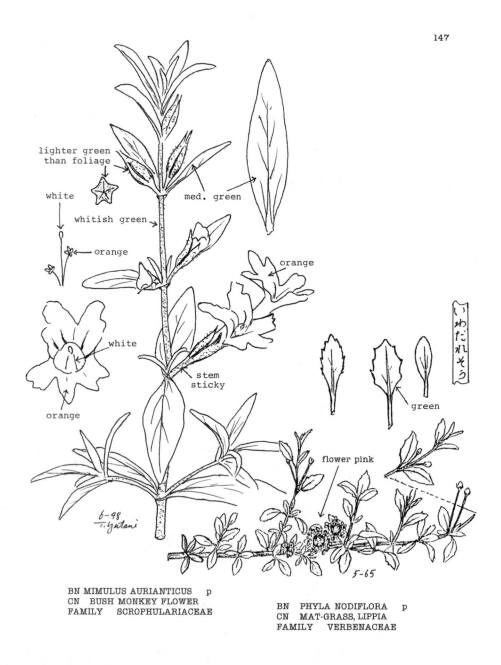

lighter green
than foliage

white

whitish green

orange

med. green

orange

white

orange

stem
sticky

green

flower pink

6-98
T. yatani

5-65

BN MIMULUS AURIANTICUS   p
CN   BUSH MONKEY FLOWER
FAMILY   SCROPHULARIACEAE

BN   PHYLA NODIFLORA   p
CN   MAT-GRASS, LIPPIA
FAMILY   VERBENACEAE

The leaves of lippia grow opposite each other on the hairy stems. They are obovate with a wedge-shaped base, finely toothed at their upper ends, dark green to gray-green, and covered with fine hairs. The stems, also covered with fine hairs, grow from 1 to 3 feet long, rooting at the nodes.

Lippia flowers are tiny, tubular, five-petaled blossoms divided into two lips, the tube white, the lips lavender. They are clustered into dense heads ⅓ inch or less across, which sit atop peduncles growing from the leaf nodes. These heads are surrounded at their base by two or three rows of overlapping bracts. The fruit is globular or slightly two-lobed.

Lippia is widely distributed throughout the tropical and subtropical regions of the world. Grown as a ground cover or lawn substitute in warm temperate climates, it tends to turn brown in winter or freeze completely in heavy frosts. Although it has not proven to be a very satisfactory lawn substitute, it can function adequately as a ground cover in dry, open ground. It will survive with no summer irrigation and will thrive with a moderate amount.

LOVE-IN-A-MIST

Nigella damascena—love-in-a-mist, devil-in-a-bush—Ranunculaceae, buttercup family

Love-in-a-mist, a delicate herbaceous plant native to the Mediterranean Basin, is an easy to grow, self-sowing winter annual. It travels freely about the garden, filling spaces that might otherwise be occupied by less attractive weeds. It is a 1- to 3-foot-tall upright plant, with leaves finely divided into narrowly linear segments. A collar of these leaves surrounds the base of each of the 1½ to 2-inch-wide flowers with many petals (five to ten, usually) that sit atop the stems. These are more often than not light blue, but may also be pale blue, pale purple, white, yellow, or pink. The abundant feathery foliage forms the "mist" through which the flowers are viewed. The flowers produce large, papery, horned seed capsules about 2 inches across, which contain many black seeds. The plant blooms in spring, then dies out in the summer heat. In regions with cool summers such as the San Francisco Bay Area, it can bloom throughout the summer if given some water. It tolerates full sun to light shade.

The dried capsules of devil-in-a-bush are often used in dry flower arrangements. There are some selected strains: Miss Jekyll has semidouble, cornflower blue blossoms; Persian Jewels is a mixture of colors.

The nigella seeds sold as a spice in Indian and Near Eastern grocery stores are from a related plant, *Nigella sativa,* which closely resembles love-in-a-mist but has flowers with fewer petals. These seeds are sometimes referred to as black cumin in English, or by various other ethnic names in countries whose cuisine they enhance.

Given its obvious virtues, it is hard to think of love-in-a-mist as a weed, except perhaps in a garden so rigidly designed that it can allow no variation of color or form. In most gardens, pulling out seedlings that crowd other desired plants should provide sufficient control.

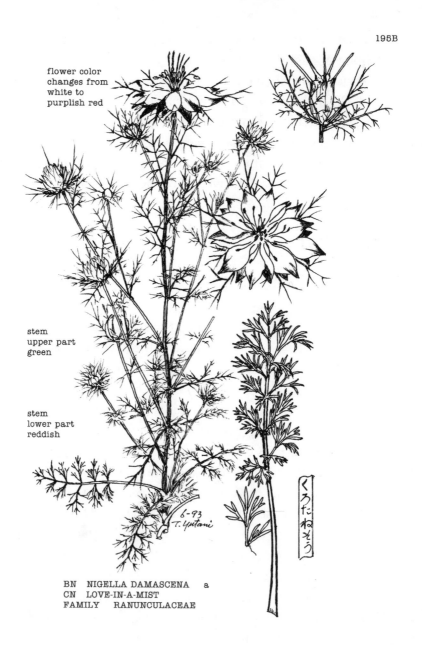

195B

flower color
changes from
white to
purplish red

stem
upper part
green

stem
lower part
reddish

6-93
T. Yutani

くろたねそう

BN   NIGELLA DAMASCENA   a
CN   LOVE-IN-A-MIST
FAMILY   RANUNCULACEAE

MINTS

Mentha pulegium—pennyroyal—Lamiaceae, Labiatae, mint family

Mentha spicata—spearmint

A number of species of the genus *Mentha,* the mints, are grown in gardens as culinary and medicinal herbs and, because of their extremely vigorous rhizomes and rooting stems, often run amok in the garden. They are best grown under some sort of containment, and the smaller this is, the more frequently they will need to be dug out, divided, and replanted. When they escape from gardens, they tend to establish themselves in areas that remain moist year round, where they can become invasive pests. They can survive, however, in drier areas because of their extensive underground stems, which store water; their behavior in these situations is considerably more subdued. The two mints that are most frequently seen outside the garden are pennyroyal and spearmint.

Pennyroyal, *Mentha pulegium*—also known in England as pulegium, run-by-the-ground, lurk-in-the-ditch, pudding grass, and pulliol-royal—is seldom cultivated anymore, being mostly found in moist to wet places outside gardens: in pastures, in wet meadows, near ditches, and on the margins of wetlands and irrigated crop lands. In urban areas, it is a common nursery weed.

The leaves of pennyroyal are elliptic, toothed or entire, grayish-green, and 1 to 1½ inches long, diminishing in size toward the tips of the stems. The stems are square, and the leaves are set on opposite sides of the nodes, as is the case with the entire mint family. They are covered with short white hairs.

The flowers of pennyroyal are blue and tubular with the five petals forming two lips; they grow in whorls around stems that arise from the leaf nodes. The fruit is a one-seeded nutlet.

As with any mint, pennyroyal can be controlled only by thoroughly digging out all the rhizomes, and perhaps following up by spraying the almost inevitable regrowth. More careful, targeted irrigation also helps keep it in check.

Pennyroyal is a prostrate plant, with stems that root at the nodes; it also spreads aggressively underground.

A native of Europe, pennyroyal has a long history of culinary and medicinal uses. The Roman naturalist Pliny the Elder called it *pulegium*, from the word *pulex*, "flea," because of its reputation for repelling these creatures (it is still sometimes used as a bug spray). It was once used in a pork stuffing known as hog's pudding, which included pepper and honey as well as pennyroyal. The medieval theologian and naturalist Albertus Magnus reports in his *Book of Secrets* that drowned flies and bees can be revived by placing them in the warm ashes of burned pennyroyal—the value of this procedure for bees is obvious, but Albertus does not explain why one might want to revive flies.

Pennyroyal is considered to be carminative, stimulant, and diaphoretic; it can be used as an emmenagogue and to soothe the stomach. Pliny the Elder recommends this herb for many ailments and says that hanging it in sleeping rooms promotes health—which it may well, if it actually does repel fleas.

The herbalist Gerard says it can be used to purify water, as well as the blood. He also recommends it as an antidote for "spasmodic, nervous, and hysterical affectations." Tea of pennyroyal and other mints is still popular for colds and for settling the stomach and promoting digestion.

Spearmint, *Mentha spicata,* is perhaps the most popular garden mint, very familiar to many people through its association with spearmint gum and mint juleps. It is generally upright in habit, a foot tall or more, spreading mostly by its rhizomes, although stems that touch the ground can root. Leaves are light green, up to 2 inches long, oblong or egg shaped, toothed, hairless but with a crinkled surface. Its flavor and aroma is somewhat less pungent than that of peppermint, but with a quality unique to itself. The flowers are usually some shade of lavender but can range from white to purple. They grow in whorls atop stems arising from the leaf nodes, forming a spike with a pointed tip. It has naturalized in many wet places in the Bay Area, including some native habitats.

Spearmint has the same medicinal uses as pennyroyal. As a culinary herb, it is used to flavor cold drinks (including mint juleps), as a tea, and to make sauces and jellies to accompany meats, especially lamb. Mint tea is especially popular in Arab cultures—cucumbers in mint-flavored yogurt are familiar palate-cleansing dishes throughout the Near East, as well as in Afghanistan and India.

NASTURTIUM

Tropaeolum majus—nasturtium, garden nasturtium—Tropaeolaceae, nasturtium family

The nasturtium is an attractive garden flower that can easily take over a yard, especially in the cool coastal zones of California, where it grows and blooms winter and summer. It is especially abundant in winter; its summer growth slows in gardens that are sparingly irrigated, but its succulent stems enable some plants to survive and continue to bloom.

Native to South America, nasturtium is perennial in wet, subtropical climates but functions as an annual where winters are cold or summer water is sparse. The plant is essentially a vine, producing succulent stems from somewhat tuberous taproots that can grow to 6 feet or more; it forms a ground cover in open areas but can climb into shrubs by using coiling petioles. These are long, often 5 or 6 inches, and end in a round leaf, 2 or 3 inches in diameter, that completely encircles them. The leaves are thin and papery so often wither in the summer; but the stems and taproots persist, producing new growth with the first substantial irrigation they receive, by rain or otherwise.

Nasturtium flowers grow singly on stalks about as long as the petioles, have five somewhat irregularly shaped petals, and are about 1 to 1½ inches across, with long, prominent spurs. The flowers are typically yellow or orange, sometimes both, but they can also be red or reddish-brown, even white. Flowers are followed by green capsules about ¼ inch in diameter, which mature to a tan color, then split into three carpels containing one seed each. These can literally cover the ground beneath the plants in late summer, producing a dense cover of seedlings when irrigated.

There are selected strains of nasturtiums that grow much more compactly, producing mounds about 1 to 1½ feet high and across; these do not grow as rampantly nor seed as freely as the vining types. Seeds for these strains are available in single or mixed colors. If you already have the vining type in your garden, however, you'll never need to plant another seed, and any attempts to replace them with the better-behaved nasturtiums will be futile.

On the bright side, the flowers, seeds, and leaves of nasturtiums have a pleasant, peppery fragrance and taste and can be used in salads; the flowers are both decorative and flavorful. Plucked nasturtium blooms last a long time in water, so they can be a useful addition to flower arrangements.

PERIWINKLE

Vinca major—periwinkle, big periwinkle—Apocynaceae, dogbane family

Periwinkle is an old European garden plant that is still widely planted as a ground cover and has been much used in California for erosion control on stream banks. It spreads both by underground rhizomes and by rooting at the nodes on the stems. Some of these stems are upright, ascending to about a foot; others lie flat on the ground, where they form adventitious roots, enabling them to cover ground very quickly. The erosion control benefit of such a plant is obvious, so much so that its propensity for crowding out native vegetation, and spreading to areas where it has not been planted, is often ignored.

The leaves of periwinkle are opposite, broadly oval, about 1 to 2 inches long, glossy dark green with a leathery texture, hairy on the margins, attached to the stem by short petioles. Flowers are a purplish blue, five-petaled, about an inch across. The fruit, a curved follicle, is seldom produced.

Periwinkle is native to Eurasia and North Africa and was introduced to America in the 1700s as an ornamental, grown primarily for its attractive flowers. It is an easy ground cover that does best in fairly moist soil, but it can survive periods of protracted drought due to its extensive rhizomes. Often grown on stream banks, it can spread when pieces break off and root in downstream areas. Restorers of native vegetation try to eradicate it or limit its spread and recommend not planting it in gardens, especially near streams. Perhaps a better choice for a garden ground cover is the small periwinkle, *Vinca minor*, which has smaller leaves and flowers and a much less rampant growth habit. This plant hugs the ground closely, does not send up ascending stems, and does best with a fair amount of moisture.

PRIDE OF MADEIRA

Echium candicans—pride of Madeira—Boraginaceae, borage family

Pride of Madeira is a rounded, 5- or 6-foot shrub growing from a bulbous base. It has been widely planted along the California coast, which provides an ideal environment for this frost-tender plant. It seeds prolifically, and in some places has escaped from gardens and naturalized in the wild. The California Invasive Plant Council lists it as having "limited" invasive potential; nonetheless, some parks and preserves along the California coast, including the Golden Gate National Recreation Area, remove it whenever it is found.

This plant is esteemed for its spring bloom; it produces flower spikes up to a foot long, covered with bluish-purple flowers with red centers at the ends of the branches, whose lower portions bear narrow, elliptical leaves covered with hairs that can cause itching when handled. It does well in poor, dry soil, as long as it is well drained. The flowers produce enormous quantities of seed, which germinates readily; keeping after the seedlings is the most work required by this plant. Deadheading the flower spikes before they drop too much is wise.

Pride of Madeira is native to Madeira, the largest island in an archipelago in the Atlantic southwest of mainland Portugal. Colonized by Portuguese settlers beginning in the 1400s, it is now part of the Portuguese Republic. It has a balmy Mediterranean climate, like Portugal and California.

A closely related species is *Echium wildpretii*, tower of jewels, native to Tenerife in the Canary Islands, which are part of Spain. A true biennial, tower of jewels spends its first year as a rounded rosette of long, narrow leaves covered with silvery gray hairs; in its second year, it shoots up on a single stem to a height of 6 to 10 feet and produces one gigantic flower spike at its tip, covered with rose to rosy-red flowers—a true Dr. Seuss plant. It dies after flowering, leaving a mass of seed at its base.

RED VALERIAN

Centranthus ruber—red valerian, Jupiter's beard—Valerianaceae, valerian family

Red valerian, also known as red-spur valerian, and, in England, as pretty Betsy, bouncing Bess, delicate Bess, drunken sailor, bovisand soldier, and keys of heaven, is an upright, branching perennial native to the Mediterranean Basin, but also naturalized in milder-winter areas of northern Europe, such as England and Ireland. It is an attractive, magenta-flowered perennial, undoubtedly first planted in California as an ornamental; but it produces copious seed and so can spread widely—and has. Its roots branch freely, so it is especially well adapted to rocky areas, crevices between stones, the bases of walls, cracks in concrete, and crowns of trees and shrubs—all locations where it is typically found. It likes sun or shade, rich or lean soil, moist or dry conditions.

Red valerian is compact and somewhat bushy and grows from 1 to 3 feet high and wide. Leaves are simple, entire or toothed at the base, and oval to lanceolate, with pointed tips. They are generally 2 to 4 inches long, sessile, and opposite on their stems. The flowers are small and fragrant, in dense terminal clusters. The most common color is a light magenta, but white and dark red variations also occur. I find these latter two much more attractive than the usual color and would try to propagate them from cuttings if I actually wanted to introduce this plant into my garden. The flowers are usually about ½ inch long, with five petals that fuse to form a slender tube with a spur at the base. The fruit is an elongated, narrow nut.

Red valerian flowers most heavily in the spring but will produce some later blooms, especially if the spent flowers are cut back. It becomes ragged and unattractive when cold weather sets in. If it is growing someplace where you want to maintain it, it is a good idea to cut it back to the crown—when the warmer weather comes, it will resprout vigorously. When older crowns get woody and lose their vigor, they can be pulled out, allowing them to be replaced by one or more of the abundant seedlings they generate.

In former times—and perhaps still, in some places—the leaves of red valerian were eaten in salads or cooked as greens. In France, the roots were sold in markets to be used in soups. This plant is in the same family as the true vale-rian, *Valeriana officinalis,* but does not have that plant's medicinal properties.

Red valerian is probably best thought of not as a weed but as an easy, overly aggressive garden plant that volunteers more freely than most gar-deners would like and needs to be kept continuously in check. This puts it in the same category as other short-lived perennials such as rose campion *(Lych-nis coronaria),* purple toadflax *(Linaria purpurea),* sweet alyssum *(Lobularia maritima),* and California poppy *(Eschscholzia californica).* The work involved in controlling these freely seeding, short-lived perennials and annuals may often be more than offset by their abundance, their free-flowering qualities, and their ability to fill spaces between larger perennials and shrubs with something other than noxious weeds. The fine line between abundance and excess must be established by each gardener; the art involved in maintaining the balance, however, is one of the more challenging and pleasurable aspects of gardening.

SLENDER FALSE BROME

Brachypodium sylvaticum—slender false brome—Poaceae, Gramineae, grass family

A native of Eurasia and North Africa that was first spotted in Eugene, Oregon, in 1930, slender false brome has invaded forests and open grasslands in that state, especially in the Willamette Valley. In forests, it often forms a dense understory that can crowd out native plants; in grasslands, it tends to become the dominant grass. It is now considered a noxious weed in Oregon, meaning that those who have it are legally obligated to control it. Recently, slender false brome has appeared in redwood forests in the Santa Cruz Mountains. The Cal-ifornia Invasive Plant Council considers it a "moderate" threat.

Slender false brome is a clump-forming perennial that grows to 3 feet tall. Leaves grow in tufts from the base and tend to droop at their ends. They are about ⅛ to ¼ inch wide, hairy, with short, membranous ligules and no auri-cles. The awned spikelets are slender, in open clusters at the tips of the stems. They droop, but are on very short pedicels, sometimes completely sessile. Slen-der false brome tends to prefer the shade of closed-canopy forests, but often spreads to woodland edges and into open grasslands, mostly in upland areas.

Although the distribution of this weed outside of Oregon is limited, it needs to be closely monitored and not allowed to spread.

STARTHISTLES

Centaurea solstitialis—yellow starthistle, St. Barnaby's thistle—Asteraceae, Compositae, aster family

Yellow starthistle has become one of the most threatening weeds in California and the western states, where it has invaded vast acreages of rangeland, pasture, and crop land and thrives along roadsides running through these infested areas. During the summer, it can be recognized easily from long distances: it forms large areas of gray-green in a landscape that is otherwise predominantly gold and brown. The bright yellow flowers, which appear throughout the summer and fall, attract bees, which produce an excellent honey from their nectar. It is thought that beekeepers may have played some part in spreading this pest, although it seems to have no difficulty spreading by the usual methods: wind, water, and movement by animals (including us).

The deep roots of this fast-growing plant take up huge amounts of water, and the dense expanses created by its prodigious seed production crowd out more desirable pasture plants, as well as native trees, shrubs, and grasses, which provide food sources for native mammals, birds, and insects. So—it must be controlled.

Yellow starthistle is a winter annual that begins its life as a rosette 2 to 3 inches long, with deeply lobed leaves with sharply pointed tips; these are covered with a soft, whitish hair, which also appears on the flower stems that emerge from the rosette, giving the entire plant a grayish appearance. A mature starthistle can grow to a height of 1 to 2½ feet tall, with extensive branching. The branch edges are covered with narrow, sessile leafy growths sometimes referred to as "wings."

The plant stays in rosette form until about May, using its energy to generate taproots that can easily grow 3 feet long—root growth as deep as 8 feet has been reported. It then begins to elongate and branch, and blooms in early summer, producing bright yellow, thistlelike flower heads surrounded by bracts with long, sharp spines. The bottom spines are three-pointed, the upper ones simple; the uppermost row of bracts has none at all. These spines give the flower head a starlike appearance when viewed from above, hence its name. Each plant produces a prodigious volume of seed, and a solid mass of starthistle can drop up to 29,000 seeds per square meter, 95 percent of which germinate.

Yellow starthistle is a serious threat to horses: the spines pierce their mouths and inject a poison that causes brain lesions and a frequently fatal neurological disorder known as chewing disease. Cattle and sheep eat it before it forms its spiny flower heads, and goats will continue to graze it even after the spines form (goats seem to be immune to chewing disease). Grazing, along with mowing, can be part of an integrated control strategy for this weed, but these practices need to be well timed; done too early, before extensive branching has occurred, they can induce flowering below the mowing level. Later in the season, cattle and sheep will not eat starthistle, and mowing of the mature flowers may spread viable seed.

Yellow starthistle germinates best in disturbed ground but persists longer in stable soil, so early summer disking could help control it, although this provides an ideal seedbed for a new generation at the beginning of the next rainy season. Therefore, this practice, as well as grazing and mowing, needs to be followed by the seeding of other plants that will compete with the starthistle. It is best to use seed of vegetation that already grows in the area: native bunch grasses and wildflowers along roadsides, in abandoned pastures and crop lands and rangelands, and desirable forage grasses in managed pastures. Grasses are more desirable than forbs, because selective herbicides can be used to spray any starthistle that regrows later in the summer. An effective and much-used herbicide for yellow starthistle is clopyralid, which provides season-long preemergent and postemergent control when applied in late winter (January through March). Dicamba is also effective and is selective for broad-leaved plants, sparing grasses, as is clopyralid. Herbicides are most effective in smaller, more intensely managed situations such as crop lands and pastures, and when employed as part of a multifaceted integrated pest management program.

Burning has also proven to be effective, although it must be done for at least two consecutive years in order to deplete the seed bank. Early summer, when the thistles are still green but the grasses and forbs have dried out, is the best time for a burn, as the dried pasture plants provide the fuel. Perennial grasses recover especially well from these burns.

Fortunately, yellow starthistle does not do particularly well in intensively cultivated ground, so it is not nearly the threat in urban environments that it is in rural areas. In the city, it sometimes infests uncultivated canyon slopes, regional park lands, and large vacant lots, but it is seldom a serious threat in parks and gardens or on well-maintained industrial and institutional campuses. Managers of urban grounds where it does occur can use some of the same strategies to control it as farmers and ranchers do.

Centaurea calcitrapa, the purple starthistle, is another Mediterranean native that is much less widely distributed than the yellow starthistle but is found in some locations in the Bay Area. Its flower clusters are similar to those of its yellow-flowered cousin, but are rose-purple. They are subtended at the base by six or seven long, narrow spines, similar to those found on yellow starthistle. Leaves and stems are covered with fine, white hairs, but the leafy structures that run up and down the stems of the yellow starthistle are absent. Leaves are lanceolate, with a long, narrow, pointed lobe at the tip and two or three shorter, sharply pointed lobes near the base. Upper leaves are often entire.

The specific epithet *calcitrapa* is the Latin base for the English word "caltrops," ancient weapons of war consisting of iron forged into small spheres with multiple projecting spikes that were scattered on the ground to impede the progress of advancing warriors and horses.

SWEET ALYSSUM

Lobularia maritima—sweet alyssum—Brassicaceae, Cruciferae, mustard family

I grew up with this low-growing, white-flowered herbaceous plant in Riverside, California, where my parents planted it on the hilltop site of the house my father had built for us, his family. It spread abundantly, filling in gaps between trees and shrubs that required frequent irrigation in the dry and scorching months of the California dry season. The woody plants had to be watered frequently to stand a chance of surviving; the sweet alyssum received no water, but continued to bloom throughout the summer.

Growing from a perennial taproot, sweet alyssum is an upright, rounded plant—almost a subshrub—with many wiry stems growing from the crown. It is covered with rounded flower clusters consisting of tiny individual four-petaled flowers. These clusters are tiny at first, but they grow to ½ inch or more as the plants mature. In typical mustard family fashion, new flowers continue to bloom at the tips of these stems, and rounded fruits (siliculas) develop along the lower stem where previous flowers grew. The leaves are narrow, linear to lanceolate, pointed at the tip, and ½ to 2 inches long, growing alternately along the stem.

Flowers bloom year round, and the plants shed large quantities of seed, which germinates anywhere there is a little moisture at the surface of the soil. Sweet alyssum grows in almost any soil, in sun or light shade. Plants that become rangy or cease to bloom will put out fresh growth and flowers; or you can just pull them out and allow them to be replaced by new seedlings.

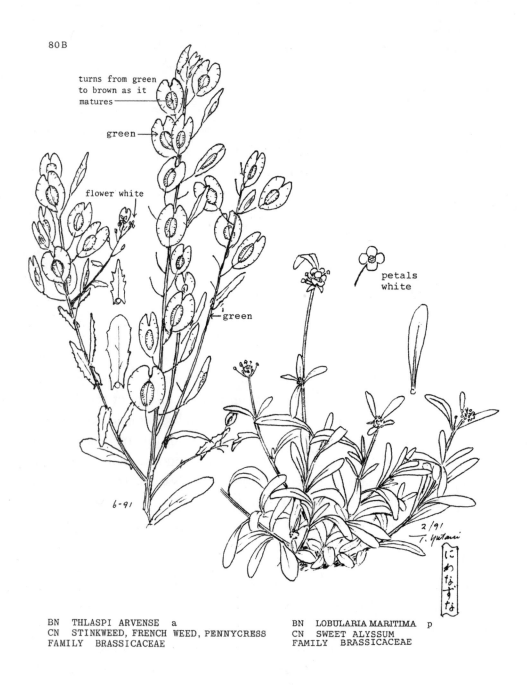

80B

turns from green
to brown as it
matures

green

flower white

green

petals
white

6-91

2/91
T. Yutani

BN   THLASPI ARVENSE   a
CN   STINKWEED, FRENCH WEED, PENNYCRESS
FAMILY   BRASSICACEAE

BN   LOBULARIA MARITIMA   p
CN   SWEET ALYSSUM
FAMILY   BRASSICACEAE

Sweet alyssum is often included in wildflower or erosion control mixes, so it is sometimes seen along roadsides. There are a number of named seed selections available, such as Carpet of Snow, a compact white, Rosie O'Day, also compact and bearing lavender-pink blooms, and Violet Queen, which grows to 5 inches and has flowers of a rich violet-purple hue. As these reproduce from seed, they slowly lose their color, producing mostly white flowers and growing taller, essentially reverting to the unselected species.

TEASELS

Dipsacus fullonum—teasel, fuller's teasel—Dipsacaceae, teasel or scabiosa family

The teasel is a sturdy, upright biennial or short-lived perennial that grows to about 3 or 4 feet high, occasionally as tall as 6 feet. This European native is a plant of wetlands and wet meadows. It seldom enters gardens, but when it manages to do so, it can be a formidable pest. It has a large, sturdy taproot that enables it to survive lengthy periods of drought, but in order to thrive it needs to grow in ground that remains very moist to wet most of the year. The leaves form a rosette; they are broad and oblong, with pointed tips, 6 inches to a foot long, opposite on the stem, with conspicuous spines on their upper surfaces. Bristly, angled flower stems arise from the rosette, branch somewhat, then grow to 3 or 4 feet tall. These also bear clasping leaves, but the rosette never disappears. A compound inflorescence develops at the tips of the stalks: this consists of a tight cluster of small, four-petaled blue-purple to pinkish flowers surrounded by short green, spiny bracts. At the base of the flower head four slender, pointed bracts grow, two long, two short. Once the spring-blooming flowers fade, the heads—green, bristly, more or less dome-shaped structures composed of hard, bristly bracts—remain, and soon turn brown.

The dried, spiny bracts are what give the fuller's teasel its name. Before the industrial revolution, fullers were workers who practiced the trade of fulling, raising the nap of newly woven cloth ("teasing" the fabric) to prepare it for dyeing. They did this with a fuller's brushes, hand tools consisting of frames holding a few teasels (the bristly flower heads of the teasel plant), which were drawn across the fabric. This laborious process was supplanted during the industrial revolution, first by water-driven machinery in fuller's mills, later by steam engines fueled by coal and oil. These early fulling machines still employed teasels to brush the cloth.

Teasels can be strikingly handsome ornamental plants, and they used to be grown in gardens as such—I haven't seen any lately. They would make an especially striking container plant, which would be suitable in a sparsely irrigated Mediterranean garden, where any volunteers wouldn't get enough water to become much of a weed problem.

VIOLETS

Viola odorata—sweet violet—Violaceae, violet or pansy family

Viola riviniana—Labrador violet, European dog violet

The sweet violet, *Viola odorata,* is a perennial wildflower native to Europe that grows in woodland clearings or at the edge of the forest. It is widely spread throughout Europe and Asia. It has been grown in gardens since ancient times, as an ornamental and for use in medicine and cookery. It is found in gardens all over the United States, including California, where it often naturalizes, spreads, and escapes.

It is a low-growing, rhizomatous plant that also produces above-ground runners that grow clusters of leaves at their tips, rising from crowns that produce new sets of roots. This plant can be very useful as a small-scale ground cover; it can also be a weedy pest where it is not wanted. Although its wild habitat is woodlands in relatively wet areas, its thick rhizomes enable it to withstand considerable drought.

The leaves of sweet violet are heart shaped, pinnate, with finely serrated edges, about 2 inches in diameter. They are medium green, set at almost right angles atop 3-inch-long petioles that are clustered at the tops of the crowns. Flowers emerge from the leaf axils, on long pedicels that curve downward at their tips. They are five-petaled, held vertically, with two earlike petals at the top, two more of similar size next to these, and a slightly larger, liplike petal at the bottom. The typical color is a dark blue-purple, the color known as violet. They can also be white, lilac, or rose colored. These flowers are typically less than ½ inch across, on peduncles 3 to 4 inches tall, and are very sweetly scented (except those growing near Toulouse, says Mrs. Grieve, which are unscented; however, they develop a pronounced fragrance when transplanted to Grasse). Traditionally, clusters of violets have been thought of as modest, even slight, gifts, but also as expressions of undying love.

Violets produce lots of nectar, which is very attractive to pollinating insects; but they tend to bloom in late winter and early spring (as early as December in California), when these insects are not available. These winter flowers do produce a modest amount of seed, but most go unpollinated.

But violets have a trick, as John Updike said in a poem about wild morning glories (which have a different trick). This trick is dubbed *cleistogamy* by scientists. Violets bloom a second time in the fall, producing inconspicuous flowers on short stems deep in the leaf axils; these have no petals and no fragrance.

They self-pollinate before they open, and produce abundant seed. In warmer climates, such as Italy, these cleistogamous buds develop into perfect flowers that can be cross-pollinated. Once this happens, they produce a small, minutely hairy, purple fruit, with many seeds.

The culinary and medicinal uses of violets are many, and are explained in detail by Mrs. Grieve; I shall summarize here. The association of the violet with erotic love goes back at least to the Greeks, who often used it in love potions. It is mentioned in the works of Homer and Virgil. Violets have also been used as a laxative, for treating wounds and bruises, as a liniment, for gout, as an emetic and purgative, and for headaches and dizziness associated with excessive drinking. The flowers are eaten in salads and used to flavor vinegar. There are many recipes for syrup of violets, a very palatable way to ingest this plant for whatever medicinal benefits it may confer. Modern chemists have identified a number of medicinal alkaloids contained in violet parts, including a glucoside known as viola-quercetin. Quercetin has recently become a popular arthritis remedy (it is listed in the British Pharmacopoeia). Violets also contain salicylic acid (the active ingredient in aspirin) and an alkaloid known as violine that resembles emetin, the purgative constituent of ipecac.

Violets also have a long history of use in perfumes. In literature, they have been associated with death as well as erotic love, especially the death of the young (the same is true of primroses). They are referred to in this context by Shakespeare in *Hamlet* and *Pericles,* and by Milton in "Lycidas." Their habit of producing abundant seed from unopened flowers does, indeed, imply immaturity and unrealized potential, and is referred to by the term *shrinking violet.*

A more or less annual viola that resembles the sweet violet, but is generally smaller, with darker foliage, and reproduces solely from seed, is widely referred to by nursery growers as *Viola labradorica,* a wildflower native to North America and widespread in boreal regions, including Greenland, but confined to higher mountains farther south. But the dark-leaved violet that we see sowing itself freely around gardens is not *V. labradorica* but a variety of a common and widespread European violet, *V. riviniana* Purpurea Group, known as the wood violet or dog violet (a name, implying inferiority, that has been applied to a number of scentless violets in Europe). This violet can be easily recognized by its very dark green leaves, almost black in appearance, and its scentless flowers. It can be a very aggressive weed and is especially annoying when it colonizes flower pots and planter boxes; but it can be very useful as a bulb cover, or growing under rhododendrons and other woodland plants, perhaps accompanied by *fraises de bois*. A few scarlet pimpernels would not be detrimental to this mixture.

WEEDY TREES

Acacia decurrens (dealbata)—Sydney blue (or green) wattle—Fabaceae, Leguminosae, bean or pea family

Acacia melanoxylon—blackwood acacia

Ailanthus altissima—Chinese tree of heaven—Simaroubaceae, quassia family

There are several trees in California that self-sow freely, form colonies, and invade wild lands, making even the most carefully chosen and sited individuals of these species potential weed generators. These all fall into the category of invasive exotics, nonnative species formerly often planted as ornamentals, but which have a tendency to proliferate.

One of the most common weed trees in urban areas is the Sydney blue (or green) wattle. This Australian native has been widely planted, mostly in its blue-green form (ssp. *dealbata),* because of its graceful broad, spreading form, substantial size (50 to 60 feet), fast growth, drought tolerance, and evergreen foliage, which consists of finely divided, bipinnate leaves, fernlike in appearance, about 6 to 8 inches long. This tree produces abundant flowers in late winter (January in the Bay Area), bright yellow clusters of small (about ⅜ inch), spherical inflorescences consisting of tiny, keeled flowers—the same general shape as pea and bean flowers. These are followed by huge quantities of legume fruits, about 2 to 3 inches long, which fall to the ground and dehisce in late spring, releasing huge numbers of dark brown or black seeds. These seeds germinate readily, forming thickets of seedlings in sun or shade (the young trees' tolerance for shady conditions goes a long way toward explaining their weediness, as does their tolerance for drought and for a variety of soil types). The offspring of the blue wattle, the most planted variety, are often the same blue-green color as their parent, but some revert to the dark green more typical of the species.

Another common weedy acacia is the blackwood acacia. This tree shares all the weedy attributes of its cousin, the blue wattle, but is quite different in appearance. It starts out as a dense tree with a broad, spreading crown but tends to become more pyramidal or roundheaded with age. It grows from 25 to 70 feet tall, forming a large, attractive street tree or garden shade tree.

The leaves of the blackwood acacia are thick, leathery, lanceolate, and parallel-veined—not leaves at all really, but enlarged leaf petioles called phyllodes. These provide the same photosynthetic function as true leaves but retain moisture more efficiently. On juvenile growth, a true leaf develops first, bipinnately compound and ferny like blue wattle leaves (but darker green and smaller), but it withers as its petioles expand into phyllodes. Many stages of this process can often be seen at the same time on young plants and root suckers. On mature woody growth, the phyllodes develop directly from the leaf bud, bypassing the juvenile leaf stage.

The inflorescences of the blackwood acacia are similar in size and form to those of the blue wattle, but the flowers are cream colored and appear in March or April. Fruits are purple-brown seed pods (legumes) that persist on the tree throughout the year and fall to the ground the following season. This acacia does not produce colonies as readily as the blue wattle, but it has a more widely spreading root system, which suckers freely; new trees can form in this way.

Despite their weediness, both these acacias can be very useful, high-functioning trees in the urban landscape, and continuing to plant them is not out of the question, as long as their tendency to spread is recognized and a plan to deal with it included in the maintenance specifications. However, it is probably best not to plant these, or a number of other weedy trees, in locations immediately adjacent to wild lands.

Yet another common weed tree and wild land invader is the Chinese tree of heaven, whose seedlings form shrubby thickets when young but can develop into groves of mature trees 20 to 60 feet tall. Trees of heaven tend to be multitrunked but can develop into single-stemmed specimens when shaded by other trees. This invader is most easily recognized by its long compound pinnate leaves, which can grow to 2 or 3 feet. Leaflets are 2 to 3 inches long, lanceolate to oval, with narrowly pointed tips and two to four teeth near their bases. The tree is deciduous, its foliage turning yellow in the fall.

The flowers of the tree of heaven are either unisexual or bisexual, with all three types occurring on the same plant, a phenomenon described by the technical term *polygamodioecious*. They are small, greenish, and occur in large terminal panicles. The male flowers have a very strong odor, which many people find objectionable (crushed leaves also have this odor). Flowers are followed by long, reddish samaras, fruits with winglike structures that enable them to be spread by the wind. The tree also spreads freely by rhizomes, and by suckering from the bases of cut stumps.

Tree of heaven is native to China and has a wide range of tolerances, including heat, cold, drought, insects, shade, and air pollution. It has been planted widely throughout the United States largely because of these tolerances—it is one of only three species that are considered dependable street trees in New York City, the others being gingkos and London plane trees. Ailanthus is also a weed of vacant lots, railroad embankments, and roadsides in many states throughout the United States. In California, colonies of tree of heaven are a very common sight along Highway 49, which runs through the Gold Country in the Sierra foothills. It is often found around abandoned dwelling sites and is popularly believed to have been introduced by Chinese miners, who would have been familiar with it as a tree often grown in temple yards in China.

The tree of heaven has a long and rich history in China. It is mentioned in the oldest extant Chinese dictionary and is listed in Chinese medical texts as a cure for ailments ranging from mental illness to baldness. The roots, leaves, and bark are still used today in traditional Chinese medicine, primarily as an astringent. Resin from the tree has been used to make varnish. Tree of heaven is a host plant for the ailanthus silk moth, an insect used in silk production, and has been grown extensively for this purpose both in China and abroad.

The tree of heaven has a cinematic claim to fame: it is the vegetative star of the movie *A Tree Grows in Brooklyn,* based on a best-selling novel by Betty Smith.

WHITE THOROUGHWORT

Ageratina adenophora—white thoroughwort—Asteraceae, Compositae, aster family

White thoroughwort, sometimes called sticky snakeroot, is a shrubby herbaceous perennial native to Mexico that was probably introduced as an ornamental and has become naturalized in a number of locations, including the San Francisco Bay Area. It grows mostly along stream banks and in areas watered by springs and seeps. Thoroughwort is not widespread, but it can easily dominate areas where it does well. A large colony can be seen along the Greenwich Steps on the east side of Telegraph Hill in San Francisco.

Thoroughwort is a branching plant 3 to 6 feet tall, with reddish stems and opposite leaves. The leaves are oval, often somewhat triangular, toothed, 2 to

4 inches long. The flower heads are about 3/16 inch across, growing in compact clusters about 2 or 3 inches wide at the ends of the branches. They are creamy white, and individual clusters consist only of disk flowers. They look like a whitish version of the garden flower ageratum, to which they are closely related. The plant blooms throughout the spring and summer and can be quite beautiful.

Also known as sticky eupatorium (its former generic name), thoroughwort has become an invader of wild lands in places such as San Bruno Mountain, and efforts are being made to control it. It thrives in gulches, canyons, and other areas where water accumulates. It is also an agricultural and pasture weed, toxic to horses and unpalatable to cattle. Eupatorium is present in the southeastern United States, and it is a very serious weed in subtropical portions of the Pacific Basin, including Australia, India, Nepal, New Zealand, Southeast Asia, and the Pacific Islands, as well as in Nigeria, South Africa, and the Canary Islands. It has become so well established in some of these places that uses have been found for it. It is the source of a green commercial dye in India and is used to heal cuts and other injuries in Nepal.

10

CALIFORNIA NATIVE WEEDS

INTRODUCTION

There are very few native plants in California that actually have weedy characteristics, but there are some. As I have already pointed out, very few California Indians practiced any agriculture, and those who did farmed only to a very limited extent. However, all the native groups were, to some extent, horticulturists—they managed the native plants they found useful for food, fiber, and building materials, and by so doing, altered their environment. The pre-European native population of California was the densest in North America, and these people moved around extensively, both on seasonal hunting and food-gathering circuits, and to trade various commodities between groups. They burned vegetation to flush game and create open vistas, and they created trails. All this disturbed ground was habitat for plants that thrive in such conditions: weeds. With the arrival of Europeans came a vast increase of human disturbance of the landscape, and a whole new flora of weedy colonizers; but the native weeds also found new opportunities, and some of them have become significant pests, both in rural areas and urban gardens. In this chapter, I describe some of the more common native weeds that thrive in urban areas.

BITTERCRESS

Cardamine oligosperma—bittercress, little western bittercress, winter cress, popweed—Brassicaceae, Cruciferae, mustard family

One of the most prolific weeds to appear in urban gardens in the west, bittercress is one of the few common weeds that are native to California. It is abundant in rich soil in moist, shady areas but will grow anywhere that the ground accumulates a fair amount of moisture in winter.

Bittercress is a winter annual that typically grows to about 4 to 6 inches but may reach a foot in rich soil. Leaves are alternate, compound pinnate, to about 4 inches long, with five to eleven round to ovate leaflets. At first the leaves form a basal rosette, which becomes suppressed as the plant elongates and flowers. Some books say bittercress has a taproot, but my experience pulling myriads tells me their roots are fibrous.

The inflorescence is a two- to ten-flowered raceme of tiny white blossoms that form at the tip of the stem, leaving slender siliques behind them as the stem elongates. These fruits are dehiscent, and when ripe they will split open with an audible pop and propel the seeds a good distance. Knowing this, a purposeful gardener will pull the plants before this stage of ripeness is reached—only experience can enable one to determine the optimum time.

Pursued aggressively and kept to a reasonable population level, this weed can be a pleasant and fun denizen of the garden—the occasional pop can be an enjoyable surprise (not all gardeners think so). The leaves are quite edible, providing a mild, mustardy spiciness to a salad of spring greens—it mixes well with chickweed and dandelions.

In natural environments, cardamine grows in wet meadows, on shady banks, and in creek bottoms. It is found throughout the western United States and Canada and turns up also in New York State—perhaps introduced there. It is closely related to another western wildflower, *Dentaria californica,* or milkmaids (a.k.a. toothwort), an early spring bloomer that grows in woodlands and has pure white flowers about ½ inch across.

Another cardamine worth noting is the lady's smock, or cuckoo flower, *Cardamine pratensis,* native to Europe and naturalized in the northeastern United States, where it is regarded as a weed. In Europe it has long been a favorite cottage garden plant, as much for its medicinal value as for its attractive silvery mauve flowers, which closely resemble those of the California milkmaids and start blooming at about the same time, in mid-March around the traditional date of the Annunciation, when an angel informed the Virgin Mary that she was going to bear Jesus. In the Catholic calendar, this is March 25, a day known as Lady Day or Ladytide, so the plant also came to be known as lady's smock. It was used traditionally in bridal bouquets (but considered unlucky in May Day garlands) and is referred to by Shakespeare in *Love's Labour's Lost:*

> *When daisies pied and violets blue*
> *And lady smocks all silvery white*
> *And cuckoo buds of yellow hue*
> *Do paint the meadows with delight*

Medicinally, lady's smock has been used, like other mustards, as a remedy for scurvy and as a cress-like salad green. It has also been regarded as efficacious for strengthening the heart, hence the name *cardamine.* This belief goes back to Dioscorides and might be associated with the shape of the leaflets. Cardamine was also used as a remedy for toothaches.

Cuckoo flower is a perennial that can be grown from seed or root divisions. Its blossoms are usually white but sometimes pink, lilac, or purple. There is a double form that was popular in cottage gardens and is still grown.

Other traditional names for lady's smock are meadow cress, spring cress, cuckoo bread, cuckoo spit, and bread and milk.

See illustration of bittercress on p. 112.

COYOTE BRUSH

Baccharis pilularis ssp. *consanguinea*—coyote brush—Asteraceae, Compositae, daisy family

Coyote brush, occasionally known as chaparral broom, is a medium-sized shrub that grows in coastal brush fields and chaparral, both in the coast ranges and the foothills of the Sierra. It ranges in size from as short as 2 feet to as tall as 10 feet but is usually seen in the 3- to 6-foot range. The leaves are medium green, sessile, alternate, broadly oval or ovate, often wedge shaped, with lighter-colored glands on the surface, ½ to 1 inch long, coarsely toothed on the margins. They are resinous and somewhat aromatic in warmer weather. This shrub is rounded and dense, about as wide as it is tall.

Baccharis blooms in the fall, producing an abundance of small white disk flowers, with male and female blooms on separate plants. It sheds massive quantities of pollen, often triggering allergies. The fruit is the typical achene with a pappus common to many composites. The shrub is anchored by a sturdy taproot, and, like most chaparral shrubs, can sprout from the crown. It tolerates summer drought but will also adapt to moist or wet soil.

Like coast live oaks and bay laurels, coyote brush will often invade gardens and disturbed areas located near native vegetation. None of these are truly rampant invaders, so some may be tolerated—it is always up to the gardener to decide whether any volunteer should be regarded as a welcome addition to the garden, or as a weed. I see coyote brush as a not terribly attractive garden shrub and would not plant it deliberately, but I have sometimes allowed it to remain indefinitely in areas where the presence of some sort of shrub seemed appropriate.

Probably the most effective way to control any woody invader is to learn to recognize it when it germinates and pull it out while it is still a seedling. Winter is an excellent time to do this in coastal California—the ground is soft from the rains, and gardeners often do not have many other urgent tasks. Fortunately, winter is when most volunteer seedlings germinate in California.

Baccharis pilularis ssp. *pilularis* is a prostrate form of coyote brush that grows along the seashore of central California, ranging inland only a short distance. It has not proven to be weedy and is often used as a woody ground cover. With some summer water, it does well in hot, dry inland areas; it can be given little or no summer irrigation near the coast. It is susceptible to a blister rust fungus—"a beautiful fungus," according to the late Dr. Bob Raabe, emeritus professor of plant pathology at UC Berkeley—but some gardeners may want to replace plantings that have suffered extensive dieback from this disease.

WOOD MINT

Stachys bullata—wood mint, hedge nettle—Lamiaceae, Labiatae, mint family

There are a number of species of *Stachys* in California that are usually referred to as wood mint in California but are known as hedge nettle in Europe, and sometimes here. They grow mostly in forests and woodlands, in shaded and open areas, but often travel to roadsides and nearby gardens. The most common species in the Bay Area is *Stachys bullata*.

Wood mint is a perennial, growing from the aggressively spreading, rhizomatous root mass so typical of the mint family. Stems are square, the pinnate leaves oblong-ovate to elliptical, squared off at the base, growing opposite each other along the stems. They are 1 to 3 inches long, scalloped at the margins, softly hairy, gray-green. The flowers grow in whorls in the leaf nodes, their upper lips purple, the lower paler with dark purple spots. The fruit is a nutlet.

When hedge nettle appears in gardens, it may be welcome as a native volunteer, but its aggressive growth habit often causes it to crowd more desirable plants. Eliminating or controlling it is difficult once it is well established, due to its extensive rhizomes, which can intertwine with the roots of perennials and shrubs, making it nearly impossible to grub out completely; from these protected locations, it can easily move back into other parts of the garden. Therefore, one needs to decide early on whether to tolerate it or not. In gardens with native oaks, it can be an attractive winter ground cover under these trees, but keeping it green in summer takes more water than is good for the oaks; so it should definitely be regarded as seasonal, flourishing when the ground is moist, perhaps withering in the driest part of summer and fall.

There is an annual stachys from Europe, *S. arvensis,* called field stachys as well as hedge nettle, an invasive found in some of the northern coastal counties, including Marin. It is about a foot tall, with leaf blades less than an inch long, and sparsely hairy. Flowers are pale purple.

Stachys byzantina, lamb's ears, is a fairly aggressive Mediterranean native often grown in sunny areas of gardens as a ground cover. It is fairly drought tolerant due to its silvery gray leaves densely covered with white hairs. The plant forms a mat and produces short flowering stems with whorls of pink flowers. Some gardeners do not like these flower heads but prefer a solid silvery mat; to please them, hybridizers have produced a form that does not bloom.

MINER'S LETTUCE AND SKUNKWEED

Claytonia perfoliata—miner's lettuce—Portulacaceae, purslane family

Navarretia squarrosa—skunkweed—Polemoniaceae, phlox family

In this section, I discuss two sometime weeds that are both California natives but occur in very different environments. Both occasionally invade gardens.

Miner's lettuce, *Claytonia perfoliata,* is a winter annual that grows in moist environments. In the wild, it is mostly found in woodlands and in open areas where moisture accumulates. It sometimes invades adjacent vineyards and orchards, where it may form a fairly solid ground cover. Some growers allow it to persist and reseed, regarding it as a good cover crop. In the city, it is mostly found on the fringes of wooded areas. When it invades gardens, it may be regarded either as a welcome volunteer native or as a weed.

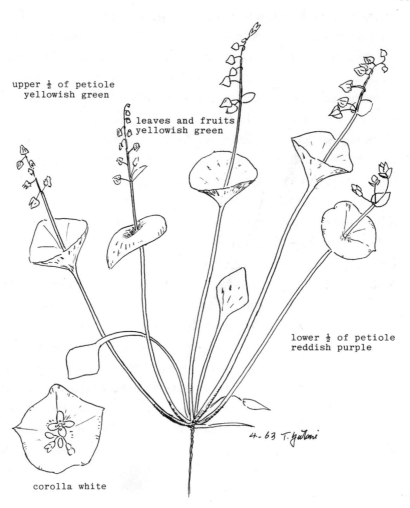

upper ½ of petiole
yellowish green

leaves and fruits
yellowish green

lower ½ of petiole
reddish purple

4-63 T. gutani

corolla white

```
BN   MONTIA PERFOLIATA   a
CN   MINER'S LETTUCE
FAMILY   PORTULACACEAE
```

The leaves of miner's lettuce are smooth, succulent, entire, with long petioles arising directly from the root crown. The basal leaves are long and narrow; as these develop, they become broadly ovate, almost triangular, then flatten and surround the stem, forming a saucerlike disk atop a stemlike petiole. A short flower stalk emerges from the middle of the disk; this branches into a panicle, bearing tiny flowers with five white or pinkish petals. The fruit is a three-valved capsule.

Miner's lettuce is native to the entire West Coast, from British Columbia to Baja. Its name derives from the discovery by early gold miners in California that it provided a succulent, tasty salad green that could be harvested easily from nearby woods. Miner's lettuce is still good salad material and is grown commercially as a winter green in Europe. It would be a good winter salad green in a home garden, as it grows more vigorously than lettuce during the colder months.

Skunkweed, *Navarretia squarrosa,* grows under conditions totally unlike those needed for miner's lettuce. It is a summer annual, and it likes sunny, dry, open ground, mostly in the countryside and urban fringe areas. It does best in heavy clay soils.

Skunkweed forms a low tuft 8 to 16 inches tall; its stems bear alternate, bipinnately compound leaves, alternate on the stems, with leaflets unequal, rigid, and spine tipped. The entire plant is glandular and pubescent and has a strong, skunk-like odor. Flowers are sessile (no petioles), in dense clusters, with many bracts enclosing purple to blue funnel-shaped corollas. The fruit is a three-celled capsule. It blooms throughout the warm summer months.

Skunkweed is native to the western United States, including California. Because of its affinity for clay, it is not likely to invade gardens with enriched soil. In urban areas, it tends to confine itself to undeveloped areas on ridge tops and to compacted shoulders on roadsides. It can be rather attractive in these areas, and I see little reason to control it.

NUTSEDGES

Cyperus eragrostis—umbrella sedge, tall flatsedge—Cyperaceae, nutsedge family

Cyperus esculentus—yellow nutsedge

The sedge family consists of a number of grasslike monocots, mostly perennial, which usually grow in wet areas: along stream banks and ditches, at the margins of lakes, ponds, and wetlands, in wet meadows and vernal pools—and in overwatered lawns. The greatest number of its species are in the immense genus *Carex;* the other genera include the family's type genus, *Cyperus,* whose plants are often referred to as nutsedges, a reference to their ability to produce underground tubers that can sprout into new plants.

The most common weedy nutsedge in coastal California is *Cyperus eragrostis,* the umbrella sedge, or tall flatsedge. It does not produce nutlets so is not commonly referred to as a nutsedge. It spreads by tillering—sending out a short rhizome from the crown, which then forms an adjacent clump. The roots of this perennial are fibrous, but thick and tough, making it difficult to pull out. As might be expected, umbrella sedge tends to pop up mostly in overwatered landscapes and lawns; but, like many sedges native to wet areas in dry climates, it can withstand considerable drying once established. *Jepson* lists it as native to California; some other sources say it is introduced.

"Sedges have edges, rushes are round," the mnemonic saying goes. These "edges" are on the leaves, which have a thickened midrib, and on the flower stalk, which is triangular in cross section. A single plant of flatsedge has six to ten leaves emerging from a basal crown; they are long (from 12 to 20 inches) and pointed at the tips, shiny yellow-green, entire, but with slightly rough margins. The triangular flower scape emerges in the midst of these leaves, producing a compact, globe-like raceme of yellow-green spikelets, which soon turn a brownish color. The inflorescence is somewhat flattened and umbrellalike; beneath the floral structures is a ring of short leaves, which renders the whole plant even more umbrellalike. The flowers are followed by brown, sharply triangular achenes.

Controlling tall umbrella sedge where it is not wanted is best accomplished by drying out the ground: watering less and improving drainage. Where it is established, flatsedge has to be dug out, often a laborious task that requires follow-through. It is somewhat difficult to kill with herbicides; in any case, spraying pesticides in wet areas can be hazardous to frogs and tadpoles. Along streams and ditches, this plant helps stabilize the banks, so controlling it there would be counterproductive.

Cyperus esculentus, yellow nutsedge, also known as yellow nutgrass, earth or ground almond, chufa, galingale, and rush nut, has leaves and stems similar to those of the umbrella sedge, but smaller—they generally do not exceed a foot in height and usually grow to 6 inches or less. The inflorescence is more open and vertical, its spikelets fewer and more widely spaced. This species, too, according to *The Jepson Manual,* is native to California, but it is also native to much of the rest of the world. In rural areas, it is an aggressive weed of irrigated crop lands; in the city, it is mostly found in and near heavily watered lawns.

The root system of yellow nutsedge is similar to that of the tall flatsedge, consisting of a cluster of tough, fibrous roots; these, however, produce tubers ("nuts") capable of generating new plants at their tips. These tubers have been dubbed earth almonds or chufa. They have an almondlike flavor and have long

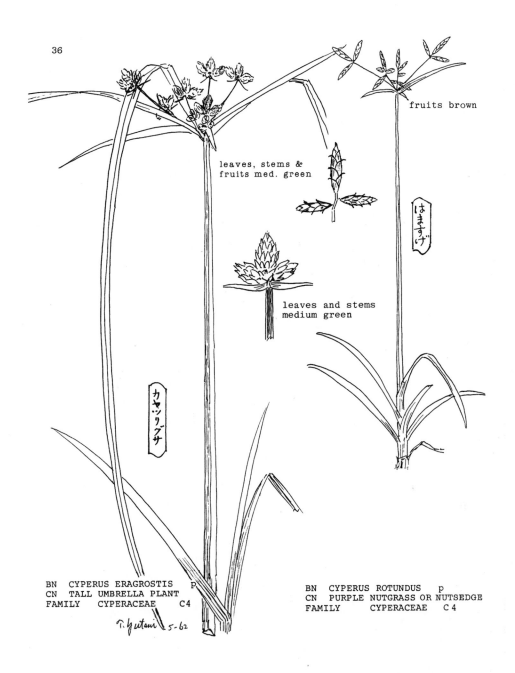

36

fruits brown

leaves, stems &
fruits med. green

leaves and stems
medium green

はますげ

カヤツリグサ

BN   CYPERUS ERAGROSTIS   p
CN   TALL UMBRELLA PLANT
FAMILY   CYPERACEAE   C4

T. Yutani 5-62

BN   CYPERUS ROTUNDUS   p
CN   PURPLE NUTGRASS OR NUTSEDGE
FAMILY   CYPERACEAE   C 4

been used as a food item, especially in the southern United States. According to Elizabeth Lawrence, a Southern garden writer of some note, they are sometimes found in markets in that region, where they are sold as *chufa*. Earth almonds are still grown to a limited extent in the Gulf States for hog food—perhaps an unwise practice, considering their weedy potential. Galingale is also the name of a tall plant that is native to Britain, western France, and the

Mediterranean region, where it grows in wet meadows or on pond edges. It is as tall as 3 feet, with creeping rhizomes and erect, triangular stems, each terminating in an inflorescence about 3 feet tall. Its tuberous roots, more water chestnut–like than those of yellow nutsedge, have a violet-like aroma and were a culinary staple in medieval Europe. They are reported to be eaten still in some places in Europe and might be worth trying in a swale or other perennially wet part of a garden.

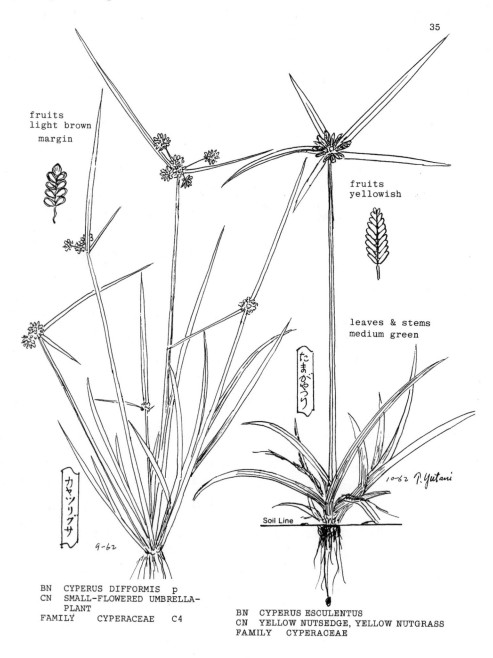

35

fruits
light brown
margin

fruits
yellowish

leaves & stems
medium green

Soil Line

9-62

10-62 P. Yutani

BN CYPERUS DIFFORMIS p
CN SMALL-FLOWERED UMBRELLA-
    PLANT
FAMILY   CYPERACEAE   C4

BN CYPERUS ESCULENTUS
CN YELLOW NUTSEDGE, YELLOW NUTGRASS
FAMILY CYPERACEAE

Recently, a number of sedges (mostly in the genus *Carex,* family Cyperaceae) have become popular as landscape plants, especially some of the reddish-colored ones from New Zealand. Their popularity has been largely due to the work of John Greenlee, a Southern California gardener and writer who focuses on grasses and grasslike plants and who strongly advocates the use of certain sedges for unmowed lawns. The ones he recommends are short-statured species that can tolerate either wet or dry soil and so are seemingly ideal for our winter-wet, summer-dry climate. I have had no experience with such lawns so cannot recommend for or against this notion; but any idea that might enable us to grow turf requiring less water and maintenance is worth considering.

POISON OAK

Toxicodendron diversilobum—poison oak—Anacardiaceae, sumac family

Of the three skin-irritating sumacs that grow in the United States, poison oak is the only one that occurs west of the Rocky Mountains; the others, poison ivy and poison sumac, confine themselves to the eastern side of the country. Poison oak is the most widespread native shrub in California, growing in many habitats below 5,000 feet in elevation. In chaparral, it is a multistemmed shrub, arising from aggressive rhizomes; when the vegetation is really dense, it can become vine-like and clamber over other shrubs. In the forest, it is a massive vine, attaching itself to the trunks of trees by adventitious roots and climbing as high as 100 feet.

Poison oak is deciduous, its leaves turning a brilliant red by mid- to late summer and dropping in the fall. The leaves are trifoliate (as in the "leaflets three" rhyme: "leaflets three, let it be"). They are alternate on the stems, shiny green, 1 to 4 inches long, the leaflets smooth and edged with rounded lobes, which make them resemble oak leaves. When they first appear, they are very bright green, becoming darker as they age. Flower clusters form in the leaf axils in April and May, panicles of greenish-white blossoms about ⅛ inch long. These give way to clusters of attractive white drupes, as toxic to people as the rest of the plant, but well loved by birds, which eat them and spread the seed. Deer also do not seem to be affected by this plant and frequently browse on it.

Shortly after contact with the skin of susceptible people (most of us), a reddish rash appears, which soon forms puss-oozing blisters, itching furiously the while. Effects last a week or two. Itching skin can be soothed temporarily by a variety of remedies, including crushed plantain leaves, dock, and aloe vera.

Some people seem to be immune and can hire themselves out to remove poison oak; but this immunity tends to come and go.

Poison oak has no place in any garden, and the best way to keep it out is to learn to recognize its seedlings and remove them before they grow and spread. Even in wild areas, poison oak has to be controlled along trails, in campgrounds, and in picnic areas. Getting rid of well-established clumps is a formidable task, requiring digging and cutting tools, gloves, long pants, and long-sleeved shirts; coveralls and face shields are also a good idea. All of these must be cleaned immediately after use, as the rash-causing oils cling to them.

Inevitably, regrowth of poison oak will occur from portions of the roots left in the ground; cutting back (or spraying—probably preferable) this new growth as soon as it sprouts will eventually starve the plant. Burning is not advisable—the smoke can be toxic. Firefighters in wild lands frequently fall victim to severe lung irritation from smoke produced by burning poison oak.

Part 3

INTEGRATED PEST MANAGEMENT— WITH AND WITHOUT PESTICIDES

11

INTEGRATED PEST MANAGEMENT— AN OVERVIEW

*W*hen I introduced the concept of integrated pest management in one of my past weeds classes, one of the students asked me whether I favored this approach over chemical pest control. I replied that integrated pest management was the only valid approach to weed control, whether or not one chose to employ chemicals. That is still my opinion.

The term *integrated pest management,* often abbreviated "IPM, is a name for a procedure for making pest control decisions. It was first used in an article published in the University of California's agricultural science journal *Hilgardia* in October 1959 (three years before the 1962 publication of Rachel Carson's *Silent Spring*) and written by four University of California entomologists: Vernon Stern, Ray Smith, Robert van den Bosch, and Kenneth Hagen. These men were concerned about what they perceived as overreliance on pesticides, materials that were not only hazardous to their handlers, to birds and animals living nearby, and to consumers of sprayed fruits and vegetables, but also capable of disrupting natural control processes by decimating organisms that parasitized or preyed upon the pests. They proposed a system based on careful and frequent monitoring of populations of pests and beneficial organisms, establishment of thresholds at which action needed to be taken, and careful selection from a variety of control methods of those that would most effectively control the pests while doing the least damage to workers, consumers, and the environment.

Of the four researchers, perhaps the most outspoken and controversial was Robert van den Bosch, whose broad social and environmental concerns led him to write and lecture widely; he often criticized the pesticide industry, which funded much of the research being conducted at the University of California. This provoked negative reactions not only from the funders but from many of his colleagues. Van den Bosch summarized his ideas in his last book, *The Pesticide Conspiracy,* published in 1978 and still in print today.

Despite the outcry, the concept of integrated pest management slowly gained traction as it was recognized both in the University and in the wider world as an idea whose time had come.

In 1979, the University of California Statewide Integrated Pest Management Project (later changed to "Program") was founded at UC Davis with the mission of further refining and implementing the ideas proposed in the *Hilgardia* article twenty years before. When Ray Smith was elected to the National Academy of Sciences in 1981, this article was cited as "the single most important paper on crop protection in this century."

The UC Statewide IPM Program is still very active today. It has produced, and continues to produce, a series of manuals explaining the best practices for achieving integrated pest management in the major crops grown in California, as well as in the landscape. The directors of this program have also taken responsibility for advocating protocols that ensure the safest possible use of pesticides through their book *The Safe and Effective Use of Pesticides,* now in its third edition, and through their Train the Trainer program, which educates and certifies instructors who can then conduct the annual trainings required by California state law for all pesticide handlers and other farmworkers who are exposed to pesticides.

The definition of integrated pest management cited in *The Safe and Effective Use of Pesticides* summarizes the current state of thinking on the subject and is the definition I shall refer to throughout the rest of this chapter. I quote it here: "[Integrated pest management (IPM)] is a pest management program that uses life history information and extensive monitoring to understand a pest and its potential for causing economic damage. Control is achieved through multiple approaches, including prevention, cultural practices, pesticide application, exclusion, natural enemies, and host resistance. The goal is to achieve long-term suppression of target pests with minimal impact on non-target organisms and the environment."

Taken step by step, the integrated pest management process begins with the identification of the pests that are attacking the plants or animals we are trying to nurture. We must also accurately identify these, and identify any organisms present that might aid in the suppression of the pests: insects that eat or parasitize other insects, or microbes that kill them; fungi that attack other fungi; desirable plants that compete well with more noxious weeds; weeds and native plants that provide nectar to insect parasites and predators when they are not actively preying upon or parasitizing their victims. This process not only provides us with a basis for creating pest control strategies, but gives us some notion of the complexity of the living system and of the need to proceed cautiously, lest we generate unintended consequences. It will, hopefully, make us think about what we might be able to leave alone, as well as what we might do proactively.

Once we have identified all the relevant organisms, we need to rank the pests through a sort of triage process, a division into groups. The first group should contain the most threatening pests, those that need to be suppressed to the greatest extent possible, even, some might say, "eradicated"; but total eradication of any pest is largely a fantasy. The second group contains those pests that can be tolerated to some extent (fortunately, this includes most of the weeds that we encounter) but need to be kept below a certain population level, or threshold, a level that is different for each pest, and that, ultimately, only the people growing the plants can define. The third group encompasses the pests that cause minimal damage and might even have some virtues, and so can be tolerated, or even enjoyed. Among weeds, some freely self-sowing annuals such as sweet alyssum or California poppy come to mind; these are admittedly weedy plants, but they mix well with other garden flowers and can, if well managed, compete with more troublesome weeds.

In commercial agriculture, population thresholds for pests can be quantified with reasonable accuracy by calculating the value of the crops being lost and comparing it to the cost of controlling the pest. When one has reached a ratio that seems to make sense, the "economic threshold," the population level at which it is more cost-effective to take action than not, has been defined. In landscape horticulture, these thresholds are more subjective, as there is no way to quantify objectively the aesthetic impact of weeds (although gardeners have lost their jobs for disagreeing with employers about how many weeds are tolerable); but unless one is willing to let weeds have their way, limits need to be set. This is so even with those beautiful and tolerable weeds in the last group—once they start dominating rather than complementing the plants with which they are being allowed to coexist, something must be done.

Once pest managers have determined population thresholds, they must begin monitoring to determine when those thresholds have been reached. In large commercial agricultural operations, some sort of scientifically valid sampling process should be used; but those monitoring smaller gardens or landscape plantings need not be so rigorous. A quick visual assessment of a large lawn can generally tell you whether the dandelions and English daisies are providing a colorful complement to the grasses or are beginning to dominate it. If you need a more quantitative method of determining when a threshold has been reached, something like the "Frisbee method" will often suffice. Decide how many of any given weed can be tolerated in any given square foot of lawn, then take a Frisbee and make several more or less random tosses onto the grass—at least a dozen for an average-sized lawn. Try not to aim, but make sure that the landings are well distributed. Count the number of weeds in the square foot of turf on which the Frisbee lands. When done, average these numbers. If the average exceeds the threshold, it is time to take action.

The main requirement of effective monitoring is to do it regularly, consistently, and with some frequency—and this is where most IPM programs fall down.

When you have decided that your threshold has been reached and action is necessary, it is time to consider all available control options and to choose those that are most likely to control the weeds effectively with the least adverse effects on workers and others nearby and on wildlife, soil, air, adjacent bodies of water, and the rest of the surrounding environment. Possible tools fall into several categories: cultural; physical or mechanical; biological; breeding; regulatory; chemical. Let us consider each of these in turn.

The cultural approach focuses directly on the well-being of desirable plants, on enabling them to grow as vigorously as possible and so compete effectively with weeds and other pests. This approach is best implemented in the planning stage, when the gardener or designer considers the natural advantages and limitations of the environment and chooses plants that are well adapted to these conditions, thus minimizing the need for special care and coming as close as it is possible to something that might be termed a "natural" garden. If the garden falls short of this "natural" state, then the horticulturist needs to modify the conditions. First, provide water when and where it is needed; withhold it when it is not needed and when irrigation would only induce the growth of weeds or trigger root rot. Next, make sure the humus level in the soil is high enough to avoid compaction, hold nutrients and water, and stimulate the microbial activity that is needed to make nutrients available to plants and suppress diseases; and adjust the level of fertility to keep plants growing vigorously during the growing season, but not so vigorously that they produce excessive, succulent foliage that attracts aphids and disease organisms. The result of all these carefully planned and timed inputs should be a garden in which the soil is well covered with vigorously growing desirable vegetation, thus providing scant bare ground in which weeds can establish themselves.

But—nothing is perfect, and even in the most meticulously planned and carefully tended garden, weeds will appear and will have to be dealt with. The most common direct methods are the physical or mechanical: digging them out; cutting or scraping them off at the surface of the soil; cultivating the ground to uproot young weeds and allow them to dry out; smothering them under layers of organic mulch, stones or gravel, or plastic.

Organic mulch is beneficial not only for keeping newly germinated weeds from developing, but for retaining moisture, regulating soil temperature, and, through slow, steady decay, adding humus to the soil; thus, mulching can be considered a cultural as well as a physical approach to weed control. Coarse woody mulch lasts longer than fine mulch and allows water and oxygen to penetrate more readily from above and excess water vapor and gases formed by decomposition to escape into the atmosphere; but finer, quickly decaying mulches can help build up the organic content of lean soils. Three inches or more is the ideal depth for good weed control, but mulch over four inches thick can seriously inhibit penetration of rain or irrigation water, exchange of gases, and drying out of saturated soil. Generally, a three- to four-inch depth is recommended for sandy soils, two to three inches for clay soils. It is very important not to allow mulch to pile up around the bases of plants (mulch "volcanoes")— this can induce crown rot.

Mulch consisting of inorganic materials, such as gravel, crushed lava rock, or small stones, is just as effective as organic mulches for conserving moisture and controlling weeds and is much longer-lasting; it does not, however, have the humus-building benefits of the organic materials. Pavement also acts as a sort of mulch and does not shift around the way that loose stones do.

Tools for removing weeds from the soil include hoes, cultivators, digging forks, shovels, and various hand-weeding implements. Hoes are used to cut off the tops of individual weeds or to scrape the ground a little below the surface and sever the crowns or roots of the plants. There are two basic kinds of hoes: the first are the conventional chopping hoes used widely in agriculture; these are the most labor intensive, and the least effective. The second, called scuffle hoes (these include the popular Hula Hoe) are dragged along the surface of the ground, cutting on the push or pull stroke, or both, depending on their design. One of the most effective is a Japanese tool with a sickle-shaped blade, called a *ko gama*. This implement cuts on the pull stroke, and the pointed blade can also be used to dig out more deeply rooted weeds. The best of these tools have thin, flexible blades, making them very lightweight and easy to sharpen (all hoes work much better if kept sharp). They come in long- and short-handled versions. Hoes and scrapers of all sorts work best on young, small, annual weeds—cutting them off or uprooting them, allowing them to lie on the surface of the ground and dry out.

Perennial weeds, as well as some deeply rooted annuals, must have most or all of their root systems removed from the ground in order to prevent resprouting; the best tools for this purpose are various digging or pulling implements that either loosen the soil around the weeds and allow them to be extracted by hand or use leverage to yank them directly from the ground. Tine cultivators, long or short handled, work well for smaller weeds and have the added benefit of aerating the soil and providing a good planting bed for more desirable plants (and an ideal environment for more weeds to sprout). Larger, more deeply rooted weeds can be extracted most easily with a sturdy digging fork, one with square tines forged from a single bar of steel (most digging forks sold in garden centers and hardware stores have flat tines and are useless in anything other than soil that has already been well cultivated).

Tools that use leverage to extract roots include the ubiquitous asparagus cutter, a metal bar with a flattened, double-pointed end designed to cut asparagus stalks beneath the surface, but just as useful for easing out the long roots of perennials such as dandelions, or cutting them off at a depth that makes them less likely to resprout. The *hori-hori* is a Japanese tool with a very sturdy, knifelike blade that is concave on one side and can be used to dig around sturdy roots and lever them out. The Weed Wrench is a tool with a long handle connected to a base that rests on the ground and has a set of moveable jaws that can be adjusted to grasp the main stem of a woody shrub or small tree. When the handle is rocked backward, the jaws tighten, and the base acts as a fulcrum to allow the plant to be pried out. An alternative method is simply to use a shovel to dig the plant out by the roots. This is more laborious and time-consuming, and leaves more dug-up ground than you get from the less disruptive process of wrenching out the weeds.

Another mechanical process is mowing, cutting weeds to nearly ground level, usually a fairly temporary control, as all perennial and many annual weeds will regrow from their undisturbed crowns. But mowing is relatively efficient and can provide a month or more of acceptable suppression along roadsides or in marginal areas. Mowing when the ground is drying out will often kill most of the annual weeds, leaving only the perennials to be dealt with by subsequent mowing or other means. Mowing tends to favor grasses over broad-leaved weeds, especially when it is done regularly. Bare ground covered mostly with grass is often looked upon as a lawn of sorts and considered more desirable than ground covered with coarse broad-leaved weeds. Mowing can be done with power tools such as mowers and Weed Eaters, but also by hand, by swinging an implement known as a sling blade, or grass whip, a tool that seems to be modeled on a combination of a scythe and a golf club. These come with heavy, rigid blades or light, flexible ones. The heavy, rigid models ("sling blades") work well in large, open areas such as fields and roadsides; the smaller, lighter, more flexible ones are better for working in tighter spaces.

Rototilling or plowing tends to bury surface weeds but can bring up seeds that have been previously buried and can stimulate the regeneration of perennial weeds from root or stem fragments. These processes are better suited to farming than urban gardening and are increasingly being seen as problematic by farmers, who are, in growing numbers, embracing various "no-till" strategies.

Biological controls for weeds often consist of releasing various insects that chew leaves, bore holes in flower heads or in the seeds themselves, or lay their eggs on certain plants to allow insects to parasitize them. Birds that eat weed seeds, such as goldfinches, should also be nurtured by insuring that they have nesting opportunities. If insects are used, species must be found that focus selectively on the weeds that need to be eradicated and do not harm other plants.

Historically, one of the most effective biological controls for weeds was the introduction of a beetle native to southern France to the rangelands of the upper Klamath basin early in 1944 to control *Hypericum perforatum,* a southern European weed known as St. John's wort (dubbed Klamath weed in the western United States), which had invaded pastures and grasslands and had proven toxic to livestock. The beetle was imported from Australia, where it had been introduced in 1929; in early 1944, southern France was still under Nazi control. This blue-green beetle, about the size of a ladybug, feeds on the leaves of the mature plants, causing some damage; but, more importantly, its larvae feed on the basal portions of the plants, often killing them. By 1959, this control had been so effective that the rangelands dominated by Klamath weed were less than 1 percent of their extent in 1944. Farmers and ranchers are still urged to look for remnant populations of Klamath weed and to use herbicides when they find it, a strategy that could be counterproductive if it wipes out the remaining population of the beetle and the weed is reintroduced. All biological control depends upon retaining at least a residual population of the controlling organism, which means maintaining a small population of the organisms they feed upon.

Various biological controls, consisting mostly of beetles and weevils, have also been introduced for control of yellow starthistle, *Centaurea solstitialis,* and puncture vine, *Tribulus terrestris,* two other weeds that have had a substantial impact on rangelands, but much less in urban areas. Whether there will be significant biological controls developed for urban weeds remains to be seen. It should be noted, however, that many weeds, especially the winter bloomers, provide a significant nectar source for beneficial insects that prey upon or parasitize insect pests. This should be kept in mind when setting population thresholds for these particular weeds.

Careful choice of plants is important for controlling pests, since those that grow vigorously and resist attacks by insects and disease organisms need fewer interventions. Plant breeders have long sought to create landscape plants that not only are more beautiful, but also need less care, less water, and less use of pesticides. Genetic engineering has added a whole new dimension to this endeavor, and despite the risks that come with manipulating the gene codes of organisms (and there are many), the potential benefits cannot be denied. However, the most important factor in choosing plants is their suitability for the particular environment into which they are being introduced. Do not underestimate the value of some of the weedier, self-sowing ornamentals: they are often happy in many different environments, mix well with many other garden plants, and quickly occupy bare ground that might otherwise be colonized by less desirable weeds.

Pests that are especially threatening are often dealt with through regulatory controls, laws and regulations mandating spraying, requiring quarantines or restrictions on the movement of infested nursery stock, labeling certain pests as "noxious," and requiring growers and farmers to take steps to control them whenever or wherever they are found. For someone practicing urban pest management, these regulations can often restrict the availability of nursery stock, impose controls on how plant wastes are handled, and require lower tolerance levels than the manager might otherwise choose.

The final approach I consider for dealing with pests is chemical control, meaning, in the case of weeds, the use of herbicides. IPM is often regarded as a way to avoid pesticides entirely, or to use them only as a last resort; but neither of these is necessarily required. Pest managers may well decide to exclude pesticides from their programs—many do; but if they do decide to use them, they must choose them carefully, seeking the least toxic and least environmentally damaging materials that will be effective, using them only when the population of the pest has exceeded the threshold level, and applying them when the pest is most vulnerable, in a manner that does not affect nontarget organisms. They should never be sprayed when field workers and passersby are near the spray site. Finally, chemical control should not work against other methods being used to control pests, such as biological control. This requires not only timing the applications carefully, but also selecting materials wisely, choosing those that kill the target pest without causing undue harm to other organisms.

I provide some more detailed guidelines for the safe and effective use of pesticides in the next chapter.

12

TO SPRAY OR NOT TO SPRAY; OR, PESTICIDES 101

*I*n my chapter on integrated pest management, I said that deciding whether or not to use pesticides is an important step in formulating a complete IPM program for a particular pest, crop, or situation. The UC State-wide IPM Program website posits a standard for making this judgment, and I repeat it here: "Pesticides are used only after monitoring indicates they are needed according to established guidelines, and treatments are made with the goal of removing only the target organism."

"Established guidelines" is a rather vague term. A number of publications, including the various IPM guides published by the UC Statewide IPM Program, suggest situations or population thresholds in which pesticide use might be the best choice; but the ultimate decision belongs to the individual grower, gardener, or pest manager and will vary widely depending on the situation and the point of view of the person making the decision. Some pest managers will not consider the use of pesticides under any circumstances; others, following organic guidelines, will use only "natural" pesticides, although these materials are not necessarily always less toxic or more environmentally benign than synthetic products. In the following pages, I shall discuss my views on how to decide whether to use pesticides at all, how to select the best pesticides for the job, and how to use them safely and effectively.

Once monitoring has indicated that a threshold has been reached where action is necessary, many options are available, and they all need to be considered. Some pest managers think of pesticides as a "last resort" and will not use them unless they have decided that there are no other effective controls available—or that other methods alone are not sufficient. Since there are many dangers associated with pesticides—to people and other creatures—and since pesticide use is expensive and becoming even more so, I agree with these managers. I think it is useful to consider whether combinations of other methods might be adequate before even contemplating pesticides use. Even so, pesticides may not always be a last resort; they may in some cases be preferable to other methods, some of which have their own toxicity issues. Take Weed Eaters and mowers, for instance, both good tools for mechanical weed control. These are hardly nontoxic; internal combustion exhaust is a known carcinogen, whereas many pesticides are not even suspected carcinogens. Mowing can destroy endangered species or their habitats, and mowing machines can definitely cause harm to their operators, even to bystanders. I have accidentally put pebbles through car windshields by using Weed Eaters in gravelly areas; flying pebbles can also put out eyes. Working safely is a consideration whether or not pesticides are used.

The Safe and Effective Use of Pesticides, the guidebook for pesticide use published by the UC Statewide IPM Program, gives equal emphasis to safety and effectiveness. If the product chosen is the least toxic available, it is still toxic, and must be used in a safe manner; and there is no point in using it at all if it does not effectively control the targeted pest. If you must resort to a more hazardous compound, using it safely becomes even more important. This book is designed to be a bible for pest managers, to serve as a training guide for workers, and to prepare students to take the Laws and Regulations section of the exams for the Qualified Applicator Certificate or the Pest Control Adviser License (more about this later).

Once you have decided that a pesticide is needed, you have to consider what type would do the job best with the fewest hazards to workers, neighbors, and the environment. Herbicides fall into several classification categories based on their chemistry, how they are used, their mode of action, and their formulation. Considering these choices before narrowing the field down to a single product (or a few alternative products) relates directly to how safe and effective their use will be.

The chemistry of herbicides falls into two main groups: organic and inorganic. This has nothing to do with organic gardening, or with using "natural" products instead of manufactured materials—the chemical definition of *organic* is a carbon-based compound, whereas *inorganic* refers to salts, compounds whose molecules are formed by the union of a metal and a nonmetal. Common table salt will kill weeds; so will many of the salts used as fertilizers if applied in sufficient amounts. Most of these salts have a long history of use for various purposes, and their hazards are well known. They are effective for burning down the top growth of plants by desiccating the leaves (they do not move into the roots), but if they build up in the soil, they can be toxic to nonweedy plants as well; salt buildup, mostly from overuse of chemical fertilizers, has become a severe problem for many farmers.

In general, little use is made today of inorganic herbicides: the carbon-based ones are more effective and employ many modes of action. Carbon molecules are the building blocks of all living tissue; with four electrons in their outer rings, they can produce branching chains to which other ions and radicals can adhere, and thus build the large, complex molecules that are the basis of living organisms. Similar molecules can be designed to interfere with the life processes of plants and animals, and thus provide a number of very effective ways to kill pest organisms. Like living molecules, these are often susceptible to fairly rapid degradation into simple compounds by soil microorganisms, and so buildup in the soil and the environment is not nearly as problematic as is the concentration of salts from repeated and excessive use. There are hazards associated with these substances, however—compounds that interfere with life processes can also have unintended consequences, such as causing cancer, genetic mutations, and birth defects. Organic compounds are the main culprits associated with the *chronic* toxicities of pesticides, that is, the long-term effects of repeated exposures. Their *acute* toxicity (the effect of a single exposure) to humans and other mammals varies widely, ranging from very high to practically nonexistent, whereas that of mineral salts, in general, is relatively low.

Pesticides are also classified according to their *modes of action,* the mechanisms by which they disrupt the life processes of plants. The inorganic herbicides, and some of the organic (such as soaps and oils), are called *contact* herbicides; they work by desiccating the leaves and stems of the plants they contact. They are very effective on annual weeds, and even small perennials, but will not kill the roots or underground stems of mature perennials. To do this, one needs to use a *translocated* material, one that is absorbed into the plant's vascular system and moves about, killing the entire plant. Translocated (also called *systemic*) herbicides and other pesticides are all in the organic category, and mostly mimic the actions of the organism's hormones, but in a disruptive way. They are far more effective in smaller amounts than contact materials, but have the potential to cause more harm to nontargeted organisms. Users of these compounds should not only read the material safety data sheets carefully, but should also keep up with continuing research and controversies concerning their dangers and effectiveness.

Contact herbicides are always applied to the leaves and stems of plants, but translocated compounds are designed to be applied in one of two ways: on the leaves, *foliage applied,* the method used for *postemergent* applications on growing plants; or in the ground, *soil applied,* which is done mostly with *preemergent* herbicides, which kill sprouting seeds and young plants still in the cotyledon stage. The translocated preemergents are virtually all organic and must be able to persist in the soil for at least a while in order to be effective. They are applied directly to the soil surface, by spraying or distributing granules, watered in (or not—read the label), and left to do their work. Short-residual preemergents, generally effective for a few weeks to a month or more, are used in areas that will be seeded after the weed seeds have germinated and died—if one is planting a lawn, this is an effective way to eliminate the reservoir of weed seeds that would otherwise compete with the grass. Long-residual (effective up to six months) herbicides can be used where weed growth needs to be suppressed for a longer period, and where germination of grass or other seed is not desired. This can be done in newly planted ground cover, with the goal of suppressing weed growth until the ground cover has filled in and is able to provide an effective barrier to subsequent weed germination. Far too often, these applications are made year after year in areas such as median strips, in order to create permanently bare ground. A better strategy would be to cover this ground with appropriate vegetation, or pavement, or both.

Herbicides and other pesticides are formulated in three ways: as *powders, granules,* or *liquid concentrates.* Powders can be *water soluble* (often designated on labels as WSP), *wettable* (WP), or *dusts.* Dusts are applied by blowing them directly onto the leaves of plants, allowing them to adhere and form a protective barrier. This is a very inefficient process, requiring use of excessive material highly subject to drifting into nontarget areas and contaminating the air for some distance around the area of application. It has never been done with herbicides, and now it is seldom done with insecticides or fungicides. One notable exception is dusting the leaves of grapevines with sulfur to prevent powdery mildew (since sulfur is "natural," this is allowed in organic agriculture), although many growers now prefer to spray organic fungicides, probably a far safer, more efficient, and more effective practice than dusting with sulfur.

Some herbicides, insecticides, and fungicides are formulated as *wettable powders,* which do not dissolve in water, but can be suspended through constant agitation and sprayed onto plants. Doing this efficiently requires the use of a tank with an agitating device that keeps the mixture in constant motion. To use one of these powders in a handheld spray tank, one must constantly shake the tank, a process that is seldom very effective: the powder tends to clump up and clog the nozzle, and it leaves residues in the tank that are difficult to clean out. Wettable powders are mostly used in agriculture, and only for applying insoluble compounds that are known to be more effective for certain uses than are soluble alternatives. Urban horticulturists, especially those spraying from handheld tanks, should avoid these—there are plenty of soluble alternatives available. Some of these are formulated as *water soluble powders* (WSP); others come in liquid form as *water soluble concentrates* (WSC).

Materials that will not dissolve in water can be formulated as *emulsifiable concentrates* (EC) by mixing them with oil, which does not dissolve in water, but tends to form tiny droplets and create what is called an *emulsion.* Emulsified oil remains dispersed with less frequent, lighter agitation than is needed for wettable powders. Emulsifiable concentrates are far easier to use in a handheld spray tank than wettable powders, but soluble powders and concentrates are still preferable.

Preemergent herbicides are often formulated as *granules,* small chunks of hard minerals coated with the active ingredient. Unlike dusts, these have some weight and can easily be spread over the ground, with a mechanical spreader or by sowing, without being carried by the wind. Once the granules are in place, the ground is irrigated, and the herbicide washes off the granules and adheres to the soil particles. Fertilizers and soil-applied insecticides are also often formulated as granules.

After deciding what type of herbicide is needed, you have to select the least toxic and least environmentally damaging material that will effectively control the pest. It is best to begin with advice from a farm adviser: their recommendations for the most currently effective products change frequently and are generally more reliable and up to date than advice from printed sources. Salespeople for chemical companies will always be eager to point out the latest whiz-bang solution to a vexing pest problem, but these should be checked with knowledgeable advisers who have no financial interest in the outcome. And, whatever the credentials of the people making the recommendations, you should always fully research any pesticide under consideration yourself before deciding whether it meets your standards for safety and effectiveness.

The *least toxic material that will be effective* is what is desired, so you must know how to evaluate toxicity. Before chemical companies can register a product with federal and state environmental protection agencies, they are required to hire an independent lab to do a toxicity evaluation that the federal and state environmental protection agencies must review before giving permission to market it; these agencies also specify what information must be on the labeling. This *labeling,* a term that includes both the label affixed to the container and all supplementary materials that come with it (typically in the form of a printed booklet in a blister pack attached to the container), has on it the name and composition of the product, a list of pests for which its use is registered, a number of precautionary statements, often fairly generic, and directions for mixing and applying the chemical and for disposing of excess mixtures and concentrates. Toxicity information is given only in the form of four fairly imprecise *signal words:* Danger—Poison for the most toxic products; Warning for those of medium toxicity; Caution for the least toxic materials.

The signal words evaluate only one type of toxicity, known as *acute,* that is, the threat to one's health or life posed by a single dose. They are category labels for groups of compounds that share a range of toxicities; each individual compound has a more precisely measured hazard level known as LD50. This is determined by laboratory tests (mandated by federal and state environmental protection agencies) on groups of lab animals (mice, rats, dogs, cats, etc.). The first test group is fed a small dose of the substance; these doses are gradually increased for subsequent groups. When a dose is given that kills (i.e., the LD, lethal dose) half the test group (50 percent), the number of milligrams of the test substance per kilogram of average body weight of the test animals becomes the LD50. Note that the smaller the number, the more lethal the substance. Take, for instance, a two-pound rat that dies after ingesting 5 milligrams of Temik, a highly toxic insecticide; if he or she dies along with half their test group mates, the LD50 of Temik is established as 5, in the Danger—Poison category. The same group of rats fed large doses of Roundup, the most commonly used herbicide, will mostly still be alive when the dose reaches 5,000 milligrams (how scientists get them to ingest that much I cannot explain). The LD50 of this product is then established as <5,000, considered practically nontoxic, and thus in the Caution category.

The oral toxicity range of the three categories is as follows: Danger: unmeasurably tiny to 50 milligrams per kilogram of body weight; Warning: 50 to 500; Caution: 500 to 5,000 and beyond. The label indicates only the category, not the precise number, and it so is a very rough indication of the toxicity of the substance. To find the LD50 number, one must consult another document, known as the material safety data sheet (MSDS), which summarizes all the data from the testing required before federal and state environmental protection agencies will allow the product to be marketed. Pesticide companies are required to make these sheets available to anyone who requests them, which they generally do by posting them online; links to these documents can be found on websites such as the UC Statewide IPM Program site (ipm.ucanr.edu). They contain fairly detailed information on how the testing was conducted and what the results were, both for acute toxicity and for another category, *chronic* toxicity.

Chronic refers to the likelihood that repeated exposures to the substance over a period of time will cause various life-threatening conditions, such as cancer (*carcinogenic* potential), genetic mutations in offspring *(mutagenic),* or birth defects *(teratogenic).* A good number of pesticides, as well as many other substances (oil and gasoline, for instance) are known to cause cancer; others are suspected carcinogens—these can be found on a list published by the California Environmental Protection Agency. That they are marketed at all reflects a decision by the EPA that careful handling and use can minimize their potential for harm. Groups like the Pesticide Action Network reject this notion and deem as "bad actors" any pesticide that contains even suspected carcinogens. Conscientious pest managers will at the very least look at the full range of alternatives to chemicals known to cause or even suspected of causing cancer, birth defects, or genetic mutations before deciding to use them. The best way to begin this process is to carefully read the labeling and the MSDS for all products under consideration before making a decision. Reading the labeling before each and every use of any pesticide is actually required by law—reading the MSDS is not, but it is a good idea, a discipline that all conscientious pesticide users should impose on themselves.

Material safety data sheets also contain information on health hazards other than cancer, birth defects, and genetic mutations; on volatility and flammability; on first-aid measures, firefighting measures, and environmental hazards; on what to do in case of spills; on handling and storage and exposure control measures; and much more detailed information on toxicology and physical and chemical properties than can be found on the label.

Conscientious pesticide applicators must take into consideration dangers to their own health and well-being and that of others nearby and take steps to mitigate them. California law does not allow spraying when wind speeds exceed ten miles per hour—staying well below this threshold is prudent. Posting warning signs stating what has been sprayed, and when, and warning people to keep out of the area until the legally mandated reentry interval has expired is often required (read the label!), and it is a good idea in public spaces even if not specifically required. If no interval is stated for the product, the default reentry period is the time it takes the sprayed material to dry on the leaves and ground. Again, pesticides that require a reentry period longer than this should probably not be used in urban parks and gardens, however much they may be needed in production agriculture. Pesticide bottles and tanks carried in vehicles must be secured to prevent spills and must be locked up whenever the applicator cannot constantly watch the vehicle, preferably in a box in the bed of the truck (they may be locked in the cab when the vehicle is unoccupied but must be carried in the back when it is being driven).

Any pesticide not in its original container (this includes spray tanks, as well as small containers used to carry premeasured amounts to the field) must be labeled with a *service container label,* which indicates the common name of the material inside (e.g., Roundup), the signal word on the original container (e.g., Caution), and a phone number for the person responsible for the application (adding the name and address of this person would also be a good idea). This is very basic, minimal information that will allow first responders to get off to a good start in case of a spill, poisoning, or discovery of an unattended or misplaced container.

Labeling will often contain very specific information on clothing and protective gear required for an application, and this must be followed. Minimal requirements for less toxic pesticides are long pants, long-sleeved shirts, and shoes and socks. I think this is too minimal; I believe chemically impervious boots and gloves, and eye protection (safety glasses and/or a face shield) should be added to this list. When one is *mixing* pesticides with water in a spray tank, these are required, along with an apron. Spraying the more toxic pesticides may require using a National Institute for Occupational Safety and Health (NIOSH)–approved respirator, wearing a chemically impervious hat and face shield (especially when spraying anywhere near one's face), and wearing coveralls, or even a rain suit (for materials that might soak through coveralls). In agricultural operations, mixing in a tank with a *closed system*—an apparatus for extracting the concentrate from the container and conveying it into the tank without opening the tank or the container—is sometimes mandated, as is spraying from a rig with an enclosed cab. Once again, any pesticides that require such extreme precautions should be ruled out for use in urban horticulture, and should be only a last resort in production agriculture.

Pesticide users need to know the environmental hazards associated with any pesticide and be able to take steps to mitigate them. Ground and surface water contamination is a major problem, whose impact often extends far beyond the area being treated. Even pesticides with low mammalian toxicity are often deadly to fish and amphibians, so they must be kept out of waterways. Spraying should never be done when rain is imminent, or directly into bodies of water, unless one is using a pesticide that has been registered to control aquatic weeds. In California, the use of certain pesticides within a minimum distance of bodies of water containing California red-legged frogs is forbidden; prudent applicators will consult state regulations before spraying anything within two hundred yards of *any* body of water. Conscientious applicators will also consult the special regulations that apply to Groundwater Management Areas that have been designated by the Department of Pesticide Regulation. These ban the use of some pesticides entirely, and require permits for others.

Drift of pesticides away from their intended targets presents another hazard to people and the environment. It can pollute the air with toxins, kill beneficial insects or desirable plants, and contaminate field workers and bystanders. Pesticide drift can be mitigated a number of ways: spray only when wind speed is less than ten miles per hour; keep nozzles aimed directly at the target at all times; keep tank pressure low and droplet size large; make sure that all applicators are properly attired, in clothing that will not allow spray drift to contact their skin; make sure all other workers and bystanders are kept well away from the area being sprayed.

Another hazard is what is called *potentiation,* unforeseen chemical reactions that occur when certain pesticides are mixed, sometimes resulting in a mixture many times more toxic than either of the materials that are being mixed. Applying more than one compound at a time is often desirable when treating more than one pest in the same area, or when the most effective compound to use on a particular pest is in doubt—but this should not be done unless one is fully aware of possible adverse effects. Labeling often contains information on what mixtures are okay and which to avoid; if applicators cannot find authoritative information about the particular mixtures they have in mind, it is best to avoid mixing.

Most organically based herbicides are decomposed relatively quickly by soil microbes, usually, but not always, into simple, harmless compounds. Applicators need to keep in mind that, among the thousands of pesticides registered for use, there are some that can break down into compounds more toxic or harmful to the environment than the original material, and that relatively harmless decomposition products in the soil can combine to produce hazardous compounds (another form of potentiation). The MSDS often gives information on how fast the material degrades in the soil and what the end products are; if it does not, further inquiry is in order.

Another environmental concern is pest resistance, something that is almost certain to develop as organisms are targeted repeatedly with the same substance. This is an inevitable outcome of natural selection: under adverse conditions, the weak die, the strongest survive and reproduce. This process has been remarkably slow to occur with Roundup, the most widely used herbicide due to its low mammalian toxicity and its effectiveness for control of a wide range of weedy plants. Some weeds have developed resistance to Roundup, however, and more are likely to as the use of this product increases. The development of Roundup Ready crops—food plants with genetically engineered Roundup resistance—seems to be driving many farmers to adopt Roundup as their principal, or exclusive, tool for weed control; this will inevitably render it virtually useless. The only way to keep this herbicide effective for weed control for as long as possible is to use it less: to alternate it with other herbicides, or, better yet, with control methods that do not employ herbicides.

Conscientious applicators are also law-abiding applicators: they obey all federal and state regulations pertaining to pesticide use. The original legislation from which all regulations are descended is known as the Federal Insecticide, Fungicide, and Rodenticide Act, passed in 1947. There has been a good deal of federal and state legislation since then, as well as a body of regulations promulgated by enforcing agencies that seek to interpret these laws as they apply to more specific situations. In California, the regulations are issued by the Department of Pesticide Regulation, a branch of the California Environmental Protection Agency. They are interpreted and enforced at the county level by county agricultural commissioners.

In California, anyone applying pesticides or giving advice on pest control "for hire" must have a license: a Qualified Applicator License, a Maintenance Gardener Business License, or a Pest Control Adviser License (other states have similar licensing requirements). These documents are issued by the Department of Pesticide Regulation, which also administers the testing. To obtain a Pest Control Adviser License, one must have extensive education in biological or agricultural sciences, or considerable work experience scouting for advisers, before being eligible to take the exam. This license entitles the holder to give advice on pest control and to issue written pesticide recommendations; pest control advisers are not licensed to *apply* pesticides. The Qualified Applicator License is required for anyone whose principal business is pest control; the Maintenance Gardener Business License is for maintenance gardeners who do pest control as an incidental part of their maintenance work.

In addition to licensing, all commercial applicators must register with the counties in which they work (there is a fee) and submit monthly reports to the county agricultural commissioner stating the products used and the amounts sprayed. This paperwork has to be submitted every month; if no pesticides are used that month, the licensee has to declare zero use. This information goes into a statewide database, which enables regulators to track pesticide use and see if any patterns emerge connecting specific materials with injuries, illnesses, or environmental damage.

Employees of private businesses or public agencies do not need licensing or certification to apply pesticides, unless they use restricted materials, pesticides that require permits. In California, these permits are issued by county agricultural commissioners, and anyone applying for one must have a Qualified Applicator Certificate or License. Testing for the certificate is virtually the same as the examination for a Qualified Applicator License, but the fee is lower; the certificate alone does not allow the holder to conduct a private pesticide application business. Employees who apply only nonrestricted pesticides, or who work under the close supervision of a licensed or certified applicator, do not need any kind of certification, only an annual training conducted by qualified trainers and paid for by their employers. This training must include information on the hazards of pesticides, how to mix and apply them safely, how to recognize symptoms of pesticide poisoning, and whom to contact in case of poisoning, a spill, or other emergency.

In addition to training, employers in California are responsible for providing workers with personal protective equipment (masks, coveralls, rubber boots, etc.), posting emergency contact information and any other documents the state requires, and making MSDSs available for all pesticides and other hazardous materials. They must provide daily changes of protective clothing to anyone using pesticides in the Warning or Danger categories and make sure that pesticides are kept in their original containers, with the labeling intact, and stored in a locked facility with a cautionary sign visible fifty feet away. They must enforce all regulations, including directives from the county agricultural commissioner regarding how regulations are to be interpreted in specific instances. Employers must also have a plan for dealing with spills, and they must train employees to implement this plan.

Dealing with spills requires four steps, carried out in the following order:

1. Alert anyone in the vicinity that a spill has occurred, and warn them to keep away.

2. Contain the spill—keep it from spreading. Use dirt or anything else immediately available on the scene, or absorbing materials or containment barriers that are included in specially designed spill kits.

3. Call the emergency response number given by the employer, report the situation, and ask for help if needed. Also, call the county agricultural commissioner, tell them what happened, and follow their directions before proceeding further. If there is more than one worker present— always a good idea when working with any hazardous materials— steps 2 and 3 can be done at once.

4. Clean up the spill: use absorbent material such as cat litter or sawdust to soak up spilled liquids, then bag it in plastic; vacuum spilled powders with a cleaner that has a disposable bag; and take the bagged materials to a hazardous waste disposal facility. If a specially trained cleanup team is sent (many large companies or institutions have these on their staffs; smaller companies often contract for such services), stand by and assist them as asked. Cleanup workers should not leave the site until someone with the authority to declare the area safe (e.g., the agricultural commissioner) has done so.

I have just outlined the basic safety regulations and licensing requirements in California, my home state, known to have some of the most stringent pesticide laws and regulations in the country. Readers not living in California will need to know the law in their own states; if they are less stringent than California's, they might well consider being extra conscientious and abiding by my state's more exacting requirements.

I shall now describe a typical procedure for doing a safe, effective, and legal pesticide application using a handheld pressurized sprayer, the most common pesticide application tool used by maintenance gardeners, landscapers, and homeowners. Before starting, conscientious applicators have chosen the least toxic pesticide they deem effective, hopefully something water soluble and in the Caution category. They are attired in at least the minimal protective clothing, including long pants, a long-sleeved shirt, rubber boots and gloves, safety glasses, perhaps hard hats with face shields. They have already read their labels. When mixing, they add chemically impervious aprons and face shields, if they are not already wearing them.

Applicators first fill their tanks about a third full of clean water: pouring pesticides into water is safer than pouring the pesticide first, which sometimes causes a violent reaction that can propel pesticide into the faces of the mixers. They then measure the correct amount of concentrate, using a device calibrated to the smallest unit that needs to be measured, pour it carefully into the tank, and add water to the fill line.

At this point, sprayers may remove their aprons and face shields (or not), pump up the tanks, and adjust the nozzles. Their aim is to keep the pressure relatively low, the droplet size fairly large, in order to minimize risk of drift. They then attach service container labels and proceed to spray, coating the top and undersides of the leaves enough to wet them, but without allowing them to drip. If at all possible, applicators empty their tanks completely, since pesticides stored in tanks lose their potency after a while. They then post warning signs around the sprayed area, and proceed to the wash area to clean tanks and protective gear.

Pesticide-contaminated equipment may be cleaned in a large sink in the storage room (one used for no other purpose), or in an outdoor area with a drain that leads into a sanitary sewer—pesticides must never be allowed to go down a storm drain. If no such facility is available, equipment may be cleaned on open ground recently sprayed or cleared of weeds, as long as runoff can be contained and prevented from contaminating waterways or adjacent areas.

The cleaning procedure for pesticide tanks, as well as empty concentrate containers, is known as the *triple rinse*. Applicators first add water to the tanks or bottles until they are about a third full, then replace the lids, shake them vigorously, and pour out the water. If they are washing empty bottles, they pour the water into the tank being mixed; if a tank is being washed, the water can go into a sanitary sewer or a holding container that is kept locked up until taken to a hazardous waste facility, or it can be spread out over ground that has been recently sprayed or is about to be sprayed—probably the preferable risk-reduction option, environmentally speaking, since it minimizes handling and allows soil microbes to decompose the pesticides.

This procedure is done three times; before tanks are emptied the third time, applicators pump them up and spray most of the water out, in order to clean the hose and wand. They then hang the tank upside down to dry and thoroughly rinse all other contaminated gear (gloves, boots, hard hats, face shields, measuring cups, etc.).

Tanks used for herbicides may be employed for other types of pesticides if they are cleaned thoroughly between uses; however, there is some risk that some residue may remain and harm the plants being sprayed. It is generally preferable to have dedicated tanks for herbicides.

Unwanted pesticide concentrates, and leftover mixtures, must never be poured out on the ground or down a storm drain—they need to be taken, labels intact (or relabeled), to a hazardous waste disposal facility. Such disposal is generally free to homeowners; companies and for-hire applicators have to pay.

I shall conclude this chapter with a list of rules of thumb for sensible pesticide use that I devised to pass out to classes I teach and that, I think, neatly summarizes most of the essential material I have covered. I have labeled it "Richard's Rules for Using Pesticides."

If you are planning, or even considering, using pesticides as part of a maintenance gardening or landscaping business, or as someone else's employee, and want to work as safely as possible with the least adverse impact on the environment, consider adopting the following rules:

1. If you get paid for gardening, **get certified.** Do this even if you don't strictly need certification—it tells you, and others, that you have the knowledge and competence to use pesticides safely and effectively. At the very least, get the Qualified Applicator Certificate or equivalent—you'll need it if you are a self-employed maintenance gardener, and it will be to your advantage if you work for someone else. If you can meet the educational requirements, try for the Pest Control Adviser License—it will enable you to make good money without actually handling pesticides.

2. **Thoroughly explore the alternatives.** Use pesticides only when there are no better options available, and only in conjunction with other methods.

3. **Avoid restricted pesticides.** If you're a maintenance gardener or landscaper, you won't need them: there are plenty of nonrestricted products that will provide adequate control. If you grow nursery crops or take care of highly specialized plantings or sports turf, you may need to break this rule from time to time—but make it a rule, anyway.

4. **Avoid carcinogens, mutagens, teratogens.** Don't use pesticides that are known to cause or are strongly suspected of causing cancer, birth defects, or genetic mutations.

5. **Don't pollute.** Work carefully, wear protective clothing, keep chemicals on target, and avoid pesticides with long-lasting residues.

6. **Avoid overkill.** Use pesticides with the lowest toxicity level that will control the pest. Try to restrict yourself to products carrying the Caution label.

Who says it is desirable to have a garden that is "pest-free"? Bugs, weeds, and fungi are all part of the web of life—and a garden is supposed to be a microcosm of the larger environment. A garden without a full range of biological activity is not a garden at all; it is merely outdoor decoration.

On the other hand, *you* have the privilege of deciding when enough is enough, and of doing what you need to do to reestablish the balance. Just do it safely, effectively, and legally.

CONCLUSION

Want your bad romance.

—LADY GAGA

The garden delves no deeper than its roots
And lifts no higher than its leaves and fruits.

—WENDELL BERRY

Our connection with weeds goes back to the very beginning of our transition from surviving five hundred millennia as hunter-gatherers to thriving for the last ten as farmers, builders, and inventors. After the last ice age, we learned to grow crops and expanded our population; villages became cities, new settlements arose, and we built roads to connect them; we domesticated animals and used them for food, fiber, and drayage. In the process, we acquired weeds: plants that had evolved to colonize the bare ground left by retreating glaciers and had continued to thrive by learning to colonize the bare ground we continually created. We adopted them as much as they adopted us—we learned which ones were good for us and our domestic animals to eat, which could be used to treat ailments, which could improve soil. Although unintentionally, we allowed them to hybridize with the crop plants we selected from the wild and thus produce improved varieties. We gave them names, sometimes proper names.

We also learned that they were a nuisance, indeed, sometimes, a threat to our very existence. They occupied ground that should be occupied by crops or fodder; when they grew alongside our desired plants, they robbed them of nutrients and water. The Tollund man's tribe took advantage of this situation by eating the seeds of some of the weeds that grew in their barley fields along with the grains of barley, a smart move, since they contained oils and nutrients that were missing from the barley; we have moved beyond that perspective. We want our grain fields to grow nothing but grain, our lawns to contain nothing but a single species of grass, our parks and home gardens to consist only of plants that conform to designs we have already established. Most of us no longer call our weeds by their names; we simply refer to them as *weeds,* usually said contemptuously and with a grimace, as if they were all members of a single demonic species.

The sacred text for most Europeans and their New World descendants, the Bible, supports this point of view. As punishment for overreaching the limits set for them, Adam and Eve were sentenced to labor incessantly, to deal with "thistles and thorns" and, by the sweat of their brows, earn the bread made from the grain they produced. We are still overreaching. We still talk about the "war on weeds" and continually create new and more destructive—and expensive—weapons to help us "win" it, even though we're as unlikely to win a war on weeds as we are to win any other war.

I'm not advocating surrender—just a peace treaty, a softer path to managing weeds that still allows us to appreciate their virtues: their toughness, their resilience, their ability to adapt to sudden changes in their environment, all virtues we will increasingly need to embrace as we struggle to work our way out of the climatic corner we seem to have painted ourselves into. We need to start calling them by their names again, eating them again, maybe even brewing concoctions (carefully) that might help us get through some of our ailments a little more easily and pleasantly. We can control them, manage them, limit them, and that is enough; we can't ever eradicate them.

Nor should we want to. Some weeds that appear unbidden in our gardens fill the empty spaces they occupy more beautifully and appropriately than anything we could buy in a nursery. Weeds are our familiars, our fellow travelers, our constant companions. They annoy us, they threaten us, and they constantly remind us of who we are—creatures with limits that we would rather not acknowledge. How can we not love them?

GLOSSARY

PLANT PARTS

I've tried to describe the weeds in this book using plain language, but sometimes this is impossible—for instance, what can you call a stamen or pistil other than a *stamen* or *pistil*? I've chosen to include definitions of some of the more common terms used to describe plants; more comprehensive lists may be found in *The Jepson Manual* and other botanical texts.

Flowers

Angiosperms: Flowering plants—almost all weeds are in this class.

Anther: The knobby structure at the top of the stamen that bears pollen grains.

Awn: A pointed tip, long or short, attached to a glume on a grass spikelet; not always present.

Banner: The vertical petal at the top of a "pea" flower.

Calyx: A ring of sepals between the base of a flower and the stem.

Composite inflorescence: Densely grouped flowers on top of a receptacle. A feature of the aster or composite family.

Corolla: The petals of a flower.

Disk flowers: Tiny blossoms without petals that are crowded onto a receptacle and sometimes surrounded by ray flowers, forming a "daisy."

Double: Describes a flower with two or more rings of petals.

Filament: The thin stem to which the anther is attached.

Glumes: Paired papery leaflike structures on the outside of grass spikelets.

Inflorescence: A cluster of flowers.

Keel: The two fused petals that form the base of typical "pea" flowers.

Involucre: The leafy structure at the base of a composite inflorescence.

Lemma: A leaflike structure beneath the glumes on grass spikelets. Paired with a shorter structure called the palea; together these enclose the flower parts.

Ovary: The bulbous structure at the base of the pistil that holds the ovules.

Ovule: An unpollinated seed, a vegetative egg.

Panicle: Like a raceme, but with the flowers on secondary branches.

Pedicel: A stalk of a single flower in an inflorescence.

Peduncle: A stalk from which pedicels branch.

Pistil: The tubular flower structure in which seeds are formed.

Raceme: Like a spike, but with the flowers on branches of the flower stalks.

Ray flowers: Blossoms with petal-like appendages that form a ring around a composite inflorescence.

Receptacle: The end of a peduncle or pedicel on which the flower parts are laid out. In composites, the flattened end of the stalk holding the inflorescence and surrounded by the involucre.

Sepal: A leaflike structure at the top of a flower stem; a ring of these comprise the calyx.

Single: A flower with one ring of petals.

Spike: Consists of stemless flowers growing on opposite sides of an unbranched stem.

Spikelet: Individual flowers comprising a grass spike.

Stamen: The pollen-bearing structure in an angiosperm flower.

Stigma: The sticky tip of the pistil to which pollen grains adhere.

Style: The tube between the stigma and the ovary.

Umbel: A flat-topped inflorescence with flower stalks branching from one point atop a stem.

Wings: The two petals below the banner on "pea" flowers.

Leaves

Alternate: On opposite sides of a branch or stem, but not opposite one another.

Blade: The portion of a leaf that does not include the petiole.

Compound leaves: Leaves with leaflets on branching stems arising from the petiole.

Cotyledon: A fleshy leaf that emerges on a stem when a seed germinates. It contains starch that nourishes the plant until the true leaves appear.

Crenate: Describes leaf margins with small, rounded indentations.

Dentate: With pointed indentations resembling teeth; fewer points than serrate leaves.

Dicotyledons: A class of plants that produce two cotyledons when a seed germinates; "broad-leaved" plants.

Entire: Describes a smooth leaf margin, without indentations.

Glandular: Describes leaf surfaces covered with tiny dots.

Hastate: A term for a pointed leaf with two pointed lobes at the base—like a spearhead.

Lanceolate: Describes a long, narrow pinnate leaf with a rounded base and pointed tip.

Lobed: Having deep indentations, rounded or pointed, along the leaf margin.

Monocotyledons: So-called narrow-leaved plants, angiosperms with one seed leaf; e.g., grasses, sedges, rushes, lilies, onions, narcissus, palms, etc.

Nerves: Veins that run the entire length of the leaf.

Oblanceolate: The same shape as lanceolate, but pointed at the base and rounded at the tip.

Obovate: Egg-shaped; pointed at the base, rounded at the tip.

Opposite: On opposite sides of a branch or stem, and opposite one another.

Ovate: Egg-shaped; pinnate, rounded at the base, pointed at the tip.

Palmate: Describes generally broad leaves with veins that fan out from the junction of the petiole and blade.

Pinnate: Describes generally narrow leaves with a branched central vein running from the base to the tip, like a feather.

Pubescent: Describes a leaf surface covered with fine, short hairs.

Rugose: Describes a wrinkled or ridged leaf surface.

Serrate: With sharp, pointed indentations; saw-toothed.

Stipule: A leafy structure at the base of a petiole.

Tomentose: Describes a leaf surface covered with dense, woolly hairs.

Veins: Thin tubes embedded in the leaf, which carry water and nutrients.

Whorled: Describes very closely set alternate leaves forming dense clusters.

Fruits and Seeds

Achene: The simplest of fruits: a seed with a hard outer coating.

Adpressed: Describes siliques with very short or no petioles that cling closely to the stems.

Berry: A fleshy fruit with seeds not encased in stones; examples are lemons, tomatoes, and grapes.

Capsule: A fruit that splits open to release its seeds, for example, peas, beans, and siliques.

Carpel: A single section of a compound pistil.

Compound fruit: A cluster of tiny fruits that adhere to one another and seem to form a single fruit; raspberries, blackberries, and thimbleberries are examples.

Dehiscent: Splitting open along a seam, often with enough force to propel the seeds some distance.

Drupe: A fleshy or pulpy fruit containing one or more stones encasing single seeds; examples are peaches, plums, cherries, almonds, and manzanita "berries."

Nut, nutlet: A dry, usually indehiscent fruit, consisting of a hard shell enclosing a single seed, for example, acorns and hazelnuts.

Pappus: A long, thin appendage with a branched tip at the top of an achene, which enables it to be carried on the wind. (Plural pappi.)

Pomes: Fleshy fruits in the rose family, for example, apples, pears, and cotoneaster and pyracantha "berries."

Stems

Angled: Not rounded in cross section; with corners; for example, mint and scarlet pimpernel stems.

Ascending: Arising from the base of the plant and curving or angling upward.

Culm: A grass stem with leaves along its length, with inflorescences at the tip or on stems growing from the leaf nodes.

Decumbent: Lying flat on the ground, but with the tips curving upward.

Erect: Growing vertically or branching from a strong central leader.

Procumbent: Lying flat on the ground.

Underground Parts

Bulb: A short underground stem consisting of fleshy leaves arising from a leaf base and surrounding a single miniature plant, complete with leaves and flowers, which emerges from the ground when the time is right. Roots grow from the bulb base.

Bulblet: A tiny bulb that develops as an offset of its parent bulb and grows underground until it is ready to emerge.

Corm: A short, thick underground stem, usually round, often surrounded by dry, papery leaf blades. Buds at the top send up clusters of leaves when conditions are right. Corms also generate tiny offspring, cormlets, which can quickly turn a single corm into a colony.

Rhizomes: Horizontal underground stems with buds capable of sending up stems through the ground, thus developing colonies of plants.

Roots: Underground appendages sprouting from the crown that anchor the plant and absorb nutrients through the root hairs.

Tubers: Short, thick underground stems that store starch; many have "eyes," clusters of buds capable of generating new plants; examples are potatoes and sweet potatoes.

MEDICINAL TERMS

Again, I've tried to use mostly plain language when describing the medicinal uses of many of the weeds in this book, but there are more technical terms that are used over and over in herbals whose meaning is not self-evident. I explain some of these in my text but am also providing a list here.

Anodyne: Relieves pain, but not strongly narcotic.

Anthelminthic: Expels worms.

Antiemetic: Stops vomiting.

Antiscorbutic: Relieves the symptoms of scurvy, or cures it.

Antiseptic: Kills microbes.

Aperient: Acts as a gentle laxative.

Aromatic: Has a stimulating fragrance.

Astringent: Closes pores, dries up discharges.

Carminative: Aids in expelling gas from the bowels.

Cathartic: Acts as a strong laxative.

Demulcent: Soothes irritated mucous membranes.

Deobstruent: Opens clogged ducts, allowing free flow of glandular fluids.

Diaphoretic: Induces sweating.

Diuretic: Induces urination.

Emetic: Causes vomiting.

Laxative: Stimulates bowel movement.

Maturating: Bringing boils, tumors, and ulcers to a head.

Mucilaginous: Full of or providing mucus, thus soothing inflamed tissue.

Nervine: Calms the nerves.

Refrigerant: Cools fevers.

Resolvent: Dissolves tumors.

Rubefacient: Stimulates blood flow, thus reddening pallid skin.

Sedative: Quiets the nerves.

Stomachic: Tones the stomach muscles, aiding digestion.

Styptic: Stops bleeding.

Sudorfic: Causes profuse sweating.

Tonic: Tones stomach muscles; also, generally refreshing and invigorating.

Vermifuge: Expels worms.

ANNOTATED BIBLIOGRAPHY

Anderson, Edgar. *Plants, Man, and Life*. Berkeley: University of California Press, Berkeley and Los Angeles, 1967.

Edgar Anderson, Carl Sauer, and Marston Bates are the three writers who revealed to me that weeds have a history that mirrors our own species' post–ice age history. Anderson, a Washington University, St. Louis botanist, was one of a number of scholars who paid close attention to the crops, ornamentals, and weeds that accompanied humans as they developed their civilizations. Anderson, Sauer, and Bates did their seminal work during the 1960s—each was aware of the work of the other two, and they all acknowledged one another. Anderson's chapter "Dump Heaps and the Origins of Agriculture" should be required reading for anyone wanting to understand the true nature of crop plants and weeds. This book, alas, has long been out of print; used copies are available.

Bailey, L. H. *How Plants Get Their Names*. New York: Dover, 1963.

Liberty Hyde Bailey was the horticulturist who created the massive encyclopedia *Hortus*. The last edition of this work, a doorstopper of a book, was *Hortus Third*, which Bailey modestly subtitled "a concise dictionary of plants cultivated in the United States and Canada." *How Plants Get Their Names* is a beautifully written little gem of a book that explains binomial nomenclature and the Linnaean system.

Baker, Herbert G. *Plants and Civilization*. Belmont, CA: Wadsworth Publishing Co., 1970.

This work on crop plants by another University of California botanist is written from a historical and geographic perspective, but includes a wealth of technical details. Baker also created a very useful list called "The Ideal (?) Weed" in an article in *Genetics of Colonizing Species,* a book he edited with G. Ledyard Stebbins, published by Academic Press, New York and London, 1965.

Baldwin, Bruce G., Douglas H. Goldman, David J. Keil, Robert Patterson, Thomas J. Rosatti, and Dieter H. Wilken, eds. *The Jepson Manual: Vascular Plants of California*. 2nd ed. Berkeley: University of California Press, 2012.

This book is the latest in the series of revisions and expansions of Willis Linn Jepson's *A Manual of the Flowering Plants of California,* first published in 1925. It revised and expanded that book so much that Jepson, ironically, is no longer credited as an author. It covers virtually every plant that grows without cultivation in California, native and alien, and adheres to the taxonomic revisions that were more or less agreed upon in 2012. I use the plant names and family classifications found in this book. By the time my book is published, a good number of these will have changed.

Bates, Marston. *The Forest and the Sea: A Look at the Economy of Nature and the Ecology of Man.* New York: New American Library, 1960.

Marston Bates published this book when he was a professor of zoology at the University of Michigan. He was one of the founders of the discipline of ecology, an integrative science that examines the interactions of biological organisms in their total environmental contexts, a field that has attracted scholars from other disciplines such as geography, botany, and history. Bates discusses the interactions of humans with the natural world throughout their time on earth and, as might be expected, has plenty to say about weeds.

Beverley, Robert, Jr. *The History and Present State of Virginia, Book II: Of the Natural Product and Conveniences in Its Unimprov'd State, before the English Went Thither,* 1705.

This is the source of the vivid and humorous description of the reaction of a group of English soldiers in Jamestown that I quoted in my write-up on jimson weed. I found the excerpt in the Wikipedia entry on *Datura stramonium.*

Crampton, Beecher. *Grasses in California.* Berkeley: University of California Press, 1974.

This well-illustrated pocket-sized guide covers wild and weedy grasses that grow in California. It is a handy field guide.

Devine, Robert. *Alien Invasion: America's Battle with Non-Native Animals and Plants.* Washington, DC: National Geographic Society, 1998.

Devine has written a fun-to-read book that verges on yellow journalism, a lively and exuberant account of some very lively and exuberant plants and animals.

Diamond, Jared. *Guns, Germs, and Steel: The Fates of Human Societies.* New York: W. W. Norton, 1997.

Jared Diamond, an ornithologist who spent a good deal of time studying bird evolution in New Guinea, wrote this book as a response to a question he was asked there by a local politician named Yali: "Why is it that you white people developed so much cargo and brought it to New Guinea, but we black people had little cargo of our own?" His answer is well summarized by the three-word title of the book, but the complete answer occupies 457 pages. The word *weeds* is not even found in the index, but "wheat" certainly is, and Diamond devotes a significant portion of his book to explaining how wheat production and the domestication of livestock led to guns, germs, and steel.

DiTomaso, Joseph M., and Evelyn A. Healy. *Weeds of California and Other Western States.* Publication 3488. Oakland, CA: University of California Agriculture and Natural Resources, 2007.

DiTomaso and Healy's massive and definitive work consists of two hefty volumes that document virtually all the weedy plants found in California and illustrate them with clear, sharp color photos. It is way too big to serve as a field guide but should be included in any reference collection pertaining to weeds and alien invaders. A researcher based at UC Davis, DiTomaso is certainly the leading authority on weeds in California.

DiTomaso, Joseph M., et al. *Weed Control in Natural Areas in the Western United States.* Davis, CA: University of California, Davis, Weed Research and Information Center, 2013.

This book contains a detailed account of the issues surrounding invasions of *Arundo donax* and the proposals to change its status from an unwelcome invader to a farmed biofuel crop, as well as discussions of control strategies for many other invasives.

Dowden, Anne Ophelia. *Wild Green Things in the City: A Book of Weeds.* New York: Thomas Y. Crowell Company, 1972.

Anne Ophelia Dowden was a lifelong botanical illustrator and a dedicated fan of the weeds that crop up wherever they find opportunities in New York City, where she lived and worked. Her beautiful color paintings of these plants are accompanied by lively text that is both celebratory and explanatory, and that makes a case for weeds as essential components of urban ecology. As a bonus, this book includes lists of weeds found not only in New York City, but in Denver and Los Angeles.

Dreistadt, Steve H. *Pests of Landscape Trees and Shrubs: An Integrated Pest Management Guide.* Publication 3359. Oakland, CA: University of California Statewide Integrated Pest Management Program, Division of Agriculture and Natural Resources, 1993.

The UC Statewide IPM Program was responsible for leading University of California agricultural researchers away from emphasis on developing pesticides to a broader, more comprehensive approach to pest control. They have produced IPM guides for many of California's crop plants and continue to do so. This particular guide is now in its third edition.

Ertter, Barbara, and Lech Naumovich. *Annotated Checklist of the East Bay Flora: Native and Naturalized Plants of Alameda and Contra Costa Counties, California.* 2nd. ed. Berkeley: California Native Plant Society, 2013.

This work documents all the wild plants growing in the East Bay Area and classifies them by the types of plant communities in which they are found. It has helped me identify wild plants by confirming or denying their presence in the areas where I find them, allowing me to eliminate some possible misidentifications. Hopefully, similar checklists exist for other parts of California, and elsewhere.

Farmer, Jared. "The Rise and Fall of the Gum Tree." *Zocalo.* www.zocalopublicsquare .org/01/93/the-rise-and-fall-of-the-gum-tree/ideas/nexus.

This article outlines the history of eucalyptus plantations in California and gives, I think, a very balanced view of how their remnants should be dealt with.

Frenkel, Robert E. *Ruderal Vegetation along Some California Roadsides.* Berkeley: University of California Press, 1970.

On the whole, this is a fairly technical study, but it is very well written and contains some fascinating essays on the history of vegetation in California, including a detailed account of the effects of human activity beginning with the Native Americans and continuing with the massive disruption caused by Hispano-American and later Anglo-American settlement. An appendix lists all the weeds introduced by 1860 and the approximate dates or time periods they first appeared.

Genders, Roy. *The Cottage Garden and the Old-Fashioned Flowers.* London: Pelham Books, 1984.

Before cottage gardening became a style, the term referred to plantings around the homes of rural workers, who grew junglelike assemblages of vegetation primarily for food and medicine. Many of these plants, especially the medicinal ones, are now considered merely weeds and probably would not be tolerated for long in contemporary cottage gardens. This is a good introduction to the flora of the historical cottage gardens.

Gilkey, Helen M. *Weeds of the Pacific Northwest.* Corvallis, OR: Oregon State College, 1957.

I don't know this book well, but I include it because it might be useful to readers of my book who live in the Pacific Northwest.

Grieve, Mrs. M. *A Modern Herbal.* New York: Dover, 1971.

Maud Grieve's work has been a very important reference for me while writing this book, a source of detailed historical, cultural, and medicinal information about plants that have traditionally been grown for medicine in physic gardens and cottage gardens in England. This two-volume work only scratches the surface of this vast subject, as it is mostly focused on England, but it provided me with more information than I could realistically include in my treatment of the weeds that grow all around me.

Hart, John, Russell Beatty, and Michael Boland. *Gardens of Alcatraz.* San Francisco: Golden Gate National Parks Association, 1996.

Prisoners on Alcatraz, a tiny rocky island near the Golden Gate in San Francisco Bay, cultivated some remarkably lush and beautiful gardens, which are now being restored using plants that had gone wild after the prison was abandoned as well as others that are particularly suited to the island's cool, foggy climate. The plants discussed in this book grow well in many other parts of the Bay Area and elsewhere along the Pacific coast; many escape into wild lands.

Haselwood, E. L., and G. G. Motter, eds. *Handbook of Hawaiian Weeds.* 2nd ed. Revised and expanded by Robert T. Hirano. Honolulu: University of Hawaii Press, 1983.

Wherever I travel, I look for weeds. I've been to the Big Island of Hawaii several times, where I have been astounded by the quantity and variety of nonnative vegetation that grows with abandon, often threatening native plant communities. This book has been very useful to me on my trips there. Many of the weeds listed came from other tropical countries, but at higher elevations, a surprising number can be found that grow all around me where I live.

Heizer, Robert F., and Albert B. Elsasser. *The Natural World of the California Indians.* Berkeley: University of California Press, 1980.

This book is one of the four sources I consulted for information about how the use of plants by California Indians affected their way of life and their environment. It is fairly brief and well illustrated. Heizer also edited a much more massive tome that I found useful—the *California* volume of the Smithsonian's multivolume *Handbook of North American Indians.*

Herodotus. *The Histories.* Translated by Robin Wakefield. Oxford: Oxford University Press, 1998.

I got my quote describing the Scythians' use of cannabis as a drug from this book.

Hersey, John. *Hiroshima*, New York: Vintage Books, 1989.

Here's a quote from the book that explains why it's included in this list:

> Over everything—up through the wreckage of the city in gutters, along the riverbanks, tangled among tiles and tin roofing, climbing on charred tree trunks—was a blanket of fresh, vivid, lush, optimistic green; the verdancy rose even from the foundations of ruined houses. Weeds already hid the ashes, and wild flowers were in bloom among the city's bones. The bomb had not only left the underground organs of plants intact; it had stimulated them. Everywhere were bluets and Spanish bayonets, goosefoot, morning glories and day lilies, the hairy-fruited bean, purslane and clotbur and sesame and panic grass and feverfew. Especially in a circle at the center, sickle senna grew in extraordinary regeneration, not only standing among the charred remnants of the same plant, but pushing up in new places, among bricks and through cracks in the asphalt. It actually seemed as if a load of sickle senna seed had been dropped along with the bomb.

Heywood, V. H., R. K. Brummitt, A. Culham, and O. Seberg. *Flowering Plant Families of the World*. Richmond Hill, ON: Firefly Books, 2007.

This looks like a coffee-table book but is actually a solid and beautifully illustrated botanical text that covers all the flowering plant families. It provides a guide to the important genera in each family, maps showing the family's distribution, and detailed write-ups on family characteristics, distribution, description, classification, and economic uses. This book is a revised edition of *Flowering Plants of the World*, which was last published in 1993 by Oxford University Press. It is much more up to date in regard to botanical names and classification.

Hitchcock, A. S. *Manual of the Grasses of the United States.* New York: Dover, 1971.

Hitchcock's book is a good source for descriptions of grasses all over the country. Even for California, it is much more comprehensive than the Beecher Crampton manual.

Holloran, Pete, Anouk Mackenzie, Sharon Farrell, and Doug Johnson. *The Weed Workers' Handbook: A Guide to Techniques for Removing Bay Area Invasive Plants.* Berkeley: The Watershed Project and California Invasive Plant Council, 2004.

The authors of this handbook discuss thirty-five of the most invasive plants growing in the Bay Area and much of the rest of coastal California and explain strategies and techniques for controlling them. It is an indispensible guide for anyone wanting to do weed work in natural areas. The entire book, including color illustrations, can be downloaded free from the Cal-IPC website (cal-ipc.org/ip/management/wwh/index.php).

Hughes, Kitty. "The Street of Weeds." In *Wandering in Paris: Luminaries and Love in the City of Light,* edited by Linda Watanabe McFerrin and Joanna Biggar. Oakland: Wanderland Writers, 2013.

This is a true story about searching for weeds in Paris, written by my wife Kitty Hughes. It has a few delightfully unexpected twists.

Lamoureux, Charles H. *Trailside Plants of Hawaii's National Parks.* Hilo: Hawaii Natural History Association, 1976.

Written by a professor of botany at the University of Hawaii, this guidebook contains color photographs and descriptions of the plants, native and introduced, that can be seen from the trails of Hawaii Volcanoes National Park on the island of Hawaii and Haleakala National Park on Maui. It begins with a short essay on the origins and evolution of Hawaiian plants, followed by descriptions organized by plant families.

Mabey, Richard. *Weeds: In Defense of Nature's Most Unloved Plants.* New York: Ecco, 2012.

Mabey's book ostensibly focuses on twelve weeds that have had significant impact on English natural and cultural history and whose common names he uses as the titles to his chapters (for example, "Triffid: The Weed at the End of the World"). But he takes his time getting to these weeds, in the process weaving the stories of many other weeds into the narrative that finally leads to the titular weed. Mabey's chapters comprise a series of vivid and complex natural history essays, beautifully written, a pleasure to read.

Margolin, Malcolm. *The Ohlone Way: Indian Life in the San Francisco–Monterey Bay Area.* Berkeley: Heyday Books, 1978.

Malcolm Margolin is not an academic but a writer who is thoroughly engaged with his subject, and he writes in a breezy, colloquial style that is easy and fun to read. He focuses on a single tribe, the Ohlone, whose homeland included the Berkeley area, where Margolin lives.

Martin, Alexander C. *Weeds.* New York: Golden Books, 1987.

This is a handy field guide to some of the more common weeds that are found almost anywhere. Good color illustrations and maps of geographic distribution are features of a number of the Golden guides, this one included. It fits easily into a back pocket.

Merlin, Mark David. *Hawaiian Forest Plants: A Hiker's Guide.* 3rd ed. Honolulu: Oriental Publishing Company, 1980.

Merlin's book consists of descriptions and color images of the more common plants that can be seen in both wet and dry forests on the Hawaiian islands. If using this book as an identification guide, readers have to thumb through it to find photos of the plants they are observing; the plants are not organized by families, and the table of contents lists only the Hawaiian names. There are excellent descriptions of the native Hawaiian uses.

Muenscher, W. C. *Weeds.* Ithaca, NY: Cornell University Press, 1984.

A fairly standard textbook for college level courses on weeds, mostly agricultural, in the eastern half of this country, Muenscher's book can be valuable for weed students in the west. Two of his opening chapters, "Dissemination and Importance of Weeds" and "The Control of Weeds" are especially insightful and universally applicable.

Randall, John M., and Janet Marinelli, eds. *Invasive Plants: Weeds of the Global Garden.* New York: Brooklyn Botanic Garden, 1996.

This slim volume has single-page write-ups, illustrated by clear color photos, of more than seventy-five invasives that grow in different habitats in every part of the world. It's a fine overview but needs to be supplemented by additional study of writings about weeds growing in specific locales.

Robbins, W. W., Margaret K. Bellue, and Walter S. Ball. *Weeds of California.* Sacramento, CA: California Department of Agriculture, 1970.

Alas, 1970 was the last year this fine book, covering rural, urban, and wild land weeds, was published. I still find it the single most useful field manual for the weeds that are found in my part of California. Many of the botanical names and family assignations have changed since it went out of print, but the latest nomenclature can be found in the most recent *Jepson Manual.* If you live in California, go online and find a used copy.

Robinson, William. *The Wild Garden.* Portland, OR: Sagapress/Timber Press, 1994.

William Robinson was a late nineteenth-century Irish estate gardener who hated the practice of carpet bedding: the practice of growing garishly colored annual plants packed tightly into beds, often in combinations of clashing colors, and producing, in his opinion, a most unnatural effect. Legend has it that, during a freezing winter night on the Irish estate where he worked, he shut off the greenhouse heaters, opened all the vents, and, having assured the demise of all the bedding plant seedlings being grown there, headed for London and a career as a gardener, writer and editor, friend and collaborator of Gertrude Jekyll, and successful stock market speculator. *The Wild Garden* advocates creating gardens that virtually design themselves, by planting species native to many areas of the world with climates and terrain similar to that of the locale in which the gardener works, and allowing them to grow, spread, and intermingle freely. In Robinson's view, volunteers from other gardens, and even weeds, are welcome, if they can find room. Robinson even advocates planting some species that are considered weeds by most gardeners, such as milk thistle. His book should give a great deal of aid and comfort to anyone who feels, as I do, that the more life forms that thrive in their gardens, the better.

Sauer, Carl O. *Agricultural Origins and Dispersals: The Domestication of Animals and Foodstuffs*. 2nd ed. Cambridge, MA: MIT Press, 1969.

This fairly short book (175 pages) was originally published in 1952, the same year as Edgar Anderson's *Plants, Man, and Life*. Both these writers cite each other as major influences. Sauer, a geographer, focuses on discussing the particularities of the domestication processes in all the regions in which they occurred, Old World and New. He characterizes crop plants as "benign weeds" that people kept around for their culinary and medicinal value, deliberately selecting and crossbreeding them to produce improved varieties. This is a theory that Anderson explains in greater detail in his work.

Sauer, Jonathan D. *Plant Migration: The Dynamics of Geographic Patterning in Seed Plant Species*. Berkeley: University of California Press, 1988.

Jonathan is Carl's son; he also became a geographer and worked at UCLA. He discusses many recent instances of large-scale plant migration, both of truly wild plants and of weeds. The chapter I find most compelling is the last, titled "The Deep Past." Here he uses studies of fossilized parts of plants, especially their pollen, to produce vivid reconstructions of vegetation communities going back as far as the Devonian era. That this can be done almost entirely by microscopic observation of tiny fossilized pollen grains boggles my mind. I once had a student in my weeds class who had engaged in this work; he agreed that it was fascinating, but had finally found it way too tedious, and was studying to become a gardener and landscaper.

Seiter, David. *Spontaneous Urban Plants: Weeds in NYC*. New York: Archer, 2016.

Just published in 2016, Seiter's book describes many of the weeds that grow in New York City and explains the roles they can play in managing the urban environment by assisting in carbon sequestration, providing wildlife habitat, aiding in storm water retention and phytoremediation (removing toxins from soil), and providing food and medicine. His views are not entirely optimistic, however; he ends the book by acknowledging that there are some weeds that do more harm than good by establishing "pervasive monocultures—reducing flora and fauna biodiversity and resulting in a destruction of native habitat." He characterizes this phenomenon as "ecological disservice" and declares that these weeds "deserve eradication." I find the assertion that weeds "deserve" anything at all to be a dubious proposition.

Simmonds, N. W., ed. *Evolution of Crop Plants*. London: Longman, 1984.

Simmonds, a professor at the University of Edinburgh Agricultural College, compiled this collection more than thirty years after Anderson and Sauer published their works, so it contains rather more detailed information on the crop plants of the world than they offer. It is organized more or less like an encyclopedia, with headings for each of the crop plants discussed (not in alphabetical order, but grouped by families) followed by an article written by an expert on that plant. These chapters include lots of genetic information.

Thomson, W. T. *Agricultural Chemicals, Book II: Herbicides*. Fresno, CA: Thomson Publications, 1986.

Anyone considering using an herbicide should read what this book has to say about the particular chemicals under consideration, then consult ipm.ucanr.edu, as well as the websites of the Pesticide Action Network and Californians for Pesticide Reform, before choosing the safest and most effective product to use in conjunction with all other methods employed.

Thoreau, Henry D. *Faith in a Seed*. Washington, D.C: Island Press, 1993.

This book contains a manuscript by Thoreau titled *The Dispersion of Seeds*, which finally made it into print in 1993. It revealed an entirely overlooked aspect of a man who had long been seen as a mystical philosopher of nature and had sometimes been characterized as a proto-hippie. This is a fair enough view but does not represent the whole person: he was also a focused and thoughtful observer of natural processes, a thoroughgoing empiricist. Nonetheless, Thoreau wrote about seed dispersal using the same poetic language that he employs in his more mystical writings.

University of California Agricultural and Natural Resources Statewide Integrated Pest Management Program. *The Safe and Effective Use of Pesticides*. 3rd ed. Publication 3324. Oakland, CA: University of California Statewide Integrated Pest Management Program, Agriculture and Natural Resources, 2016.

After accomplishing its goal of leading University of California agricultural researchers away from a heavy focus on developing herbicides and inspiring them to embrace a more integrated approach, the UC Statewide IPM Program took on the task of training agricultural workers to use pesticides safely and effectively whenever their use was required as part of an integrated pest management program. This book was designed to serve as a training manual. It is also a useful study guide for those seeking certification as pest control advisers and applicators.

Vessel, Matthew F., and Herbert H. Wong. *Natural History of Vacant Lots*. Berkeley: University of California Press, 1987.

The fiftieth in the California Natural History Guides series published by UC Press, *Natural History of Vacant Lots* describes and explains the interactions among plants, insects, mollusks, worms, reptiles, birds, and mammals that take place in urban environments such as vacant lots, construction sites, roadways, and other disturbed areas through written descriptions and analyses, drawings, charts, diagrams, and photographs. The late Matthew Vessel was a professor emeritus of natural science at San Jose State University when this book was published, and the late Herbert Wong was the administrator of the UC Laboratory School at Washington Elementary School in Berkeley, where he created an environmental education site by removing the asphalt from the schoolyard and letting the students create a garden. At the time I discovered this magnificent book, I knew him only as a disc jockey on KJAZ, which was then the leading jazz station in the Bay Area, where he was as knowledgeable and passionate about jazz as he was about environmental education at Washington School.

White, Lynn, Jr. *Medieval Technology and Social Change.* London: Oxford University Press, 1962.

Lynn White was a professor of history at UCLA whose main interest was medieval technology. This book, written well before Jared Diamond's *Guns, Germs, and Steel,* is based on the same thesis: that food production capacity correlates with political power. White shows that in the early Middle Ages two key technological advances— the invention of the improved horse harness and the moldboard plow—allowed the heavier and richer clay soils of northern Europe to be tilled, resulting in much greater wheat production than had ever occurred in the lighter soils of the Mediter- ranean Basin, thus leading to the development of European kingdoms and urban societies that were able to dominate the rest of the world in modern times—and, of course, to the spread of European crops and weeds.

Whitson, Tom D., ed., Larry C. Burrill, Steven A. Dewey, David W. Cudney, B. E. Nelson, Richard D. Lee, and Robert Parker. *Weeds of the West.* Rev. ed. Western Society of Weed Science in cooperation with the Western United States Land Grant Universi- ties Cooperative Extension Services, 1992.

In a *New York Times* interview (January 12, 2017), novelist Paul Auster was asked what his favorite book nobody had ever heard of was. He cited *Weeds of the West,* saying how entranced he was by all the poetic plant names it mentioned. I'm entranced by common plant names too, but have to say that the "nobody" the interviewer referred to includes a great number of farmers, ranchers, agricultural extension advisers, scientists, scholars, writers, and teachers in the western part of the country who deal with weeds on a daily basis. More than forty weed experts collaborated to produce this massive volume, full of beautiful color photographs of the plants the book discusses. As I said in my opening chapter, I tried assigning this book as a text one year, but found it left out too many weeds that are important in urban environments but don't seem to cause much concern in the rural West.

LIST OF WEEDS BY
BOTANICAL NAME

Acacia decurrens (dealbata)—Sydney blue (or green) wattle—Fabaceae
Acacia melanoxylon—blackwood acacia—Fabaceae
Acanthus mollis—acanthus—Acanthaceae
Achillea millefolium—yarrow—Asteraceae
Ageratina adenophora—white thoroughwort—Asteraceae
Ailanthus altissima—Chinese tree of heaven—Simaroubaceae
Allium neapolitanum—Neapolitan onion—Alliaceae
Allium triquetrum—wild onion—Alliaceae
Amaranthus blitoides—prostrate pigweed—Amaranthaceae
Amaranthus deflexus—pigweed, low amaranth—Amaranthaceae
Anagallis arvensis—scarlet pimpernel—Primulaceae
Anthriscus caucalis—bur chervil—Apiaceae
Artemisia vulgaris—mugwort—Asteraceae
Arum italicum—Italian arum—Araceae
Arundo donax—giant reed, river cane—Poaceae
Asparagus asparagoides—smilax asparagus, bridal creeper—Asparagaceae
Atriplex prostrata—arrowleaf saltbush, spearscale
Avena fatua—wild oats—Poaceae
Baccharis pilularis ssp. *consanguinea*—coyote brush—Asteraceae
Bellis perennis—English daisy—Asteraceae
Brachypodium sylvaticum—slender false brome—Poaceae
Brassica rapa—yellow mustard—Brassicaceae
Briza maxima, B. minor—quaking grass—Poaceae
Bromus catharticus—rescue grass, Shraeder's grass—Poaceae
Bromus diandrus—ripgut brome—Poaceae
Bromus hordeaceus—soft chess—Poaceae
Bromus madritensis—Spanish brome—Poaceae
Cannabis sativa—marijuana, common hemp—Cannabinaceae
Capsella bursa-pastoris—shepherd's purse—Brassicaceae
Cardamine oligosperma—bittercress, popweed—Brassicaceae
Carduus pycnocephalus—Italian thistle—Asteraceae
Centaurea calcitrapa—purple starthistle—Asteraceae
Centaurea solstitialis—yellow starthistle—Asteraceae
Centranthus ruber—red valerian, Jupiter's beard—Valerianaceae
Cerastium fontanum ssp. *vulgare*—perennial mouse-eared chickweed—Caryophyllaceae
Cerastium glomeratum—annual mouse-eared chickweed—Caryophyllaceae
Chamaesyce maculata—prostrate spotted spurge—Euphorbiaceae
Chamaesyce prostrata—prostrate spurge—Euphorbiaceae
Chasmanthe floribunda—African corn flag—Iridaceae
Chenopodium album—lamb's quarters—Chenopodiaceae
Cichorium intybus—chicory—Asteraceae
Cirsium vulgare—bull thistle—Asteraceae
Claytonia perfoliata—miner's lettuce—Portulacaceae
Conium maculatum—poison hemlock—Apiaceae
Convolvulus arvensis—bindweed—Convolvulaceae

Conyza bonariensis—flax-leaved fleabane—Asteraceae
Conyza canadensis—horseweed, Canadian fleabane—Asteraceae
Coronopus didymus—swine cress—Brassicaceae
Cortaderia jubata—jubata grass—Poaceae
Cotoneaster franchetii, Cotoneaster pannosa—cotoneaster—Rosaceae
Cotula australis—Australian or southern brass buttons—Asteraceae
Cotula coronopifolia—common brass buttons—Asteraceae
Crocosmia × crocosmiiflora—montbretia, crocosmia—Iridaceae
Cuscuta spp.—dodder, love vine, hairweed—Convolvulaceae
Cyclospermum leptophyllum—marsh parsley—Apiaceae
Cymbalaria muralis—Kenilworth ivy—Plantaginaceae
Cynara cardunculus—cardoon, wild artichoke—Asteraceae
Cynodon dactylon—Bermuda grass—Poaceae
Cyperus eragrostis—umbrella sedge—Cyperaceae
Cyperus esculentus—yellow nutsedge—Cyperaceae
Cytisus scoparius—Scotch broom—Fabaceae
Dactylis glomerata—orchard grass, cocksfoot—Poaceae
Datura stramonium—jimson weed, thornapple, tolguacha—Solanaceae
Daucus carota—wild carrot, Queen Anne's lace—Apiaceae
Delairea odorata (Senecio mikanoides)—Cape ivy, German ivy—Asteraceae
Digitaria ischaemum—smooth crabgrass—Poaceae
Digitaria sanguinialis—hairy crabgrass—Poaceae
Dipsacus fullonum—teasel, fuller's teasel—Dipsacaceae
Duchesnea indica—Indian mock strawberry—Rosaceae
Dysphania ambrosioides—epazote, Mexican tea—Chenopodiaceae
Echium candicans—pride of Madeira—Boraginaceae
Ehrharta erecta—panic veldt grass—Poaceae
Epilobium angustifolium—fireweed—Onagraceae
Epilobium brachycarpum—panicled willow herb—Onagraceae
Epilobium ciliatum—fireweed, willow herb—Onagraceae
Epipactis helleborine—wild orchid, helleborine—Orchidaceae
Equisetum arvense—field horsetail—Equisetaceae
Equisetum hyemale—scouring rush—Equisetaceae
Erigeron karvinskianus—Mexican fleabane, Santa Barbara daisy—Poaceae
Erodium botrys—broadleaf filaree—Geraniaceae
Erodium cicutarium—redstem filaree—Geraniaceae
Erodium moschatum—whitestem filaree—Geraniaceae
Eucalyptus camaldulensis—river red gum—Myrtaceae
Eucalyptus globulus—blue gum—Myrtaceae
Euphorbia peplus—petty spurge—Euphorbiaceae
Festuca arundinacea—tall fescue—Poaceae
Festuca rubra—fine fescue, creeping red fescue—Poaceae
Foeniculum vulgare—fennel—Apiaceae
Fumaria officinalis—fumitory—Papaveraceae
Galium aparine—bedstraw—Rubiaceae
Genista monspessulana—French broom—Fabaceae
Geranium carolinianum—Carolina geranium—Geraniaceae
Geranium dissectum—birdsfoot geranium, cutleaf geranium—Geraniaceae
Geranium molle—dove's foot geranium—Geraniaceae
Geranium robertianum—herb Robert—Geraniaceae
Hedera canariensis—Algerian ivy—Araliaceae
Hedera helix—English ivy—Araliaceae
Helminthotheca echioides—bristly oxtongue—Asteraceae
Hemizonia spp.—hayfield tarweed or tarplant—Asteraceae
Heterotheca subaxillaris—camphor weed, telegraph weed—Asteraceae

Hirschfeldia incana—shortpod mustard—Brassicaceae
Hordeum jubatum ssp. *jubatum*—foxtail barley—Poaceae
Hypochaeris glabra—smooth cat's ear—Asteraceae
Hypochaeris radicata—hairy cat's ear, coast dandelion—Asteraceae
Juncus bufonius—toad rush—Juncaceae
Kickxia elatine—sharp-pointed toadflax, Fluellin—Plantaginaceae
Lactuca saligna—willow-leaved lettuce—Asteraceae
Lactuca serriola—prickly lettuce—Asteraceae
Lactuca virosa—wild lettuce, opium lettuce—Asteraceae
Lamium amplexicaule—dead nettle, henbit—Lamiaceae
Lamium purpureum—red dead nettle—Lamiaceae
Lobularia maritima—sweet alyssum—Brassicaceae
Lolium multiflorum—Italian ryegrass—Poaceae
Lotus corniculatus—birdsfoot trefoil—Fabaceae
Lythrum hyssopifolium—hyssop loosestrife—Lythraceae
Madia elegans—common madia—Asteraceae
Madia sativa—coast madia, Chilean tarweed—Asteraceae
Malva nicaeensis—bull mallow—Malvaceae
Malva parviflora—cheeseweed, small mallow—Malvaceae
Matricaria discoidea—pineapple weed—Asteraceae
Medicago arabica—spotted bur clover—Fabaceae
Medicago lupulina—black medic—Fabaceae
Medicago polymorpha—bur clover—Fabaceae
Medicago sativa—alfalfa—Fabaceae
Melilotus alba—white sweet clover—Fabaceae
Melilotus indica—yellow sweet clover—Fabaceae
Mentha pulegium—pennyroyal—Lamiaceae
Mentha spicata—spearmint—Lamiaceae
Modiola caroliniana—bristly mallow—Malvaceae
Myosotis sylvatica—forget-me-not—Boraginaceae
Navarretia squarrosa—skunkweed—Polemoniaceae
Nigella damascena—love-in-a-mist—Ranunculaceae
Nothoscordum inodorum—false garlic—Alliaceae
Oxalis corniculata—yellow oxalis, creeping wood sorrel—Oxalidaceae
Oxalis pes-caprae—Bermuda buttercup, sour grass—Oxalidaceae
Parietaria judaica—Jerusalem pellitory—Urticaceae
Paspalum dilatatum—dallis grass—Poaceae
Pennisetum clandestinum—Kikuyu grass—Poaceae
Persicaria capitata (Polygonum capitatum)—rose carpet knotweed—Polygonaceae
Phalaris aquatica—Harding grass—Poaceae
Phyla nodiflora—lippia—Verbenaceae
Plantago coronopus—saltmarsh plantain—Plantaginaceae
Plantago lanceolata—buckhorn plantain, ribgrass—Plantaginaceae
Plantago major—common plantain—Plantaginaceae
Poa annua—annual bluegrass—Poaceae
Polycarpon tetraphyllum—four-leaved allseed—Caryophyllaceae
Polygonum aviculare—common or prostrate knotweed—Polygonaceae
Polypogon monspeliensis—rabbit's foot grass—Poaceae
Portulaca oleracea—purslane—Portulacaceae
Prunella vulgaris—self-heal—Lamiaceae
Pseudognaphalium luteoalbum—white cudweed—Asteraceae
Pteridium aquilinum var. *pubescens*—western bracken fern—Dennstaedtiaceae
Ranunculus repens—creeping buttercup—Ranunculaceae
Raphanus raphanistrum—wild radish—Brassicaceae
Raphanus sativum—wild radish—Brassicaceae

Ricinus communis—castor bean—Euphorbiaceae
Rubus armeniacus—Himalayan blackberry—Rosaceae
Rubus lacinatus—cutleaf blackberry—Rosaceae
Rubus unifolius var. *inermis*—thornless elm-leaf blackberry—Rosaceae
Rubus ursinus—California blackberry—Rosaceae
Rumex acetosella—sheep sorrel, sour dock—Polygonaceae
Rumex conglomeratus—cluster dock, green dock—Polygonaceae
Rumex crispus—curly dock—Polygonaceae
Rumex pulcher—fiddle dock—Polygonaceae
Salpichroa origanifolia—lily of the valley vine—Solanaceae
Salsola tragus—Russian thistle, tumbleweed—Chenopodiaceae
Scandix pecten-veneris—shepherd's needle—Apiaceae
Senecio vulgaris—groundsel—Asteraceae
Sherardia arvensis—field madder—Rubiaceae
Silybum marianum—milk thistle—Asteraceae
Sisymbrium altissimum—tumble mustard—Brassicaceae
Sisymbrium irio—London rocket—Brassicaceae
Sisymbrium officinale—hedge mustard—Brassicaceae
Solanum americanum—American black nightshade, white nightshade—Solanaceae
Solanum nigrum—European black nightshade
Soliva sessilis—soliva—Asteraceae
Sonchus asper—prickly sowthistle—Asteraceae
Sonchus oleraceus—common sowthistle—Asteraceae
Spartium junceum—Spanish broom—Fabaceae
Spergula arvensis—corn spurry—Caryophyllaceae
Spergularia rubra—sand spurry—Caryophyllaceae
Stachys bullata—wood mint, hedge nettle—Lamiaceae
Stellaria media—common chickweed—Caryophyllaceae
Stipa miliacea—smilo grass, San Diego grass—Poaceae
Tanacetum parthenium—feverfew—Asteraceae
Taraxacum officinale—dandelion—Asteraceae
Torilis nodosa—hedge parsley—Apiaceae
Toxicodendron diversilobum—poison oak—Anacardiaceae
Tragopogon porrifolius—salsify, oyster plant—Asteraceae
Tragopogon pratensis—John-go-to-bed-at-noon—Asteraceae
Trifolium hirtum—rose clover—Fabaceae
Trifolium pratense—red clover—Fabaceae
Trifolium repens—white clover—Fabaceae
Tropaeolum majus—nasturtium—Tropaeolaceae
Ulex europaeus—gorse—Fabaceae
Urtica dioicia ssp. *holosericea*—creek nettle—Urticaceae
Urtica urens—dwarf nettle—Urticaceae
Verbascum thapsus—mullein—Scrophulariaceae
Veronica arvensis—corn speedwell—Plantaginaceae
Veronica persica—bird's eye speedwell—Plantaginaceae
Veronica serphyllifolia—thyme-leaf speedwell—Plantaginaceae
Vicia faba—fava bean, horse bean—Fabaceae
Vicia sativa—common vetch—Fabaceae
Vicia sativa ssp. *nigra*—narrow-leaved vetch—Fabaceae
Vinca major—periwinkle—Apocynaceae
Viola odorata—sweet violet—Violaceae
Viola riviniana— Labrador violet, European dog violet—Violaceae
Vulpia myuros—rattail fescue, zorro fescue—Poaceae
Zantedeschia aethiopica—calla lily, common calla—Araceae

LIST OF WEEDS BY COMMON NAME

Despite attempts to create them, there are no universally agreed-upon common names. For each plant I'm listing one or two names that I judge to be the most commonly used, at least where I live and work.

Acacia, blackwood—*Acacia melanoxylon*—Fabaceae
Acacia, Sydney blue (or green) wattle—*Acacia decurrens (dealbata)*—Fabaceae
Acanthus—*Acanthus mollis*—Acanthaceae
African corn flag—*Chasmanthe floribunda*—Iridaceae
Alfalfa—*Medicago sativa*—Fabaceae
Annual bluegrass—*Poa annua*—Poaceae
Arrowleaf saltbush, spearscale—*Atriplex prostrata*
Australian or southern brass buttons—*Cotula australis*—Asteraceae
Bedstraw—*Galium aparine*—Rubiaceae
Bermuda buttercup, sour grass—*Oxalis pes-caprae*—Oxalidaceae
Bermuda grass—*Cynodon dactylon*—Poaceae
Bindweed—*Convolvulus arvensis*—Convolvulaceae
Birdsfoot trefoil—*Lotus corniculatus*—Fabaceae
Bittercress, popweed—*Cardamine oligosperma*—Brassicaceae
Black medic—*Medicago lupulina*—Fabaceae
Black nightshade, American, white nightshade—*Solanum americanum*—Solanaceae
Black nightshade, European—*Solanum nigrum*—Solanaceae
Blackberry, California—*Rubus ursinus*—Rosaceae
Blackberry, cutleaf—*Rubus lacinatus*—Rosaceae
Blackberry, Himalayan—*Rubus armeniacus*—Rosaceae
Blackberry, thornless elm-leaf—*Rubus unifolius* var. *inermis*—Rosaceae
Bracken fern, western—*Pteridium aquilinum* var. *pubescens*—Dennistaedaceae
Brass buttons, common—*Cotula coronopifolia*—Asteraceae
Bristly mallow—*Modiola caroliniana*—Malvaceae
Bristly oxtongue—*Helminthotheca echioides*—Asteraceae
Brome, Spanish, red brome—*Bromus madritensis, B. madritensis* ssp. *rubens*—Poaceae
Broom, Scotch—*Cytisus scoparius*—Fabaceae
Broom, Spanish—*Spartium junceum*—Fabaceae
Bull thistle—*Cirsium vulgare*—Asteraceae
Bur chervil—*Anthriscus caucalis*—Apiaceae
Bur clover—*Medicago polymorpha*—Fabaceae
Bur clover, spotted—*Medicago arabica*—Fabaceae
Calla lily, common calla—*Zantedeschia aethiopica*—Araceae
Cape ivy, German ivy—*Delairea odorata (Senecio mikanoides)*—Asteraceae
Cardoon, wild artichoke—*Cynara cardunculus*—Asteraceae
Castor bean—*Ricinus communis*—Euphorbiaceae
Cat's ear, hairy, coast dandelion—*Hypochaeris radicata*—Asteraceae
Cat's ear, smooth—*Hypochaeris glabra*—Asteraceae
Chickweed, common—*Stellaria media*—Caryophyllaceae

Chicory—*Cichorium intybus*—Asteraceae
Chinese tree of heaven—*Ailanthus altissima*—Simaroubaceae
Clover, red—*Trifolium pratense*—Fabaceae
Clover, rose—*Trifolium hirtum*—Fabaceae
Clover, white—*Trifolium repens*—Fabaceae
Corn spurry—*Spergula arvensis*—Caryophyllaceae
Cotoneaster—*Cotoneaster franchetii, C. pannosa*—Rosaceae
Coyote brush—*Baccharis pilularis* ssp. *consanguinea*—Asteraceae
Crabgrass, hairy—*Digitaria sanguinialis*—Poaceae
Crabgrass, smooth—*Digitaria ischaemum*—Poaceae
Creeping buttercup—*Ranunculus repens*—Ranunculaceae
Cudweed, white—*Pseudognaphalium luteoalbum*—Asteraceae
Dallis grass—*Paspalum dilatatum*—Poaceae
Dandelion—*Taraxacum officinale*—Asteraceae
Dead nettle, henbit—*Lamium amplexicaule*—Lamiaceae
Dock, cluster—*Rumex conglomeratus*—Polygonaceae
Dock, curly—*Rumex crispus*—Polygonaceae
Dock, fiddle—*Rumex pulcher*—Polygonaceae
Dodder, hairweed—*Cuscuta* spp.—Convolvulaceae
English daisy—*Bellis perennis*—Asteraceae
Epazote, Mexican tea—*Dysphania ambrosioides*—Chenopodiaceae
Eucalyptus, blue gum—*Eucalyptus globulus*—Myrtaceae
Eucalyptus, river red gum—*Eucalyptus camaldulensis*—Myrtaceae
False garlic—*Nothoscordum inodorum*—Alliaceae
Fava bean, horse bean—*Vicia faba*—Fabaceae
Fennel—*Foeniculum vulgare*—Apiaceae
Fescue, fine, creeping red fescue—*Festuca rubra*—Poaceae
Fescue, tall—*Festuca arundinacea*—Poaceae
Feverfew—*Tanacetum parthenium*—Asteraceae
Field madder—*Sherardia arvensis*—Rubiaceae
Filaree, broadleaf—*Erodium botrys*—Geraniaceae
Filaree, redstem—*Erodium cicutarium*—Geraniaceae
Filaree, whitestem—*Erodium moschatum*—Geraniaceae
Fireweed—*Epilobium angustifolium*—Onagraceae
Fireweed, willow herb—*Epilobium ciliatum*—Onagraceae
Flax-leaved fleabane—*Conyza bonariensis*—Asteraceae
Forget-me-not—*Myosotis sylvatica*—Boraginaceae
Four-leaved allseed—*Polycarpon tetraphyllum*—Caryophyllaceae
Foxtail barley—*Hordeum jubatum* ssp. *jubatum*—Poaceae
French broom—*Genista monspessulana*—Fabaceae
Fumitory—*Fumaria officinalis*—Papaveraceae
Geranium, birdsfoot or cutleaf—*Geranium dissectum*—Geraniaceae
Geranium, Carolina—*Geranium carolinianum*—Geraniaceae
Geranium, dove's foot—*Geranium molle*—Geraniaceae
Giant reed, river cane—*Arundo donax*—Poaceae
Gorse—*Ulex europaeus*—Fabaceae
Groundsel—*Senecio vulgaris*—Asteraceae
Harding grass—*Phalaris aquatica*—Poaceae
Hayfield tarweed or tarplant—*Hemizonia* spp.—Asteraceae
Hedge parsley—*Torilis nodosa*—Apiaceae
Herb Robert—*Geranium robertianum*—Geraniaceae
Horsetail, field—*Equisetum arvense*—Equisetaceae
Horseweed, Canadian fleabane—*Conyza Canadensis*—Asteraceae
Hyssop loosestrife—*Lythrum hyssopifolium*—Lythraceae
Indian mock strawberry—*Duchesnea indica*—Rosaceae
Italian arum—*Arum italicum*—Araceae

Italian ryegrass—*Lolium multiflorum*—Poaceae
Italian thistle—*Carduus pycnocephalus*—Asteraceae
Ivy, Algerian—*Hedera canariensis*—Araliaceae
Ivy, English—*Hedera helix*—Araliaceae
Jerusalem pellitory—*Parietaria judaica*—Urticaceae
Jimson weed, thornapple, tolguacha—*Datura stramonium*—Solanaceae
John-go-to-bed-at-noon—*Tragopogon pratensis*—Asteraceae
Jubata grass—*Cortaderia jubata*—Poaceae
Kenilworth ivy—*Cymbalaria muralis*—Plantaginaceae
Kikuyu grass—*Pennisetum clandestinum*—Poaceae
Knotweed, prostrate or common—*Polygonum aviculare*—Polygonaceae
Lamb's quarters—*Chenopodium album*—Chenopodiaceae
Lettuce, wild, opium lettuce—*Lactuca virosa*—Asteraceae
Lettuce, willow-leaved—*Lactuca saligna*—Asteraceae
Lettuce, prickly—*Lactuca serriola*—Asteraceae
Lily of the valley vine—*Salpichroa origanifolia*—Solanaceae
Lippia—*Phyla nodiflora*—Verbenaceae
London rocket—*Sisymbrium irio*—Brassicaceae
Love-in-a-mist—*Nigella damascena*—Ranunculaceae
Madia, coast, Chilean tarweed—*Madia sativa*—Asteraceae
Madia, common—*Madia elegans*—Asteraceae
Mallow, bull—*Malva nicaeensis*—Malvaceae
Mallow, small, cheeseweed—*Malva parviflora*—Malvaceae
Marijuana, common hemp—*Cannabis sativa*—Cannabinaceae
Marsh parsley—*Cyclospermum leptophyllum*—Apiaceae
Mexican fleabane—*Erigeron karvinskianus*—Poaceae
Milk thistle—*Silybum marianum*—Asteraceae
Miner's lettuce—*Claytonia perfoliata*—Portulacaceae
Montbretia, crocosmia—*Crocosmia* × *crocosmiiflora*—Iridaceae
Mouse-eared chickweed, annual—*Cerastium glomeratum*—Caryophyllaceae
Mouse-eared chickweed, perennial—*Cerastium fontanum* ssp. *vulgare*—Caryophyllaceae
Mugwort—*Artemisia vulgaris*—Asteraceae
Mullein—*Verbascum thapsus*—Scrophulariaceae
Mustard, hedge—*Sisymbrium officinale*—Brassicaceae
Mustard, shortpod—*Hirschfeldia incana*—Brassicaceae
Mustard, tumble—*Sisymbrium altissimum*—Brassicaceae
Mustard, yellow—*Brassica rapa*—Brassicaceae
Nasturtium—*Tropaeolum majus*—Tropaeolaceae
Neapolitan onion—*Allium neapolitanum*—Alliaceae
Nettle, creek—*Urtica dioicia* ssp. *holosericea*—Urticaceae
Nettle, dwarf—*Urtica urens*—Urticaceae
Oats, wild—*Avena fatua*—Poaceae
Onion, wild—*Allium triquetrum*—Alliaceae
Orchard grass, cocksfoot—*Dactylis glomerata*—Poaceae
Orchid, wild—*Epipactis helleborine*—Orchidaceae
Oxalis, yellow, creeping wood sorrel—*Oxalis corniculata*—Oxalidaceae
Panic veldt grass—*Ehrharta erecta*—Poaceae
Pennyroyal—*Mentha pulegium*—Lamiaceae
Periwinkle—*Vinca major*—Apocynaceae
Petty spurge—*Euphorbia peplus*—Euphorbiaceae
Pigweed, low amaranth—*Amaranthus deflexus*—Amaranthaceae
Pigweed, prostrate—*Amaranthus blitoides*—Amaranthaceae
Pineapple weed—*Matricaria discoidea*—Asteraceae
Plantain, buckhorn, ribgrass—*Plantago lanceolata*—Plantaginaceae
Plantain, common—*Plantago major*—Plantaginaceae
Plantain, saltmarsh—*Plantago coronopus*—Plantaginaceae

Poison hemlock—*Conium maculatum*—Apiaceae
Poison oak—*Toxicodendron diversilobum*—Anacardiaceae
Pride of Madeira—*Echium candicans*—Boraginaceae
Prostrate spotted spurge—*Chamaesyce maculata*—Euphorbiaceae
Prostrate spurge—*Chamaesyce prostrata*—Euphorbiaceae
Purslane—*Portulaca oleracea*—Portulacaceae
Quaking grass—*Briza maxima, B. minor*—Poaceae
Queen Anne's lace, wild carrot—*Daucus carota*—Apiaceae
Rabbit's foot grass—*Polypogon monspeliensis*—Poaceae
Radish, wild—*Raphanus raphanistrum, R. sativum*—Brassicaceae
Rattail fescue, zorro fescue—*Vulpia myuros*—Poaceae
Red dead nettle—*Lamium purpureum*—Lamiaceae
Red valerian, Jupiter's beard—*Centranthus ruber*—Valerianaceae
Rescue grass, Shraeder's grass—*Bromus catharticus*—Poaceae
Ripgut brome—*Bromus diandrus*—Poaceae
Rose carpet knotweed—*Persicaria capitata*—Polygonaceae
Russian thistle, tumbleweed—*Salsola tragus*—Chenopodiaceae
Salsify, oyster plant—*Tragopogon porrifolius*—Asteraceae
Sand spurry—*Spergularia rubra*—Caryophyllaceae
Scarlet pimpernel—*Anagallis arvensis*—Primulaceae
Scouring rush—*Equisetum hyemale*—Equisetaceae
Self-heal—*Prunella vulgaris*—Lamiaceae
Sharp-pointed toadflax, Fluellin—*Kickxia elatine*—Plantaginaceae
Sheep sorrel, sour dock—*Rumex acetosella*—Polygonaceae
Shepherd's needle—*Scandix pecten-veneris*—Apiaceae
Shepherd's purse—*Capsella bursa-pastoris*—Brassicaceae
Skunkweed—*Navarretia squarrosa*—Polemoniaceae
Slender false brome—*Brachypodium sylvaticum*—Poaceae
Smilax asparagus, bridal creeper—*Asparagus asparagoides*—Asparagaceae
Smilo grass, San Diego grass—*Stipa miliacea*—Poaceae
Soft chess—*Bromus hordeaceus*—Poaceae
Soliva—*Soliva sessilis*—Asteraceae
Sowthistle, common—*Sonchus oleraceus*—Asteraceae
Sowthistle, prickly—*Sonchus asper*—Asteraceae
Spearmint—*Mentha spicata*—Lamiaceae
Speedwell, bird's eye—*Veronica persica*—Plantaginaceae
Speedwell, corn—*Veronica arvensis*—Plantaginaceae
Speedwell, thyme-leaf—*Veronica serphyllifolia*—Plantaginaceae
Starthistle, purple—*Centaurea calcitrapa*—Asteraceae
Starthistle, yellow—*Centaurea solstitialis*—Asteraceae
Sweet alyssum—*Lobularia maritima*—Brassicaceae
Sweet clover, white—*Melilotus alba*—Fabaceae
Sweet clover, yellow—*Melilotus indica*—Fabaceae
Swine cress—*Coronopus didymus*—Brassicaceae
Teasel, fuller's teasel—*Dipsacus fullonum*—Dipsacaceae
Telegraph weed, camphor weed—*Heterotheca subaxillaris*—Asteraceae
Thoroughwort, white—*Ageratina adenophora*—Asteraceae
Toad rush—*Juncus bufonius*—Juncaceae
Umbrella sedge—*Cyperus eragrostis*—Cyperaceae
Vetch, common—*Vicia sativa*—Fabaceae
Vetch, narrow-leaved—*Vicia sativa* ssp. *nigra*—Fabaceae
Violet, European dog, Labrador violet—*Viola riviniana*—Violaceae
Violet, sweet—*Viola odorata*—Violaceae
Willow herb, panicled—*Epilobium brachycarpum*—Onagraceae
Wood mint, hedge nettle—*Stachys bullata*—Lamiaceae
Yarrow—*Achillea millefolium*—Asteraceae

INDEX

ABOUT THE AUTHOR

Photo by Stephen Loewinsohn

RICHARD ORLANDO worked for more than twenty-five years as a lead gardener at University of California, Berkeley, and has taught classes taught classes on weeds and gardening for nearly thirty years. For decades he taught at Merritt College in Oakland, including a course entitled "Weeds in the Urban Landscape." He has led trainings for pesticide handlers and continues to offer consulting services as an arborist.

About North Atlantic Books

North Atlantic Books (NAB) is an independent, nonprofit publisher committed to a bold exploration of the relationships between mind, body, spirit, and nature. Founded in 1974, NAB aims to nurture a holistic view of the arts, sciences, humanities, and healing. To make a donation or to *learn more about our books, authors, events, and newsletter, please visit www.northatlanticbooks.com.*

North Atlantic Books is the publishing arm of the Society for the Study of Native Arts and Sciences, a 501(c)(3) nonprofit educational organization that promotes cross-cultural perspectives linking scientific, social, and artistic fields. To learn how you can support us, please visit our website.